Commentaries
on the Cantatas of
Johann Sebastian Bach

Commentaries on the Cantatas of Johann Sebastian Bach

A Selective Guide

HANS-JOACHIM SCHULZE

Translated by
JAMES A. BROKAW II

© 2024 by the Board of Trustees
of the University of Illinois
All rights reserved
1 2 3 4 5 C P 5 4 3 2 1
∞ This book is printed on acid-free paper.

Commentaries on the Cantatas of Johann Sebastian Bach: A Selective Guide is copublished by the University of Illinois Press (print and ebook) and Windsor & Downs Press (online digital edition, https://doi.org/10.21900/wd.21).

Sponsored by the Ruth and Noel Monte Fund of the American Bach Society.

Ruth and Noel Monte were deeply devoted to Bach and his music, sensing its great impact on the human brain and culture throughout the world. To them, Bach represents a bright planet appearing in the sky only once, requiring centuries for the human mind to observe and fully comprehend. The Monte Fund has the goal of supporting and promoting this living musical treasure for present and future generations.

Library of Congress Cataloging-in-Publication Data

Names: Schulze, Hans-Joachim, author. | Brokaw, James Albert, 1951– translator.
Title: Commentaries on the cantatas of Johann Sebastian Bach : a selective guide / Hans-Joachim Schulze; translated by James A. Brokaw II. Other titles: Bach-Kantaten. Selections. English
Description: Urbana : University of Illinois Press, 2024. | Includes bibliographical references and index.
Identifiers: LCCN 2023043126 (print) | LCCN 2023043127 (ebook) | ISBN 9780252045820 (cloth) | ISBN 9780252087929 (paperback) | ISBN 9780252056703 (ebook)
Subjects: LCSH: Bach, Johann Sebastian, 1685–1750. Cantatas. | Cantatas—Analysis, appreciation.
Classification: LCC ML410.B13 S4313 2024 (print) | LCC ML410.B13 (ebook) | DDC 782.2/4092—dc23/eng/20230925
LC record available at https://lccn.loc.gov/2023043126
LC ebook record available at https://lccn.loc.gov/2023043127

Contents

Translator's Note xi
Abbreviations xv

CHAPTER 1. BACH AT ARNSTADT AND
MÜHLHAUSEN FROM 1703 TO 1708

Aus der Tiefen rufe ich, Herr, zu dir (BWV 131)
Penance Service, 1707 1

Nach dir, Herr, verlanget mich (BWV 150)
Homage, ca. 1707 4

Christ lag in Todes Banden (BWV 4)
Easter Sunday, April 24, 1707? 10

Gottes Zeit ist die allerbeste Zeit (BWV 106)
Memorial Service, ca. 1707–1708 13

Gott ist mein König (BWV 71)
Mühlhausen City Council Inauguration, February 4, 1708 17

CHAPTER 2. BACH AT WEIMAR AND KÖTHEN
FROM MARCH 25, 1708, TO TRINITY SUNDAY 1723

Was mir behagt, ist nur die muntre Jagd (BWV 208)
Court of Saxe-Weissenfels, 1713 23

Widerstehe doch der Sünde (BWV 54)
Oculi, 1708–1717 27

Himmelskönig, sei willkommen (BWV 182)
Palm Sunday, March 25, 1714 32

Weinen, Klagen, Sorgen, Zagen (BWV 12)
Jubilate, April 22, 1714 37

Ich hatte viel Bekümmernis (BWV 21)
Third Sunday after Trinity, June 17, 1714. 41

Nun komm der Heiden Heiland (BWV 61)
First Sunday of Advent, December 2, 1714 46

Der Himmel lacht, die Erde jubilieret (BWV 31)
Easter Sunday, April 21, 1715 51

Komm, du süße Todesstunde (BWV 161)
Sixteenth Sunday after Trinity, September 27, 1716. 55

CHAPTER 3. BACH'S FIRST YEAR AT LEIPZIG
FROM THE FIRST SUNDAY AFTER TRINITY 1723
TO TRINITY SUNDAY 1724

Die Elenden sollen essen (BWV 75)
First Sunday after Trinity, May 30, 1723 61

Die Himmel erzählen die Ehre Gottes (BWV 76)
Second Sunday after Trinity, June 6, 1723. 65

Herz und Mund und Tat und Leben (BWV 147)
Visitation of Mary, July 2, 1723. 70

Herr, gehe nicht ins Gericht mit deinem Knecht (BWV 105)
Ninth Sunday after Trinity, July 25, 1723 75

Preise, Jerusalem, den Herrn (BWV 119)
Leipzig City Council Inauguration, August 30, 1723 79

Christus, der ist mein Leben (BWV 95)
Sixteenth Sunday after Trinity, September 12, 1723. 84

Wachet! betet! betet! wachet (BWV 70)
Twenty-Sixth Sunday after Trinity, November 21, 1723. 88

Sie werden aus Saba alle kommen (BWV 65)
Epiphany, January 6, 1724 92

Jesus schläft, was soll ich hoffen? (BWV 81)
Fourth Sunday after Epiphany, January 30, 1724. 96

CHAPTER 4. BACH'S SECOND AND THIRD YEARS AT LEIPZIG FROM THE FIRST SUNDAY AFTER TRINITY 1724 TO TRINITY SUNDAY 1726

O Ewigkeit, du Donnerwort (BWV 20)
First Sunday after Trinity, June 11, 1724 102

Ach Gott, vom Himmel sieh darein (BWV 2)
Second Sunday after Trinity, June 18, 1724......................108

Wer nur den lieben Gott läßt walten (BWV 93)
Fifth Sunday after Trinity, July 9, 1724..........................113

Was willst du dich betrüben (BWV 107)
Seventh Sunday after Trinity, July 23, 1724......................118

Jesu, der du meine Seele (BWV 78)
Fourteenth Sunday after Trinity, September 10, 1724............122

Liebster Immanuel, Herzog der Frommen (BWV 123)
Epiphany, January 6, 1725 126

Herr Jesu Christ, wahr' Mensch und Gott (BWV 127)
Estomihi, February 11, 1725 131

Wie schön leuchtet der Morgenstern (BWV 1)
Annunciation, March 25, 1725....................................135

Ihr werdet weinen und heulen (BWV 103)
Jubilate, April 22, 1725 141

Unser Mund sei voll Lachens (BWV 110)
Christmas Day, December 25, 1725..............................145

CHAPTER 5. BACH'S FOURTH YEAR AT LEIPZIG FROM THE FIRST SUNDAY AFTER TRINITY 1726 TO TRINITY SUNDAY 1727

Brich dem Hungrigen dein Brot (BWV 39)
First Sunday after Trinity, June 23, 1726 149

Es erhub sich ein Streit (BWV 19)
St. Michael's Day, September 29, 1726 154

Wer weiß, wie nahe mir mein Ende (BWV 27)
Sixteenth Sunday after Trinity, October 6, 1726 160

Ich will den Kreuzstab gerne tragen (BWV 56)
Nineteenth Sunday after Trinity, October 27, 1726..............164

Vereinigte Zwietracht der wechselnden Saiten (BWV 207.1)
University of Leipzig, December 11, 1726 169

Ich bin in mir vergnügt (BWV 204)
For Various Purposes, 1726 or 1727 174

Ich habe genung (BWV 82)
Purification of Mary, February 2, 1727 177

O ewiges Feuer, o Ursprung der Liebe (BWV 34.2)
Pentecost, June 1, 1727 181

CHAPTER 6. BACH AT LEIPZIG AFTER TRINITY 1727

Schwingt freudig euch empor (BWV 36)
First Sunday of Advent, 1726–1730 186

Laß, Fürstin, laß noch einen Strahl (BWV 198)
Funeral, Electress Christiane Eberhardine, October 17, 1727 191

Sehet, wir gehn hinauf gen Jerusalem (BWV 159)
Estomihi, February 27, 1729 195

Geschwinde, geschwinde, ihr wirbelnden Winde (BWV 201)
For Various Purposes, Autumn 1729.......................... 200

Weichet nur, betrübte Schatten (BWV 202)
Secular Wedding, before 1730................................ 201

Jauchzet Gott in allen Landen (BWV 51)
Fifteenth Sunday after Trinity, September 17, 1730............ 206

Wachet auf, ruft uns die Stimme (BWV 140)
Twenty-Seventh Sunday after Trinity, November 25, 1731 210

Schweigt stille, plaudert nicht (BWV 211)
For Various Purposes, mid-1734............................. 215

Jauchzet, frohlocket, auf, preiset die Tage (BWV 248 Part I)
Christmas Day, December 25, 1734........................... 218

Gott ist unsere Zuversicht (BWV 197.2)
Wedding Ceremony, 1736–1737............................. 221

Kommt, eilet und laufet, ihr flüchtigen Füße (BWV 249.4)
Easter Sunday, April 6, 1738 226

Lobet Gott in seinen Reichen (BWV 11)
Ascension Day, May 15, 1738 228

Ein feste Burg ist unser Gott (BWV 80)
Reformation Day, 1739?................................... 233

Mer han en neue Oberkeet (BWV 212)
For Members of the Aristocracy, August 30, 1742.............. 238

Notes 247
References 257
Index 263
BWV Index.. 279

Translator's Note

It is impossible to overstate the pervasive influence and enduring place held by Hans-Joachim Schulze's contributions to Bach scholarship over nearly three-quarters of a century. Schulze began his long tenure with Bach-Archiv Leipzig in 1957, becoming its director in 1992 and serving until 2000. He is author of the first comprehensive study of the source traditions of Bach's music in the eighteenth century; coeditor with Christoph Wolff of *Bach-Jahrbuch* from 1975 to 2000 and author of countless articles in its pages; and compiler of the *Bach Compendium*, also with Christoph Wolff, a chronological catalog of the works of Bach. Schulze's foundational contribution is undoubtedly his work with Werner Neumann in conceiving and preparing the supplemental volumes to the Neue Bach-Ausgabe (New Bach Edition), compiling and transcribing the first, second, third, and fifth volumes of the Bach-Dokumente (Bach Documents) series.

Although Schulze has dedicated the greater part of his work to the rarified, arcane world of Bach scholarship, he has occasionally directed his attention to a broader public. Beginning in 1991 and running until 1994, he presented a weekly series of half-hour radio broadcasts on all of the extant cantatas by Johann Sebastian Bach. Addressing the interested newcomer to Bach's music directly but also keeping the seasoned connoisseur in mind, Schulze strenuously avoided technical language and musical examples, choosing instead to describe the cantatas in terms easily understood by nonprofessionals. The series was quite popular and was repeated several times until 2000. In 2006 Schulze published his scripts as *Die Bach-Kantaten: Einführungen zu sämtlichen Kantaten Johann Sebastian Bachs*. His lively and engaging discussions provide a wealth of rewarding insights and perspectives focused on individual cantatas and their particular features, their contexts, and the problems of chronology and evolution that attend them.

Schulze begins nearly every discussion with a careful examination of the work's libretto, turning only afterward to describing the music's structure and how it amplifies the text. In his foreword to the German edition of 2006, Schulze makes clear that this approach is intended to redress a long-standing bias. Since the early nineteenth century, Bach's libretti—often rooted in the German Baroque poetic traditions of the seventeenth century—have been disparaged as mediocre and unsuitable (a judgment perhaps arising from the inevitable comparison with the classicists of the later eighteenth century). "The deliberate or careless disregard for the texts chosen by Bach for composition," writes Schulze, "and the underestimation of their authors, known or unidentified, can easily lead into a dead end, perpetuating a hagiography that will inevitably loosen the connection between text and music, opening the door to a frivolous consideration of these elements."[1] For Schulze, text and music inherently belong together. Particularly in the church cantatas, the overwhelming majority of the works in question, theological ideas, language, and musical expression are inseparably unified.

This volume presents a selection of Schulze's essays in English. (All essays will be available online at Illinois Open Publishing Network [IOPN], at the University of Illinois Library.) Schulze's essays are arranged according to the Bach Compendium: by church calendar for the sacred works and chronologically within each Sunday or holiday, and, for secular works, chronologically by patron or occasion. I have arranged the selected essays chronologically by first performance according to BWV3, the recently issued expanded edition of Wolfgang Schmieder's catalog of Bach's works. I have grouped them in chapters according to the cities and courts in which Bach worked and within the Leipzig sacred cantatas, by far the largest share, by annual cycle. In selecting essays for inclusion here, I have tried to choose not simply those that treat the best-known and most beloved works but also those that illuminate a wide range of biographical and cultural features of Bach's life and creative milieu. All three of Bach's oratorios are represented, although I chose to include only the first cantata from the Christmas Oratorio because it provides a fascinating, detailed, and wide-ranging consideration of the parody procedures so fundamental to Bach's composition of the oratorios and other late vocal works. I include two of the six cantatas for town council inaugurations, *Gott ist mein König* BWV 71 and *Preise, Jerusalem, den Herrn* BWV 119; they present details regarding the elaborate rituals these ceremonies involved, their place in the municipal structures of Mühlhausen and Leipzig, and even the names and occupations of their principals. We have detailed discussions of the customs, locations, and expenses entailed by cantata performances for wedding ceremonies and celebrations in *Gott ist unsre Zuversicht* BWV 197 and *Weichet nur, betrübte Schatten* BWV 202. Schulze's discussions of BWV 207 and other homage and congratulatory works are wonderful for their profiles of those being honored, as well as the institutions in which they worked.

Schulze uses minimal references: one to at most three endnotes per essay, indicated by asterisks. I have preserved these endnotes with the individual essays rather than placing all of them in a separate section. Where I have deemed additional references or commentary useful—either to supply original language or to briefly describe advances since the publication of Schulze's book in 2006—I have added them as numerical chapter endnotes. Since the publication of Schulze's book there have in fact been several significant advances in our knowledge about Bach's cantatas. An important body of new evidence has been discovered in St. Petersburg with direct bearing on the chronology of sacred cantatas at Leipzig: a large cache of text booklets distributed to congregations at St. Thomas Church. This discovery has resulted in the redating of several cantatas, in one case—*O ewiges Feuer, o Ursprung der Liebe* BWV 34—by several decades. Second, German musicologist Christine Blanken (2015a) has discovered a previously unknown annual cycle of cantata texts that was published in Nuremberg by Christoph Birkmann, a former theology student at the University of Leipzig from 1724 to 1727. The presence of several texts composed by Bach in the cycle makes it likely that their librettist, previously unidentified, was Birkmann. Finally, I have included one work, *Nach dir, Herr, verlanget mich* BWV 150, because of its perplexing nature and genesis—which Schulze himself brought us closer to clarifying after his book was published. Schulze himself recognized an acrostic in the free strophes of the text, thus identifying the cantata's dedicatee, an official closely associated with Bach.

I have done my best to preserve the author's approachable and sympathetic voice while making several changes in format to make the essays more lucid for an English-speaking readership. Because Bach's libretti and their origins, evolution, and structure are at the very center of Schulze's discussions, I felt it important that the original German cantata texts be included with their English translations.

Producing a felicitous English translation of texts used by Bach has frankly not been my primary goal. Rather, my aim has been to illuminate German syntax, structure, and meaning, even if this results in what might occasionally seem to be an awkward English rendering. In terms of word position, each line of translation corresponds as closely as possible to the German original.

I have striven to apply this same principle to the translation of the extensive biblical passages quoted in Schulze's discussions, especially in order to make clear the relationship between cantata text and its biblical origin where it applies. I provide the original German only when it is useful in understanding the libretto; I do not include German text for secondary literature. While my translations often echo the New Revised Standard Version, I have worked to stay as close as possible to the German as quoted by Schulze, presumably from a modern edition of the Lutheran Bible. I relied heavily on Alfred Dürr, *The Cantatas of J. S. Bach*, as well as Michael Marissen and Daniel Melamed's website, www.bachcantatatexts.org, which presents historically informed translations of Bach's cantata and oratorio texts. Unless otherwise noted, all translations are my own.

I express my sincere thanks to mentors and colleagues who have assisted me in this project: Stephen Crist, who initially suggested it to me; Laurie Matheson, director of the University of Illinois Press, who received my proposal with immediate enthusiasm; two anonymous peer readers, who offered substantive criticisms; Bernd Koska, Markus Rathey, and Peter Burkholder, who read extensive portions of the draft and offered very helpful suggestions; Christoph Wolff, Robert Marshall, and Russell Stinson, who offered encouragement and valuable advice; Hans-Joachim Schulze, who has enthusiastically supported the project from the very beginning; my wife, Mollie Sandock, who carefully read every essay and offered wonderful observations and insights as to style; and, finally, I dedicate this translation to the memory of Adelaide Brokaw Tolberg.

James A. Brokaw II
Brunswick, Maine, United States
April 2023

Abbreviations

BC	Hans-Joachim Schulze and Christoph Wolff. 1985. *Bach Compendium: Analytisch-bibliographisches Repertorium der Werke Johann Sebastian Bachs.* Vol. 1, *Vocalwerke.* Leipzig: C. F. Peters. A multivolume reference to the works of J. S. Bach. Alphabetical letters denote genre groupings: A = sacred cantatas for occasions in the church calendar; B = sacred cantatas for special occasions; C = motets; D = passions and oratorios; G = secular cantatas for court, nobility, and university events, as well as weddings and other occasions. BWV and *BC* numbers appear together in chapter subheads.
BD I	Werner Neumann and Hans-Joachim Schulze, eds. 1963. *Schriftstücke von der Hand Johann Sebastian Bachs: Kritische Gesamtausgabe.* Vol. 1 of Bach-Dokumente. Leipzig: Bach-Archiv. Complete critical edition of documents handwritten by J. S. Bach.
BD II	Werner Neumann and Hans-Joachim Schulze, eds. 1969. *Fremdschriftstücke und gedruckte Dokumente zur Lebensgeschichte Johann Sebastian Bachs, 1685–1750: Kritische Gesamtausgabe.* Vol. 2 of Bach-Dokumente. Leipzig: Bach-Archiv. Complete critical edition of other documents, printed and handwritten, from Bach's lifetime (1685–1750).
BD III	Hans-Joachim Schulze, ed. 1972. *Documente zum Nachwirken Johann Sebastian Bachs, 1750–1800.* Vol.

	3 of Bach-Dokumente. Leipzig: Bach-Archiv. Documents relating to Bach from the half century after his death (1750–1800).
BJ	*Bach-Jahrbuch*. 1904–. Leipzig and Berlin. Edited by Arnold Schering, 1904–39; Max Schneider, 1940–52; Alfred Dürr and Werner Neumann, 1953–74; Hans-Joachim Schulze and Christoph Wolff, 1975–2005; Peter Wollny, 2005–. The principal journal of Bach research, issued annually.
BTLM	Christoph Wolff. 2000. *Johann Sebastian Bach: The Learned Musician*. New York: Norton.
BWV	Wolfgang Schmieder, ed. 1950. *Thematisch-systematisches Verzeichnis der musikalischen Werke von Johann Sebastian Bach: Bach-Werke-Verzeichnis*. Leipzig: Breitkopf & Härtel.
BWV2	Wolfgang Schmieder, ed. 1990. *Thematisch-systematisches Verzeichnis der musikalischen Werke von Johann Sebastian Bach: Bach-Werke-Verzeichnis*. Second, revised, and expanded edition. Wiesbaden: Breitkopf & Härtel.
BWV3	Christine Blanken, Christoph Wolff, and Peter Wollny, eds. 2022. *Thematisch-systematisches Verzeichnis der musikalischen Werke von Johann Sebastian Bach*. Third, expanded edition. Wiesbaden: Breitkopf & Härtel.
JRBI	*Bach: Journal of the Riemenschneider Bach Institute*. 1970–. Baldwin Wallace University, Berea, Ohio.
NBA	Neue Bach-Ausgabe, referring to Johann Sebastian Bach (1685–1750): Neue Ausgabe sämtliche Werke. Edited under the auspices of the Johann-Sebastian-Bach Institut, Göttingen, and the Bach-Archiv, Leipzig. Kassel, Leipzig: Bärenreiter, 1954–.
NBR	Hans T. David and Arthur Mendel, eds. 1999. *The New Bach Reader: A Life of Johann Sebastian Bach in Letters and Documents*. Revised and expanded by Christoph Wolff. New York: Norton. A documentary biography of Bach containing many of the sources in the Bach-Dokumente series in English translation.
NHDM	Don Michael Randel, ed. *The New Harvard Dictionary of Music*. Cambridge, MA: Harvard University Press, 1986.

Commentaries
on the Cantatas of
Johann Sebastian Bach

CHAPTER 1

Bach at Arnstadt and Mühlhausen from 1703 to 1708

Aus der Tiefen rufe ich, Herr, zu dir
BWV 131 / BC B 25
Penance Service, 1707

The cantata *Aus der Tiefen rufe ich, Herr, zu dir* BWV 131 (Out of the depths, Lord, I call to you) is a relatively early composition, if not the earliest vocal work by Johann Sebastian Bach available to us at present. Bach composed the work while at Mühlhausen between June 1707 and June 1708, possibly closer to the beginning of this brief period than the end. Evidence for this chronological placement comes from Bach's autograph score. At the beginning of the nineteenth century it was in the possession of the Leipzig publishing house Breitkopf, and after frequent changes of ownership, it today graces a private collection in New York. The precious manuscript displays the finely chiseled text and musical script typical of Bach's early period. In addition, it displays a watermark characteristic of Mühlhausen: an eagle with wings spread, symbolic of the rank of free imperial city; the mill wheel, the sign of its name and tradition; and the initials of the Mühlhausen paper manufacturer Becker.

As if he wanted to eliminate any doubt beforehand, Bach made another inscription at the close of his manuscript that confirms its Mühlhausen origins with welcome clarity: "At the request of Herr Dr. Georg Christian Eilmar, set to music by Johann Sebastian Bach, Organist at Mühlhausen."[1] Whether this notation was just meant as a simple statement of fact or as a precaution to defuse any potential disputes cannot be known at present. Since Dr. Christian Eilmar was a clergyman at St. Mary's Church in Mühlhausen and Bach was employed as organist at St. Blasius Church, it is unlikely that the two had much to do with one another officially. On the basis of several surviving polemics, older scholarship concluded that Bach's supervisor, the superintendent at St. Blasius, Johann Adolph Frohne, was engaged in long-running, far-reaching, and fundamental disputes with Eilmar. According to this line of thinking, Bach was in a difficult position because of the men's irreconcilable differences, so to speak, and he left his position as organist at Mühlhausen after only one year. However, more recent studies have shown that while there was indeed a remarkably competitive situation that was hardly free of personal discord, there was no falling out nor any breakdown in diplomatic relations.* Bach's relationship with Eilmar was indeed better than his relationship with Frohne, his superintendent, as shown by the fact that, half a year after Bach left Mühlhausen, it was Eilmar and not Frohne who served as godfather to Catharina Dorothea, the first child of Bach's marriage with his cousin Maria Barbara. Contemporaries characterized Eilmar as emotional and in possession of a powerful sense of justice—characteristics that one finds in Bach's personality as well.

Such documents understandably have little to say about the occasion for commissioning Bach to write a cantata. Thus one must rely on the relatively vague clues provided by the sources of the text. Any search for a librettist would be an exercise in futility. For unexplained reasons but obviously in keeping with local tradition, in 1707 Mühlhausen the fashionably modern operatic forms of recitative and aria were not allowed any role in church music. Nor can what is commonly known as "mixed text form"—consisting of biblical passages, chorales, and free madrigalistic poetry in the form of recitatives and arias—be found in the cantata *Aus der Tiefen rufe ich* or in any other of Bach's Mühlhausen cantatas. The biblical passage comprises Psalm 130 in its entirety, a prayer for the forgiveness of sins:

> Aus der Tiefen rufe ich, Herr, zu dir. Herr, höre meine Stimme, laß deine Ohren merken auf die Stimme meines Flehens! So du willst, Herr, Sünde zurechnen, wer wird bestehen? Denn bei dir ist die Vergebung, daß man dich fürchte. Ich harre des Herrn; meine Seele harret, und ich hoffe auf sein Wort. Meine Seele wartet auf den Herrn von einer Morgenwache bis zu der andern. Israel, hoffe auf den Herrn; denn bei dem Herrn ist die Gnade und viel Erlösung bei ihm, und er wird Israel erlösen aus allen seinen Sünden.

> Out of the depths I cry, Lord, to you. Lord, hear my voice, let your ears receive the voice of my pleading! If you would, Lord, mark sins, who will withstand? For with you there is forgiveness, that one might fear you. I await the Lord; my soul awaits, and I hope upon his word. My soul waits for the

Lord from one morning watch to the next. Israel, hope upon the Lord; for with the Lord there is grace and much redemption with him, and he will redeem Israel from all of his sins.

In the libretto, this psalm text is combined with two chorale strophes from the hymn *Herr Jesu Christ, du höchstes Gut* (Lord Jesus Christ, you highest good), written by Bartholomäus Ringwaldt in 1588.

According to ancient tradition, Psalm 130 is associated with the eleventh Sunday after Trinity, and its Gospel reading is from Luke 18, the parable of the Pharisees and the customs officers. Thus it is possible that the cantata was performed on September 4, 1707, in Mühlhausen. On the other hand, Psalm 130 belongs to the seven penitential psalms, to be sung on days of penance, fasting, and prayer. Since the hymn just mentioned by Bartholomäus Ringwaldt appears in hymnaries of the period under the rubric "Von der Buße und Beichte" (Of penance and confession), the theory that the cantata is for a penitential service has the most in its favor, pending further investigation. Whether such things were common in Mühlhausen remains to be investigated.

Not only textually but also musically Bach's cantata looks to the past. In remarkable ways it shows itself to be the descendant of traditions of the seventeenth century. It would be worth investigating whether only elements of personal style are at work here and whether the work reflects the level of Bach's compositional abilities in 1707 or whether there was a kind of resistance to current trends** and hence a situation akin to that of the Mühlhausen source texts.

Typical of the style of the seventeenth century and of our cantata as well is the small-segmented approach that follows the text step-by-step, related to the procedure for writing motets. In multifarious gradations of solo and polyphonic vocal textures and the choral alternation between vocal and instrumental parts, new facets continually reveal themselves in a virtually inexhaustible wealth of invention. Large-scale relationships and closed forms, on the other hand, are rather more exceptional. They are found in the two multitextual chorale arrangements: the quartet "So du willst, Herr, Sünde zurechnen" (If you should, Lord, mark sins) with the chorale strophe "Erbarm dich mein in solcher Last" (Have mercy upon me, under such burden) for bass, soprano, obbligato oboe, and basso continuo, as well as in the trio "Meine Seele wartet auf den Herrn" (My soul waits upon the Lord) with the chorale strophe "Und will ich denn in meinem Sinn" (And since I then in my mind) for tenor, alto, and continuo. Both sections of the cantata display an unmistakable affinity to writing for organ and show Bach, the

Mühlhausen organist, in his element. The same applies to the elaborately fugal final movement, in which a playful motive of instrumental character for the text "Und er wird Israel erlösen" (And he will redeem Israel) is combined with an ascending linear passage in half steps for the text portion "aus allen seinen Sünden" (from all of his sins). According to more recent studies, this double motive with simultaneous contrast is not an invention of Bach's but rather a thematic structure that Bach—perhaps by way of his oldest brother—adopted from Johann Pachelbel. Its roots reach far back, at least past Jan Pieterszoon Sweelinck into the sixteenth century.

*Petzoldt (1992, 133).
**Ernst (1987, 76ff.).

Nach dir, Herr, verlanget mich
BWV 150 / BC B 24

Homage, ca. 1707

The cantata *Nach dir, Herr, verlanget mich* BWV 150 (For you, Lord, I do long) has been handed down to us without any assignment to the church calendar. In other respects, it is the source of headaches for performers as well as scholars. Indeed, the legitimacy of the attribution to Johann Sebastian Bach was in doubt for a very long time. In particular, it was Arnold Schering, one of the most significant music scholars of the first half of the twentieth century, who with immoderate oratory attempted to convince the experts of the cantata's inauthenticity. Schering closed a 1913 special study* with a kind of sweeping statement with which he described the quality and transmission of the work: "It is all the same, whatever name of a minor Saxon or Thuringian cantor we may put on it. In any case it would be irresponsible, as far as the present case is concerned, if we were to allow the letters 'di J. S. Bach' by the teenage St. Thomas student Penzel, put there perhaps through ignorance or foolishness, to lead us astray ever again in our understanding of the personal style and powerful spirit of our Bach."[2]

Strong words, certainly. The analysis that precedes it spares nothing in criticizing compositional technique and text declamation, complains about the lack of clarity of form, and mocks errors of counterpoint. A good explanation for deficits of this sort would be that it could be an early work, making pardonable the sins against the rules of composition and declamation. Although even Arnold Schering cannot deny this idea, he remains true to his intention of striking this cantata from the Bachian canon. He takes advantage of the fact that the cantata has survived the ages only in a copy made shortly after 1750 by the St. Thomas School student Christian Friedrich Penzel and gives full rein to his eloquence:

> The formal layout and style of this so-called ... Bachian cantata place it in the period around or shortly after 1700, where one can still occasionally find the segmented structure as well as simple chaconnes in $\frac{3}{2}$ meter. Leipzig masters of the first rank such as Knüpfer and Schelle are to be disregarded, as well as even Kuhnau, although as a cantata composer he occasionally came off badly. After such brilliant church pieces as he composed around 1710, he would not have offered Leipzig something so hackneyed and old-fashioned. It strikingly demonstrates the total immaturity in judgment of the young Penzel, as he copied this particular cantata that no one could have appreciated in 1750. Or was it piety before an ancient, yellowed manuscript in Sebastian's music case that he in careless haste signed with the name of the great one? Precisely because of his immaturity, he scarcely would have thought of an intentional deception.[3]

If one reduces this verbal cascade to its core substance, what remains is the assertion that the cantata would already have been regarded as distinctly unmodern when it was copied shortly after 1750 and was therefore—particularly with regard to its pronounced, finely segmented structure—to be placed hypothetically around 1700. What kept Schering and others from placing the work around 1705 and regarding it as a youthful work by Johann Sebastian Bach? In addition to several musical blunders one would not want to ascribe to the master of the St. Matthew Passion, even in his younger years, it was above all the form of the text that did not conform to the prevailing opinion as to the course of development. It was believed that the combination of biblical passages and free poetry found in the cantata *Nach dir, Herr, verlanget mich* could not have originated before 1710 because it presupposed a specific change in the form of cantata libretti. For decades there had been talk of a "text reform" and of its supposed originator, Erdmann Neumeister, chief pastor in Hamburg at the end of his career. It is said to have been Neumeister who, after introducing free poetry into the church cantata in 1702, eleven years later created the so-called mixed text form consisting of free poetry as well as biblical passages and chorale verse. In no way is this true, and it doesn't apply to the cantata *Nach dir, Herr, verlanget mich* anyway. For the mere presence of free poetry in the text has nothing to do with the modern formal world of recitative and aria drawn from opera, which Erdmann Neumeister had in fact made accessible to the church cantata. Instead, what we have here are strophic forms of an older style, suggesting that they may be the verses of a very rare, as yet unidentified chorale. To use texts of this sort for composition—even in connection with biblical text—was not at all unusual for the seventeenth century. Further, nothing speaks against the hypothesis that in choosing the text, the young Johann Sebastian Bach was following conventions of the age as well as the traditions of the Bach family. Another question concerns when and to what purpose the cantata may have been composed. There are securely dated works for comparison from Bach's Mühlhausen period, from mid-1707 to mid-1708, but these are distinguished by a visibly more advanced compositional technique. Accordingly, the cantata *Nach dir, Herr, verlanget mich* must have been composed during Bach's years in Arnstadt, from the summer of 1703 to the summer of 1707. But at least until February 1706, the young Arnstadt organist refused to make music in the church with students at the lyceum, precluding the performance of cantatas. So the question remains open whether the cantata really belongs to the Arnstadt period and in Arnstadt itself or whether it may have been performed in one of the surrounding villages.

Further, no details have been established regarding the author and origin of the text.[4] Of its six sections, three are taken from Psalm 25:

Nach dir, Herr, verlanget mich. Mein Gott, ich hoffe auf dich. Laß mich nicht zuschanden werden, daß sich meine Feinde nicht freuen über mich. (1–2)
   Leite mich in deiner Wahrheit und lehre mich; denn du bist der Gott, er mir hilft, täglich harre ich dein. (5)
   Meine Augen sehen stets zu dem Herrn; denn er wird meinen Fuß aus dem Netze ziehen. (15)

After you, Lord, I long. My God, I place my hopes in you. Let me not be ashamed, so that my enemies do not triumph over me.
   Lead me in your truth, and teach me; for you are the God who helps me, daily I await you.
   My eyes always look to the Lord; for he will pull my foot out of the net.

The succession of these three psalm verses can be described with the key words "Prayer," "Confession," and "Certainty." At the center stands "Confession"; it is flanked by two six-line strophes that are interrelated, although they are structured differently. At the same time, they, as well as the concluding eight-line strophe, can be understood to interpret the psalm verses that precede them. To this extent, the cantata text can be said to be elegantly structured and consciously formed, in spite of its simplicity and brevity.

The same can be said of the composition, with the proviso that the work depicts the young Bach's search for his own musical language and, further, his struggle for mastery of his musical craft. Yet even at this putative early stage there is no lack of self-confidence: right away in the first movement, a sinfonia of fewer than twenty measures and a quite modest ensemble of two violins, bassoon, and basso continuo sets forth the main theme in all of its parts for the following vocal movement in the style of an Italian trio sonata. This theme consists mainly of a series of half-tone steps that fill out the interval of the fourth—the traditional *lamento*—so that the text "Nach dir, Herr, verlanget mich" is presented as a passionate lamentation. In a rapid succession of lively and measured phrases, an extended fugal exposition is reached in which the text "daß sich meine Feinde nicht freuen über mich" is combined with a variant of the *lamento* theme, for which the coloratura on the keyword "freuen" (triumph) helps to reveal new aspects.

The first freely versified text "Doch bin und bleibe ich vergnügt" (Yet I am and remain content) is set as an aria for soprano and obbligato violins. "Aria" is admittedly a high-flown designation for the short-segmented structure, in which hardly two measures follow one another without being separated by a cadence. Motet-like short segmentation also characterizes the second choral movement, on a passage from Psalm 25. Here, sustained single pitches stand out, an illustrative element depicting the word "harren" (await). The second aria is set up as a trio of alto, tenor, and bass, in parallel for the most part. Their text, beginning "Zedern müßen von den Winden / Oft viel Ungemach empfinden" (Cedars must, from the winds / Often suffer much hardship), provides the composer the occasion to depict, through the incessant figuration of the basso continuo, the raging of the forces of nature. The ensuing psalm verse follows the model of the first, beginning with the short-breathed exchange of phrases that culminates in a fugal intensification, here, however, with the more challenging procedure of permutation fugue.

The closing and consummate tutti on the freely versified text that begins "Meine Tage in dem Leide / Endet Gott dennoch zur Freude" (My days of suffering / God will nevertheless end with joy) is designed as a chaconne, a series of variations above a constantly repeating theme in the bass. The solemnity of the step dance in $\frac{3}{2}$ meter and its rigorously managed procedures of repetition and variation produce a constant earnestness that creates a unity of character amid the diversity of variations. Thus a large-scale coherence is ultimately established that had been lacking from the previous movements. This "lack" obviously presupposes the perspective of Bach's later oeuvre; in that early period to which the cantata belongs, diversity and variety within a confined space were undoubtedly a virtue, proof of richness of invention, and without this criterion a just assessment of the early works for keyboard and organ would be hardly conceivable.

---

*Schering (1913); Glöckner (1988).

Addendum

Only a few years after his book's publication, Schulze was able to resolve several significant mysteries attending this cantata, clarifying the work's purpose and producing a quite compelling hypothesis as to the author of its text.[5] Within the seven-movement scheme, the three strophes of free verse (movements 3, 5, and 7) read as follows:

3.
Doch bin und bleibe ich vergnügt,
Obgleich hier zeitlich toben
Kreutz, Sturm und andre Proben,
Tod, Höll und was sich fügt.
Ob Unfall schlägt den treuen Knecht,
Recht ist und bleibet ewig Recht.

Yet I am and remain cheerful,
Although here briefly rage
Cross, storm, and other trials,
Death, hell, and all that follow.
Though misfortune may strike the loyal servant,
Right is and must ever remain right.

5.
Zedern müssen von den Winden
Oft viel Ungemach empfinden,
Oftmals werden sie verkehrt.
Rat und Tat auf Gott gestellt,
Achtet nicht was widerbellet,
Denn sein Wort ganz anders lehrt.

Cedars must, from the winds,
Often feel much hardship,
Often are they uprooted.
Counsel and action based on God,
Ignore that which howls back,
For his word teaches quite differently.

7.
Meine Tage in dem Leide
Endet Gott dennoch zur Freude:
Christen auf den Dornenwegen
Führen Himmels Kraft und Segen.

Bleibet Gott mein treuer Schutz,
Achte ich nicht Menschentrutz;
Christus, der uns steht zur Seiten,
Hilft mir täglich sieghaft streiten.

My days in suffering
God nevertheless ends in joy:
Christians on their thorny paths
Are led by heaven's power and blessing
If God remains my loyal defense,
I may ignore human spite;
Christ, who stands at our side,
Helps me daily to fight victoriously.

In 2005 an alert Belgian blogger named Johan DeWael noticed that the last four lines of the concluding eight-line strophe, the chaconne, begin with the letter sequence B-A-C-H and that in the third movement—the first strophe of free poetry—the six lines begin with D-O-K-T-O-R.[6]

The online discussion focused on speculation that Bach had applied his signature to the text of his first cantata, and little further progress in solving the riddle was made. However, by correcting several errors of spelling and usage, Schulze was able to decipher an acrostic that involved all lines of free poetry in the text:

The solution to this puzzle did not present any particular difficulties. All that was required were a few changes to the text as it has stood until now. In the fifth movement, verse 1 (measure 5), the reading "Zedern"—which accords with the primary source, Christian Friedrich Penzel's copy of 1755 (P 1044)—must be restored to its historical spelling "Cedern":[7]

Cedern müssen von den Winden

Similarly, in movement 5, verse 3 (measure 15), the nonsensical reading "Oftmals" (often)—obviously the result of a handwriting error, unnoticed until now—had to be corrected to "Niemals" (never), appropriate to the "steadfastness of these trees":

Niemals werden sie verkehrt

In movement 7, verse 4 (measure 28), the imprecise word "Führen" (to lead)—hardly appropriate to "Himmels Kraft und Segen" (Heaven's power and blessing)—was replaced by the—conjectural—"Kühren" (old spelling, here used in the sense of "elect"):

Küren Himmels Kraft und Segen

The freely versified strophes, corrected by means of these minor edits, yield the acrostic *Doktor Conrad Meckbach* and thus refer to one of the most important Mühlhausen personages during the era of young Johann Sebastian Bach.[8]

A year after publishing these revelations in *Bach-Jahrbuch* 2010, Schulze followed up with several corrections and clarifications.[9] The spelling "DOCTOR" is more historically appropriate to the early eighteenth century and hence preferable to "DOKTOR"; moreover, the Penzel copy has "Creutz, Sturm und andere Proben" instead of "Kreutz," as seen in recent editions. Second, a presentation print of the text must have been produced in addition to the performance, since the acrostic could not easily have been perceived aurally alone.

Meckbach was a Mühlhausen burgomaster and town councilor who spoke in favor of hiring Bach as organist at Divi Blasii on May 24, 1707, and, a bit more than a year later, on June 26, 1708, recommended that Bach's dismissal be granted to allow him to accept a new position at the court of Weimar.

Schulze tentatively suggested that Georg Christian Eilmar, archdeacon at St. Mary's in Mühlhausen, may have been the librettist, based on his authorship of several funeral odes for Meckbach's wife in 1709. And in 2011 Schulze ventured the possibility that the work might have been in honor of Meckbach's seventieth birthday on April 19, 1707. Locating the work at Mühlhausen, Schulze concluded in 2010, should make possible a fairer view of its musical merits, help to clarify its compositional superiority to works by contemporaries, and draw attention to commonalities and differences with its sister works *Aus der Tiefen rufe ich, Herr, zu dir* BWV 131 and *Gott ist mein König* BWV 71.

Christ lag in Todes Banden
BWV 4 / BC A 54
Easter Sunday, April 24, 1707?

The Easter cantata *Christ lag in Todes Banden* BWV 4 (Christ lay in the bonds of death) belongs to a group of fewer than a dozen works that Johann Sebastian Bach composed using pure, unmodified chorale texts. This technique was hardly his own invention; it appears rather frequently in the seventeenth and early eighteenth centuries, and it enjoyed a certain favor among cantors of St. Thomas. Ernst Ludwig Gerber, organist at the court of Sondershausen, writing in his dictionary of composers published in

Leipzig in 1790, describes Johann Friedrich Doles, Bach's second successor at St. Thomas: "For the most part he performs his own compositions in the churches. And in the interest of greater variety, since 1766 he has set entire chorales through in the manner of the famous Kuhnau, occasionally recasting the contents of the strophes as recitatives, arias, duets and choruses, and performed them to great acclaim instead of the usual church cantatas."[10]

The year given by Gerber lends his account considerable credence because he matriculated at the University of Leipzig early in the same year. Hence his account apparently reflects the first impressions of music he encountered in the trade-fair city at a time when the young Goethe also frequented the *Alma mater Lipsiensis*. Moreover, Gerber's allusion to the *Manier* of Bach's predecessor Johann Kuhnau was hardly baseless; the dictionary article states: "He was not the initiator but rather the fortunate follower of the manner of church cantatas in which a chorale serves as text, the content of every strophe worked through. I own the chorale *Wer nur den lieben Gott läßt walten* in this style by him."[11] Two centuries later, scholars have supplemented Gerber's brief accounts with a multitude of names, illustrating the continuity of the procedure, whose roots reach back well into the seventeenth century and whose adherents are still found in the middle of the eighteenth. Later examples such as those by Mendelssohn in the nineteenth century are clearly retrospective in nature. In the seventeenth and early eighteenth centuries the most outstanding examples are by the northern German masters Dieterich Buxtehude, Nicolaus Bruhns, and Joachim Gerstenbüttel and in central Germany Johann Philipp Krieger, Friedrich Wilhelm Zachow, and Johann Pachelbel, as well as the Leipzig cantors of St. Thomas Knüpfer, Schelle, and Kuhnau. What is remarkable in all this is that the lexicographer Gerber, in praising the achievements of Kuhnau and Doles in connection with the chorale cantata, completely neglects the contributions of Johann Sebastian Bach. This is particularly difficult to explain since his father, Heinrich Nicolaus Gerber, studied in Leipzig beginning in 1724 and must have heard a large part of Bach's annual cycle of chorale cantatas—including the performance of the cantata *Christ lag in Todes Banden* BWV 4.2 at Easter in 1725.

This performance in early 1725 was the conclusion—earlier than planned—of the annual cycle begun in the summer of the previous year. Cantatas performed after Easter of 1725 do not belong to the chorale cantata type. Strictly speaking, the cantata *Christ lag in Todes Banden* was just a straggler. Only a few days previously, Bach had completed the last newly composed work for his chorale cantata cycle: *Wie schön leuchtet der Morgenstern* BWV 1 (How brightly shines the morning star) for March 25, the feast day of the Annunciation of Mary. *Christ lag in Todes Banden*, on the other hand, involved the reperformance of an existing work: it had been heard the year before, the current version having cornet and trombones added to three of the seven vocal movements.

In the context of Bach's chorale cantata cycle begun in June 1724, the first Leipzig performance of the Easter cantata in April 1724 might be understood as a testing of the waters, so to speak. But there are qualifications: features of the work's style exclude the possibility that *Christ lag in Todes Banden* originated in 1724. Its musical diction instead points to the era of the young J. S. Bach. Specifically, the work is comparable to his Mühlhausen cantatas of 1707–8; one might suppose that the work (BWV 4.1) was meant for Easter 1708 and performance at St. Blasius Church. An even more likely hypothesis is that the work was composed a year earlier and served as audition music for Bach's application to the position of organist at St. Blasius. That Bach's audition took place on Easter Sunday in 1707 is explicitly attested to by the report of the so-called *Eingepfarrten*—the city council's representative for church music.

There are certainly problems with these hypotheses as well. Strictly speaking, the stylistic attributes that point to Bach's early style pertain only from the first movement through the next to the last; the concluding movement is a four-part chorale setting typical of Bach's Leipzig compositional style. If one wanted to postulate a Mühlhausen early version (and very little speaks against such an endeavor), then one would have to consider a completely different concluding movement, of which no trace remains.

Bach's first Leipzig performance of the cantata—possibly with a replacement for the last movement—was a part of the bicentennial celebration of Luther's hymn. It first appeared in 1524, a particularly significant year for the Lutheran Reformation, in a collection printed in Wittenberg entitled *Geystlichen gesangk Buchleyn*, as well as in Erfurt under the title *Enchiridion Oder eyn Handbüchlein*. The oldest version of the hymn appears beneath the heading "Christ ist erstanden, gebessert" (Christ is arisen, improved). In fact, both text and melody go back to the pre-Reformation era, in particular to the sequence traced to the eleventh century, *Victimae paschali laudes*, to the Gregorian Easter Alleluia *Christus resurgens ex mortuis*, and to the twelfth-century Easter hymn *Christ ist erstanden*.[12] However, these are not the only sources that nourish the vivid scenario of Luther's hymn. Essential to Luther's language are, in addition, direct reference to the Bible, on the one hand, and the centuries-old tradition of Easter plays with their transfer of Passion and resurrection to the everyday language of the waning Middle Ages, on the other.

Johann Sebastian Bach's composition transposes this textual and liturgical connection into the musical realm by clothing the cantata in the regalia of the chorale partita. In keeping to the same key in all movements and in its succession of different movement characters, the chorale partita is the counterpart of the secular variation suite. At the time of the cantata's presumed origin, the chorale partita was already in its final stages. It remains debatable whether the young Bach was aware of this historical development when he was occupied with Luther's chorale. If the work was indeed an audition piece, he may have decided that he could place many facets of his compositional art on display and in particular make clear that the close connection between strophic content and musical form was of paramount concern to him.

The palette of models on display ranges from ostinato variation, to trio texture with lively obbligato parts, to canon and *alternatim* forms, to motet with fugal treatment of individual chorale lines.[13] Viewed superficially, the results of his compositional effort resemble organ writing. But in contrast to the instrumental chorale partita, which can pursue purely musical objectives, the cantata in the form of a chorale partita is strictly bound by the sequence of strophes and their contents. The manner in which the composer met this challenge demonstrates how absorbed the young Bach was in mastering complicated, multidimensional tasks. The quality of the result is shown simply by the fact that the composer himself, after nearly two decades, felt it appropriate to include the work almost without change in the ambitious project of the chorale cantata annual cycle.

Gottes Zeit ist die allerbeste Zeit
BWV 106 / *BC* B 18
Memorial Service, ca. 1707–1708

The cantata *Gottes Zeit ist die allerbeste Zeit* BWV 106 (God's time is the best time of all), also known as the *Actus tragicus*, has always been among the most beloved of Bach's vocal works. In his 1908 biography of Bach, Albert Schweitzer even maintained that "there is hardly an admirer of his who has not felt that we would give the two hundred church cantatas for one hundred works in the style of the *Actus tragicus*."[14] Schweitzer formulated his opinion in connection with a critical examination of the range of forms in the church cantatas. Recitatives and da capo arias found little favor here; instead, Schweitzer preferred the "animated alternation between solo and chorus" in the style of Bach's early cantatas.[15] With this assessment, he was continuing a conversation that had begun soon after the cantata's appearance in print in 1830. In March 1835 Felix Mendelssohn wrote to his father: "Incidentally there is one peculiar aspect of this music—it must be either very early or very late, for it differs entirely from his usual style of writing in middle age; the first choral movements and the final chorus are of a kind that I would never have thought to be by Sebastian Bach, but rather some other composer of his era, while no other man in the world could have written a single bar of the middle movements." A bit later, *Thomaskantor* Moritz Hauptmann, writing to Otto Jahn, praised the "wundervolle Innerlichkeit" (wonderful interiority) of the work, in which "everything and every detail was so precise and appropriate to the musical meaning and its expression." Hauptmann continued, very much in keeping with his classicizing view of music, "But if one wanted to and could, for a moment, look beyond his feeling for this aspect of beauty and regard the whole as a work of musical architecture, then it is a curious monstrosity of phrases piled on top of one another, grown into one another, just as the text phrases are thrown together without grouping or high points." Judgments of this sort had no place in the later nineteenth century. At the time it was composed, the pieced-together or supposedly fractured form of the *Actus tragicus* was a relic of the seventeenth century; but in the era of Richard Wagner, it was regarded as modern, while the closed form of the da capo aria, preferred by Bach from 1714 onward, was seen as conventional and moribund. From today's standpoint we regard the *Actus tragicus*, along with its few sibling works, as the culmination and conclusion of a development that reaches far back into the seventeenth century—but not at all as an underdeveloped precursor to Bach's later vocal works.

An assessment of this kind presupposes an extensive chronological understanding of Bach's musical legacy. But this poses several problems. The earliest copy originated in Leipzig and is inscribed with the date 1768; it thus can hardly provide evidence as to chronology. Stylistic criteria suggest that the work originated in the context of the earliest of Bach's surviving cantatas. Insofar as these can be dated, they all belong to Bach's Mühlhausen period from June 1707 to June 1708. The rather unusual term *Actus* for a cantata—or, rather, a sacred concerto—is not to be seen as a clue to other nonsurviving parts of the work; instead, it implies an independent, coherent sequence of events. One finds work titles of this sort now and again, for example, a work by Bach's second predecessor as cantor of St. Thomas School, Johann Schelle, his *Actus musicus auf Weihnachten*. Clearly, it is terminology of the seventeenth instead of the eighteenth century.

We could say more about this if we knew more about the occasion for which our cantata was composed. Although it clearly was composed for a memorial service, there is no reliable evidence.[16] For the most part, this also applies to the text. As recent research has shown, the text follows a "form" that can be seen, for example, in the *Christliche Bet-Schule* by Johann Olearius, printed in Leipzig in 1668,* beneath the rubric "Tägliche Seuffzer und Gebet üm ein seliges Ende." Whether several deviations from the printed text reflect Bach's choices or perhaps were the last wish of the deceased remains unknown. This applies in particular to the beginning, which has not been found elsewhere, except for a formulation in Acts of the Apostles 17:

> Gottes Zeit ist die allerbeste Zeit.
> In ihm leben, weben und sind wir, solange er will. In ihm sterben wir zur rechten Zeit, wenn er will. (28)

> God's time is the best time of all.
> In him we live, move, and exist, as long as he wills. In him we die at the right time, when he wills.

Moreover, the continuation is singular, with its slightly modified verse from Psalm 90:12: "Ach Herr, lehre uns bedenken, daß wir sterben müssen, auf daßs wir klug werden" (Ah Lord, teach us to remember that we must die in order that we become wise). The rest of the text is found in Olearius, in the order given there:

ISAIAH 38:1

Bestelle dein Haus; denn du wirst sterben und nicht lebendig bleiben.

Set your house in order, for you will die and not remain living.

SIRACH 13:18

Es ist der alte Bund: Mensch, du mußt sterben.

It is the ancient covenant: Man, you must die.

REVELATION OF ST. JOHN 22:20

Ja komm, Herr Jesu!

Yes come, Lord Jesus!

PSALM 31:5

In deine Hände befehl ich meinen Geist; du hast mich erlöset, Herr, du getreuer Gott.

Into your hands I commit my spirit; you have redeemed me, Lord, you faithful God.

LUKE 23:43

Heute wirst du mit mir im Paradies sein.

Today you will be with me in Paradise.

Cross-references in Johann Olearius's prayer book point to both of the chorale strophes included in our cantata: the opening strophe of Martin Luther's German version of the Nunc Dimittis, *Mit Fried und Freud fahr ich dahin* of 1524, as well as the seventh strophe from Adam Reusner's only slightly more recent hymn *In dich hab ich gehoffet, Herr*:

> Glorie, Lob, Ehr und Herrlichkeit
> Sei dir, Gott Vater und Sohn bereit',
> Dem Heilgen Geist mit Namen!
> Die göttlich Kraft
> Mach uns sieghaft
> Durch Jesum Christum, Amen
>
> May glory, praise, honor, and majesty
> Be bestowed upon you, God Father and Son,
> [And] to the Holy Spirit by name!
> May the divine power
> Make us victorious
> Through Jesus Christ, Amen.

This libretto presented the composer with the task of realizing the diversity of the text as far as possible, on the one hand, while not endangering the coherence of the overall work, on the other. Bach's solution offers a balanced grouping of movements and their parts around a center that is at once musical, spiritual, and theological. In the section beginning with the words "Es ist der alte Bund: Mensch du mußt sterben," there are several levels layered on top of one another. The three lower voices begin with a choral fugue that soon breaks off and is answered by the soprano's "Ja komm, Herr Jesu." Shortly afterward, the chorale melody *Ich hab mein Sach Gott heimgestellt* (I have left all that I have to God) is heard in instrumental three-part harmony. This sequence of choral fugue, soprano solo, and instrumental chorale appears four times in total at ever shorter intervals, giving the impression of acceleration and compression. In the fourth and final iteration, this impression is intensified by the simultaneous sounding of choral fugue and instrumental chorale, while the soprano trades places with the latter and, in a lonely solo, unaccompanied at the end, brings the "antithesis ... between the Hebrew Bible fear of death and the New Testament joy in death" to a preliminary culmination.[17]

Even in the opening measures of the instrumental prelude, it is clear that the other movements of the cantata do not recede behind this central complex. As Albert Schweitzer writes, this "stille musique," a sonatina for two flutes, two violas da gamba, and continuo, "is based on a motive in E-flat, expressive of transfigured grief; this runs through the whole work. To grasp these harmonies is to be transported far from all earthly pain; the words from the Apocalypse come into one's mind that Bach probably had in his—'And God shall wipe away all the tears from their eyes, and there shall be no more death, neither sorrow, nor crying, neither shall there be any more pain; for the former things are passed away.'"[18]

---

*Steiger (1989).

Gott ist mein König
BWV 71 / BC B 1
Mühlhausen City Council Inauguration, February 4, 1708

The cantata *Gott ist mein König* BWV 71 (God is my king) belongs to Bach's church music for special occasions. One such special occasion in the middle-class cities of Bach's era was the annual inauguration of the city council. Our cantata, composed in 1708, owes its origin to the town council inauguration in Mühlhausen, Thuringia.

Mühlhausen, a free imperial city subject only to the Holy Roman emperor, was governed by a plenary council of forty-eight members. Of these forty-eight, three subcouncils of sixteen members each rotated at established intervals in conducting city affairs. Each council of sixteen comprised fourteen councilmen and two mayors. A description from the eighteenth century recorded how another such transfer of business proceeded in Mühlhausen:

> On February 3 the new councilmen were elected, and thus on the day afterward the inauguration of the new council occurred. The great bell, all alone, was rung between seven and eight o'clock in the morning. Then the council walked in procession from the town hall to the church. The path there was strewn with sand. The rifle company and young citizens formed a line on either side. The old, outgoing council walked ahead; the new one followed; and the council servants brought up the rear. Meanwhile, two bands of musicians with trumpets and drums played opposite one another in front of the bread market and the treasury. At the beginning of the church service two hymns were sung, then the regent's sermon was delivered, and after the sermon a concert was held to wish the new council good fortune,

vocally and instrumentally. This lasted an entire hour, and only the little council piece was named. On each occasion this was repeated in St. Blasius Church on the afternoon of the following Sunday. Another hymn was sung after the blessing. Afterward the new council led the procession and positioned itself by rank before the church door, where, beneath the open sky and the image of His Imperial Roman Majesty, they took their oath, administered by the general counsel standing in the doorway. Afterward the procession returned the way they had come, only that the new council took the lead. Then a great festival was held at the town hall, where the bakers' guild presented a cake, called *Mahlplatz*, to honor the new council.

The first performance of the "council piece" took place in spacious St. Mary's Church. By ancient custom the organist at the second main church, St. Blasius, was responsible for the composition. Frequently, although not always, the text and music of the composition were reproduced in printed form by the council's administrative office and, presumably, distributed as commemorative gifts. Very few of these printed Mühlhausen council pieces have been preserved, but, happily, Bach's cantata is among them. Actually, one needs to speak of "Bach's cantatas," since in 1709 Bach also provided the Mühlhausen council piece and issued it in print. Unfortunately, nothing further is known about this second print, not even the title of the lost cantata, which Bach must have composed and prepared for performance from his new post at the court of Weimar.

The names of the two mayors in the sitting council chosen in February 1708 are given in the old-fashioned folio distributed along with the music print, which serves as a text supplement as well as an overall title. The names of the other councilmen, also honored by the sounds of Bach's music as they were conducted into office, can be gleaned from the archives. They are Beyreiß and Stüler, Backmeister and Schmidt, Bellstedt, Stephan, and Hagedorn. Their professions are postal administrator, city scribe, master clothier and lawyer, master baker, and garment maker. The older of the two mayors, Adolf Strecker, was certainly more significant with regard to the cantata than his colleague, the master butcher Georg Adam Steinbach, who in 1708 entered high office for the first time; Strecker, on the other hand, had already presided over the council several times. Four months after his inauguration Strecker turned eighty-four years old, and death overtook him three months after that in the middle of his term. One remained mayor or councilman for life, even as advancing years robbed him of his powers.

The unidentified librettist, perhaps a member of the Mühlhausen clergy, furnished a selection of Bible verses, all from the Hebrew Bible, as well as a chorale strophe with a high incidence of allusion to the biblical age of the first mayor. In any case, a verse from Psalm 74 begins the text, which at the time was understood as dealing "with divine salvation": "Gott ist mein König von alters her, der alle Hilfe tut, so auf Erden geschieht" (God is my king from of old who works all salvation that happens on Earth). But this is followed by a conflation of two verses from 2 Samuel 19. These verses are about aged Barsillai of Gilead, who was at least eighty years old. He led King David and his people across the Jordan and replied to the request that he go along to Jerusalem thusly:[19]

> Ich bin nun achtzig Jahr. . . .
> Warum soll dein Knecht sich mehr beschweren? (35) Laß mich
>   umkehren
> Daß ich sterbe in meiner Stadt
> Bei meines Vaters
> Und meiner Mutter Grab. (37)
>
> I am now eighty years old. . . .
> Why should your servant be burdened more? Let me return
> That I may die in my city Beside my father's
> And my mother's graves.

This biblical passage is attached to a chorale strophe from Johannes Heerman's hymn *O Gott du frommer Gott* (O God you pious God), a "tägliches Gebet um göttlichen Gnade und Beistand" (daily prayer for divine grace and assistance). There, strophes 4 through 6 focus on "geduldiges Leiden" (patient suffering), and the sixth strophe, connected in the cantata to the passage from Samuel, reads:

> Soll ich auf dieser Welt
> Mein Leben höher bringen
> Durch manchen sauren Tritt
> Hindurch ins Alter dringen
> So gib Geduld, für Sünd und Schanden mich bewahr
> Auf daß ich tragen mag
> Mit Ehren graues Haar.
>
> Should I in this world
> Bring my life further
> Through many a bitter step
> Pushing further into old age
> Then grant patience, protect me from sin and disgrace
> That I may wear
> With honor my gray hair

The objection is occasionally raised that this strophe does not properly fit the biblical passage, since the strophe points to a future era while the passage takes it for granted. This objection can be dismissed as overdrawn. The biblical passage that follows is the last one that focuses on age. It comprises two verses from Deuteronomy and Genesis: "Dein Alter sei wie deine Jugend" (Deuteronomy 33:25; May your old age be as your youth) and "Und Gott ist mit dir in allem, das du tust" (Genesis 21:22; And God is with you in everything that you do).

Everything further is aimed at the council election in general and focuses directly or indirectly on the usual wishes for a peaceful government serving the common good without disruption by external enemies. Psalm 74 is drawn upon again, with verses 16 and 17:

> Tag und Nacht ist dein. Du machest, daß beide, Sonn und Gestirn, ihren gewissen Lauf haben. Du setztest einem jeglichen Lande seine Grenze.
>
> Day and night are yours. You make it that both, sun and stars, have their certain course. For each and every country you set its borders.

And later:

> Du wollest dem Feinde nicht geben die Seele deiner Turteltauben.
>
> You do not wish to give the enemy the souls of your turtledoves.

The close of the first psalm verse is developed further in a freely versified aria text:

> Durch mächtige Kraft
> Erhältst du unsre Grenzen.
> Hier muß der Friede glänzen,
> Wenn Mord und Kriegessturm
> Sich allerort erhebt.
>
> Through mighty strength
> You maintain our borders.
> Here peace must shine forth
> If murder and storm of war
> Everywhere arise.

This sort of thing was not simply a continuation of convention, for in those years central Germany in particular suffered the rampaging military campaigns of Swedish king Charles XII. And the free poetry based on the second psalm quotation once again prays for "Friede, Ruh und Wohlergehen" (peace, calm, and prosperity) for the government before wishing "Glück, Heil und großer Sieg" (good fortune, salvation, and great victory) for Emperor Joseph I, reigning since 1705.

Bach's composition largely reflects the rather backward-looking profile of this text, in which recitative and aria, elements that had been common since the beginning of the eighteenth century, are avoided as much as possible. For that reason, recent scholarship has classified this Mühlhausen cantata and its sibling works as the crowning culmination of stylistic developments of the seventeenth century* instead of regarding them as precursors by which Bach prepared himself for his later composition of cantatas. Whether local tradition may have played a role here or even if the possibility of restrictive proscriptions should be considered lies beyond our knowledge at this point.

Any such restrictions in place in 1708 can only have affected the text and array of musical forms—certainly not, however, the musical forces involved. For here, Bach ensured that nothing was missing. Eighteen or if necessary twenty-two voices can participate, unfolding in five to six sonic groups of voices and instruments above the common organ basso continuo: three trumpets and drums; violins, viola, and bass viol; two oboes and bassoon; two recorders and cello; and four voices and four further reinforcing voice parts.

This considerable contingent obviously calls for the spaciousness of Mühlhausen's St. Mary's Church. Since the council piece was traditionally performed a second time on the Sunday following the election in St. Blasius, the composer had to find a way to accommodate the piece within the markedly more confined space of the second main church. In view of the fact that most instrumental parts would have been only minimally set—the woodwinds and brass in particular—arranging the performing forces would have presented no great problem. It would have been more difficult to get together the necessary singers and instrumentalists in Mühlhausen. Presumably, assistants were used, volunteers mostly from surrounding villages who came into the city to help with the performance. Since the first performance fell on February 4, 1708, a Saturday, the second performance in St. Blasius would have taken place the following day, posing no serious organizational difficulties.

It is not easy to say what caused Bach to assemble such elaborate and diverse performing forces, thereby distancing himself from traditions in Mühlhausen that were focused on moderation. Possibly, he was prompted to do so by the memory of the famous, festive *Abendmusiken* that he had experienced two years earlier in Lübeck during his visit with Dieterich Buxtehude.[20]**

Bach's cantata—or, to use his own term, "Motetto"—evinces a rather backward-looking character musically as well as textually. Characteristic in this regard are style elements of the seventeenth century such as small segmentation and frequent cadences. These elements affect not only the ensemble movements at the beginning and end but also the pastorale bass arioso "Tag und Nacht sind dein" (Day and night are yours) and the brass-accompanied alto aria "Durch mächtige Kraft" (Through mighty power). All the more surprising, then, is the expansive breadth with which closed developments of great intensity are created in the other movements. This sort of thing applies first of all to the tenor aria "Ich bin nun achtzig Jahr," which combines its vocal part with the cantus firmus on the melody *O Gott, du frommer Gott*, richly ornamented and performed line by line. Second, it concerns the two motet-like fugues "Dein Alter sei wie deine Jugend" and "muß täglich von neuem dich, Joseph, erfreuen," in which a permutation procedure handed down from the seventeenth century makes possible a spacious and architectonically convincing structure and—in the second fugue—an impressive intensification. In spite of all this, the crown jewel is the filigree akin to chamber music with which the twenty-three-year-old organist delivered his masterpiece in this cantata: the deeply emotional composition on the final psalm verse "Du wollest dem Feinde nicht geben die Seele deiner Turteltauben."

---

*Krummacher (1991).
**Karstädt (1962).

CHAPTER 2

Bach at Weimar and Köthen from March 25, 1708, to Trinity Sunday 1723

Was mir behagt, ist nur die muntre Jagd
BWV 208 / BC G 1

Court of Saxe-Weissenfels, 1713

The significance of Bach's secular vocal compositions is often underestimated. Seen as occasional works of middling rank and as too closely bound to the spirit of the age, they often provide us the only opportunity to discuss the whole complex of Bach's parody technique in its entirety, based on the transfer of individual arias and choruses into his sacred vocal music and his procedure for providing them with new texts. Philipp Spitta, the most prominent Bach scholar of the nineteenth century, actually maintained, categorically, that Bach's compositional style was principally sacred and that he was practically unable to produce secular works; rather, his music was only temporarily on loan to texts that were inappropriate: "His secular occasional works were, rather, nonsecular, and as such they did not fulfill their purpose. The composer returned them to their true home when he transformed them to church music."[1]

But even such a broadside—which recalls Christian Morgenstern's formulation that "was nicht sein kann, nicht sein darf" (that which cannot, must not be)—cannot erase an entire field of creativity.[2] To the fifty or so such works from Bach's pen whose music or at least text is preserved, at least as many have been lost without a trace. Nothing justifies the assumption that the composition and performance of a secular vocal work seemed a burdensome obligation to Bach or that he was never in more of a hurry than when he supposedly rushed to integrate such a piece in his sacred vocal works.

Instead, closer study of the secular cantatas shows that they were not handled any differently than church cantatas, oratorios, masses, or passions. In other words, they were treated as repertoire pieces to be reperformed at the next appropriate occasion with as little effort devoted to revision as possible. This procedure shows, on the one hand, that Bach valued these works as essential components of his entire oeuvre in the way Goethe did, so to speak, and, on the other, that he was as unwilling to tolerate any lapses in quality in this area as in any other. Instead, he always gave his best here and considered the results to be presentable on any occasion.

The *Hunt Cantata* BWV 208 can serve as a perfect example for Bach's management of his secular vocal works as outlined here. The composition originated rather early, no later than 1713 (BWV 208.1); Bach performed it for the last time about thirty years later, in the summer of 1742 (BWV 208.2). In the intervening years, three of its movements were provided with new texts and adopted by various church cantatas; yet this did not affect the continued presence and reperformance of the entire work in Bach's last decade.

Bach's autograph score gives no hint as to the original reason for the work's composition. In it the work is simply entitled "Cantata," although either "Serenata" or "Dramma per musica" would have probably been more appropriate. More clarity is provided by a 1716 reprint of the text, found in part 2 of Salomon Franck's *Geistliche und Weltlichen Poesien* (Sacred and secular poetry). There, the four mythological personages in the libretto are named, along with the following remark: "At the High-Princely Birthday Celebration for Lord Duke Christian of Saxe-Weissenfels, Performed at a Banquet Concert Following a Sport Hunt held in the Princely Hunting Lodge."[3] Christian's birthday fell on February 23 and was usually celebrated on that day or immediately before or afterward. Christian became duke upon the death of his older brother Johann Georg in May 1712. Since the features of Bach's handwriting exclude any later date, the *Hunt Cantata* consequently was composed in February 1713 and dedicated to Christian's first birthday as regent.*

The "Princely Hunting Lodge" belonged to the Weissenfels castle complex. What a "Sport Hunt" looked like in practice can be deduced from certain traditions that continue up to the present day (or the recent unhappy past). In order to spare the potentate the exertion of a real hunt, the game to be killed was driven into an enclosed area, where it fell victim to the hunting party.

The title of the banquet music performed in the Weissenfels hunting lodge is found neither in Bach's score nor in Salomon Franck's reprint of the text. Instead, it is contained in a handwritten note accompanying the score in which the outlines of a dedication can be seen for a print that must have been produced in the past but of which not a single exemplar survives. The note reads: "Frolockender GötterStreit bey des etc. Hochfürstlichen Geburths Tage Unterthänigst aufgeführet von etc." (Jubilant battle of gods at the etc. high-princely birthday, most humbly performed by etc.). While the first "et cetera" can be deciphered easily—here Duke Christian can only be meant; the writer spared himself the duke's complete and longwinded title—we would love to know more about the "Performed by etc." It cannot simply be assumed that the name of the composer and his rank and title stood here ("Fürstlich Sachsen-Weimarischer Hof-Organist und Cammer-Musicus"); the performing ensemble, the Weissenfels Hof-Capelle, might also have been mentioned here.

Finally, the title "Jubilant dispute of the gods" gives us an indication as to the structure of the libretto. In accordance with the way the aristocracy of the era understood themselves, a congratulation could only be accepted from a person of equal birth rank. In the age of the divine right of kings, "equal birth rank" included the gods and heroes of antiquity, and so nearly every librettist helped themselves to the nearly inexhaustible arsenal of ancient mythology. In order to bring at least a hint of plot into the course of a text of this sort (whose function of homage and tribute inherently destined it to one-sidedness), one happily set up a sham dispute about rank between those to be honored, which would be resolved at the end as quickly as the quarrel had been picked out of thin air at the beginning. Admittedly, even this element is inadequately developed in the text for Bach's *Hunt Cantata*, and the libretto—the work of Weimar ducal consistory secretary Salomon Franck—lacks dramatic tension. Four gods of the antique world are mustered: Diana, the goddess of the hunt, also known as Artemis by the Greeks; Pales, the goddess of shepherds and pastures; Endymion, an Aeolian legendary figure, a son of Zeus, who gave him eternal sleep and eternal youth; and Pan, the goat-footed god of mountains and flocks whose home is Arcadia.

All four enter the stage with a recitative and aria, one after the other. Diana begins, praising the hunt as "pleasure of the gods" and an appropriate activity for heroes. Endymion lodges a weak protest and recalls being a prisoner in the "snares of Cupid." Diana takes him to task, saying that such things cannot now be thought of, because the "high birthday feast" for "dear Christian" must be celebrated. Pan rushes to lay down his shepherd's staff and praise the duke as the "Pan of his country," without whom the country would seem like a body without a soul. Pales aims in the same direction, praising serenity, peace, and good fortune as the blessings of the regent who protects his subjects as a good shepherd watches over his flock. All four join together in the song of praise "Lebe, Sonne dieser Erden" (Live, sun of this earth), with which things might be brought to an end. However, all four speak up again: Diana and Endymion together, Pales and Pan at odds, and only a second song of praise at last provides the finale: "Ihr lieblichste Blicke, ihr freudige Stunden, euch bleibe das Glücke auf ewig verbunden" (You loveliest sights, you joyous hours, may good fortune remain yours forever).

Details about how the musical performance proceeded must remain largely a matter of conjecture. In comparison to the four soloists, who probably had no additional support even in the two ensemble pieces, the orchestra was relatively richly scored: two hunting horns, two recorders, three oboes, strings, and basso continuo. One can assume that all participants came from Weissenfels, with the exception of the composer, who may have conducted from the cembalo. The demands on the virtuosity of soloists and instrumentalists remain limited for the most part; evidently, Bach was more interested in textual characteristics and the effective use of timbre. Thus the hunting horns are naturally assigned to Diana's aria, the oboe trio to Pan's song of praise, the bucolic coloration of recorders moving in parallel thirds and sixths to Pales's first aria, and a solo violin to Diana and Endymion's duet. On the other hand, Endymion's aria and each of Pales's and Pan's second arias forgo obbligato instruments; their only instrumental accompaniment is the basso continuo. Bach himself may have artistically enriched this part improvisationally, but the only score handed down to us shows no trace of this. Alert observers at the time may have taken critical note of the way that Bach, in the last two arias, ignored the jurisdiction of the mythological figures of Pan and Pales as he gave the text on "Felder und Auen" (fields and valleys), appropriate for Pales, the goddess of shepherds and fields, to Pan, just as Bach allowed Pales to enthuse about "wollenreichen Herden" (large flocks rich with wool).

The two ensemble movements are partly homophonic and chordal and partly canonic or fugal. In the late 1720s Bach transferred the closing movement of the *Hunt Cantata* to a church cantata for St. Michael's Day and did so again in 1740 for a cantata for the Leipzig city council election.[4] In 1725 Pan's aria, accompanied by three oboes, found its way into the Pentecost cantata *Also hat Gott die Welt geliebt* BWV 68 (God so loved the world), as did Pales's second aria, after extensive revision. With its new text, "Mein gläubiges Herze, frohlocke, sing, scherze" (My faithful heart, rejoice, sing, play), it became widely known in later eras.

As mentioned, these borrowings did not inhibit further performances of the *Hunt Cantata* in its original or slightly modified form. Only a few years after its premiere in Weissenfels, a second performance is likely to have occurred in Weimar to honor Duke Ernst August. Another performance in

Weissenfels is at least within the realm of the possible. There is evidence of another performance in Leipzig at a concert by Bach's Collegium Musicum. One would very much like to know how listeners in *galant* Leipzig may have responded to the music, then thirty years old. It can hardly escape the alert listener that the last six movements are all in F major. The composer may have sought relief by working in one or another instrumental movement from his repertoire as an introduction or interlude—a possibility, given the practices common at the time, that one must also consider for the performances in Weissenfels and Weimar. Many questions remain open in this regard.

---

*Schulze (2000).

Widerstehe doch der Sünde
BWV 54 / *BC* A 51

Oculi, 1708–1717

It is only since 1970 that we have known that Johann Sebastian Bach's cantata *Widerstehe doch der Sünde* BWV 54 (Resist sin indeed) was written for Oculi, the fourth Sunday before Easter. This is due to Elisabeth Noack's discovery of the cantata text cycle *Gottgefälliges Kirchen-Opffer*, published by the Darmstadt court librarian Georg Christian Lehms for the Darmstadt Court Chapel for "Früh- und Mittags-Erbauung" (Early and midday devotion). Johann Sebastian Bach took at least ten texts from this cycle, originally written for the court music director Christoph Graupner, who set much of it to music in 1711 and 1712. Of the ten texts set by Bach, two were composed in Weimar (thus 1717 at the latest), and eight more were composed during his third year in office as cantor of St. Thomas in Leipzig.

In Lehms's cycle, the cantata text *Widerstehe doch der Sünde* appears beneath the heading "Andacht auf den Sonntag Oculi" (Devotion for the Sunday of Oculi). There was church music on Oculi Sunday in Weimar and several other cities but not in Leipzig during Lent, also known as *tempus clausum* (closed time), during which polyphonic church music fell silent. This fact by itself would allow one to conclude that the cantata originated during Bach's Weimar period. In addition, there is a peculiarity of the source transmission: the only manuscript source from the eighteenth century to preserve this work was copied in part by the Weimar city organist, Johann Gottfried Walther, a contemporary and cousin of Bach, and mostly by Johann Tobias Krebs the Elder, father of the better-known organist, composer, and Bach student Johann Ludwig Krebs. The elder Krebs was active as an organist in Buttelstedt near Weimar between 1710 and 1717, but as Johann Gottfried Walther reports in his *Musikalisches Lexikon* of 1732, he continued to study composition and keyboard playing with Walther himself at first and with Johann Sebastian Bach later. In sum, everything supports the view that Walther and his student Johann Tobias Krebs copied Bach's cantata no later than 1717, making it without doubt an early composition.

Certainly, this does not solve all the puzzles, for the score of *Widerstehe doch der Sünde* appears under the heading "Cantata" without naming the point in the church calendar intended by the composer. The text itself shows only a loose relationship to the Gospel reading for Oculi Sunday, the account in Luke 11 of Jesus driving out the devil. The not terribly close relationship between cantata libretto and Sunday Gospel reading should certainly not be given too much weight: Georg Christian Lehms himself expressly wrote his rhymed "Andacht" (Devotion) for Oculi Sunday in the printed text collection of 1711, and Bach must have used exactly this publication. It is therefore not significant that the cantata text *Widerstehe doch der Sünde* was performed in 1739 and 1748 in Leisnig, Saxony (whether or not composed by Bach, remains to be seen), one occasion on Trinity Sunday and the other on the twentieth Sunday after Trinity. Scholars have considered an assignment to Bach's Weimar performance schedule on the seventh Sunday after Trinity in 1714, but this remains hypothetical.

However, another question was definitively answered by the recently discovered text source, namely, whether Bach's cantata is complete. The suspicion has frequently been expressed that the cantata, which contains only three movements, might be a fragment of what was originally a more extensive work. This suspicion arose, on the one hand, from the relative brevity of the composition and, on the other, from the apparently narrow scope of ideas in its text, which revolves around sin and the devil, using powerful Baroque vocabulary. But the evaluation must proceed from the opposite direction. With *Widerstehe doch der Sünde* we are dealing with a cantata in the literal sense, an example of that construct that the theologian and poet Erdmann Neumeister in 1720 characterized as having the appearance of "a piece from an opera, assembled of recitatives and arias" (ein Stück aus einer Oper, von Stylo Recitativo und Arien zusammen gesetzt).[5] Two arias with an intervening recitative are practically the minimum needed to fulfill the definition of a cantata. In this context, concentration of ideas is not a fault; it is a virtue. Georg Christian Lehms, with above average experience for his young age, knew how to work with rigor and freedom as well as unity and contrast, as he created both opera libretti and texts for church music.

Lehms's great skill is demonstrated in the cantata text for Oculi Sunday, although it contains no more than two dozen verses. The first aria begins:

> Widerstehe doch der Sünde,
> Sonst ergreifet dich ihr Gift.

> Resist sin indeed,
> Lest its poison take hold of you.

After this admonition, the consequences of defiance are described:

> Laß dich nicht den Satan blenden
> Denn die Gottes Ehre schänden
> Trifft ein Fluch, der tödlich ist.

> Do not let Satan blind you,
> For those who disgrace God's honor
> Are struck by a curse that is deadly.

In the text as published by Lehms, the closing line reads "Trifft ein Fluch, der tödlich trifft" (Are struck by a curse that strikes fatally); one must assume that the repeated "trifft" was intentional and not the result of oversight or ineptitude. The version in the Bach cantata avoids the repetition of the word but at the cost of the now-missing rhyme for the word "Gift."

The second aria—the cantata's closing movement—proceeds in the opposite direction from the first movement. It begins with the consequences of defiance:

> Wer Sünde tut, der ist vom Teufel
> Denn dieser hat sie aufgebracht

> Whoever commits sin, he is of the devil,
> For the devil has brought it forth.

It then points to "rechte Andacht" (proper devotion) as a promising remedy:

> Doch wenn man ihren schnöden Banden
> Mit rechter Andacht widerstanden
> Hat sie sich gleich davongemacht.

> Yet if its vile bonds
> With proper devotion are resisted
> It has made off immediately.

The beginning of the aria proves to be a direct quotation from 1 John 3:8: "Wer Sünde tut, der ist vom Teufel; denn der Teufel sündigt vom Anfang.

Darzu ist erschienen der Sohn Gottes, daß er die Werke des Teufels zerstöre" (He that commits sin is of the devil, for the devil sins from the beginning. For this purpose the Son of God was manifested, that he might destroy the works of the devil).

The reciprocal relationship between the two aria texts is reflected in the recitative that connects them in an opposition of external appearance and inner reality:

> Die Art verruchter Sünden
> Ist zwar von außen wunderschön.
> . . . .
> Von außen ist sie Gold
> Doch, will man weitergehn
> So zeigt sich nur ein leerer Schatten
> Und übertünschtes Grab.
>
> The nature of wicked sins
> Is certainly wonderfully beautiful from the outside.
> . . . .
> From outside it is gold.
> Yet if one goes further,
> It proves only an empty shadow
> And whitewashed sepulchre.

The concept "außen Gold" (outwardly gold) and inner "leerer Schatten" (empty shadow) targets hypocrites and conceited Pharisees. The same is true of the image of the "whitewashed sepulchre": it comes from Jesus's sermon against the scribes and Pharisees from Matthew 23:27–28: "Woe unto you, scribes and Pharisees, you hypocrites, for you are like the whitened sepulchres, which indeed appear beautiful outwardly, but inwardly they are full of bones of the dead, and of all uncleanness. Even so you also outwardly appear righteous before people, but within you are full of hypocrisy and iniquity." One finds similar language in Luke 11 and thus in the immediate vicinity of the Gospel reading for Oculi Sunday, obviously taken up by the librettist Lehms.

At the time, a favorite vehicle for the comparison between outward appearance and inner condition—as well as the "übertünschter Gräber"—was the *Sodomsapfel* (apple of Sodom), the fruit of a shrub living near the Dead Sea. "Sie ist den Sodomsäpfeln gleich" (It is like the apple of Sodom), reads Lehms's recitative regarding sin. What is meant—according to a description from 1721—is "a lovely fruit to look at, white and reddish, like small apples of Paradise. Inside, however, they are full of white seeds, like unripe apples, without juice, bitter and tasteless. Those left on the vine dry out and turn black, and if one breaks them open they emit dust like ashes. . . . Tacitus thought the same thing, almost in the same manner, as did the Jewish historian Josephus. Several scholars consider them a remnant or reminder of the destruction of Sodom."[6] The history of the Jews, quoted here from Flavius Josephus in the first century CE, was in Bach's library. Whether he consulted it in order to enlighten himself about the concept "Sodomsäpfel" must remain an open question.

That Bach's composition belongs to his Weimar period is shown not only by the source of the printed text (the presumed liturgical placement as well as its manuscript score copy) but also by particular musical details. Among these are the setting of the first movement, with two violins and two violas. Violas divisi are characteristic of Bach's early work, but not that of Köthen or Leipzig. Also pointing to Weimar is the remarkably deep range of the voice: the solo alto operates mostly in the region of what is known as the "small octave" and frequently must descend as far as F below middle C.[7] This could have to do with the specifics of the Weimar musical establishment, such as, for example, the performance of the cantata by a male falsettist. But the most likely reason is the relatively high tuning of the organ at Weimar castle church, which had the effect that the performance pitch of E-flat, relative to the chamber pitch at that time, sounded at least as high as F. The deep timbre of the strings, with glistening sixteenth-note figuration enveloping the voice, and the seductive dissonances, evocative of the modern Italian concerto, characterize the enticing pull of sin; at the words "sonst ergreifet dich ihr Gift" the voice too falls away. The long-held tones on the word "widerstehe" against dissonant cross-relations embody resistance, as do the rousing dissonances with which the movement suddenly begins, intended as a wakening call, together with the unaccompanied and hence clearly audible words of warning in the middle part of the first movement. The recitative begins restfully but flows into animated sixteenth-note passages in the accompanying part as sin is compared to a "scharfer Schwert" (sharp sword) in the text "das uns durch Leib und Seele fährt" (that slices through our body and soul). We are met with a sharper pace in the last movement: violins and violas are constantly in unison, whereby the number of voices as compared to the first movement shrinks from six to four. In place of the seductive, euphonious sonorities and the deceptive security of a slumber scene, there enters the alert vigilance of a vocal-instrumental fugue in which the strict half-tone steps assigned to the keywords "Sünde" (sin) and "Teufel" (devil) and the single-minded determination of the permutation technique so favored by Bach no longer allow any deviation from the prescribed path of virtue, embodied by "rechte Andacht" (proper devotion).[8]

In terms of its textual concept as well as its musical substance, the cantata *Widerstehe doch der Sünde* proves to be a masterwork despite its early origin. Johann Sebastian Bach was also aware of the lasting value of his composition: in 1731, as he began work on a passion according to Mark, he recalled his Weimar cantata of nearly twenty years earlier and engaged his Leipzig librettist to write a new text for its first movement, allowing the aria to be included in his passion.

Himmelskönig, sei willkommen
BWV 182 / BC A 53

Palm Sunday, March 25, 1714

In several respects, the cantata *Himmelskönig, sei willkommen* BWV 182 (King of heaven, be welcomed) occupies a special place among the works of Johann Sebastian Bach. One of these is the fact that this is the work with which Bach began his regular composition of cantatas at Weimar. Another exceptional feature concerns the work's intended place in the church year.

For Bach, the move from Mühlhausen to Weimar in the early summer of 1708 meant a change from a position as city organist to a similar one at court. He served for nearly six years as court organist and chamber musician before he gained a promotion. If his main focus had previously been on organ performance and composition and, according to family lore, gaining "the goodwill of his gracious employers," he now had to turn to a new, more strictly regimented realm of activity. The earliest biography states: "In the year 1714 he was named Concertmaster at the same court. Now, the functions connected with this post then consisted mainly in composing church pieces and performing them."[9] At present we have no further detail about the appointment because part of the archive was destroyed in 1774 when a lightning strike and resulting fire consumed much of the Weimar castle.

Fortunately, at the beginning of the twentieth century an alternative was found for the lost records. The notes of a court secretary, akin to a diary, were examined in the Weimar archive, providing fairly precise points of reference. In the volume for 1714 the notes state: "Friday, the 2. of March, 1714, His Serene Highness the Reigning Duke most graciously conferred upon the quondam Court Organist Bach, at his most humble request, the title of Concertmaster, with official rank below that of Vice-Capellmeister Drese, for which he is to be obliged and to be held accountable to perform new works monthly."[10]

Bach's "most humble request" has not been handed down. Even so, it is worth considering what it probably contained. The court organist would have referred to his appointment in 1708 with "most humble gratitude," to the continuing grace and kind benevolence of the entire princely house, and to his obligations with respect to the castle church organ and the court chapel ensemble. At this point, Johann Sebastian Bach would have started to speak of the high cost of living, the need to support his ever-increasing family, and the urgency of either receiving an increase in salary at court or seeking advancement elsewhere. For this last possibility he held a trump card in his sleeve: in mid-December 1713, having successfully passed an audition, he had been chosen as organist at the Church of Our Lady in Halle and had a written contract in hand, ready for countersigning, and was at that moment engaged in drawing out negotiations with more monetary demands.

If he wanted to retain his capable court organist, Duke Wilhelm Ernst of Saxe-Weimar had no other option than to give in to the pressure and strike a compromise acceptable to both sides. The appointment of a certain Georg Christoph Strattner in 1695 could serve as a model. Strattner was named vice music director with the requirement that he "in the absence of the current Capellmeister Johann Samuel Drese, or when he is unable to come out because of his known physical infirmity, shall direct the entire chapel, and in such cases hold the usual rehearsals in Drese's quarters, and not less frequently than every fourth Sunday, perform a piece of his own composition in the ducal castle church under his own direction." Strattner died in 1704; his position was taken over by a son of music director Drese, who was still in office in 1704 as well as 1714—and still sick.

And so, in early 1714, the new position of concertmaster was arranged for Johann Sebastian Bach, together with the age-old obligation to provide newly composed *Stücke* (pieces)—in today's parlance, church cantatas—in the castle church every month, in other words, on a four-week rotation. Traditionally, rehearsals were to be held outside the church, but there appear to have been problems with this. The notes of the court secretary make quite clear: "NB. Rehearsing of the musical pieces at home or one's own lodgings was changed as of March 23, 1714, and it was expressly ordered that it should always take place in the church chapel."[11] Two days after the issuance of this direct order, Bach's cantata *Himmelskönig, sei willkommen* was heard for the first time in the Kirchen-Cappelle, the elevated music gallery in the church.

Certainly, this work was not the very first Weimar church cantata by Bach. Two solo cantatas on texts by the Darmstadt court librarian Georg Christian Lehms probably preceded it: the cantatas *Mein Herze schwimmt im Blut* BWV 199 and *Widerstehe doch der Sünde* BWV 54. In addition, a composition on a text by Erdmann Neumeister could have originated before 1714: the Sexagesima cantata *Gleichwie der Regen und Schnee vom Himmel fällt* BWV 18. But it is just as clear that Bach's *Himmelskönig* cantata is his first work composed "von Amts wegen" (officially in his new position). It is for Palm Sunday, the last Sunday before Easter. The Gospel reading for this Sunday, Matthew 21:4–8, is an account of Christ's entry into Jerusalem:

> All this was done, that it might be fulfilled which was spoken by the prophets, saying, "Tell ye the daughter of Zion, Behold, thy King cometh unto thee, meek, and sitting upon an ass, and a colt, the foal of an ass." And the disciples went, and did as Jesus commanded them, And brought the ass, and the colt, and put on them their clothes, and they set him thereon. And a very great multitude spread their garments in the way; others cut down branches from the trees, and scattered them in the way.

It is here that the cantata's librettist begins. We do not know who it was; suggestions focus on the Weimar ducal consistory secretary Salomon Franck. Evidence in favor of Franck, twenty-six years older than Bach, includes the relatively conservative form of the text. Although it does not avoid the modern aria form, it seems to regard the contemporary recitative with undisguised mistrust. At the beginning of his text he placed a short strophe, meant for the chorus, that compares the arrival of Christ in Jerusalem to the human heart:

> Himmelskönig, sei willkommen,
> Laß uns auch dein Zion sein!
> Komm herein,
> Du hast uns das Herz genommen.
>
> King of heaven, be welcomed,
> Let us too be your Zion!
> Come in,
> You have stolen our hearts.

A recitative follows, yet it contains no modern madrigalistic versification. Instead, it cites Psalm 40:7, certainly words of the psalmist yet unmistakably placed in the mouth of Jesus and binding the events of Palm Sunday and Holy Week:

> Siehe, ich komme; im Buch ist von mir geschrieben.
> Deinen Willen, mein Gott, tu ich gerne.

See, I come; in the book it is written of me.
I delight to do thy will, my God.

In various ways, this logical connection characterizes all of the movements that follow: three arias, a chorale, the concluding chorus. The second of the three arias takes up the "garments" mentioned in Matthew; it now appears as "unbeflecktes Kleid" (spotless garment), a metaphor for the cleansing of sin:

> Leget euch dem Heiland unter,
> Herzen, die ihr christlich seid!
> Tragt ein unbeflecktes Kleid
> Eures Glaubens ihm entgegen.
>
> Lay yourselves underneath the savior,
> Hearts that are Christian!
> Offer up a spotless garment
> Of your faith to him.

The texts of the first and third arias speak of crucifixion and a martyr's death:

> Starkes Lieben,
> Das dich, großer Gottessohn,
> Von dem Thron
> Deiner Herrlichkeit getrieben,
> Daß du dich zum Heil der Welt
> Als ein Opfer vorgestellt.
>
> What strong love,
> That you, great Son of God
> From the throne
> Of your glory were driven,
> That you, to heal the world,
> Presented yourself as a sacrifice.

Later:

> Jesu, laß durch Wohl und Weh
> Mich auch mit dir ziehen!
> Schreit die Welt nur, "Kreuzige,"
> So laß mich nicht fliehen.
>
> Jesus, through wealth and woe
> Let me also go with you!
> Though the world may only cry "Crucify!"
> So let me not flee.

Even the text of the closing chorus is unable to free itself from this dynamic:

> So lasset uns gehen in Salem der Freuden,
> Begleitet den König in Lieben und Leiden.
> Er gehet voran
> Und öffnet die Bahn.
>
> Then let us go into the Salem of joys,
> Accompany the King in love and sorrow.
> He goes ahead
> And opens the way.

Just as the opening chorus is separated from the three arias by the psalm verses, the concluding free verse does not follow this group directly. Instead, it is preceded by the only chorale in the cantata, the next to last strophe from Paul Stockmann's passion hymn *Jesu Leiden, Pein und Tod* (Jesus's suffering, pain, and death), whose text begins "Jesu, deine Passion ist mir lauter Freude" (Jesus, your Passion is pure joy to me).

The rather austere libretto inspired Bach to one of his most richly imaginative cantata creations. The words of the evangelist, "Siehe, dein König kommt zu dir sanftmütig" (Behold, your King comes meekly unto you), hover, unspoken, over the opening sonata: in their luminous upper ranges, recorder and solo violin proceed in solemn rhythm above dabbed chords in the strings—a procession experienced from afar, intangible as the ether, almost surreal, descending only at the close to the earth from heavenly heights. The first chorus is by contrast earthbound, alternating between the architectonic discipline of a permutation fugue, free canonic structures, and—in the central section—a dialogue between singers and instruments.

The psalm verses given to the bass, the *vox Christi*, shift quickly from free recitative to the more appropriate arioso. The first aria is also given to the bass, the voice that embodies "Strength"; the self-confident, powerful texture of strings, led by the lively figuration of the violins, seems to be directly developed from the text's opening phrase, "starkes Lieben." The expressive alto aria, "Leget euch dem Heiland unter," is characterized by constantly descending arabesques of melody, alternating between the voice and obbligato flute. In several respects, the tenor aria, "Jesu, laß durch Wohl und Weh," goes even farther: in a key distant from the bass and alto arias, the accompanying instrumental ensemble is reduced to basso continuo, intensifying the expression and achieving the strongest sense of inwardness. The ensuing chorale is composed as a motet movement in which the singers are in part supported by the instruments; the chorale melody *Jesu Kreuz, Leiden und Pein* (Jesus's cross, suffering, and pain) is performed in long note values by the soprano, together with violin and the recorder, at the octave in the manner of a four-foot register on an organ. In formal design, compositional technique, and treatment of text, the closing choral movement "So lasset uns gehen in Salem der Freuden" is the precise counterpart of the first chorus, so that the increasing anticipation of Holy Week in the course of the cantata ends with the return to the world of Palm Sunday.

Johann Sebastian Bach reperformed his first Weimar masterpiece several times in Leipzig. He designated the work "Tempore Passionis. In specie Dominica Palmarum" (For Lent: Particularly for Palm Sunday), knowing well that in Leipzig, Palm Sunday fell during the period without music. "Tempore Passionis aut Festo Mariae Annunciationis" reads Bach's title at another place, thereby focusing on the Feast of the Annunciation, an occasion when the cantata might be used in Leipzig. Upon the distribution of Bach's estate in 1750, Philipp Emanuel Bach added to the three designations a fourth, for Estomihi Sunday. It is certainly a unique case among Bach's cantatas and, to that extent, an estimation of the singular esteem held for this cantata.

Weinen, Klagen, Sorgen, Zagen
BWV 12 / BC A 68
Jubilate, April 22, 1714

Bach composed this cantata in April 1714, a few weeks after his promotion to concertmaster of the court chapel at Weimar, in accordance with his new obligation to perform new cantatas on a monthly rotation. The work is for the third Sunday after Easter, or Jubilate Sunday. While the libretto contains no literal quotation from the Gospel reading of the day, it is related in many respects. In particular, it concerns that part of the Gospel reading in John 16:19, 20, and 22 that refers to Jesus's farewell speeches: "For a little while, you will not see me; and however for a little while, you shall see me. Truly, truly I say to you: You shall weep and wail; yet your sadness will be turned into joy. . . . And you have now sorrow; but I will see you again, and your hearts will rejoice, and no one shall take your joy from you."

The librettist of the cantata is not known. It is conceivable that the libretto is the work of the Weimar chief ducal consistory secretary Salomon Franck, whose libretti Bach set fairly frequently beginning in late 1714. In any case, the librettist was a well-educated author who demonstrates his erudition right away at the beginning of the first aria. As recent research has shown, the parataxis (a sequence of words or phrases unconnected by conjunctions) found here goes back to a Latin cry of lament often used in ancient times.* Only the conclusion, therefore, is new; it creates a connection to the sorrow that is the subject of the Gospel reading:

> Weinen, Klagen,
> Sorgen, Zagen,
> Angst und Not
> Sind der Christen Tränenbrot,
> Die das Zeichen Jesu tragen.

> Weeping, wailing,
> Sorrows, trembling,
> Anguish and need
> Are the Christian's bread of tears,
> They who bear the mark of Jesus.

In the following movement, the poetic effusion of this beginning turns to the sober seriousness of a passage from Acts 14:22: "Wir müßen durch viel Trübsal in das Reich Gottes eingehen" (We must go through much tribulation to enter the Kingdom of God). But immediately afterward, the librettist once again gives free rein to his predilection for wordplay: this time it is alliteration ("Kreuz," "Kronen," "Kampf," "Kleinod"), the stave rhyme, that marks the line beginnings in the next aria text:

> Kreuz und Kronen sind verbunden,
> Kampf und Kleinod sind vereint.
> Christen haben alle Stunden
> Ihre Qual und ihren Feind,
> Doch ihr Trost sind Christi Wunden.

> Cross and crowns are bound together,
> Contest and prize medal are united.
> Christians have, at every hour,
> Their suffering and their enemy.
> Yet Christ's wounds are their comfort.

In spite of the verbal artifice, the content of the strophe is clear: the cross stands for suffering and redemption, the crown for ascension into heaven.

The paraphrase of the emulation of Christ in the ensuing aria thus appears as a logical continuation:

> Ich folge Christo nach,
> Von ihm will ich nicht lassen
> Im Wohl und Ungemach,

In Leben und Erblassen.
Ich küsse Christi Schmach,
Ich will sein Kreuz umfassen.
Ich folge Christo nach,
Von ihm will ich nicht lassen.

I follow after Christ,
I will not let go of him,
In well-being and misfortune
In life and in death.
I kiss Christ's humiliation,
I will embrace his cross,
I follow after Christ,
I will not let go of him.

The aria that follows promises a reward for this fidelity, associated with the high trumpet's quotation of the chorale melody *Jesu meine Freude*:

Sei getreu, alle Pein
Wird doch nur ein Kleines sein.
Nach dem Regen
Blüht der Segen,
Alles Wetter geht vorbei.
Sei getreu, sei getreu!

Stay faithful, all pain
Will indeed be but a little while.
After the rain
Blessing blooms,
Every storm passes.
Stay faithful, stay faithful!

The concluding chorale strophe, the last in Samuel Rodigast's 1674 hymn, functions catechetically as it summarizes the threads of thought in the entire cantata text:

Was Gott tut, das ist wohlgetan,
Dabei will ich verbleiben,
Es mag mich auf die rauhe Bahn
Not, Tod und elend treiben,
So wird Gott mich
Ganz väterlich
In seinen Armen halten:
Drum laß ich ihn nur walten.

> What God does, that is done well,
> I will abide by this,
> Though I may, on the rough road,
> Be driven by need, death, and misery,
> Then God will,
> Quite fatherly,
> Hold me in his arms:
> Therefore, I just let him rule.

Bach begins his composition of this text—which is entirely free of recitatives—with a sinfonia in F minor that outwardly resembles the slow movement of a concerto. The accompaniment—tightly regulated, nearly static, and consisting of four string instruments above a spare basso continuo—and the intensely expressive voice of the oboe enter into a distinctively tense relationship with each other. The accompaniment's unusual dimensions point to a barely restrained, individual, and emotional interpretation of the cry of lament drawn from the ancient tradition. The phrase "Weinen, Klagen, Sorgen, Zagen" in four-part choral setting appears with the greatest possible expressive power, with many sighing suspensions and chromatic modulations but disciplined and restrained at the same time. The framing sections of this tripartite movement prove to be a sequence of twelve variations on the archaic *lamento* bass, which descends by half steps through the interval of the fourth. One sees how greatly Bach treasured this strictly constructed yet intensively expressive chaconne in the fact that he adopted it, without its middle sections, as the Crucifixus in his "great Catholic mass"—later known as the Mass in B Minor BWV 232.

The accumulated solemnity of this beginning radiates over the movements that follow. The biblical passage recitative, given to the alto, begins in a dark C minor. But the space unexpectedly opens; as the basso continuo descends to low C, the solo violin, undeterred, strides upward along the C major scale as it leads the accompaniment, a fine interpretation of the text "Wir müßen durch viel Trübsal in das Reich Gottes eingehen"—a subtle means of interpreting the text, trusting in the imagery of such symbols. In the ensuing aria, also for alto and obbligato oboe, the density of texture seems to want to outdo the terse stave rhymes of "Kreuz und Kronen sind verbunden, Kampf und Kleinod sind vereint." The stubbornness in keeping to one and the same motivic idea could be conditioned by the text passages containing "Kampf" and "Feind."

The aria that follows, for bass and two obbligato violins, is similarly tenacious in its adherence to motivic material formulated at the very start. Certainly, the prevailing idea is clear enough: the characteristic rising head motive is given to the text beginning "Ich folge Christo nach," and, wherever possible, it is woven into imitative textures, a manifest image of "following."

The cantata's last aria is an elaborately sophisticated chorale arrangement, a tribute to the art of Bach, the widely known Weimar court organist. Above an obstinately repeating bass foundation (idiomatic to the organ pedal), an expressive tenor, rich in coloratura, unfolds its "Sei getreu, alle Pein wird doch nur ein Kleines sein" (Stay faithful, all pain will indeed be but a little while). In addition, a high trumpet, undeterred, sounds the chorale melody *Jesu meine Freude*. Musically, it functions as the cornerstone to the movement structure; at the same time, it is an invitation to the listener to consider the aria text in conjunction with the words of the chorale, as a second level, so to speak.

With the concluding chorale in a bright B-flat major on the chorale melody *Was Gott tut, das ist wohlgetan*, from the late seventeenth century, Bach underscores the completed ascent from the sorrow of the cantata's beginning. He adds a fifth, high-range instrumental part to the four voices that not only enriches the movement technically and harmonically but also lends it an unexpected dimension similar to the undaunted soaring ascent of the violin in the accompanied recitative "Wir müßen durch viel Trübsal in das Reich Gottes eingehen."

―――――――
*Ambrose (1980).

Ich hatte viel Bekümmernis
BWV 21 / BC A 99
Third Sunday after Trinity, June 17, 1714

The cantor of St. Thomas School, Johann Sebastian Bach, presented the cantata *Ich hatte viel Bekümmernis* BWV 21.3 (I had much grieving) for the first time in Leipzig on June 13, 1723, the third Sunday after Trinity. This date, only a few weeks after his official assumption of office, marks an important shift in his production plans. In addition to new compositions of concerted church music, there were also reperformances of older works, cantatas that Bach had composed for Mühlhausen and, in particular, for Weimar and brought with him to Leipzig by way of Köthen. By all appearances, the Leipzig performance of our cantata was preceded by one at Hamburg (BWV 27.2) as part of Bach's application (made from Köthen*) for the position of organist at St. Jacobi and thus took place in the autumn of 1720, according to our knowledge today. Bach was not awarded the Hamburg position; however, the cantata performance had a later, unexpected echo.

In his journal, *Critica Musica*, published in 1725, the composer and influential music theorist Johann Mattheson mocked what in his view were unnecessary, irrational text repetitions in movements 2, 3, and 8 of Bach's cantata. After taking issue with a work by the Halle music director Friedrich Wilhelm Zachow, Mattheson took aim at Bach's "kurzweillig" (amusing) and, in his opinion, laughable diction as follows:

> In order that good old Zachau [Handel's teacher] might have company, and not be quite so alone, let us set beside him an otherwise excellent practicing musician of today, who for a long time does nothing but repeat: "I, I, I, I had much grief, I had much grief, in my heart, in my heart. I had much grief, etc., in my heart, etc., etc., etc., etc. I had much grief etc., in my heart, etc., etc." Then again: "Sighs, tears, sorrow, anguish (rest), sighs, tears, anxious longing, fear and death (rest) gnaw at my oppressed heart, etc." Also: "Come, my Jesus, and refresh (rest) and rejoice with Thy glance (rest), come, my Jesus (rest), come, my Jesus, and refresh and rejoice ... with Thy glance this soul, etc."[12]

Mattheson's biting ridicule does not appear to have bothered Bach. On the contrary, the cantata *Ich hatte viel Bekümmernis* seems to have had pride of place in his oeuvre. Evidence for this is seen not only in the note in his own hand on the title folder containing the performance materials, explaining that the work could be used "in ogni tempo" (at all times) of the church year, but also in the performances on important occasions: the application to Hamburg of 1720 and the start of reperformances of older cantatas in Leipzig in 1723. In his own hand, Bach entered yet another date worth mentioning: the indication of a performance on the third Sunday after Trinity 1714 in Weimar (BWV 21.1). This was a special situation insofar as the young Prince Johann Ernst, a gifted composer and violinist who had returned to Weimar a year earlier from a grand tour through many countries, was now about to leave again for the baths at Taunus in order to seek a cure for an ailment that was steadily worsening. According to the monthly rotation schedule, Bach was expected to perform a cantata in the castle church on June 17, 1714; this would be his final opportunity to offer the departing prince a note of consolation by way of a composition. The eighteen-year-old Prince Johann Ernst was probably the most important point of contact at court for the organist and concertmaster, older by ten years. Bach certainly had reason enough to present his patron with a representative church cantata before his departure—a departure that no one had any way of knowing would be forever.

The extensive, eleven-movement cantata was probably not newly composed for this occasion; it seems more likely that the Weimar production of 1714 was itself a reperformance. A predecessor of our cantata with ten or even eleven movements may itself have been preceded by one or more older versions, each with six movements, whose dates and occasions can only be sketchily guessed at. It seems unlikely that any of these dimly perceivable early versions were assigned to the third Sunday after Trinity,** since neither the text in the form handed down to us nor the short version of the supposedly oldest components shows any relation to the Gospel reading for that Sunday. More likely is a connection to the Epistle from the fifth chapter of the first letter of Peter and its core phrase, "Alle eure Sorge werfet auf ihn; denn er sorget für euch" (7; Cast all of your cares upon him, for he cares for you).

In fact, this thought—sorrow and affliction, on the one hand, consolation and hope, on the other—courses through the entire text of the cantata. At its beginning stands a verse from Psalm 94: "Ich hatte viel Bekümmernis in meinem Herzen; aber deine Tröstungen erquicken meine Seele" (19; I had much affliction in my heart, but your consolations restore my soul). The free poetry that follows at first stays close to the keyword "Bekümmernis." The first aria begins "Seufzer, Tränen, Kummer, Not" (Sighing, tears, trouble, need); the ensuing recitative laments God's turning away from his child; the second aria compares the tears of affliction to a sea of mortal dangers. A verse from Psalm 42 provides temporary relief: "Was betrübst du dich meine Seele, und bist so unruhig in mir? Harre auf Gott; denn ich werde ihm noch danken, daß er meines Angesichtes Hilfe und mein Gott ist" (11; Why are you aggrieved, my soul, and so disquieted within me? Wait upon God, for I shall yet thank him, that he is the help of my countenance, and is my God). This concludes the first part of the cantata, to be performed before the sermon.

With the beginning of the second part, the genre changes. Jesus and the soul hold a dialogue*** clearly inspired by the Song of Songs, and the classic search theme must be included:

> Ach Jesu, meine Ruh,
> Mein Licht, wo bleibest du?
>   O Seele sieh! Ich bin bei dir.
> Bei mir? Hier ist ja lauter Nacht.
>   Ich bin dein treuer Freund,
>   Der auch im Dunkeln wacht,
>   Wo lauter Schalken seind.

> Ah Jesus, my repose,
> My light, where do you tarry?
>   O soul, look! I am with you.

With me? Here it is surely darkest night.
I am your loyal friend,
Who keeps watch also in the darkness,
Where true rogues are.

After this recitative dialogue, the two join together in a duet that, in the diction typical of the Song of Songs poetry of the Baroque, ends with these lines:

Ach Jesu, durchsüße mir Seele und Herze
Entweichet, ihr Sorgen, verschwinde, du Schmerze.

Ah Jesus, sweeten my soul and heart
Flee, you cares, vanish, you pains.

The last aria exhibits the same meter and nearly the same vocabulary. Beforehand, however, there appears another psalm passage, connected to two chorale strophes. Psalm 116 provides the verse "Sei nun wieder zufrieden, meine Seele, denn der Herr tut dir Guts" (May you once again be at peace, my soul, for the Lord has done for you good things); the two strophes are from Georg Neumark's 1657 hymn *Wer nur den lieben Gott läßt walten* (Whoever only lets the dear God rule). The text abruptly concludes with a passage from the fifth chapter of the Revelation of St. John: "Das Lamm, das erwürget ist, ist würdig zu nehmen Kraft und Reichtum und Weisheit und Stärke und Preis und Lob. . . . Lob und Ehre und Preis und Gewalt sei unserm Gott von Ewigkeit zu Ewigkeit. Amen. Alleluja" (12–13; The Lamb, which was slain, is worthy to receive power and riches and wisdom and might and glory and blessing. . . . Tribute and honor and praise and power to our God from eternity to eternity. Amen. Alleluia).

Bach's composition matches the diversity of the source texts; indeed, it seems intended to unify the heterogeneity. A stately sinfonia in the mold of a slow concerto movement begins with an oboe and solo violin in expressive dialogue. Its sorrowful effusions form a transition to the first choral movement, whose two contrasting sections seem to prefigure the overall course of the entire cantata. Close canonic structures, which are symbolic of multitude, and striking dissonances of the second, which are in the style of Italian concertos of the era, characterize the first section with its boundless, intensifying "Bekümmernis." Only in the last third of the movement, where consolation is at issue, do things brighten with a more lively tempo and relaxed diction. Sorrow and doubt predominate once again in the following three movements. The motivically uniform soprano aria is full of torment, with its expressive dialogue between oboe and voice. In contrast, the tenor aria develops a Baroque abundance with its comparison of "Tränenbächen" (streams of tears) and a "Meer voller Trübsal" (sea of affliction), strengthened by the full complement of strings. The choral movement on the verse from Psalm 42 provides a calming conclusion to the first part. With its fragmented structure and concluding fugue, it strongly recalls Bach's compositional style of the Mühlhausen period around 1707 and thereby strengthens the hypothesis of an early origin.

A significantly more modern formal world opens with the beginning of the cantata's second half in the duet movements for soprano and bass, traditionally assigned to the soul and Jesus. The same is true for the lively, animated tenor aria in the next to last position. On the other hand, the severe chorale motet "Sei nun wieder zufrieden" (May you once again be at peace) is again indebted to an older style. In two expositions, of which the second is intensified by colla parte instrumentation, the motet connects its psalm text to the melody and text of the hymn *Wer nur den lieben Gott läßt walten*. The magnificent concluding movement probably belonged originally to another composition, the rest of which is lost. It combines a slow opening part in which voices and instruments alternate in blocklike fashion with a quick fugue. In the combination of fugal voice exchange procedure and concerto form, it carries out a thrilling, gradual intensification that culminates in an abrupt "Alleluia" conclusion that seems to anticipate the finale of Mozart's Symphony no. 39 in E-flat Major, K. 543.

In all, the cantata *Ich hatte viel Bekümmernis* seems intentionally to present a cross section of the work of Johann Sebastian Bach, barely thirty years old, that draws upon all registers of his abilities as a representational work for application, even at the cost of unity. This brimming abundance could explain the appearance of the cantata at important stations of the composer's life in 1714, 1720, and 1723, just as it demonstrates the high estimation of the work held by the composer himself, his contemporaries, and posterity.

---
*Maul and Wollny (2003).
**Petzoldt (1993).
***Wolff (1996).

Nun komm der Heiden Heiland
BWV 61 / BC A 1

First Sunday of Advent, December 2, 1714

There are two Bach cantatas that begin with the first strophe of Martin Luther's chorale *Nun komm der Heiden Heiland* (Now come, savior of the Gentiles), and both are for the first Sunday of Advent. This one, the older of the two, originated in Weimar in 1714. The other was composed a decade later in Leipzig. The work composed in 1714 is based on a text by Erdmann Neumeister. Born near Weissenfels (Thuringia) in 1671 and active at first in various positions near this royal seat, in 1714 Neumeister was working as senior court chaplain and superintendent in Sorau, Silesia. In that year he published a new annual cycle of cantata texts in Frankfurt am Main under the title *Geistliche Poesien mit untermischten biblischen Sprüchen und Choralen auf alle Sonn- und Festtagen* (Sacred poems with interspersed biblical sayings and chorales for all Sundays and feast days), intended to be set by Georg Philipp Telemann, the director of music at Frankfurt. In March 1714 Telemann stood as godfather at the baptism of Bach's son Carl Philipp Emanuel. Six decades later, Carl Philipp Emanuel reported regarding his father that "in his younger years he was often together with Telemann—who also lifted me out of the baptismal font."[13] It seems likely that this close relationship, featuring godparenthood, enabled an exchange of news and recent developments that included Neumeister's new annual cycle of texts.

Annual text cycles normally were arranged according to the church year, beginning, as this one does, with the first Sunday of Advent. The Gospel reading for this Sunday, found in the twenty-first chapter of Matthew and nearly identically in Mark and Luke, describes the entry of Jesus into Jerusalem and, thus, the arrival of the savior:

> When they now came near to Jerusalem, at Bethphage on the Mount of Olives, Jesus sent two of his disciples and said to them, "Go into the village that lies before you, and immediately you shall find an ass tied, and a colt with her: loose them, and bring them unto me! And if anyone says something to you, you shall say, the Lord needs them, and immediately he will release them to you." All this was done, that it might be fulfilled which was spoken by the Prophet, saying, "Tell the daughter of Zion, 'Behold, thy king comes to you, meek, and sitting upon an ass, and a colt, the foal of an ass.'" The disciples went forth, and did as Jesus commanded them, and brought the ass and the colt, and put their clothes on them, and they set him thereon. But many people spread their garments in the way, others cut down branches from the trees, and scattered them in the way. But the people

however, those that went before followed, cried and said, Hosanna to the son of David! Blessed is he that comes in the Name of the Lord! Hosanna in the highest! (1–9)

As the title of his annual cycle indicates, Erdmann Neumeister's cantata poetry belongs to the genre of mixed text form; that is, it contains free poetry—recitatives and arias—alongside chorale strophes and biblical passages. This form of mixed text was long regarded as Neumeister's most important contribution to the development of the Protestant Church cantata, until it turned out that Neumeister neither invented this hybrid text nor particularly preferred it. His domain was free cantata poetry without chorale strophes or biblical passages, with which he surprised his contemporaries in 1702.* He completed the transition to mixed text subsequently and perhaps even reluctantly; according to a predecessor in Thuringia in 1704 whose identity remains unknown to scholarship, the roots of the practice reach far back into the seventeenth century.

At the beginning of his libretto, Neumeister placed the first strophe of Luther's German translation of the ancient church hymn *Veni redemptor gentium*, published in 1524:

> Nun komm der Heiden Heiland,
> Der Jungfrauen Kind erkannt,
> Des sich wundert alle Welt,
> Gott solch Geburt ihm bestellt.
>
> Now come, savior of the Gentiles,
> Known as the child of the Virgin,
> Of this, all the world marvels,
> God ordained him such a birth.

A chorale fragment concludes the libretto, the *Abgesang* (second part) of the last strophe of Philipp Nicolai's 1599 hymn *Wie schön leuchtet der Morgenstern* (How brightly gleams the morning star). Nicolai's strophe begins with the words "Wie bin ich doch so herzlich froh" (How am I though so sincerely glad); the *Abgesang* reads:

> Amen! Amen!
> Komm du schöne Freudenkrone, bleib nicht lange!
> Deiner wart ich mit Verlangen.
>
> Amen! Amen!
> Come, you beautiful crown of joy, tarry not long!
> I await you with longing.

"Kommen" (come) is the most important keyword of the entire cantata libretto; it is missing only from the one movement that cites a passage from the Gospel. The free portions of the text are characterized by this keyword, as in movement 2, a recitative:

> Der Heiland ist gekommen,
> Hat unser armes Fleisch und Blut
> An sich genommen
> Und nimmet uns zu Blutsverwandten an.
>
> The savior is come,
> Has taken our poor flesh and blood
> Upon himself
> And accepts us as blood relatives.

And at the conclusion:

> Was tust du nicht
> Noch täglich an den Deinen?
> Du kömmst und läßt dein Licht
> Mit vollem Segen scheinen.
>
> What do you not do
> Still daily for your people?
> You come and let your light
> Shine with full blessing.

The accompanying aria prays for this blessing at the outset of the newly begun church year:

> Komm, Jesu, komm zu deiner Kirche
> Und gib ein selig neues Jahr!
> Befördre deines Namens Ehre
> Erhalte die gesunde Lehre
> Und segne Kanzel und Altar.
>
> Come, Jesus, come to your church
> And grant a blessed new year!
> Promote your name's honor,
> Uphold the sound teaching,
> And bless pulpit and altar.

Words of Jesus give the answer to this prayer from the third chapter of the Revelation of St. John: "Siehe, ich stehe vor der Tür und klopfe an. So jemand meine Stimme hören wird und die Tür auftun, zu dem werde ich eingehen und das Abendmahl mit ihm halten und er mit mir" (3:20; See, I stand before the door and knock. Should anyone hear my voice and open the door, to him I will go in and have the evening meal with him and he with me). The meaning of "Tür auftun" and "eingehen"—to open the door and go in—is expressed by the penultimate movement of the cantata, an aria whose text paraphrases the classic metaphor of the human heart as the dwelling of God:

> Öffne dich, mein ganzes Herze,
> Jesus kommt und ziehet ein.
> Bin ich gleich nur Staub und Erde,
> Will er mich doch nicht verschmähn,
> Seine Lust an mir zu sehen,
> Daß ich seine Wohnung werde.
> O wie selig werd ich sein!

> Open yourself, my whole heart,
> Jesus comes and enters.
> Though I am but dust and earth,
> He will, nevertheless, not disdain me,
> His pleasure in me to see,
> That I become his dwelling.
> O how blessed will I be!

As mentioned, Johann Sebastian Bach's composition based on this text originated in late 1714 for the service in the Weimar castle chapel. A reperformance is documented in Leipzig in 1723, Bach's first year of service there. It is remarkable that on this occasion Bach outlined the rather complicated sequence of the church service in the score, including the organist's duties—which he himself did not have to perform:

1. Preluding.
2. Motet.
3. Preluding on the Kyrie, which is performed throughout in concerted manner [*musiciret*].
4. Intoning before the altar.
5. Reading of the Epistle.
6. Singing of the Litany.
7. Preluding on [and singing of] the Chorale.
8. Reading of the Gospel [*crossed out*: and intoning of the creed].
9. Preluding on [and performance of] the principal music [cantata].
10. Singing of the Creed [Luther's *Credo* hymn].
11. The Sermon.

12 After the Sermon, as usual, singing of several verses from a hymn.
13 Words of Institution [of the Sacrament].
14 Preluding on [and performance of] the Music [probably the second half of the cantata]. And after the same, alternate preluding and the singing of chorales until the end of the Communion, *et sic porro* [and so on].[14]

Accordingly, the "principal music" (after number 9) or the "Music" (during number 14)—that is, the cantata—would have been performed with the first part before the sermon, between the reading of the Gospel and the singing of the creed, *Wir glauben all' an einen Gott,* and the second part after the Words of Institution and before or during Communion or the Offertory. But whether the cantata *Nun komm der Heiden Heiland* in fact was performed in two parts, the first part ending after the third movement, cannot be determined. It is also conceivable that the entire cantata was performed as principal music and that for the presentation of music during Communion or the Lord's Supper the work of another composer was drawn upon.

The Weimar Advent cantata *Nun Komm der Heiden Heiland* displays the thirty-year-old court organist at the height of his powers. The first movement meets a self-imposed challenge, as it integrates an arrangement of an ancient church hymn with the modern instrumental form of the French overture. This is in three parts; its first and last sections have dotted rhythms and sweeping scales that go back to the fanfares at the French opera in the seventeenth century that announced the arrival of the king. It is thus clear that Bach's compositional experiment was meant to symbolize, formally, the entrance of Jesus in Jerusalem and the arrival of the savior at the same time. That no radiant major is allowed to sound, and instead a melancholy, shadowy minor, is conditioned by the modal nature of the ancient hymn tune. A change of tempo and meter in the middle section enables the buoyant fugal development of the text line "des sich wundert alle Welt." Buoyant as well is the tenor aria, following a brief recitative extended by an arioso at its conclusion. Here, the upper strings—two violins and two violas—unite to form a pastose obbligato voice of sonorous timbre. The Gospel recitative, "Siehe, ich stehe vor der Tür und klopfe an" (See, I stand before the door and knock), is taken by the bass, the *vox Christi* (voice of Christ). The pizzicato interspersed with rests more reflects tense anticipation and preliminary uncertainty than simply tone painting of "knocking at the door." Sincere naivete and the use of the most modest instrumental forces define the soprano aria, "Öffne dich, mein ganzes Herze," whose increasingly joyous excitement flows directly into the closing chorale. The two violins form an obbligato part that gives it festive splendor, transiting the entire compass of the two instruments and climbing to the highest possible peak at the closing fermata, certainly conducted and performed in person by the composer and concertmaster, Johann Sebastian Bach.

*See Hobohm (2002); Rucker (2000); and Krausse (1986).

Der Himmel lacht, die Erde jubilieret
BWV 31 / BC A 55

Easter Sunday, April 21, 1715

This cantata belongs to the surprisingly small group of compositions by Johann Sebastian Bach for Easter Sunday. The relatively modest corpus of works for this high-ranking feast day suggests that there may have been losses in the transmission of sources, possibly after Bach's death and in association with the distribution of his musical estate, but possibly during his lifetime as well. (Dilatory borrowers come to mind in this regard.) However, a more plausible theory would seem to be that after 1750 Bach's feast day cantatas—among them those meant for Easter—went to the oldest son, Wilhelm Friedemann, who, as music director of the Liebfrauenkirche in Halle at midcentury, had great need of exactly that sort of church music and that they went astray in his later years for various reasons.

And so, at present there are three known cantatas meant for the first day of Easter: the partita *per omnes versus Christ lag in Todes Banden* BWV 4, presumably a very early work; the composition known as the Easter Oratorio BWV 249.4, an arrangement of a secular cantata BWV 249.1; and the cantata *Der Himmel lacht, die Erde jubilieret* BWV 31 (Heaven laughs, the earth rejoices). This work (BWV 31.1) originated in 1715, a year after Bach's promotion to concertmaster at the court of Weimar. It was the first Easter cantata by the newly appointed concertmaster for the congregation at the Weimar castle church. The situation was similar nine years later in Leipzig, when *Der Himmel lacht, die Erde jubilieret* was performed in April 1724 (BWV 31.2); it was the first Easter cantata by Bach in his new position as the cantor of St. Thomas School. A surviving text booklet from that year confirms that, in accordance with the custom in Leipzig, the work was performed in the morning main service in St. Nicholas and in the afternoon at vespers in St. Thomas. The same sequence demonstrably took place again in 1731, and we have documentation of some further performances, while others are hinted at.

Thus our cantata assumed a permanent, immovable place in Bach's repertoire. But this is in no way obvious, and indeed for reasons regarding the text. Several decades ago, Arnold Schering formulated the problems thusly:

> For ourselves, who since ancient times have associated the concept of Easter with thoughts of triumph, victory, and resurrection, Salomon Franck's ... text takes a turn that is difficult to understand insofar as it turns away from the joy of Easter in its course and ultimately leads to thoughts of death. The usual path would have been to take up the deathly horrors of the earlier Passion and gradually transition to the brightness of Easter morning. Instead, poet and musician write pieces for the last two movements that could just as well appear in a funeral cantata.[15]

Johann Sebastian Bach found the text in a collection entitled *Evangelisches Andachts-Opffer* (Protestant Devotional Offering), which he was obliged to use for his cantata compositions after its publication by Salomon Franck, the Weimar ducal consistory secretary, in early 1715. "Triumph, victory, and resurrection" are found particularly at the beginning of Franck's cantata text for Easter in the aria that Bach composed as a choral movement:

> Der Himmel lacht! Die Erde jubilieret
> Und was sie trägt in ihrem Schoß;
> Der Schöpfer lebt! der Höchste triumphieret
> Und ist von Todesbanden los.
> Der sich das Grab zur Ruh erlesen,
> Der Heiligste kann nicht verwesen.

> The heavens laugh! The earth rejoices
> And what it carries in its bosom;
> The Creator lives! the Most High triumphs
> And is from the bonds of death released.
> Who chose the grave for rest,
> The holiest cannot be decayed.

With the last line, the poet alludes to a verse in Psalm 16 that belongs to the lesson for Easter Monday: "Denn du wirst meine Seele nicht dem Tode lassen und nicht zugeben, daß dein Heiliger verwese" (10; For you will not leave my soul in death and will not allow your holy one to be decayed). If this reference to death seems simply apt, what follows increasingly strengthens the "turning away from the joy of Easter," as Schering calls it. Instead of the Gospel reading for the Sunday from Matthew 16, the second movement, a recitative, draws on the Revelation of St. John on several occasions, as in these verses from the first chapter: "Fürchte dich nicht! ich bin der Erste und der Letzte und der Lebendige; ich war tot, und siehe, ich bin lebendig von Ewigkeit zu Ewigkeit und habe die Schlüssel der Hölle und des Todes" (17–18; Fear not! I am the first and the last and the living one; I was dead, and behold, I am living from eternity to eternity and have the keys of hell and of death). The recitative's conclusion proclaims:

> Der sein Gewand
> Blutrot bespritzt in seinem bittern Leiden,
> Will heute sich mit Schmuck und Ehren kleiden.
>
> He whose clothing
> Was spattered blood red in his bitter suffering
> Will today be clothed in jewels and honor.

It is also quoting the Revelation of St. John where, in the nineteenth chapter, it says of the appearance of Christ: "Und er war angetan mit einem Kleide, das mit Blut besprengt war; und sein Name heißt 'Das Wort Gottes'" (13; And he was dressed in a garment that was spattered with blood, and his name was "The Word of God"). "Fürst des Lebens, starker Streiter" (prince of life, powerful champion) begins the text of the aria that follows, rhymed immediately, however, with "des Kreuzes Leiter" (of the ladder of the Cross) and speaking of chains and "Purpurwunden" (purple wounds).

It is not until the closing lines of the ensuing recitative that the Resurrection from the Gospel of St. Mark is taken up, depicting the scene with Mary Magdalene and Mary Jacobi at the grave:

> Ein Christe flieht
> Ganz eilend von dem Grabe!
> Er läßt den Stein,
> Er läßt das Tuch der Sünden
> Dahinten
> Und will mit Christo lebend sein.
>
> A Christian flees
> Quite quickly from the grave!
> He leaves the stone,
> He leaves the cloth of sins
> Behind
> And wishes to be alive with Christ.

It seems to be symptomatic for the author's conception of the text that while he indeed pursues the idea of resurrection further in the next aria text, he does so indirectly by way of Adam's Fall:

> Adam muß in uns verwesen,
> Soll der neue Mensch genesen,
> Der nach Gott geschaffen ist.
>
> Adam must decay within us
> If the new man is to be saved
> Who is created in God's image.

Dying as a precondition of resurrection is also at the center of the last movement pair, a recitative and the aria that begins "Letzte Stunde, brich herein, / Mir die Augen zuzudrücken" (Last hour, break in, / And close my eyes). Salomon Franck's cantata libretto closes with the chorale strophe "So fahr ich hin zu Jesu Christ" (Then I go forth to Jesus Christ), which was added as early as 1575 to Nikolaus Herman's chorale *Wenn mein Stündlein vorhanden ist* (When my final hour is at hand).

For the composer, this wide-ranging but rather problematic text posed a challenge that he was willing to employ any and all means to overcome. "Employ any and all means" is to be understood as both compositional and technical details of performance. Only rarely did Bach deploy more extensive performance forces than he did here. Five each of strings and woodwinds, as well as trumpets and drums, contest one another in the opening movement alone, a sonorously magnificent sonata featuring unison fanfare motives by the entire orchestra, whose subtle concertizing reflects Bach's ongoing engagement with the works of his Italian contemporaries. Augmented by a five-part chorus, the choral movement "Der Himmel lacht, die Erde jubilieret" begins with the entire magnificent ensemble and indeed with two identical fugue expositions that differ only in the text that underlies them—lines 1 and 2, then lines 3 and 4. The fugal voices are alternately unaccompanied or heralded by unison fanfare motives by the entire orchestra. At times, it seems to anticipate the "et Resurrexit" from the Mass in B Minor BWV 232. At the text line "Der sich das Grab zur Ruh erlesen" the outward splendor turns to quiet inwardness, although after a few adagio measures the quick opening tempo is resumed. The closing section is determined by the line of text "Der Heiligste kann nicht verwesen," whereby the formal principle of canon becomes symbolic, representing Law, Dogma, the Unshakable.

Canonic constructions with the same significance also characterize the larger part of the bass recitative. Essential to the aria that follows, "Fürst des Lebens, starker Streiter," are the bass voice as embodiment of power and the angular, marchlike rhythm symbolizing bravery and majesty. In contrast, the recitative and aria for tenor that follow, with their harmony-saturated texture for strings, yield scarcely any hint of the character of their text. Philipp Spitta, writing in the first volume of his Bach biography, published in 1873, called Salomon Franck's "Adam muß in uns verwesen" "one of those sets of words which express no emotion, but are of purely dogmatic import."[16] The soprano aria probes even deeper, its pensive dialogue between voice and obbligato oboe blending with the sonorous voices of the united string instruments and sounding like a choral movement. The "Letzte Stunde, brich herein" of the contemporary text is connected with a quotation of the melody, whose meaning cannot be in doubt: the first strophe of Nikolaus Herman's chorale: "Wenn mein Stündlein vorhanden ist, werd ich im Grab nicht bleiben" (When my final hour is at hand, I shall not remain in the grave). The cantata concludes with the last strophe of the same chorale, quite subdued after the brilliance of its beginning. An instrumental voice ascends to celestial heights, so to speak, an eloquent symbol for the lines "So fahr ich hin zu Jesu Christ" and "der wird die Himmelstür auftun, mich für'n zum ew'gen Leben" (Who will open the door of heaven, leading me to eternal life).

Komm, du süße Todesstunde
BWV 161 / *BC* A 135

Sixteenth Sunday after Trinity, September 27, 1716

Johann Sebastian Bach wrote the cantata *Komm, du süße Todesstunde* BWV 161 (Come, you sweet hour of death) at the age of about thirty for the worship service in the castle chapel at the court of Weimar. The Weimar ducal consistory secretary, Salomon Franck, provided the libretto, published in his collection *Evangelisches Andachts-Opffer*, which appeared in print in 1715 in Weimar. The composition is for the sixteenth Sunday after Trinity. The Gospel reading for this Sunday, in Luke 7, gives the account of Jesus's raising of the widow's son at Nain. Salomon Franck's libretto is based on this Gospel reading only to the extent that the text is suffused with longing for death and the certainty of resurrection. The story itself is not recounted.

In the view of the music historian Arnold Schering,

> with its strengthening of faith in Jesus, Pietism had fostered a human race that anticipated death with joy and regarded the repose in the little burial chamber as but a brief nap from which Jesus would awaken the Soul to unearthly glory. . . . What is terrifying and horrible about this process of passing away is indeed not ignored but mitigated and covered by images and feelings that lead directly to consolation and hope. . . . Freely and with poetic power . . . the librettist develops that which will make the moment of

death seem happy and attractive to faithful souls. All is dissolved in longing and ardent yearning.[17]

Schering's description applies to the text of our cantata in general and is helpful for understanding most of the verses. Even so, the opening movement, an aria, calls for close consideration. Salomon Franck's text reads:

> Komm, du süße Todesstunde,
> Da mein Geist
> Honig speist
> Aus des Löwen Munde.
> Mache meinen Abschied süße,
> Säume nicht,
> Letztes Licht,
> Daß ich meinen Heiland küße.

> Come, you sweet hour of death,
> When my spirit
> Dines on honey
> Out of the lion's mouth.
> Make my departure sweet,
> Do not linger,
> Last light,
> That I might kiss my savior.

Here Franck has drawn a reference to Samson's battle with the lion, found in Judges 14. With his bare hands, Samson had killed a young lion. After several days, he found honey in the cadaver. At his wedding celebration, he gave the guests a riddle to solve. A late seventeenth-century sermon provides an exegesis of this passage: "When Samson found honey in the lion, he devised this riddle in the Book of Judges Chapter 14 verse 14: 'Sweetness poured out of the horrible.' What is more horrible than death when it crushes bones like a lion? . . . Nevertheless, a Christian finds honey in lions and consolation in death." Apart from this rather remote allusion in the unidentified sermon, Erdmann Neumeister's influence can be discerned in Franck's aria text. In Neumeister's first annual text cycle, prepared in Weissenfels in 1702, the libretto for the fifteenth Sunday after Trinity (immediately before the Sunday in question) contains the following formulation:

> Komm doch, komm doch, süße Stunde!
> Da mein Geist
> Sich der Eitelkeit entreißt.
> . . . .

Mich verlangt von Herzens-Grunde.
Komm doch, komm doch, süße Stunde!

But come, but come, sweet hour!
When my spirit
Wrests itself from vanity.
. . . .
I long for you from the bottom of my heart.
But come, but come, sweet hour!

The second movement of Franck's cantata libretto, a recitative, characterizes the transitoriness of existence with opposing concepts:

Welt, deine Lust ist Last,
Dein Zucker ist mir als ein Gift verhaßt,
Dein Freudenlicht
Ist mein Komete,
Und wo man deine Rosen bricht,
Sind Dornen ohne Zahl
Zu meiner Seele Qual.

World, your pleasure is a burden,
Your sugar is hateful to me as poison,
Your joyful light
Is my comet.[18]
And where one picks your roses,
There are thorns without number
To the torment of my soul.

Truly poetic expressions stand out effectively from the preceding:

Der blasse Tod ist meine Morgenröte,
Mit solcher geht mir auf die Sonne
Der Herrlichkeit und Himmelswonne.

Pale death is my sunrise,
With it arises for me the sun
Of glory and heavenly delight.

The recitative closes with a paraphrase of Philippians 1:23. The biblical passage reads, "Ich habe Lust abzuscheiden, und bei Christo zu sein" (I desire to depart and be with Christ); in Franck's words:

Ich habe Lust bei Christo bald zu weiden,
Ich habe Lust, von dieser Welt zu scheiden

> I desire soon to graze with Christ,
> I desire to part from this world.

The beginning of the third movement, another aria, continues in this vein almost without change:

> Mein Verlangen
> Ist, den Heiland zu empfangen
> Und bei Christo bald zu sein.

> My longing
> Is to embrace the savior
> And soon to be with Christ.

The fourth movement, a recitative, proceeds purposefully with this chain of ideas with these expressions:

> Der Schluß ist schon gemacht,
> Welt, gute Nacht!
> . . . .
> So brich herein, du froher Todestag,
> So schlage doch, du letzter Stundenschlag.

> The decision is already made,
> World, good night!
> . . . .
> So break forth, you joyous day of death,
> So strike, you stroke of the final hour.

The last aria, whose text begins "Wenn es meines Gottes Wille" (If it is my God's will), culminates in the exclamation:

> Jesu, komm und nimm mich fort!
> Dieses sei mein letztes Wort!

> Jesus, come and take me away!
> This shall be my last word!

The fourth strophe from Christoph Knoll's 1611 hymn *Herzlich tut mich verlangen* (Sincerely do I long) finishes the cantata text and concludes the chain of ideas with the pertinent "Was schädt mir denn der Tod?" (How then does death harm me?).

Johann Sebastian Bach may have intended to set this text for the sixteenth Sunday after Trinity in 1715; the performance would have been due in early October. But a tragic event at court thwarted his plan: at barely nineteen years of age, the extraordinarily musically gifted Prince Johann Ernst died after a long illness at Frankfurt am Main. Shortly afterward, an official period of mourning was decreed in the principality during which even polyphonic music at the court church was silenced for some time.* Hence the first performance would have taken place the following year, at the end of September 1716, and the work probably was composed at that time. It shows the Weimar concertmaster and court organist at the height of his creative powers. In invention and design, the opening movement presents itself masterfully: urgent and seductive in equal measure, a pair of recorders, playing mostly in parallel thirds and sixths, intensifies the alto's "Komm, du süße Todesstunde." Counterpoint is provided by the organ, which performs the melody "Herzlich tut mich verlangen" phrase by phrase in long note values. Since the melody inevitably elicits a textual association, a dual textuality results for the listener comprising Franck's aria poetry and Christoph Knoll's chorale strophe. At the same time, the apparently freely composed aria proves to be a wide-ranging chorale arrangement worthy of the art of a court organist.

The ensuing tenor recitative flows into an arioso section, which expressively underscores the "Ich habe lust, von dieser Welt zu scheiden" through stubbornly repeated bass figures. The tenor aria "Mein Verlangen ist, den Heiland zu umfangen" (My desire is to embrace the savior), accompanied by the strings, is also characterized by intensive text declamation, combined with a measured, dancelike stride. The alto recitative, accompanied by all the instruments, "Der Schluß ist schon gemacht," enters the realm of tone painting. Sinking figuration and sustained tones symbolize sleep, just as ascending passages evoke "awakening"; the pealing sounds of the plucked string instruments and the flutes suggest the "striking of the last hour." The last freely versified movement, "Wenn es meines Gottes Wille," was designated an aria by Franck but composed as a chorus or at least a four-part ensemble of soloists by Bach. Its thematic material harks back to the opening movement; judging by its nearly ecstatic longing it is rather filled by an inner joy, expressed by the dancelike, animated meter as well as the playful passagework of the two woodwind instruments. In the concluding chorale setting, the flute and oboe form an obbligato part in high register, rich in syncopations, that expands the texture to five parts and lends it the character of a figurative chorale prelude. The bridge back to the opening movement is created not only by the identity of the chorale melody but also by its compositional procedure, which is similar to several movements from the Orgelbüchlein BWV 599–644, to which it is close chronologically.

By all appearances, the cantata *Komm, du süße Todesstunde* was heard not simply in Weimar in 1716 but also in Bach's Leipzig period.[19] In addition to several changes in setting, the Leipzig version is different from the Weimar one in particular because the chorale melody in the opening movement is given to a voice, so that the multitextuality is not simply an associative effect but an actual occurrence. In his last years, the cantor of St. Thomas undertook a final change: he augmented the designation for the sixteenth Sunday after Trinity with an assignment to the Feast of the Purification of Mary and thereby converted the longing for death in the cantata text associated with the story of the boy at Nain to the account of the ancient Simeon found in the Gospel of Luke.

---

*Glöckner (1985).

CHAPTER 3

Bach's First Year at Leipzig from the First Sunday after Trinity 1723 to Trinity Sunday 1724

Die Elenden sollen essen
BWV 75 / BC A 94
First Sunday after Trinity, May 30, 1723

In late May 1723, the newly appointed cantor of St. Thomas School, Johann Sebastian Bach, introduced himself to the people of Leipzig with the cantata *Die Elenden sollen essen* BWV 75 (The afflicted shall eat). Eight days earlier, he had moved with his family to the trade-fair city. For unknown reasons, this event found its way into the press, and in Hamburg in fact, in a correspondent's report from Leipzig: "This past Saturday at noon, four wagons loaded with household goods arrived here from Köthen; they belonged to the former Princely Capellmeister there, now called to Leipzig as *Cantor Figuralis*. He himself arrived with his family on 2 carriages at 2 o'clock and moved into the newly renovated apartment in the St. Thomas School."[1] Several chroniclers have documented a cantata performance on May 30, 1723. One of them wrote: "The 30th instant [May], being the First Sunday after Trinity, the new Cantor and Director of the *Collegium Musicum*, Mr. Johann Sebastian Bach, who has come hither from the Prince's Court at Cöthen, produced his first music here, with great success."[2] A press report, also from Hamburg, is not aware of "great success." It says, however, that Bach "made his debut by performing his music before and after the sermon." Finally, a third report indicates that the new cantor had recently "assumed his office in the city churches with the first music for St. Nicholas Church."[3]

We have no information as to how the new cantor of St. Thomas prepared for this important day. One could imagine that he composed his inaugural cantata before moving to Leipzig. That would, however, presume that the date of the first performance had been set within the medium term and that a text for the composition was available. Nothing more precise can be established, however; even the name of the text author remains unknown. In its first part at least, the libretto hews closely to the Gospel reading of the Sunday, the parable of the rich man and Lazarus the pauper, from Luke 16:19–25:

> There was, however, a rich man who clothed himself with purple and expensive linen and lived all his days gloriously and in joy. There was, however, a pauper of the name Lazarus who lay before his door full of sores and wanted to satisfy himself with the crumbs that fell from the rich man's table; but the dogs came and licked his sores. But it came to pass that the pauper died and was carried by the angels to the bosom of Abraham. The rich man also died and was buried. As he now was in Hell and in torment, he lifted his eyes up and saw Abraham from afar and Lazarus in his bosom. And he called and spoke: Father Abraham, have mercy upon me and send Lazarus, that he dip his fingertips in water and cool my tongue, for I suffer pain in these flames. Abraham however spoke: Consider, son, that you have received your good fortune in your life, and Lazarus by contrast received evil; now, however, he is comforted and you are tormented.

At the beginning of his cantata libretto, the unknown text poet places a verse from Psalm 22, the Passion psalm of Christ, that approximates the parable from the Gospel reading: "Die Elenden sollen essen, daß sie satt werden; und die nach dem Herrn fragen, werden ihn preisen; euer Herz soll ewiglich leben" (26; The afflicted shall eat, so that they become satisfied; and those that ask after the Lord, shall praise Him; your heart shall live eternally). He then paraphrases the Sunday Gospel reading with free poetry: three recitatives and two arias. The first movement pair—recitative and aria—allude to the beginning of the reading by referring to the purple robe of the rich man:

> Was hilft des Purpurs Majestät,
> Da sie vergeht?
> Was hilft der größte Überfluß,
> Weil alles, so wir sehen,
> Verschwinden muß?
>
> What help is the majesty of purple,
> Since it fades?
> What help is the greatest surplus,
> Since all that we see
> Must disappear?

And in the aria:

> Mein Jesu soll mein alles sein.
> Mein Purpur ist sein teures Blut,
> Er selbst mein allerhöchstes Gut,
> Und seines Geistes Liebesglut
> Mein allersüß'ster Freudenwein.
>
> My Jesus shall be my all.
> My purple is his precious blood,
> He himself my all-highest good,
> And his spirit's loving glow
> My all-sweetest wine of joy.

The next movement pair treats the opposing fates of the rich man and the pauper, the way to hell or to the bosom of Abraham. "Gott stürzet und erhöhet in Zeit und Ewigkeit" (God casts down and lifts up in time and eternity), reads the recitative. The aria states:

> Ich nehme mein Leiden mit Freuden auf mich.
> Wer Lazarus' Plagen
> Geduldig ertragen,
> Den nehmen die Engel zu sich.
>
> I take my suffering upon myself with joy.
> Whoever has borne Lazarus's torment
> Patiently,
> The angels shall take him to themselves.

A third recitative leads to the hymn that closes the first half of the cantata before the sermon, the fifth strophe from Samuel Rodigast's 1564 chorale *Was Gott tut, das ist wohlgetan* (What God does, that is done well). Except for the psalm verse at the beginning, the succession of movements in the second half is the same as the first: three recitatives, two arias, and a chorale strophe. Wealth and poverty—the themes of the parable from the Gospel reading—are now related to the individual's world of belief. If the first recitative of the second half laments "des Geistes Armut" (poverty of the spirit) and failing strength, the ensuing aria answers with "Jesus macht mich geistlich reich" (Jesus makes me spiritually rich), whereby a phrase from the Sermon on the Mount, "Selig sind, die da geistlich arm sind" (Blessed are the poor in spirit), might stand in the background. If the next recitative demands self-renunciation and the avoidance of all that is earthly "Daß er in Gottes Liebe / Sich gläubig übe" (That he, in God's love, / May exercise himself in faith), here again the ensuing aria gives the confident answer with its text beginning "Mein Herze glaubt und liebt" (My heart believes and loves). With "O Armut, der kein Reichtum gleicht" (O poverty that no wealth equals), the last recitative summarizes the core of the parable, leading to the concluding chorale strophe, once again drawn from Rodigast's hymn *Was Gott tut, das ist wohlgetan*.

Bach's composition of this wide-ranging text assumes dimensions that are appropriate to a new beginning in a prominent and vibrant city. Hence the idea of the sumptuous French overture, here in two parts, stands behind the extensive opening chorus. In this case, as befits the psalm passage, it stands in the elegiac key of E minor, the key of sorrow and solace. The faster fugal concluding section on the text "Euer Herz soll ewiglich leben" (Your heart shall live eternally) is rather short compared to the melancholic beginning. The bass recitative is followed by a dancelike, animated aria with tenor solo "Mein Jesus soll mein alles sein" (My Jesus shall be my all). The restful serenity of the text statement is matched by the measured rhythmic motion, but without bringing a contemporary dance type to mind. One is prompted to wonder whether this unusually extensive aria goes back to an earlier work from Bach's time at Köthen.

The second aria, following a brief tenor recitative, also has no clear connection to any particular dance type. Here, in the buoyant collaboration of soprano and obbligato oboe d'amore on the text that begins "Ich nehme mein Leiden mit Freuden auf mich," the subtle handling of "Leiden" (suffering) is opposed by an all but unbridled unfolding of "Freude" that gradually gains the upper hand. After a third equally brief recitative, a chorale movement concludes the first half of the cantata. Instead of being restricted to a simple four-part harmonization, it takes on the dimensions of an elaborate chorale arrangement with instrumental prelude, postlude, and interludes.

The same chorale melody, *Was Gott tut, das ist wohlgetan* appears at the beginning of the cantata's second half as part of an instrumental movement: above a fugal quartet of stringed instruments, the melody is performed line by line by the trumpets. As in the first half of the cantata, the first recitative is accompanied by string instruments; in unison these also form the obbligato part in the alto aria that follows, "Jesus macht mich geistlich reich." This movement is also dancelike, although without any recognizable connection to the text. It is only in the fourth and last aria of the cantata that Bach—perhaps out of necessity and owing to the problematic nature of the text—abandons this procedure and combines solo bass, obbligato trumpet, and strings in concerted virtuosity. The beginning of the text "Mein Herze glaubt und liebt" is thus interpreted in the sense of confidence in victory.

The chorale arrangement at the end of the first part is repeated to conclude the entire cantata. Only the text differentiates this from its predecessor, now the last strophe of Samuel Rodigast's chorale *Was Gott tut, das ist wohlgetan*.

Thus ends the cantata whose unusual demands are appropriate to its context: the composer's recent appointment to the cantorate at St. Thomas School. At the same time, the work outstripped the possibilities and boundaries of concerted church music, particularly for the first Sunday after Trinity. Hence Bach quickly gave up the outsized dimensions of the fourteen-movement model and returned to more normal proportions—at least with respect to the length of his works.

Die Himmel erzählen die Ehre Gottes
BWV 76 / BC A 97

Second Sunday after Trinity, June 6, 1723

Johann Sebastian Bach composed the cantata *Die Himmel erzählen die Ehre Gottes* BWV 76 (The heavens are telling the honor of God) in early June 1723; it was his second composition after officially assuming office as cantor of St. Thomas School in Leipzig. As in the case of the cantata that came before it, *Die Elenden sollen essen* BWV 75, this work is unusually extensive and thereby signals the newly appointed cantor's intent to create an unmistakable standard reflecting his artistic goals. It remains unclear whether such an expenditure of effort and resources matched the rank of the second Sunday after Trinity.

The unidentified poet of the cantata—perhaps identical to the librettist for its sister composition—hews closely to the Gospel reading for the Sunday, found in Luke 14:16–24. It tells of Jesus's parable of the great evening meal.

> He, however, spoke to him: There was a man who prepared a great evening meal and invited many to it. And he sent out his servant at the hour of the evening meal to say to those invited: Come, for everything is ready! And they began, one after another, to excuse themselves. The first said to him: I have just bought an acre and must go out and inspect it; please excuse me. And the other spoke: I have bought five yoke of oxen and am just going now to inspect them; I beg you, please excuse me. And the third spoke: I have just taken a wife; therefore, I cannot come. And the servant came and repeated this to his master. Then the man of the house became angry and said to his servant: Go out quickly onto the streets and alleys of the city and lead the poor, the crippled, the lame, and the blind in here. And the servant spoke: Lord, it is done, what you have ordered; but there is still room. And

the master said to his servant: Go out to the country roads and the fences and insist that everyone come, that my house is full. Yet I say to you, that of the men who were invited, none shall taste my evening meal.

The text of our cantata takes up this parable but places two verses from Psalm 19 at the beginning, praising the honor of God in nature and in his word: "Die Himmel erzählen die Ehre Gottes, und die Feste verkündiget seiner Hände Werk. . . . Es ist kein Sprache noch Rede, da man nicht ihre Stimme höre" (1, 3; The heavens are telling the honor of God, and the firmament declares his handiwork. . . . There is no language nor speech where one does not hear their voice). This is followed by the first recitative:

> So läßt sich Gott nicht unbezeuget!
> Natur und Gnade red't alle Menschen an!

> So God does not leave himself without witness!
> Nature and grace speak to all people!

It concludes with these lines:

> Gott selbst hat sich zu euch geneiget
> Und ruft durch Boten ohne Zahl:
> Auf, kommt zu meinem Liebesmahl!

> God himself has turned to you
> And calls through messages without number:
> Arise, come to my feast of love!

The ensuing aria answers this invitation, drawn from the Gospel reading:

> Hört, ihr Völker, Gottes Stimme,
> Eilt zu seinem Gnadenthron.
> Aller Dinge Grund und Ende
> Ist sein eingeborener Sohn:
> Daß sich alles zu ihm wende.

> Hear, you peoples, God's voice,
> Hasten to his throne of grace.
> The foundation and end of all things
> Is his only begotten son:
> That all things may turn to him.

The movement pair that follows is focused on the contrary behavior depicted in the parable in the Gospel reading. In regard to the invitation in the preceding movement, the recitative asks:

> Wer aber hört,
> Da sich der größte Haufen
> Zu andern Göttern kehrt?
>
> But who hears,
> Since the greatest multitude
> Turns to other gods?

It closes with resignation:

> Die Weisen brüten Torheit aus,
> Und Belial sitzt wohl in Gottes Haus,
> Weil auch die Christen selbst von Christo laufen.
>
> The wise concoct foolishness,
> And Belial sits in the house of God,
> For even Christians themselves run from Christ.

But the aria counters:

> Fahr hin, abgöttische Zunft!
> Soll sich die Welt gleich verkehren,
> Will ich doch Christum verehren,
> Er ist das Licht der Vernunft.
>
> Be gone, idolatrous mob!
> Should the world be perverted,
> I will still honor Christ,
> He is the light of reason.

The last recitative of the cantata's first half provides words of thanks, once again drawn from the Gospel reading:

> Du hast uns, Herr, von allen Straßen,
> Zu dir geruft,
> Als wir im Finsternis der Heiden saßen,
> Und, wie das Licht die Luft
> Belebet und erquickt....
>
> You have, Lord, from all highways,
> Called us to you
> As we sat in the darkness of the Gentiles;
> And as the light the air
> Enlivens and refreshes....

The opening strophe from Martin Luther's chorale *Es woll uns Gott genädig sein* (May God be gracious to us) follows; it provides the "demütiges Gebet" (humble prayer) mentioned in the recitative's conclusion.

The second half of the cantata, to be performed after the sermon, turns to God's "treue Schar" (faithful host) and their works with a recitative:

> Sie ist der Himmel auf der Erden
> Und muß durch steten Streit
> Mit Haß und mit Gefahr
> In dieser Welt gereinigt werden.

> This host is heaven on earth
> And must, through continuous conflict
> With hate and with danger,
> Be purified in this world.

The ensuing aria immediately takes up a battle position:

> Hasse nur, hasse mich recht,
> Feindlichs Geschlecht!
> Christum gläubig zu umfassen,
> Will ich alle Freude lassen.

> Hate then, hate me truly,
> Hostile generation!
> To embrace Christ faithfully
> I would forgo all joy.

But the true task is not withstanding hate but rather embracing the love of Christ and extending its brotherhood: this is the focus of the last three freely versified movements before another strophe from Luther's hymn summarizes and closes the libretto:

> Es danke, Gott, und lobe dich
> Das Volk in guten Taten;
> Das Land bringt Frucht und bessert sich,
> Dein Wort ist wohlgeraten.
> Uns segne Vater und der Sohn,
> Uns segne Gott, der Heil'ge Geist,
> Dem alle Welt die Ehre tu,
> Für ihm sich fürchte allermeist
> Und sprech von Herzen Amen.

> May the people thank and praise you,
> God, in good deeds;

The land bears fruit and improves itself,
Your word brings prosperity.
May Father and Son bless us,
May God, the Holy Spirit, bless us,
May all the world honor him,
Fear him most of all,
And say from the heart Amen.

In Bach's composition of this extensive libretto, a significant role is played by "striking up" a tune, as well as taking it up and joining in. With a shout of joy, the trumpets start the opening movement "Die Himmel erzählen die Ehre Gottes"; they are answered by the woodwinds and strings. Call and echo interlock ever more closely together until the bass intones the first biblical passage and the four-part chorus picks it up. The development of more than sixty measures finally intensifies to a fugue, begun by soloists in the four voice ranges, taken up by the chorus, and brought to its conclusion. After a tenor recitative accompanied by strings, in which the most important statements in the text broaden to arioso, soprano and solo violin combine for the first aria. Here again, echo-like literal repetition plays a significant role as the interplay of calling and listening makes manifest the text "Hört, ihr Völker, Gottes Stimme."

The fifth movement, the second aria of the cantata, is framed by two recitatives. It is set with bass and obbligato trumpet with the collaboration of the other instruments. What is striking here is the twisted melody and rhythm, whose intentional instability is obviously meant to amplify the ideas in the text of "Fahr hin, abgöttische Zunft!" and "Sollt sich die Welt gleich verkehren."

The closing chorale of the first part of the cantata is Johann Walter's melody *Es woll uns Gott genädig sein* (May God be gracious to us). First documented in 1524, the hymn clearly goes back to pre-Reformation ancestry. Here again, the dynamic of leading and joining in is fundamental: each line of the chorale is played by the instruments and then presented by the entire ensemble.

The second part of the cantata begins with an instrumental movement, a trio for oboe d'amore, viola da gamba, and basso continuo. The two-part sinfonia also exists in a version for two manuals and pedal, the opening movement in Bach's Trio Sonata in E Minor for Organ BWV 528. Both versions may well go back to a common ancestor composed in Weimar with different setting, probably a sonata in G minor for oboe, viola da gamba, and basso continuo.*

The bass recitative, accompanied by strings, "Gott segne noch die treue Schar" (May God bless the faithful host), is followed by the aria "Hasse nur, hasse mich recht" for tenor, accompanied only by basso continuo. Here Bach uses diminished and augmented intervals in particular to illuminate the negative affect. The last aria, once again framed by two recitatives, is for alto: "Liebt, ihr Christen in der Tat" (Love, you Christians, in your action) unites a rocking $\frac{9}{8}$ meter, charming melody, and softly flowing harmonies in service of the text. The instrumental setting of oboe d'amore, viola da gamba, and basso continuo reflects that of the sinfonia at the beginning of the cantata's second half. Bach may have intended to form the overall character of the second half in this way, bridging the "hate aria" just mentioned.

The cantata concludes with a repetition of the chorale movement that concluded the first part with its instrumental preludes for each line, affirming the procedure that characterizes so much of the cantata.

During Bach's lifetime, the cantata was repeated many times, as a whole as well as in part—certainly an indication of the composer's estimation of its success.

---

*Dirksen (2003).

Herz und Mund und Tat und Leben
BWV 147 / BC A 174

Visitation of Mary, July 2, 1723

This cantata belongs to a small group of works that Johann Sebastian Bach composed near the end of his time at Weimar and that he reworked radically in his first few months after arriving in Leipzig in 1723, integrating them into his repertoire as cantor of St. Thomas School.[4] The reason for the revisions was the fact that he had written these cantatas for the second, third, and fourth Sundays of Advent, which made them unusable in Leipzig. Those three Sundays belonged to the *tempus clausum*, during which no musical performances took place in church. Our cantata's text is found in a collection by Salomon Franck, the chief consistorial secretary at Weimar, that appeared in 1717 in Weimar and Jena with the title *Evangelische Sonn- und Fest-Tages-Andachten* (Protestant Sunday and feast day devotions). This print contains the cantata text *Herz und Mund und Tat und Leben* (Heart and mouth and deed and life) beneath the heading "Auf den vierten Advent-Sonntag" (On the fourth Sunday of Advent). In contrast to the ten-movement Leipzig work, the Weimar version comprises only six movements. After the opening chorus, four arias follow, and the piece closes with a strophe from Johann Kolrose's *Ich dank dir, lieber Herre* (I thank you, dear Lord), whose text begins "Dein Wort lass mich bekennen" (Let me bear witness to your word).

Salomon Franck's cantata libretto is closely bound to the Gospel reading for the fourth Sunday of Advent. Found in John 1, it recounts the witness of John the Baptist. The opening chorus in Franck's libretto alludes to this foundational idea with the lines "Herz und Mund und Tat und Leben / Muß von Christo Zeugnis geben" (Heart and mouth and deed and life / Must bear witness of Christ).

The revision of the Advent cantata, probably composed in December 1716, to a cantata for the Visitation of Mary required extensive alterations to the text in order to produce a connection to the Gospel reading for that feast day. This Gospel reading is found in Luke 1 and tells of Mary's visit with Elizabeth. The account closes with Mary's song of praise, known in Latin as the Magnificat.

The unknown arranger in Leipzig inserted substantial portions of this canticle into the new version of the cantata libretto. The recitative that follows the brief Weimar opening chorus thus begins:

> Gebenedeiter Mund!
> Maria macht ihr Innerstes der Seelen
> Durch Dank und Rühmen kund;
> Sie fänget bei sich an, des Heilands Wunder zu erzählen,
> Was er an ihr als seiner Magd getan.
>
> Blessed mouth!
> Mary makes her innermost soul
> Known by thanksgiving and praise;
> She begins with herself to tell of the savior's wonders,
> What he has done for her as his handmaiden.

The corresponding place in Luke 1 reads "Meine Seele erhebet den Herrn" (46; My soul magnifies the Lord) and "denn er hat die Niedrigkeit seiner Magd angesehen" (48; for he has looked upon the lowliness of his maid), as well as "denn er hat große Dinge an mir getan" (49; for he has done great things for me). As the recitative continues, it leaves this tone and ventures the possibility of denial. This foreshadows the following aria, whose second part deals with exactly this sort of denial. The first part, on the other hand, is devoted to the confession of belief:

> Schäme dich, o Seele, nicht,
> Deinen Heiland zu bekennen
> Soll er dich die seine nennen
> Vor des Vaters Angesicht.

> Be not ashamed, O soul,
> To acknowledge your savior
> Should he name you as his own
> Before the Father's countenance.

These are Salomon Franck's formulations, although slightly moderated: the original version of 1717 reads, in reference to the Song of Solomon, "Soll er seine Braut dich nennen / Vor des Vaters Angesicht" (Should he name you his bride / Before the Father's countenance). The beginning of the ensuing recitative paraphrases another section from the Canticle of Mary. Luke 1:51 reads: "Er übet Gewalt mit seinem Arm und zerstreut, die hoffärtig sind in ihres Herzens Sinn. Er stößt die Gewaltigen vom Stuhl und erhebt die Niedrigen" (He shows power in his arm and disperses those who are arrogant in their heart's mind. He throws the mighty from their seats and exalts the lowly), but the librettist writes:

> Verstockung kann Gewaltige verblenden,
> Bis sie des Höchstens Arm von Stuhle stößt;
> Doch dieser Arm erhebt,
> Obschon vor ihm der Erde Kreis erbebt,
> Hingegen die Elenden,
> So er erlößt.

> Obstinacy can blind the powerful
> Until the arm of the Most High throws them from their seats;
> Yet this arm,
> Although the earth's orb trembles before it,
> Exalts the miserable,
> Whom he redeems.

The associated aria deviates in two respects from the Weimar cantata. Here is Franck's version:

> Bereite dir, Jesu, noch heute die Bahn!
> Beziehe die Höhle
> Des Herzens, der Seele,
> Und blicke mit Augen der Gnade mich an.

> Prepare the way to you, Jesus, even today!
> Move into the cavern
> Of the heart, of the soul,
> And look with eyes of grace upon me.

In Leipzig that version became:

> Bereite dir, Jesu, noch itzo die Bahn,
> Mein Heiland, erwähle
> Die gläubende Seele
> Und siehe mit Augen der Gnade mich an!
>
> Prepare the way to you, Jesus, even now,
> My savior, choose
> The believing soul
> And look with eyes of grace upon me!

Further, in the Leipzig libretto this aria changed places with the one that followed it in the Weimar text. The former, whose text begins "Hilf, Jesu, hilf daß ich auch dich bekenne" (Help, Jesus, help that I also acknowledge you), introduces the second half of the Leipzig cantata. The first half closes with a strophe from the chorale *Jesu, meiner Seelen Wonne* (Jesus, delight of my soul). In contrast to the two movements that precede it, the only recitative in the second half of the cantata does not take up the Canticle of Mary but rather the beginning of the Gospel reading for the feast day, Mary's entrance into the house of Zacharia, and her first encounter with his pregnant wife, Elizabeth: "Und es begab sich, als Elisabeth den Gruß Marias hörte, hüpfte das Kind in ihrem Leibe" (Luke 1:41; And it came to pass, as Elizabeth heard the greeting of Mary, the child in her body leaped). In closing with an expression announcing "Dank und Preis" (thanksgiving and praise), this recitative opens the way for an aria filled with praise and thanks:

> Ich will von Jesu Wundern singen
> Und ihm der Lippen Opfer bringen,
> Er wird nach seiner Liebe Bund
> Das schwache Fleisch, den irdschen Mund
> Durch heilges Feuer kräftig zwingen.
>
> I want to sing of Jesus's wonders
> And to him bring offerings of the lips.
> He will, according to his covenant of love,
> Subdue the weak flesh, the earthly mouth
> Through his holy fire.

This text had to be fundamentally reformulated by the Leipzig librettist so that the Weimar composition could be used again. What was required was the use of what is known as parody procedure, because the first version all too clearly alluded to the Gospel reading for Advent and the witness of John the Baptist:

Laß mich der Rufer Stimmen hören,
Die mit Johannes treulich lehren.
Ich soll in dieser Gnadenzeit
Von Finsternis und Dunkelheit
Zum wahren Lichte mich bekennen.

Let me hear the callers' voices,
Which, with John, teach faithfully.
I shall, in this time of grace,
From gloom and darkness
Confess myself to the true light.

The second part of the cantata closes as the first one did, with a strophe from Martin Janus's hymn *Jesu, meiner Seelen Wonne*.

Bach's composition of this extensive libretto is a distinctive mix of older and newer movements. The opening chorus and four arias are of Weimar origin, as seen in the attributes of their text and musical style; in Leipzig the four recitatives were added, as well as the chorale movements closing the first and second parts of the cantata. The original Weimar closing chorale was discarded and lost.

In spite of the brevity of its text, the opening chorus is spacious and complex in its design. An introductory sinfonia returns many times throughout the movement, enriched by a vocal component in a technique known as *Choreinbau*, in alternation with unaccompanied choral episodes and two fugal expositions.[5] This elegant and balanced architecture, which encompasses fewer than seventy measures, combines a delight in music making with a wealth of thematic invention and inimitable concentration.

The four arias embody a procedure characteristic of Bach's Weimar compositional style: they omit a formal da capo and only repeat the instrumental ritornello at the end. The first aria, "Schäme dich, o Seele, nicht," is set for alto and oboe d'amore. The original Weimar version almost certainly used a different obbligato instrument. It has no small challenge in contending with the negative statements in its text. The soprano and tenor arias have head motives that are eloquently expressive and hence formative: the soprano voice, with its "Bereite dir, Jesu, noch itzo die Bahn," is assisted by a solo violin; the tenor, accompanied only by basso continuo, has the even shorter and extremely pregnant "Hilf, Jesu, hilf." Bach added an obbligato trumpet to the bass aria, the next to last movement in the cantata. In view of this, in a secular context the aria could be a vehicle for the allegorical figure of Fama, the personification of Fame. Its song of praise within a church cantata achieves, at minimum, the special status of "music within music."

The movements that close both halves of the cantata are identical musically. In them, the vocal component is embedded in a sonorous, hovering figuration of strings and woodwinds. That these choral movements seem rather out of place today has less to do with the composition itself than with its reception history and is the inevitable result of wearing out a favorite piece.

Herr, gehe nicht ins Gericht mit deinem Knecht
BWV 105 / *BC* A 114

Ninth Sunday after Trinity, July 25, 1723

In late July 1723, two months after he entered office as cantor of St. Thomas School in Leipzig, Johann Sebastian Bach performed his cantata *Herr, gehe nicht ins Gericht mit deinem Knecht* BWV 105 (Lord, do not enter judgment with your servant) in the two main churches of the city. The work is for the ninth Sunday after Trinity; its text takes up the Gospel reading for that day, found in Luke 16:1–9, the parable of the unjust householder:

> He, however, spoke to his disciples: There was a rich man who had a steward of whom it was rumored that he had wasted his goods. And he called him and spoke to him: How is it that I hear this of you? Give me an account of your stewardship, for henceforth you cannot be my steward! The steward said to himself: What shall I do? My lord has taken away my job; I cannot dig, and I am ashamed to beg. I am resolved what to do so that, if I am now discharged from my job, that they welcome me into their homes. And he called all debtors to his lord and spoke to the first one: How much do you owe my lord? He spoke: A hundred casks of oil. And he spoke to him: Take your letter, sit down quickly, and write fifty. Then he spoke to the other: You, however, how much do you owe? He said a hundred bushels of wheat. And he said to him: Take your letter and write eighty. And the lord praised the unrighteous steward, that he had dealt cleverly; for the children of this world are more clever than the children of the light in their generation. And I say to you: Make friends with unrighteous mammon, so that when you fail, they may take you into the eternal dwellings.

Along with its application, this parable—together with several related biblical passages—has been interpreted as *sacrum commercium*, as "heavenly business," in which Jesus as the "heavenly storekeeper" takes the debts of people upon himself and then tears up the promissory note and, as mediator between God and humanity, pays ransom for sinful humankind.

The text of our cantata, whose author remains unknown, revolves around sin as debt and the difficulty of debt cancellation. The first three movements avoid any mention of the Sunday Gospel reading. Instead, the librettist begins with a passage from Psalm 143, which prays for divine salvation and guidance: "Herr, erhöre mein Gebet, vernimm mein Flehen um deiner Wahrheit willen, erhöre mich um deiner Gerechtigkeit willen und gehe nicht ins Gericht mit deinem Knechte; denn vor dir ist kein Lebendiger gerecht" (1; Lord, hear my prayer, hear my plea for the sake of your truth, hear me for the sake of your righteousness and do not enter judgment with your servant; since before you no one living shall be justified). The first freely versified movement, a recitative, also takes up the psalter. Psalm 51, David's plea for atonement, reads: "Verwirf mich nicht von deinem Angesicht und nimm deinen heiligen Geist nicht von mir" (11; Do not cast me away from your countenance and do not take your holy spirit away from me). The cantata text based on the psalm reads:

> Mein Gott, verwirf mich nicht,
> Indem ich mich in Demut vor dir beuge,
> Von deinem Angesicht.
> Ich weiß, wie groß dein Zorn und mein Verbrechen ist,
> Daß du zugleich ein schneller Zeuge
> Und ein gerechter Richter bist.

> My God, do not cast me aside
> As I bow down before you in humility.
> From your countenance
> I know how great your fury and my offense is,
> That you are at once a swift witness
> And a righteous judge.

The ensuing aria indicates that salvation is not yet in sight:

> Wie zittern und wanken
> Der Sünder Gedanken,
> Indem sie sich untereinander verklagen
> Und wiederum sich zu entschuldigen wagen.
> So wird ein geängstigt Gewissen
> Durch eigene Folter zerrissen.

> How tremble and waver
> The sinner's thoughts
> As they accuse one another
> And again dare to excuse themselves.
> Thus a distressed conscience
> Is torn upon its own rack.

This is a paraphrase of a passage from the letter of the Apostle Paul to the Romans 2:15, which speaks of sinners and their "Gedanken, die sich untereinander verklagen oder entschuldigen" (thoughts that accuse or excuse one another). The second recitative text, which alludes to a place in the Epistle of Paul to the Colossians, is the first to mention forgiveness of sin. In the sense of the metaphor of the "heavenly shopkeeper," the Epistle of Paul reads: "Er . . . hat uns geschenkt alle Sünden und ausgetilgt die Handschrift, so wider uns war, welche durch Satzungen entstand und uns entgegen war, und hat sie aus dem Mittel getan und auf das Kreuz geheftet" (2:13–14; He . . . has forgiven us all our sins and erased the manuscript that was so against us, which arose from statutes and was against us, and took them out of the way and lifted them upon the cross).

Following a theme from the Passion tradition, the cantata poet formulated:

> Wohl aber dem, der seinen Bürgen weiß,
> Der alle Schuld ersetzet,
> So wird die Handschrift ausgetan,
> Wenn Jesus sie mit Blute netzet.
> Er heftet sie ans Kreuze selber an.

> But goodness comes to him who knows his guarantor,
> Who redeems all debt.
> Thus the note is blotted out
> When Jesus wets it with blood.
> He lifts it on the cross himself.

And, taking up these words of Jesus, "Make friends with unrighteous mammon," the ensuing aria text concludes the "shopkeeper" reflections:

> Kann ich nur Jesum mir zum Freunde machen,
> So gilt der Mammon nichts bei mir.
> Ich finde kein Vergnügen hier
> Bei dieser eitlen Welt und irdischen Sachen.

> If only I can make Jesus my friend,
> Mammon will mean nothing to me.
> I find no pleasure here
> In this vain world and among earthly things.

This strict opposition ignores the possibility of proper use of earthly goods allowed for by the Gospel reading. In conclusion, an end to the crisis of conscience is signaled by a stanza from Johann Rist's 1641 hymn *Jesu, der du meine Seele* (Jesus, you who my soul), whose penultimate strophe begins:

Nun ich weiß, du wirst mir stillen
Mein Gewissen, das mich plagt.

Now I know you will calm for me
My conscience, which torments me.

Bach's composition is just as diverse and exciting as this source text with its wealth of oppositions. He assigns two contrasting sections to the psalm passage at the very beginning of the opening movement: the imploring "Herr, gehe nicht ins Gericht mit deinem Knecht" develops from a densely chromatic, instrumental Adagio. Anxiously repeated eighth notes connect a weary ascent that shows only minimal gain with a slow descent accompanied by many different sighs before the fervent, elegantly interleaved voices become perceptible. A fugue in quick tempo underscores the almost unassailable "Denn vor dir wird kein Lebendiger gerecht" (For before you no one living shall be justified) with implacable, hammering leaps of the fourth in the theme's beginning, as well as the apparent immutability of the permutation fugue procedure. A diminuendo to *piano* and *pianissimo* shortly before the close persists, together with the softening brought by the return of the theme's beginning.

The aria for soprano "Wie zittern und wanken der Sünder Gedanken" follows a short alto recitative; it is one of those movements in which Bach characterizes the extraordinary by refusing to rely upon the security of the familiar. The essential bass foundation is omitted, and the viola functions as the deepest voice, a "bassetto"; as a whole, the texture symbolizes the circumstance in which one's firm stability has been lost. Anxiously repeated tones, slower in the viola/bassetto, faster in the two violins, illustrate the "trembling and wavering" central to the text. The voice and oboe hold a lonely dialogue full of questioning, uncertainty, and anxiety whose outcome remains open, notwithstanding all expressions of pain.

Buoyed by gentle harmonic motion of the strings, security and faith beyond the grave characterize the bass recitative "Wohl aber dem, der seinen Bürgen weiß." Security and steadfastness also define the ensuing tenor aria "Kann ich nur Jesum mir zum Freunde machen." With their rock-solid diction, the voice along with the horn ascending to its highest range and the other instruments confront the glistening and seductive virtuoso solo violin; they allow contemptible mammon no quarter. Even so, the trembling of sinners before judgment makes another appearance: the four-part closing chorale on the melody *Jesu, der du meine Seele* is accompanied by a three-part texture of strings, anxiously repeating the first phrase of the melody. Faithful to the title "Nun ich weiß, du wirst mir stillen" (Now I know you will calm for me), the repeated tones slow from line to line, with sixteenth notes in $\frac{4}{4}$ meter becoming triplets in $\frac{12}{8}$, then eighths in duple meter, and so forth, until quarter-note motion after the close of the final line of the chorale grants a restful conclusion. Even in this section's serene chromaticism, however, one hears the hopeless situation at the cantata's beginning recalled.

Preise, Jerusalem, den Herrn
BWV 119 / BC B 3

Leipzig City Council Inauguration, August 30, 1723

With the cantata *Preise, Jerusalem, den Herrn* BWV 119 (Praise, Jerusalem, the Lord), Johann Sebastian Bach returned to a field he had not tilled for fourteen years, namely, the performance of festive music to celebrate the installation of new city councils in larger cities. Now in his first year as cantor of St. Thomas School in Leipzig, Bach encountered a long-standing custom similar to that in Mühlhausen, whereby council members served for life but were divided among several committees, each headed by a mayor.[6] These committees rotated on a multiyear basis in conducting city business. At any given time, about thirty councilmen and three mayors made up a sitting council and two resting councils. Plenary meetings, with all councilmen present, took place only on extraordinary occasions and for important reasons—such as the election of a new cantor for St. Thomas School in April 1723.

In Leipzig the change of councils took place on the Monday following St. Bartholomew's Day, celebrated on August 24. The significance of the day and the dignity of the council were matched by the rather old-fashioned rituals that preceded the event. These involved the town clerk, who was a senior councilman, meeting with the superintendent several days before the church service to formally ask him to deliver the sermon for the introduction of a new council. At the same time, a councilman of slightly lower rank with the obsolete title *Thürknecht* (door servant) would appear at the offices of the cantor to commission him for "the procurement of church music for the stipulated Monday" (die Besorgung der Kirchen Music auf besagten Montag). Both cantor and superintendent could have easily skipped their meetings, since both understood the significance of the day and knew their duties well. But for the council to do away with a "Brauch von alters her" (custom from time immemorial) would have required a formal decision on the part of the council that would have decreased its stature—an outcome hardly to be expected.

A letter of 1741 from Bach's cousin Johann Elias Bach demonstrates how seriously the celebration of the annual council election was taken.

He related several pieces of worrying news regarding the health of Anna Magdalena to the cantor, who was visiting his son Carl Philipp Emanuel in Berlin at the time, and followed it with the anxious observation: "To which is added the fact that St. Bartholomew's Day and the Council election here will occur in a few weeks, and we should not know how we should conduct ourselves in respect to the same in Your Honor's absence."[7] It was obviously inconceivable that Bach might have allowed himself to be represented by a substitute. Consequently, it seems that in his twenty-seven years of service in Leipzig, Bach conducted just as many performances of town council election cantatas.[8]

We have no way of knowing today what repertoire Bach employed to fulfill this ongoing obligation. Four Leipzig town council cantatas have been preserved along with their music, and another exists in fragmentary form. In addition, we have evidence of several texts. Even considering the possibility of repeated performances, we must assume that many such works are lost.

It is all the more gratifying that with the cantata *Preise, Jerusalem, den Herrn* we have Bach's very first such composition in Leipzig. We do not know who prepared the text for the work of nine movements. Traditionally, such a libretto had to combine praise of God with gratitude for the blessing of a godly government. Preferably, the libretto began with a psalm verse, as in this case, with verses from Psalm 147: "Preise, Jerusalem, den Herrn, lobe, Zion, deinen Gott! Denn er machet fest die Riegel deiner Tore und segnet deine Kinder drinnen, er schaffet deinen Grenzen Frieden" (12–14; Praise, Jerusalem, the Lord, praise, Zion, your God! For he strengthens the bars of your gates and blesses your children within, he makes peace within your borders). Then, with the recitative "Gesegnet Land, glückselge Stadt" (Blessed land, happy city), the "song of praise" turns to its own community. Here again, psalm verses are used. From Psalm 85, the plea of the previously pardoned nation for new blessings, come these verses: "Doch ist ja seine Hilfe nahe denen, die ihn fürchten, daß in unserm Lande Ehre wohne; daß Güte und Treue einander läßt begegnen; Gerechtigkeit und Friede sich küssen" (9–10; Yet his help is certainly near to those who fear him, that honor may dwell in our country; that goodness and devotion meet one another; justice and peace kiss one another). In the librettist's poetry, the passage sounds like this:

> Wie kann Gott besser lohnen,
> Als wo er Ehre läßt in einem Lande wohnen?
> Wie kann er eine Stadt
> Mit reicherm Nachdruck segnen,

> Als wo er Güt und Treu einander läßt begegnen,
> Wo er Gerechtigkeit und Friede
> Zu küssen niemals müde.
>
> How can God bestow greater benefit
> Than where he allows honor to dwell in a country?
> How can he bless a city
> With richer eminence
> Than where he lets goodness and devotion meet one another,
> Where he never wearies of justice and peace kissing.

The first aria apostrophizes Leipzig using the familiar translation of its name, City of Lindens:

> Wohl dir, du Volk der Linden,
> Wohl dir, du hast es gut.
> Wieviel an Gottes Segen
> Und seiner Huld gelegen,
> Die überschwenglich tut,
> Kannst du an dir befinden.
>
> Happy are you, you people of the lindens,
> Happy are you, it is well with you.
> How much dependent on God's blessing
> And his grace,
> Which manifests itself extravagantly,
> You can find within yourself.

The praise of the city continues in a recitative:

> So herrlich stehst du, liebe Stadt;
> Du Volk, das Gott zum Erbteil sich erwählet hat.
>
> So gloriously you stand, dear city;
> You people that God has chosen for his inheritance.

Here again, the psalter—Psalm 33:12—stands as godparent: "Wohl dem Volk, des Gott der Herr ist, dem Volk, das er zum Erbe erwählet hat" (Happy the nation whose God is the Lord, the nation that he has chosen for his inheritance). In a tone of utter conviction, the librettist announces that everything

> was wir Gutes bei uns sehn,
> Nächst Gott durch kluge Obrigkeit
> Und durch ihr weises Regiment geschehn.

that we regard as good around us
Happens, next to God, through prudent rulers
And through their wise governance.

Who would contradict such a statement? But there is better to come: the next aria calls it by its name:

Die Obrigkeit ist Gottes Gabe,
Ja selber Gottes Ebenbild.
Wer ihre Macht nicht will ermessen,
Der muß auch Gottes gar vergessen:
Wie würde sonst sein Wort erfüllt?

Authority is God's gift,
Yes, the very image of God himself.
Anyone unwilling to measure its power,
He must also forget God's entirely:
How otherwise would his word be fulfilled?

This is actually a paraphrase of Romans 13, which begins with the words "Jedermann sei untertan der Obrigkeit, die Gewalt über ihn hat. Denn es ist keine Obrigkeit ohne von Gott; wo aber Obrigkeit ist, die ist von Gott verordnet" (Let everyone be subject to the authority that has power over him. For there is no authority unless from God; where, however, authority exists, it is ordained by God). Thanking God for the authorities is the concern of the two cantata movements that follow, whereby authority includes those being relieved of their duties, as well as those about to assume them with renewed energy. Once again, the librettist borrows from the psalter; he chooses the beginning of a strophe from Psalm 126 for a choral movement: "Der Herr hat Großes an uns getan, des sind wir fröhlich" (3; The Lord has done great things for us, of which we are glad). Inexplicably, the word "Großes" (great things) in the cantata text was transformed to "Guts" (good things). By way of introduction, a final recitative asks that an "arm Gebet" (poor prayer) be heard; what is meant is the fourth strophe of Luther's German version of the Te Deum:

Hilf deinem Volk, Herr Jesu Christ,
Und segne, was dein Erbteil ist.
Wart und pfleg ihr zu aller Zeit
Und heb sie hoch in Ewigkeit.
Amen.

Help your people, Lord Jesus Christ,
And bless what is your inheritance.

Tend and nourish them at all times
And raise them high in eternity.
Amen.

For the opening chorus with the verses from Psalm 147, Bach chooses the greatest possible festive setting: four trumpets and drums, three oboes and two recorders, string orchestra and chorus, and, in the bass, cellos, bassoons, and bass viols in unison with the organ. How these maximal demands were reconciled with the notoriously cramped loft of Leipzig's St. Nicholas Church must remain an open question. Solemnity, dignity, and self-assurance characterize the broad beginning, whose dotted rhythms and pathos-laden, expansive scales indicate the magnificently ostentatious instrumental form of the French overture. The flow of the strings and woodwinds pauses three times, allowing fanfares in the trumpets and drums to be heard. Led by the trumpets in their high clarino range, the quick middle portion, only thirty measures in length, allows the psalm verse to pass by quickly in well-considered alternation of contemplation and celebration. Immediately, the slow instrumental introduction returns, achieving a thematic integration of the brass by way of a harmonic detour and thereby bringing about a climax and conclusion. Today scholars are seriously considering the possibility that this movement was not entirely newly composed but goes back in large part to a purely instrumental predecessor.*[9]

The tenor aria, a paean to the City of Lindens, radiates serenity and contentment with its gently ambling rhythm and songlike, catchy melody, its loosely arranged, rondo-like form, and the dark coloration of the two deep oboes. The alto aria "Die Obrigkeit ist Gottes Gabe" is tuneful and quite dancelike, with the recorders representing the upper reaches of the woodwind range. Its buoyancy of mood seems conceived more in conjunction with a varied and diverse overall structure rather than primarily projection of the text. Still, it would have seemed logical to use any and all means to demonstrate the omnipotence of the authorities installed by God to those in attendance. The altered version of the psalm verse "Der Herr hat Großes an uns getan" is clothed in a brilliant choral fugue that grows in intensity; it is surely no coincidence that its theme suggests the chorale melody *Nun danket alle Gott* (Now thank all you God). The fugue itself is the centerpiece of an elaborately layered structure comprising instrumental ritornelli and various choral complexes. The simple closing chorale uses the melody of the Te Deum, whose Reformation-era form is based on materials handed down from the old church (altkirchlicher Tradition). Recent scholarship suggests that the trumpets provided improvisatory fanfares at the end of each line,** lending the concluding chorale movement additional brilliance.

Remarkably, even the press took notice of the performance of Johann Sebastian Bach's first town council cantata for Leipzig. An account published in a Hamburg newspaper in early September 1723 mentions not only the Leipzig town council election but also the "superb council election music"— but without mentioning the name of the composer.

And this work received still another distinction in 1843 when it was heard in the Leipzig Gewandhaus under the direction of Felix Mendelssohn as part of a gala performance to inaugurate Leipzig's first monument to Bach, funded by Mendelssohn and still to be found in the park before St. Thomas Church.

*Dürr (1986).
**Hofmann (2001).

Christus, der ist mein Leben
BWV 95 / BC A 136
Sixteenth Sunday after Trinity, September 12, 1723

In terms of the number and variety of chorales they include, none of the surviving cantatas by Johann Sebastian Bach can compare with *Christus, der ist mein Leben* BWV 95 (Christ, he is my life). In the course of only seven movements, there are no fewer than four different church hymns from the sixteenth and seventeenth centuries, all with very different melodies. Therefore, this cantata, composed in mid-September 1723, together with its sister works in previous weeks, shows the cantor of St. Thomas experimenting with the possibilities of the chorale.*

An undertaking of this sort would have been unthinkable without the services of a dedicated librettist. With considerable skill, the unknown author of our cantata text connected strophes from four main chorales from the sixteenth Sunday after Trinity—without, however, including the Gospel reading for the stipulated Sunday at any point. Nevertheless, the account of Jesus raising the boy of Nain, found in Luke 7, is present insofar as its ideas revolve around the longing for death and resurrection. The text begins with the brief opening strophe from a chorale first documented in 1609, mostly in anonymous transmission:

> Christus, der ist mein Leben,
> Sterben ist mein Gewinn;
> Dem tu ich mich ergeben,
> Mit Freud fahr ich dahin.

Christ, he is my life,
To die is my reward,
To which I surrender myself,
With joy I travel there.

The allusion in the last line to the canticle of the ancient Simeon, in Luther's paraphrase of 1524, is soon verified with the adoption of the first strophe of that hymn:

Mit Fried und Freud ich fahr dahin,
Nach Gottes Willen,
Getrost ist mir mein Herz und Sinn,
Sanft und stille.
Wie Gott mir verheißen hat:
Mein Tod ist mein Schlaf worden.

With peace and joy I travel there,
According to God's will,
My heart and mind are comforted,
Soft and still.
As God has promised me:
My death has become my sleep.

The librettist connects the two strophes with a recitative that at the beginning paraphrases "Mit Fried und Freud fahr ich dahin" and at its end prepares the second strophe with the words "Mein Sterbelied ist schon gemacht, / Ach dürft ichs heute singen!" (My funeral dirge is already arranged, / O that I might sing it today!). A second recitative takes up the Luther strophe and expresses the enticements and temptations of this world using the familiar image of the apple of Sodom, lustrous without but disgusting within, and leads to yet another chorale strophe, the beginning of the chorale written by Valentin Herberger in 1619:

Valet will ich dir geben,
Du arge, falsche Welt,
Dein sündlich böses Leben
Durchaus mir nicht gefällt.
Im Himmel ist gut wohnen,
Hinauf steht mein Begier.
Da wird Gott ewig lohnen
Dem, der ihm dient allhier.

I want to bid you adieu,
You evil, false world,

Your sinfully wicked life
Thoroughly displeases me.
In heaven it is good to live,
Above stands my desire.
There God will eternally reward
Him who serves him here.

The readiness for death formulated in the freely versified text sections and the departure from this world are followed, after the third chorale strophe, by a prayer for a swift and blessed end, at first in a short recitative akin to soliloquy and then in a sigh of relief in the form of an aria:

Ach schlage doch bald, selge Stunde,
Den allerletzten Glockenschlag!
Komm, komm, ich reiche dir die Hände,
Komm, mache meiner Not ein Ende,
Du längst erseufzter Sterbenstag!

Ah, but strike soon, blessed hour,
The final toll of the bell!
Come, come, I reach my hands out to you.
Come, put an end to my misery,
You long-sighed-for day of death!

A final recitative speaks of the certainty of resurrection:

Denn ich weiß dies
Und glaub es ganz gewiß
Daß ich aus meinem Grabe
Ganz einen sichern Zugang zu dem Vater habe.
Der Tod ist nur ein Schlaf,
Dadurch der Leib, der hier von Sorgen abgenommen,
Zur Ruhe kommen.

For I know this
And believe it is quite certain
That I, from my grave,
Have wholly certain access to the Father.
Death is but a sleep
By which the body, here wasted away by care,
Will come to rest.

The line of thought concludes with the fourth strophe from Nikolaus Herman's hymn *Wenn mein Stündlein vorhanden ist* (When the hour of my death is at hand):

Weil du vom Tod erstanden bist,
Werd ich im Grab nicht bleiben;
Dein letztes Wort mein Auffahrt ist,
Todsfurcht kannst du vertreiben.
Denn wo du bist, da komm ich hin,
Daß ich stets bei dir leb und bin,
Drum fahr ich hin mit Freuden.

Because you from death are risen,
I will not remain in the grave;
Your last word is my ascension,
The fear of death you can drive away.
For where you are, I will come there,
That I may always be and live beside you,
Therefore with joy I travel there.

Bach's composition of this libretto, whose structure is decisively shaped by chorale strophes, begins with a complex three-part movement that unmistakably reflects a search for new solutions. In an almost comfortable, rolling triple meter, the chorale melody *Christus, der ist mein Leben* by Melchior Vulpius is a reserved dialogue between the two oboi d'amore accompanied by the strings, into which the undaunted, ascending scales of the first violin do not quite want to fit. A bitter dissonance in the choral voices on the word "Sterben" and the overall reserved motion seem to want to prepare an untimely end to the idyll. But with the words "ist mein Gewinn" (is my reward) the ideal world, so to speak, is restored. The syncopated motives of the beginning maintain the upper hand; their effects are even heard in the animated tenor recitative in the middle of the movement. A radical reversal takes place after this: the key changes from G major to G minor, an alla breve meter dispels the previous tranquility, and with firm determination and no concern for possible ways out the phrase "Mit Fried und Freud fahr ich dahin" is sounded.

The rest of the cantata is also complex in structure. The soprano recitative moves directly into the strophe set as a chorale trio, "Valet will ich dir geben", where a rhythmically constant triadic figure in the basso continuo accompanies both the soprano and a melodic figure in the unison oboi d'amore that is at once eloquent, elegantly dancelike, and unified. A bit later, the oboes take on a crucial function in the cantata's only aria. While the strings continuously maintain a steady pizzicato depicting the "letzter Glockenschlag" (last bell stroke), the two oboi d'amore alternate lamenting parallel fourths and calming thirds. The lamenting intervals flow into calling motives, echo effects that lend a sense of spatial depth yet go unanswered.

With the next to last movement, a bass recitative, a different world is reached that begins with unexpected certainty and ends in animated joy. In the concluding chorale movement, longing for death and certainty of resurrection are not limited to the normal four-part setting: a fifth voice, an obbligato solo violin, climbs high above the chorus to luminous heights above.

---

*Krummacher (1995, 49).

Wachet! betet! betet! wachet
BWV 70 / BC A 165
Twenty-Sixth Sunday after Trinity, November 21, 1723

As it now exists, the cantata *Wachet! betet! betet! wachet* BWV 70.2 (Watch! pray! pray! watch) is assigned to the twenty-sixth Sunday after Trinity. It was first performed in Leipzig for this particular Sunday in late November 1723, one week before the first Sunday of Advent, the beginning of the new church year. However, most of the work was composed seven years earlier for the worship service in the castle church at Weimar. In this earlier form (BWV 70.1) it belongs to a group of three cantatas that Johann Sebastian Bach, then concertmaster, presented one week apart in December 1716.[10] This unusual flurry of performances is perhaps best explained by his desire to succeed the *Kapellmeister* in the Ernestine royal seat, who had died at the beginning of the month, and to put his compositional capabilities on display—as well as his unusual stamina.[11]

Bach took all three texts from a collection by Salomon Franck that became available in late 1716, *Evangelische Sonn- und Fest-Tages-Andachten*. The remarkable feature of these 1716 texts by Salomon Franck is that they consist entirely of free poetry, except for the closing chorale. Thus they avoid biblical passages. An opening movement for chorus is followed by four arias, and a chorale strophe closes the libretto. In contrast to other cantata texts of the period—even those by Salomon Franck himself—these texts avoid not only biblical passages but also the fashionable poetic form of the recitative.

The freely versified core element of the Weimar cantata *Wachet! betet! betet! wachet*—the opening chorus and the arias—is for the second Sunday in Advent, whose Gospel reading is found in Luke 21:25–36; it contains— following on Jesus's speech about the destruction of Jerusalem—predictions about his future:

And there shall be signs in the sun and moon and stars; and on the earth the people will be distressed, and they will have trepidation, and the sea and the waves will rage, and the people will faint for fear and in expectation of the things that shall happen on the earth, for also the powers of heaven will be in motion. And then they will see the Son of Man come in a cloud with great power and glory. When, however, this begins to happen, then look up and lift your heads, for your salvation draws near. And he recounted to them a parable: Look at the fig tree and all the trees: When they now begin to bud, you see them and notice that now summer is near. So also you: when you see these things happen, you know that the kingdom of God is near. Truly I say to you: This generation shall not pass away until all is fulfilled. Heaven and earth shall pass away, but my words shall not pass away. Take heed of yourselves, however, that your hearts are not consumed with eating and drinking and with concerns for nourishment, lest that day come quickly upon you, for like a snare it will come over all that live on earth. So now watch at all times and pray that you might be worthy, to escape all that will happen, and to stand before the Son of Man.

In accordance with this account, Salomon Franck's cantata text is situated between fear and hope, at one moment calling up the end times, at the next longing for rescue through Jesus. The text of the opening chorus takes up the close of the Sunday Gospel reading "So seid nun wach allezeit und betet, daß ihr würdig werden möget" (So now watch at all times and pray that you might be worthy):

> Wachet! betet! betet! wachet!
> Seid bereit
> Allezeit,
> Bis der Herr der Herrlichkeit
> Dieser Welt ein Ende machet.
>
> Watch! pray! pray! watch!
> Be prepared
> At all times
> Until the Lord of Glory
> Makes an end of this world.

With alarming immediacy in the first aria, the current dangerous situation is exemplified by the torment of the people of Israel in Egypt and the destruction of Sodom and Gomorrah:

> Wenn kömmt der Tag, an dem wir ziehen
> Aus dem Ägypten dieser Welt?
> Ach! laßt uns bald aus Sodom fliehen,

> Eh uns das Feuer überfällt!
> Wacht, Seelen, auf von Sicherheit,
> Und glaubt, es ist die letzte Zeit!
>
> When will come the day, when we will withdraw
> Out of the Egypt of this world?
> Ah, let us flee soon from Sodom
> Before the fire attacks us!
> Awaken, souls, out of complacency
> And believe it is the end of time!

The second aria speaks against this, with confidence in the foretold appearance of the Son of God:

> Laßt der Spötter Zungen schmähen,
> Es wird doch und muß geschehen,
> Daß wir Jesum werden sehen,
> Auf den Wolken, in den Höhen.
> Welt und Himmel mag vergehen,
> Christi Wort muß fest bestehen.
>
> Let the tongues of the mockers scorn,
> Yet it will and must occur
> That we will see Jesus
> Upon the clouds, in the heights.
> World and heaven may pass away,
> Christ's word must stand firm.

The third aria paraphrases the words "sehet auf und erhebet eure Häupter" (look up and lift your heads) from the Gospel reading, while in the fourth aria the end of days is evoked:

> Seligster Erquickungstag,
> Führe mich zu deinen Zimmern.
> Schalle, knalle, letzter Schlag,
> Welt und Himmel geht zu Trümmern!
> Jesus führet mich zur Stille,
> An den Ort, da Lust die Fülle.
>
> Most blessed day of refreshment,
> Lead me to your mansions.
> Resound, crack, final stroke,
> World and heaven go to ruin.
> Jesus leads me to quiet,
> At the place where pleasure is abundant.

Salomon Franck's libretto closes with the fifth strophe of Christian Keymann's 1658 hymn, *Meinen Jesum laß ich nicht* (I will not leave my Jesus).

In contrast to Weimar, in Leipzig church music fell silent between the first Sunday of Advent and the first day of Christmas—the period known as *tempus clausum*. Bach thus had no further use for a cantata written for the second day of Advent. The late Trinity period suggested itself as an alternative, in particular the twenty-sixth Sunday after Trinity, whose Gospel reading in Matthew 25 contains Jesus's speech about the Last Judgment, beginning with formulations that are similar to those of the Advent Gospel: "When, however, the Son of Man shall come in his glory and all holy angels with him, then he will sit upon the throne of his glory and all nations shall be gathered before him. And he will separate them from one another, just as a shepherd places the sheep to his right and the goats to his left" (31–32). The address to the righteous destined for eternal life culminates in the words "Was ihr getan habt einem unter diesen meinen geringsten Brüdern, das habt ihr mir getan" (Whatever you have done to one among these, the least of my brothers, that you have done to me), while the unmerciful meet their punishment with the justification, "Was ihr nicht getan habt einem unter diesen Geringsten, das habt ihr mir auch nicht getan" (Inasmuch as you have not done it to one of the least of these, you have not done it to me).

Taking up these concepts of the fall from grace and the Last Judgment, a librettist, possibly in Leipzig but unknown by name, expanded Salomon Franck's Advent libretto with four recitatives. These are formulated, respectively, as a reprimand to hardened sinners, a lament over the inadequacies of mortals, a threat of relentless punishment, and the confident hope in salvation. In addition, a strophe from the hymn *Freu dich sehr, o meine Seele* (Rejoice greatly, O my soul) was inserted so that the six-movement text of 1716 became an eleven-movement libretto, with two chorale strophes, four Leipzig recitatives, and five Weimar aria movements.

Bach's composition of this extensive libretto makes every effort to eliminate any discrepancy between the original components and those composed later. Even so, one cannot fail to recognize that the opening chorus, the arias, and even the concluding chorale clearly embody Bach's "Weimar style."

Fanfare motives and restless rising and falling scales characterize the sense of expectation in the opening chorus, whereby on the word "betet" the harmony darkens and the motion seems to pause. The entire instrumental ensemble, comprising a trumpet, an oboe, and strings, is also used for the first recitative. Continuously interrupted by the excited tone repetitions of the stile concitato, the recitative begins as a castigation of obdurate sinners.[12] It soon takes on a gentler tone for the "erwählte Gotteskinder" (chosen children of God), and for the phrase "Anfang wahrer Freude" (beginning of true joy), it includes an extended coloratura passage. The first aria about the withdrawal from the "Ägypten dieser Welt" (Egypt of this world), given to the alto, is characterized by a deep melancholy earnestness. Its key of A minor is closely related to E minor, the key of the soprano aria "Laßt der Spötter Zungen schmähen." Here the voice is accompanied by a sonorous obbligato part formed by all the strings, out of which the concertante first violin emerges briefly or for longer sections. The first part of the cantata, to be performed before the sermon, closes with a simple chorale movement in the "Leipzig style" on the melody *Wie nach einer Wasserquelle* (As from a spring of water).

The second half of the cantata begins with the tenor aria "Hebt euer Haupt empor" (Lift up your heads), its rather abrupt cheerfulness seeming to continue the text of the preceding chorale, "Freu dich sehr o meine Seele und vergiß all Not und Qual" (Rejoice greatly, O my soul, and forget all distress and torment). In the ensuing bass recitative, the apocalyptic scenario of the Last Judgment descends upon this apparently ideal world. Above plunging scales and anxiously diverging chords, the trumpet menacingly sounds the melody *Es ist gewißlich an der Zeit* (The time is certainly drawing near). Yet even here, Jesus's mercy is not far away, and an extended coloratura evokes the joyousness with which the faithful can leave this earthly existence. Still, peace and blessedness must once more shrink before the horrors of the apocalypse as, in the three-part bass aria, the contrasts characterizing the two recitatives and the first part of the opening aria are heard again. The Leipzig style of the chorale at the end of the first half now steps aside for a movement in the "Weimar style." The four choral voices are joined by three independent parts in the strings in their high registers so that the cantata is granted a full-textured finale in seven voices.

Sie werden aus Saba alle kommen
BWV 65 / BC A 27
Epiphany, January 6, 1724

The Feast of Epiphany, also known as High New Year or Three Kings' Day, is celebrated on January 6. As the feast of the birth and baptism of Christ, it has been among the most popular holidays of the church year since ancient times. The Gospel reading for this feast day, the story of the Wise Men from the East found in the second chapter of Matthew, and the Epistle of the day, from the sixtieth chapter of the prophet Isaiah, have proven to be virtually inexhaustible sources of inspiration for artistic creativity, although certainly with different emphasis. According to Arnold Schering, "The old Italian and Netherlands painters . . . conceived the scenes of the Three Kings' worship of the child Jesus as a rule as major state affairs. They placed mother and child in the center of the painting, both surrounded, however, with such an abundance of animated humanity and heaps of garments, jewelry, and beasts of burden, so confused that one feels present at a sumptuous homage to royalty rather than at a silent devotion in a Bethlehem manger."[13]

A "silent devotion in a Bethlehem manger" would match the section of the Gospel reading as Johann Sebastian Bach composed it for the sixth cantata of the Christmas Oratorio: "As they saw the star, they became overjoyed [11] and went in the house and found the little child with Mary, his mother, and fell to their knees and prayed to him and brought out their treasures and gave him gold, frankincense, and myrrh" (Matthew 2:10–11). By contrast, one indeed encounters a "sumptuous" scenario in Isaiah 60:4–6, which reads:

> Lift up your eyes and look around: these all gathered together come to you. Your sons shall come from afar, and your daughters will be carried in arms. Then you shall see your pleasure, and flow together, and your heart shall fear, and be enlarged; because the abundance of the sea shall be converted unto thee, the forces of the Gentiles shall come unto thee. For the multitude of camels shall cover you, the young camels of Midian and Ephah; they will from Sheba all come, they shall bring gold and incense; and they shall sing forth the praises of the Lord.

The Sabaean people alluded to here have been known to inhabit southern Arabia at least from the eighth century BCE through the second century CE. Trade routes between India, Ethiopia, and northern lands brought the area great affluence. Its star declined as transport by caravan on land was gradually replaced by ships at sea.

This context becomes significant when one goes about bringing Bach's score to life. In particular, the instrumental part in the opening movement is as rich as it is attractive; in it, horns, recorders in the upper regions of their range, and hunting oboes—oboi da caccia—appear in pairs. The horns move partly in the harmony-filling "horn range" and partly in the higher clarino register. The oboi da caccia—reed instruments originally in half-round, curved form with a large bell—have a darkly sonorous, distinctively attractive sound in the context of the original instruments of the Bach era. Together with the strings and the recorders in their upper ranges, the hunting horns and oboes produce a multicolored array of sonorities that seem entirely appropriate to the pomp of a royal procession. The $\frac{12}{8}$ meter chosen by Bach also can be seen to fit with this scenario: it can symbolize "completeness," "church," or "angels"—but also royalty. An older interpretation of our opening movement ascribed a pastorale coloring and hence had the horns tuned in C, sounding an octave lower than notated. This practice is in no way justified, although it is still stubbornly adhered to. Instead, what is meant is a heraldic symbolism focusing on the kings from Sheba apostrophized in the second movement of the cantata, where the horns must sound in their upper range.

After eight purely instrumental measures, the chorus enters with "Sie werden aus Saba alle kommen," the incoming throng symbolized by the overlapping, canonic entries of thematic material. Ten measures later, the bass begins a rocking, then lively fugue theme, taken up immediately by tenor, alto, and soprano, at first in permutation procedure and then in stretto. How seriously the composer took his task here can be seen in an extensive set of sketches—a relatively rare case for Johann Sebastian Bach—which were preserved by chance in a cantata score of the same period.[14] Above all, they show the evolution of the fugue theme from a rather clumsy, uncharacteristic tune with many pitch repetitions, reworked until it received its final, elegant form. Contrary to earlier interpretations, the choice and implementation of fugue do not point to an "anwachsenden und sich vergrößernden Strom" (growing and increasing stream); instead, they point to the general sense of order, dignity, pomp, and high rank, befitting the scenario at the crib at the birth of Christ the king.* The movement's close takes up the initial theme again and concludes with, so to speak, the global text line in unison, "Und des Herren Lob verkündigen" (And announce the praise of the Lord). The thematic correspondence with the Prelude in C Major BWV 547 for organ is palpable. Which of the two pieces came first and what hides behind the similarity of course remain unknown at this point.

Following such an overpowering opening, it is difficult for the other movements to assert themselves. The chorale strophe "Die Kön'ge aus Saba kamen dar" (The kings came out of Sheba) connects in meaningful ways with the text of the opening movement. Here we are dealing with a section of the 1545 hymn *Ein Kind geborn zu Bethlehem* (A child is born in Bethlehem), a German version of the ancient Latin *Puer natus in Bethlehem*, whose fourth strophe, "Reges de Saba veniunt," is the source. The chorale has a direct relationship to the liturgy for Epiphany, since the *Puer natus* hymn was heard at the beginning of the service.

After this simple chorale movement one could imagine a caesura in the cantata's course, closing the first half before the sermon. If so, the bass recitative that follows would have begun the cantata's second half. Free poetry appears here for the first time; its author remains unknown. The prophecy of Isaiah is recounted, along with the events in Bethlehem; and gold, frankincense, and myrrh appear as "priceless presents" in the recitative. However, the following lines seem rather wooden and clumsy:

> Mein Jesu, wenn ich itzt an meine Pflicht gedenke,
> Muß ich auch zu deiner Krippe kehren
> Und gleichfalls dankbar sein,
> Denn dieser Tag ist mir ein Tag der Freuden.

> My Jesus, if I now remember my duty,
> I must also return to your crib
> And likewise be thankful,
> For this day is to me a day of joys.

If one recalls the fact that the cantata *Sie werden aus Saba alle kommen* was written for January 6, 1724, it may have been that Bach occasionally encountered problems finding suitable texts, especially in his first year in office.

No less infelicitous is the text of the ensuing aria, whose didactic tone is not exactly conducive to musical inspiration:

> Gold aus Ophir ist zu schlecht,
> Weg, nur weg mit eitlen Gaben,
> Die ihr aus der Erde brecht,
> Jesus will das Herze haben.

> Gold from Ophir is too poor,
> Away, but away with idle gifts
> That you break out of the earth.
> Jesus wants to have your heart.

Bach helps himself here with a quartet texture—bass voice, basso continuo, two oboi da caccia—in which the rhythm of the opening line, "Gold aus Ophir ist zu schlecht," persists in every measure. "Ophir" here means a fabulous country that turns up occasionally in the Hebrew Bible, such as in 1 Kings 9:27–28: "And Hiram sent his servants by ship, shipmen that had knowledge of the sea, with the servants of Solomon. And they came to Ophir, and fetched from thence gold, four hundred and twenty talents, and brought it to King Solomon." This land was thought to be in the Near East or India, in South Africa, or even in distant Peru (although this is difficult to reconcile with navigational capabilities in biblical times). Bach may have meant the exotic sound of the oboi da caccia as an allusion to this far-off, unknown land of gold.

After the recitative and aria for bass, the tenor voice has its say with the same sequence. "Des Glaubens Gold, der Weihrauch des Gebets, die Myrrhen der Geduld sind meine Gaben" (The gold of faith, the frankincense of prayer, the myrrh of patience are my gifts)—these are the "köstliche Geschenke" (precious gifts) in the earlier recitative for bass, now declared to be personal offerings of thanksgiving. Musical development is possible only with difficulty at this point. It succeeds again only in the aria for tenor, "Nimm mich dir zu eigen hin" (Take me unto yourself as your own), whose joyous testament, with its yearning leaps of the sixth at the beginning of the theme, almost has a touch of sentimentality about it, which is hardly moderated by the dancelike $\frac{3}{8}$ meter but instead intensified by the orchestra's blaze of color. The interchange between the instrumental groups and, above all, the octave doublings between registers recall the brilliant array of timbral juxtapositions in the first movement. And so the progression from the outward display of "Sie werden aus Saba alle kommen" to the turn to the personal in "Nimm mich dir zu eigen hin" seems to be the conceptual core of the cantata text, elucidated and made clear musically.

A simple four-part chorale movement on the melody *Was mein Gott will, das g'scheh allzeit* (What my God wills is for all time) concludes the cantata. It is only by a circuitous path that we know which strophe Bach intended to underlie the melody. An entry in the original score indicates a strophe from Paul Gerhardt's hymn *Ich hab in Gottes Herz und Sinn* (I have to God's heart and mind). According to a recent investigation,** the entry is in the hand of Johann Christoph Friedrich Bach, Johann Sebastian's second-youngest son, and may go back to the missing original parts, and to this extent can claim a significant degree of authority.

---

*Wetzel (1985, 145).
**Wollny (2001).

Jesus schläft, was soll ich hoffen?
BWV 81 / BC A 39
Fourth Sunday after Epiphany, January 30, 1724

The cantata *Jesus schläft, was soll ich hoffen?* BWV 81 (Jesus sleeps, what hope have I?) is for the fourth Sunday after Epiphany, a date that appears only when Easter Sunday falls on April 8 or later in the church calendar—on average, every three years. Such a situation arose in 1724, Johann Sebastian Bach's first year as cantor of St. Thomas in Leipzig. Scholars long assumed that the present cantata must have been assigned to January 30 of that year, and source studies in the twentieth century solidified this conclusion. A printed text discovered in the former Imperial Library in St. Petersburg in 1970 provided the final confirmation.* The booklet to be used by a congregation member bears the title *Texts for Leipzig Church Music, on the Second, Third, Fourth Sundays after the Revealing of Christ, the Feast of the Purification of Mary, and the Sundays Septuagesimae, Sexagesimae, Esto mihi, as well as the Feast of the Annunciation of Mary 1724*.[15] Among the cantata texts to be consulted during performance, *Jesus schläft, was soll ich hoffen?* also appears beneath the heading "On the fourth Sunday after the Revealing of Christ. In the Church of St. Thomas."[16]

The libretto, the work of an unknown author, closely follows the Gospel reading for the Sunday. Found in Matthew 8, it recounts a sea journey taken by Jesus and his disciples that briefly brought them into danger. The Evangelist Matthew places this event on an unspecified "ocean"; according to the parallel account in Luke 8, it involves the Sea of Galilee and a crossing in a southeasterly direction toward the Land of the Gadarenes. In Matthew 8:23–27 the passage reads:

> And he entered into the ship, and his disciples followed him. And, behold, there arose a great tempest in the sea, insomuch that the ship was covered with the waves: and he slept. And his disciples came to him and awoke him, saying, Lord, help us: we perish. And he said unto them, You of little faith, why are you so fearful? Then he arose and rebuked the winds and the sea; and there was a great calm. But the men marveled, saying, What manner of man is this, that even the winds and the sea obey him!

In the first cantata movement, an aria, the poet describes the slumber of Jesus as an existential danger for the individual in which sleep is perceived as a complete absence, in the sense of the "search motif":[17]

> Jesus schläft, was soll ich hoffen?
> Seh ich nicht
> Mit erblaßtem Angesicht
> Schon des Todes Abgrund offen?
>
> Jesus sleeps, what hope have I?
> Do I not see,
> With pale countenance,
> The abyss of death already open?

Question after question follow in the next movement as well, a recitative, alluding to the first verse of Psalm 10, which reads: "Herr, warum trittst du so ferne, verbirgst dich zur Zeit der Not?" (Lord, why do you walk so far away, do you hide yourself in time of trouble?). The recitative derived from this reads:

> Herr, warum trittst du so ferne?
> Warum verbirgst du dich zur Zeit der Not,
> Da alles mir ein kläglich Ende droht?
> Ach, wird dein Auge nicht durch mein Not beweget,
> So sonsten nie zu schlummern pfleget?

> Lord, why do you walk so far away?
> Why do you hide yourself in time of trouble,
> When everything threatens me with a miserable death?
> O, does not my distress move your eye,
> Which otherwise is never wont to sleep?

With an allusion to the Star of Bethlehem it continues:

> Du wiesest ja mit einem Stern
> Vordem den neubekehrten Weisen,
> Den rechten Weg zu reisen,
> Ach, leite mich durch deiner Augen Licht,
> Weil dieser Weg nichts als Gefahr verspricht.

> You certainly pointed with a star,
> Before the newly converted Wise Men,
> The right way to journey.
> O lead me through the light of your eyes,
> For this way promises only peril.

What danger awaits is depicted by the second aria, which compares the turbulent sea to "Belial's streams," a torrent that threatens to wash the human soul into the abyss of hell, should the soul's firm grasp of faith be lost:

> Die schäumende Wellen von Belials Bächen
> Verdoppeln die Wut.
> Ein Christ soll zwar wie Wellen [wie Felsen?] stehn,
> Wenn Trübsalswinde um ihn gehn,
> Doch suchet die stürmende Flut
> Die Kräfte des Glaubens zu schwächen.

> The foaming waves of Belial's streams
> Redouble their fury.
> A Christian should stand like waves [like crags?]
> When the winds of tribulation swirl about him.

> Yet the storming flood seeks
> To weaken the powers of faith.

Whether this truly means that the Christian should stand in the storm "wie Wellen" (like waves) remains a mystery known only to Bach and his librettist. In any case, the word "Wellen" stands in Bach's autograph score, in the original performance part for the singer, as well as in the printed text just mentioned. However, the substitution of a word suggesting greater strength of resistance, "Felsen" (crags), for example, is by no means forbidden.[18]

If the evangelist's narrative up to now has served as a kind of foil for the reflections without being itself the object of depiction, it speaks directly with the words of Jesus in Matthew and names the source of all evils: "Ihr Kleingläubigen, warum seid ihr so furchtsam?" (You of little faith, why are you so fearful?). And now the heart of the scene can appear in an aria as Jesus enters as rescuer amid the storm at sea:

> Schweig, aufgetürmtes Meer!
> Verstumme, Sturm und Wind!
> Dir sei dein Ziel gesetzt,
> Damit mein auserwähltes Kind
> Kein Unfall je verletzet.
>
> Silence, towering ocean!
> Quiet, storm and wind!
> Let your goal be so restricted
> That my chosen child
> By no accident is injured.

A brief recitative expresses the gratitude of those rescued:

> Wohl mir, Jesus spricht ein Wort,
> Mein Helfer ist erwacht,
> So muß der Wellen Sturm, des Unglücks Nacht
> Und aller Kummer fort.
>
> Blessed am I, Jesus speaks a word,
> My helper is awakened;
> So must the wave's storm, the night of misfortune,
> And all tribulation be gone.

The cantata text closes with the second strophe from Johann Franck's hymn of 1650, *Jesu, meine Freude* (Jesus, my joy):

> Unter deinem Schirmen
> Bin ich vor dem Stürmen

Aller Feinde frei.
Laß den Satan wittern,
Laß den Feind erbittern,
Mir steht Jesus bei.
Ob es itzt gleich kracht und blitzt,
Ob gleich Sünd und Hölle schrecken,
Jesus will mich decken.

Beneath your shelter
I am free from the storms
Of all enemies.
Let Satan prowl about,
Let the enemy grow enraged,
Jesus stands with me.
Though it right now thunders and lightnings,
Though now sin and hell terrify me,
Jesus will shelter me.

Johann Sebastian Bach's composition of this text is as rich in contrasts as it is in imagery, and it exploits its possibilities fully. The alto aria "Jesus schläft, was soll ich hoffen?" develops in a region of tension between outer calm and increasing inner agitation. The chordal texture of the strings suggests a familiar scene of slumber as they sound in their deep register, brightened by a pair of recorders at the upper octave and combined with restful repeated notes in the basso continuo, as well as long sustained tones in the vocal part, but they are countered by the constant presence of sigh motives, the entrance of sharp dissonances, and the disjunct questions of the voice. The tenor recitative that follows takes up its lamenting tone and intensifies it to an ardent plea.

In the aria that follows, a depiction of nature unclouded and cheerful is briefly evoked by the virtuoso competition between the voice and the cascading passagework of the string texture, led by the first violins. After only a few measures, sharper dissonances make clear that these are not just any "foaming waves" but the dangerous rapids of "Belial's streams." In spite of three ruminative pauses, the breakneck momentum in this aria retains the upper hand. A change is first heard with the words of Jesus from the Gospel reading. Performed by the bass, the *vox Christi*, it unfolds with impressive repeated motives that follow in quick succession between voice and accompanying parts in a musical progression that, if not truly fugue, is strongly related to the spirit of fugue and appropriate to the severe question, "Ihr Kleingläubigen, warum seid ihr so furchtsam?"

The aria "Schweig, aufgetürmtes Meer," derived from the Gospel text, is also given to the bass. The turbulence of the elements, expressed in massive repeated unisons in the strings, is countered by the voice with similar effects, supported by the calming timbre and more restful motion of the two oboi d'amore. The last freely versified movement, expressing thanks for the rescue of body and soul, is also given to the alto voice, which at the cantata's beginning was trapped by fear and doubt. As resolute and collected as it began, the cantata ends with a four-part setting of the melody *Jesu, meine Freude*.

―――――――――
*Hobohm (1973)

CHAPTER 4

Bach's Second and Third Years at Leipzig from the First Sunday after Trinity 1724 to Trinity Sunday 1726

O Ewigkeit, du Donnerwort
BWV 20 / BC A 95
First Sunday after Trinity, June 11, 1724

For Johann Sebastian Bach, the cantata *O Ewigkeit, du Donnerwort* BWV 20 (O eternity, you word of thunder) represented the initial spark of a plan that, beginning in June 1724, would claim the greater part of his creative energy for many months. His idea was to create, within a year's time, a complete annual cycle of church cantatas that were based on appropriate chorales, textually as well as musically, with preference for the main hymns for each Sunday and feast day where possible. No one knew better than the *Thomaskantor* himself what such a concept would entail with regard to the never-abating demands of his position, as well as his own high standards of quality. We cannot say whether at the outset he could foresee that he would be able to complete only three-quarters of the project as he had conceived it. In any case, he started work without hesitation and without sparing any effort, even at the beginning.

The new cycle did not begin with Advent, the start of the church year. This deviation from the norm had to do with Bach's professional situation. He had made his debut as cantor of St. Thomas School exactly a year earlier, on the first Sunday after Trinity. Now, exactly a year later, he wanted to introduce the Leipzig public to a complete annual cycle of church cantatas of a new type.

The chorale he chose for this exemplary first work was a principal hymn for the first Sunday after Trinity. Written by Johann Rist in 1642, it was published the same year with a melody by Johann Schop, a city musician in Hamburg. In hymnals of the era it is found beneath the rubric "Von der Hölle" (Of hell) or "Von der Ewigkeit und Hölle" (Of eternity and hell) with the subtitle "Das Weh der Ewigkeit" (The torment of eternity). The Gospel reading for the Sunday is found in Luke 16, which contains Jesus's parable of the rich man and Lazarus. The chorale text is related in that it takes up the fate of the rich man. In the parable, the rich man lived "alle Tage herrlich und in Freuden" (all his days gloriously and in joy), only after his death to land "in der Hölle und in der Qual" (in hell and in torment).

Johann Rist's unabridged hymn contains sixteen strophes, each with eight lines. The cantata text is derived from the hymn in the fashion common to nearly all works in Bach's chorale cantata cycle: some individual chorale strophes remain unchanged, others are reshaped to become recitatives and arias even as one or more lines maintain their original wording, while still others are reformulated without direct quotation of the original. In the case of *O Ewigkeit, du Donnerwort*, Bach's unknown librettist drew upon all but three of the chorale's sixteen strophes. As usual, the first strophe in Rist's poem is adopted literally:

> O Ewigkeit, du Donnerwort,
> O Schwert, das durch die Seele bohrt,
> O Anfang sonder Ende!
> O Ewigkeit, Zeit ohne Zeit,
> Ich weiß vor lauter Traurigkeit
> Nicht, wo ich mich hinwende.
> Mein ganz erschrocken Herz erbebt,
> Daß mir die Zung am Gaumen klebt.
>
> O eternity, you word of thunder,
> O sword that bores through the soul.
> O beginning without end!
> O eternity, time without time,
> I know not, in deep sadness,
> Where I should turn.
> My quite terrified heart so trembles,
> That my tongue cleaves to the roof of my mouth.

The eleventh strophe, "Solang ein Gott im Himmel lebt" (All the while that a God in heaven lives), and the concluding strophe, beginning with

"O Ewigkeit, du Donnerwort," were also brought into the cantata libretto without change.

The fifth movement of the cantata provides an example of how Bach revised the chorale strophes while preserving several of the original lines. Its text is based on the ninth strophe of Rist's chorale:

> Ach Gott, wie bist du so gerecht,
> Wie strafest du die bösen Knecht
> Im heißen Pfuhl der Schmerzen.
> Auf kurze Sünden dieser Welt
> Hast du so lange Pein bestellt,
> Ach nimm dies wohl zu Herzen.
> Betracht es oft, o Menschenkind,
> Kurz ist die Zeit, der Tod geschwind.

> O God, how just you are
> As you punish the evil servants
> In a seething pool of sorrows.
> For the brief sins of this world
> You have ordained such lengthy pain,
> O take this well to heart.
> Consider it often, O child of humankind,
> Brief is time, death is swift.

As an aria text, it takes the following form:

> Gott ist gerecht in seinen Werken:
> Auf kurze Sünde dieser Welt
> Hat er so lange Pein bestellt;
> Ach wollte doch die Welt dies merken.
> Kurz ist die Zeit, der Tod geschwind,
> Bedenke dies, o Menschenkind!

> God is righteous in his works:
> For the brief sins of this world
> He has ordained such lengthy pain.
> Oh, if only the world wanted to heed this.
> Brief is time, death is swift,
> Consider this, O child of humankind!

Rist's thirteenth strophe was handled more freely:

> Wach auf, o Mensch, vom Sündenschlaf,
> Ermuntre dich, verlorenes Schaf,
> Und beßre bald dein Leben.

> Wach auf, es ist sehr hohe Zeit,
> Es kömmt heran die Ewigkeit,
> Dir deinen Lohn zu geben;
> Vielleicht ist heut der letzte Tag
> Wer weiß, wie man noch sterben mag.

> Wake up, O man, from the sleep of sin,
> Rouse yourself, lost sheep,
> And quickly improve your life.
> Wake up, it is very high time.
> Eternity approaches
> To give your reward to you;
> Perhaps today is the last day.

The aria text associates this wakening call with an allusion to the trumpet of the Last Judgment:

> Wacht auf, wacht auf, verlorenen Schafe,
> Ermuntert euch vom Sündenschlafe
> Und bessert euer Leben bald.
> Wacht auf, eh die Posaune schallt,
> Die euch mit Schrecken aus der Gruft
> Zum Richter aller Welt vor das Gerichte ruft!

> Wake up, wake up, lost sheep,
> Rouse yourselves from the sleep of sin
> And improve your lives quickly.
> Wake up before the trumpet sounds
> That calls you with terror from the crypt
> To the judge of all the world for judgment!

Rist's penultimate strophe was revised in yet another fashion. Out of its beginning:

> O du verfluchtes Menschenkind,
> Von Sinnen toll, von Herzen blind,
> Laß ab, die Welt zu lieben!

> O you accursed child of humankind,
> Mad of senses, blind of heart,
> Leave off to love the world!

The aria text became:

> O Menschenkind,
> Hör auf geschwind,

> Die Sünd und Welt zu lieben,
> Daß nicht die Pein,
> Wo Heulen und Zähnenklappen sein,
> Dich ewig mag betrüben!
> Ach spiegle dich am reichen Mann,
> Der in der Qual
> Auch nicht einmal
> Ein Tröpflein Wasser haben kann!
>
> O child of humankind,
> Cease quickly
> To love sin and the world,
> So that the pain,
> Where howling and gnashing of teeth,
> May never eternally aggrieve you!
> Oh, see your image in the rich man
> Who, in torment,
> Not even once
> Can have a droplet of water!

Clearly, this refers to the Gospel reading for the first Sunday after Trinity, in particular to Luke 16:23: "As he now was in hell and in torment, he lifted his eyes up and saw Abraham from afar and Lazarus in his bosom."[1]

Bach's composition of this extremely wide-ranging libretto, with three each of chorale movements and recitatives, as well as five arias, highlights the special nature of the situation in many ways. An outward feature of his holograph score indicates this: the first page of the score contains, instead of the standard abbreviation of the invocation "Jesu Juva" (Jesus, help me), a sequence of six letters whose solution reads "In Nomine Domini Nostri Jesu Christi" (In the name of our lord Jesus Christ). Moreover, the form of the opening movement is sharply distinguished from the familiar. Certainly, the model for the majority of cantata first movements is clearly recognizable here: the chorale melody is presented line by line in one voice; other voices provide either harmonic support or motet-like counterpoint; there is a motivically unified, independent instrumental component. But there is another dimension: the formal outlines of the French overture. This is seen in the complete three-part form: two solemn, slow outer sections with dotted rhythms and sweeping scales enclosing a quicker, imitatively worked central section. Bach's choice of this characteristic form, signaling inauguration and a new beginning, was certainly no coincidence. It represents the entrance portal to the comprehensive new opus the composer had just embarked upon, the "Kantatenjahrgang über Kirchenlieder" (annual cantata cycle on chorales). Its traditional function is to announce what is about to happen; in the context of the text it can be seen to depict the anxious anticipation of eternity to come. Moreover, it allows the penultimate line of text, "Mein ganz erschrocken Herz erbebt" (My quite terrified heart trembles), to be set by the concluding slow section with its *zerrissen* (ripped, or dotted) rhythms.

This fully developed chorale movement is contrasted by two simple four-part chorales that conclude the cantata's two sections, performed before and after the sermon. The eight solo movements are all influenced by the linguistic richness of the libretto. In order to control this and keep the work's dimensions within tenable limits, Bach was forced to forgo the da capo form for the most part. Only the fifth movement, an aria for bass with three oboes, uses the phrase "Gott ist gerecht in seinen Werken" as a framing device. It is worth noticing that the head motif for this movement appears in two different forms: a broken-chord motif with an unassailable, chanted quality, and a melodic, mellifluous gesture. Both are connected to the voice with the text "Gott ist gerecht"; when these motives appear in the instrumental component they can be understood as an untexted quotation. The composer works in a similar fashion in the next to last movement, a duet for alto and tenor whose text begins, "O Menschenkind, hör auf geschwind, die Sünd und Welt zu lieben." Here, the untexted "evocative" motive is given to the basso continuo and creates the constant presence of the "O Menschenkind—hör auf geschwind."

In addition to these architectonic devices, specific text interpretations are found everywhere. Chromaticism, sigh motives, harmonic clashes, and other effects are given to key words such as "Schmerz" (hurt), "Qual" (torment), "Hölle" (hell), and "Pein" (pain). Rarely is the composer's method simply one-dimensional. In the third movement, an aria for tenor and strings, the text beginning "Ewigkeit, du machst mir bange" (Eternity, you make me frightened) is set by sustained chords for "Ewigkeit" and sigh motives for "bange." Later, the voice's extended coloraturas depict the word "Flammen" (flames)—yet these are artfully combined with the sustained tones and sighs just mentioned, for the text speaks of "Flammen, die auf ewig brennen" (flames that burn eternally).

A more complicated interpretation appears in movement 6, an aria for alto and strings whose text begins "O Mensch, errette deine Seele" (O human, deliver your soul). What is striking about this movement is the change of meter from $\frac{3}{4}$ to $\frac{3}{2}$ by means of suspensions and accent displacement. It is conceivable that this "bound" style is aimed at a depiction of the shackles from which the soul must be rescued. More transparent is the bass aria found at the beginning of the second half of the cantata, "Wacht auf, wacht auf, verlornen Schafe" (Wake up, wake up, lost sheep) with its energetic, upward-striving scales, pounding, insistent rhythms, and penetrating trumpet signals.

Ach Gott, vom Himmel sieh darein
BWV 2 / BC A 98

Second Sunday after Trinity, June 18, 1724

This cantata, composed in 1724, is based on the chorale of the same name, the main hymn for the second Sunday after Trinity. The content of the chorale is closely associated with the Sunday Gospel reading, the parable of the great evening meal from the dinner table teachings of Jesus in Luke 14. The path is not long from this account to the source of the chorale, Psalm 12. The Gospel reading recounts the dismay over the absence of the invited guests at dinner and their threadbare excuses; the chorale is drawn from Psalm 12:1–8 and its complaint of the decline of the pious and the superior strength of the wicked, but also its trust in divine assistance:

> Help Lord! The Holy are in decline, and the believers are few among the children of humankind. Each speaks useless things with the others; they are hypocrites and teach out of divided hearts. May the Lord eradicate all hypocrisy and the tongues that speak pridefully, that say: With our tongues we shall prevail, we shall speak: Who is our Lord? Because the needy are destroyed and the poor sigh, I will arise, speaks the Lord, I want to create a help for him who longs thereafter. The speech of the Lord is purer than refined silver in an earthen crucible, purified seven times. You, Lord, shall keep them and protect us from this generation for ever! For everywhere there are the godless, where such worthless men rule among the people.

The hymn, documented as early as 1524, on Psalm 12, *Salvum me fac, Domine*, belongs to a series of "etliche Psalm, zu geistlichen Liedern / deutsch gemacht / Durch Dr. Martinum Luther" (several psalms made into sacred songs in German by Dr. Martin Luther) as they appear in hymnaries of the period. Luther's six-strophe translation hews closely to the psalmist's train of thought while expanding, explaining, and clarifying the source text. Luther formed the first strophe from "Hilf Herr! Die Heiligen haben abgenommen und der Gläubigen ist wenig unter den Menschenkindern" (Help, Lord! The saints have diminished, and the faithful are few among the children of humankind). The chorale version reads:

Ach Gott, vom Himmel sieh darein
Und laß dichs doch erbarmen!
Wie wenig sind der Heilgen dein,
Verlassen sind wir Armen;
Dein Wort man nicht läßt haben wahr,
Der Glaub ist auch verloschen gar
Bei allen Menschenkindern.

Ah God, look down from heaven
And indeed have mercy!
How few are your saints,
We wretches are abandoned;
Your word is not believed,
Faith is also quite extinguished
Among all children of humankind.

The version set to music by Bach, adapted from the chorale by an unknown poet, is much more distant from the psalmist's original. As seen so frequently in Bach's chorale cantatas, only a few strophes are adopted word for word from the chorale text; all the others are more or less freely adapted. The version of Psalm 12:2, "Einer redet mit dem andern unnütze Dinge; sie heucheln und lehren aus uneinig Herzen" (Each speaks useless things with the others; they are hypocrites and teach out of divided hearts), takes the following form in Luther's conception:

Sie lehren eitel falsche List,
Was Eigenwitz erfindet;
Ihr Herz nicht eines Sinnes ist,
In Gottes Wort gegründet;
Der wählet dies, der andre das,
Sie trennen uns ohn alle Maß
Und gleißen schön von außen.

They teach idle, false cunning,
Invented by their own wit;
Their heart is not of one mind,
Founded in God's word;
One chooses this, the other that,
They divide us without all measure
And gleam beautifully outwardly.

From this, the cantata librettist forms a recitative that clearly refutes any attempt to substitute understanding (here called "Witz" [wit]) and reason for faith. It closes with a powerful comparison to the pair of opposites, "outwardly beautiful / inwardly evil" (außen schön / innen schlimm), choosing the grave to do so; he could have used the same vocabulary to describe the so-called apples of Sodom:[2]

> Sie lehren eitel falsche List,
> Was wider Gott und seine Wahrheit ist;
> Und was der eigen Witz erdenket
> O Jammer! der die Kirche schmerzlich kränket—,
> Das muß anstatt der Bibel stehn.
> Der eine wählet dies, der andre das,
> Die töricht Vernunft ist ihr Kompaß.
> Sie gleichen denen Totengräbern,
> Die, ob sie zwar von außen schön,
> Nur Stank und Moder in sich fassen
> Und lauter Unflat sehen lassen.

> They teach idle, false cunning,
> Which opposes God and his truth
> And which their own wit invents.
> O misery! That painfully afflicts the church,
> That must stand in place of the Bible.
> The one chooses this, the other that,
> Foolish reason is their compass.
> They resemble those graves of the dead,
> Which, though they indeed are outwardly beautiful,
> Contain only stench and rot
> In which nothing but filth can be seen.

The associated aria is developed from the psalmist's complaint of hypocrisy, pride, and self-importance by way of Luther's chorale strophe:

> Tilg, o Gott, die Lehren,
> So dein Wort verkehren!
> Wehre doch der Ketzerei
> Und allen Rottengeistern,
> Denn sie sprechen ohne Scheu:
> Trotz dem, der uns will meistern!

> Erase, O God, the teachings
> That pervert your word!
> But resist the heresy
> And all the spirit-rabble,
> For they speak without shame:
> Resist him who wants to master us!

The ensuing recitative is devoted in full to the assurance of God's assistance; the words of Psalm 12:5, "Weil denn die Elenden verstöret werden und die Armen seufzen" (Because the needy are destroyed and the poor sigh), resound unmistakably in its opening lines:

> Die Armen sind verstört,
> Ihr seufzend Ach, ihr ängstlich Klagen
> Bei soviel Kreuz und Not,
> Wodurch die Feinde fromme Seelen plagen,
> Dringt in das Gnadenohr des Allerhöchsten ein.
> Darum spricht Gott: Ich muß ihr Helfer sein!
>
> The poor are destroyed,
> Their sighing ah, their anxious plaints,
> At so much cross-bearing and distress,
> Whereby the enemies plague pious souls,
> Penetrate the ear of grace of the Most High.
> Therefore, God says: I must be their helper!

The last aria uses Psalm 12:6: "Die Rede des Herrn ist lauter wie durchläutert im irdenen Tiegel, bewähret siebenmal" (The speech of the Lord is purer than refined silver in an earthen crucible, purified seven times), as well as the ideas introduced in Luther's poem of probation through the cross:

> Durchs Feuer wird das Silber rein,
> Durchs Kreuz das Wort bewährt erfunden.
> Drum soll ein Christ zu allen Stunden
> Im Kreuz und Not geduldig sein.
>
> Through fire the silver becomes pure,
> Through the cross the Word is proven.
> Therefore, a Christian should at all times,
> In cross-bearing and distress, be patient.

The cantata's conclusion is provided, as usual, by the unaltered final strophe of the source chorale:

> Das wollst du, Gott, bewahren rein
> Für diesem arg'n Geschlechte,
> Und laß uns dir befohlen sein,
> Daß sichs in uns nicht flechte.
> Der gottlos Hauf sich umher findt,
> Wo solche lose Leute sind
> In deinem Volk erhaben.

> Would you keep it pure, God,
> In the face of this evil generation,
> And let us be commended to you,
> That they do not mingle with us.
> The godless mob is found all around,
> Where such vile folk are
> Exalted among your people.

What is particularly striking about Bach's composition is the form of the opening movement. In contrast to the majority of Bach's chorale cantatas, the instrumentation does not perform an independent structural function. Instead, we have a texture that is purely vocal in its conception; it is a chorale motet, intentionally archaic in design. The chorale melody, whose ancestry lies in the pre-Reformation era, is heard line by line in the alto, while the other three voices prepare the chorale lines with fugal material and then provide counterpoint. Four trombones provide timbral support to the four voices; the three upper voices also have strings, and the alto, the cantus firmus part, has two oboes as well. The basso continuo is the only independent instrumental part. Its function as an autonomous bass foundation is the only deviation from what is otherwise a pure motet principle.

With his decision in favor of this compositional model,* Bach was able to realize several objectives at the same time: he could provide variety with regard to the opening movements in his recently begun cycle of chorale cantatas, and he could arrange the ancient melody of *Ach Gott, vom Himmel sieh darein* in the tradition of the organ chorale and chorale motet, thereby obviating the otherwise unavoidable obstacle that a modern concerted treatment of the Phrygian melody would have presented.

In the first recitative for tenor and basso continuo, two short sections are highlighted by the shift to an arioso Adagio: here, two verses from Luther's second chorale strophe are quoted in their original form. A similar emphasis is found in the following aria, roughly at the beginning of the last third of the piece. Otherwise, this aria is characterized by lively competition between the alto and a solo violin, in particular because of the nearly continuous presence of the head motive, which seems to want to bring to mind the entreaty "Tilg, o Gott, die Lehren."

The second recitative embeds the bass voice in four-part chords in the strings. The assurance of God's assistance is highlighted; it is sounded as a contoured arioso. In the tenor aria "Durchs Feuer wird das Silber rein," a four-part accompanimental texture, unusually dense harmonically, is similarly characteristic—although a motive for the ambitious five- and six-part textures remains unclear. In contrast to this, the warning "ein Christ soll zu allen Stunden in Kreuz und Not geduldig sein" is effectively emphasized, as it is performed without the protective sound of the instruments. The simply set closing chorale rounds out a work that attracted considerable attention as early as the eighteenth century. Copies of the entire work are documented in Saxony and Thuringia, as well as copies of the motet-like opening chorus in Berlin and even Vienna.

———————

*Krummacher (1995).

Wer nur den lieben Gott läßt walten
BWV 93 / BC A 104

Fifth Sunday after Trinity, July 9, 1724

This cantata, which belongs to Bach's annual cycle of chorale cantatas, was first performed on July 9, 1724. There were presumably other performances, although we have no documentation of them except for one that probably took place in 1732. We would like to know more about a reperformance that may have taken place in 1756, after Bach's death. Although the musical estate of the greatest cantor of St. Thomas School left Leipzig for the most part when it was distributed to his family, the chorale cantata cycle remains an important and famous exception. At one time comprising fifty or more compositions, its composing scores passed to the oldest son, Wilhelm Friedemann, while the performing parts went to Bach's widow, Anna Magdalena. Since she was unable to make use of them, she presented them to St. Thomas School in 1750 in exchange for several favors from city officials. Forty-four complete compositions remain in the possession of Leipzig's St. Thomas School, thereby representing a unique, unbroken tradition over the nearly three centuries from the time of their composition. Several of the part collections show signs of use after Bach's death, among them the cantata *Wer nur den lieben Gott läßt walten* BWV 93 (Whoever only lets dear God rule), which Bach's student and second successor, Johann Friedrich Doles, must have performed in 1756 when he took office or shortly afterward.

This cantata is for the fifth Sunday after Trinity; its text is based on "einem Kernlied dieses Sonntags" (the principal hymn for that Sunday), Georg Neumark's seven-strophe chorale published in 1657 with the motto "Wie Gott es fügt, bin ich vergnügt" (As God decrees, I am pleased). In the manner typical for Bach's chorale cantatas, several strophes of the chorale text were adopted without change, and others were adjusted through word replacements, contractions, and interpolation of free poetry to satisfy the musical requirements of recitative and aria forms.

The opening strophe remained unchanged:

> Wer nur den lieben Gott läßt walten
> Und hoffet auf ihn allezeit,
> Den wird er wunderlich erhalten
> In allem Kreuz und Traurigkeit.
> Wer Gott, dem Allerhöchsten, traut,
> Der hat auf keinen Sand gebaut.

> Whoever only lets the dear God rule
> And hopes in him at all times,
> He will wondrously preserve him
> In all cross-bearing and tribulation.
> Whoever God, the all-highest, trusts,
> He has surely not built upon sand.

The second strophe, on the other hand, was reshaped in the manner typical of Bach's chorale cantatas. Neumark's version reads:

> Was helfen uns die schweren Sorgen?
> Was hilft uns unser Weh und Ach?
> Was hilft es, daß wir alle Morgen
> Beseufzen unser Ungemach?
> Wir machen unser Kreuz und Leid
> Nur größer durch die Traurigkeit.

> What good to us are heavy sorrows?
> What good to us our woe and alas?
> What good to us that we, every morning,
> Sigh over our misfortune?
> We make our cross-bearing and suffering
> Only greater through sadness.

The unknown poet working for Bach produced the following mixture of lines taken directly from the chorale and free recitative poetry:

> Was helfen uns die schweren Sorgen?
>   Sie drücken nur das Herz
>   Mit Zentnerpein, mit tausend Angst und Schmerz,
> Was hilft uns unser Weh und Ach?
>   Es bringt nur bittres Ungemach.
> Was hilft es, daß wir alle Morgen
>   Mit Seufzen von dem Schlaf aufstehn

> Und mit beträntem Angesicht des Nachts zu Bette gehn?
> Wir machen unser Kreuz und Leid
> Durch bange Traurigkeit nur größer.
>   Drum tut ein Christ viel besser,
>   Er trägt sein Kreuz mit christlicher Gelassenheit.

> What good to us are heavy sorrows?
>   They only oppress the heart
>   With a hundredweight of pain, with a thousand fears and agonies.
> What good to us our woe and alas?
>   It brings only bitter hardship.
> What good to us that we, every morning,
> Arise from our sleep with sighs
>   And with tearful countenance at night go to bed?
> We make our cross-bearing and suffering
> Through anxious sadness only greater.
>   Therefore, a Christian does much better.
>   He carries his cross with Christian serenity.

In contrast to this thoroughgoing revision, the fourth and seventh strophes of Neumark's chorale—in the middle and at the end of the cantata libretto—were left unchanged: strophe 4, "Er kennt die rechten Freudenstunden" (He knows the right hours of joy), and strophe 7, "Sing, bet und geh auf Gottes Wegen" (Sing, pray, and go upon God's ways). The aria texts found at the third and sixth positions in the cantata libretto—"Man halte nur ein wenig stille" (One must keep only briefly quiet) and "Ich will auf den Herren schauen" (I want to look upon the Lord)—contain only a few parts of Neumark's poetry. On the other hand, the fifth movement has been reshaped in the same manner as the second movement—a combination of chorale and recitative. Here it reads at the beginning:

> Denk nicht in deiner Drangsalshitze,
> Wenn Blitz und Donner kracht,
> Und dir ein schwüles Wetter bange macht,
> Daß du von Gott verlassen seist.

> Think not, in the heat of your ordeal,
> When thunder and lightning strike
> And threatening weather makes you anxious,
> That you have been forsaken by God.

"Blitz und Donner" and "schwüles Wetter" were added by the unknown poet; later in the recitative he shows his knowledge of the Bible particularly clearly:

Du darfst nicht meinen,
Daß dieser Gott im Schoße sitze,
Der täglich wie der reiche Mann,
In Lust und Freuden leben kann.
Der sich mit stetem Glücke speist,
Bei lauter guten Tagen,
Muß oft zuletzt,
Nachdem er sich an eitler Lust ergötzt,
"Der Tod in Töpfen" sagen
Die Folgezeit verändert viel!
Hat Petrus gleich die ganze Nacht
Mit leerer Arbeit zugebracht
Und nichts gefangen:
Auf Jesu Wort kann er noch einen Zug erlangen.

You must not think
That this one sits in God's lap,
Who, daily, like a rich man,
Can live in happiness and joy.
Who feeds on constant good happiness,
With good days all around,
Must often at last,
After he has taken delight in vain pleasure,
Say, "There is death in the pots."
The coming time will alter much!
If Peter indeed the whole night
With fruitless toil spent
And caught nothing:
At Jesus's Word he can still make a catch.

The allusion to the "reichen Mann" points to the eleventh chapter of the book of Sirach, which Georg Neumark used as the source for his chorale text. Here it reads:

> Mancher kargt und spart und wird dadurch reich und denkt, er habe etwas vor sich gebracht, und spricht: "Nun will ich gutes Leben haben, essen und trinken von meinen Gütern;" und er weiß nicht, daß sein Stündlein so nahe ist, und muß alles ändern lassen und sterben. (18–19)

> Many a person stints and saves and thereby becomes rich and believes he has accomplished something and says: "Now I will lead a good life, and eat and drink from my goodness"; and he does not know how close his hour is and that he must allow everything to change and die.

The somewhat obscure biblical allusion to "Tod in Töpfen" (death in pots) refers to the fourth chapter of 2 Kings and the depiction of how the prophet Elisha, in the time of inflation, apparently cooked inedible vegetables for his people: "And as they poured it out for the men to eat, and they ate the vegetables, they cried out and spoke: O Man of God, the death in the pot! For they could not eat it" (2 Kings 4:40).[3] The reference to Peter at the end and his "leere Arbeit" (fruitless toil) every night refers to the Gospel reading for the fifth Sunday after Trinity, the description in Luke 5:4–5 of Peter's miraculous catch of fish, with the words of Jesus, "Launch into the deep water and cast your nets out, that you make a catch," and the answer of Simon Peter, "Master, we have worked through the entire night and caught nothing, but upon your Word I will cast out my net."[4]

Bach's composition of this rich and wide-ranging text is characterized, on the one hand, by adherence to Neumark's chorale melody of 1657 and, on the other, by the free and diverse treatment of its substance, in other words, the adoption and further development of the traditions of chorale variation. Thus the extensive opening movement offers a classic example of Bach's chorale arrangements for chorus: a concerted, motivically unified orchestral part that is largely independent of the chorale's melodic substance, framing the presentation of the chorale melody in long note values in one of the voices and the motet-like counterpoint in the three other voices. The contrast between polyphonic and chordal textures in the vocal parts helps create extra liveliness, just as does the prominence of the two oboes against the strings.

The two recitative-aria movement pairs are alike in their layout. The two recitatives swing back and forth between loose declamation of the freely versified portions of the text and a more regulated style of the passages containing the chorale text and melody.

The arias are even more distant from the substance of the chorale. In the tenor aria, the third movement in the cantata, "Man halte nur ein wenig stille," the melody modulates from C minor to E-flat major and amplifies the "keeping still" with short motives interspersed with rests. The next to last movement, an aria for soprano, symbolizes the trust in God sketched out in the text through a brightly animated figuration of voice and obbligato oboe. The greatest concentration in the performance of the chorale is undoubtedly achieved in the final movement with its harmonically rich four-part setting.

The fourth strophe, "Er kennt die rechten Freudenstunden" (He knows the best times for joy), in the middle of the cantata, presented the highest compositional challenge. Here, an imitative duet between soprano and alto is joined by basso continuo to form a trio; the violins and viola form an instrumental voice in the tenor range with the chorale melody. The result is an elaborate arrangement of the chorale in the form of a quartet. In the mid-1740s this was included in a collection of six similar compositions printed in Zella, Thuringia, by the publisher Johann Georg Schübler. Known later as the Schübler Chorales (BWV 645–50), these organ works were circulated widely. That Bach chose to include a movement from the cantata *Wer nur den lieben Gott läßt walten* unmistakably testifies to the composer's high esteem for this cantata in particular.

Was willst du dich betrüben
BWV 107 / BC A 109

Seventh Sunday after Trinity, July 23, 1724

This cantata, for the seventh Sunday after Trinity, was performed for the first time on July 23, 1724, six weeks after the beginning of Bach's second annual cycle of cantatas at Leipzig, as part of the chorale cantata annual cycle. Our cantata proves to be something of an outlier in the chorale cantata cycle because here for the first time in the cycle—and for some time afterward—a chorale serves as the source text with original wording of all of its strophes. We do not know why, in this particular case, Bach avoided the usual reshaping of the inner strophes of his source hymn to form verses suitable for recitatives and arias. It is possible that external circumstances may have played a role: one week earlier, Bach had to rely on a substitute for performance of the Sunday's church music because he and his wife, Anna Magdalena, were giving a guest performance at his former post, the court of Anhalt-Köthen. It may be that as a result there were difficulties with the poet who was to have prepared the libretto for the upcoming week.

The seven-strophe chorale *Was willst du dich betrüben* BWV 107 (Why would you grieve) is certainly not among the main hymns for the seventh Sunday after Trinity. The hymnaries of the period only place it generally under the heading "Kreuz- und Trostlieder" (Hymns of cross-bearing and consolation). At the same time, its exhortation to maintain trust in God in the face of challenge fits the Sunday Gospel reading very well, the account in Mark 8 of the feeding of the four thousand. For many years, the disciples' distressed question at the center of the account, "Where can we find bread in the desert?" (Woher nehmen wir Brot in der Wüste?), had a tragic actuality for the poet Johann Heermann. Nearly half of his life from 1585 to 1647 was marked by the horrors of the Thirty Years' War, which allowed Heermann's homeland, Silesia, scarcely a moment of peace.

Chronically ill and under multiple external threats, Heermann reacted with impressive poetic productivity: his contributions to the Protestant hymnary number over four hundred chorales. With Martin Opitz, Andreas Gryphius, and Matthäus Apelles von Löwenstern, Heermann therefore ranks among the most influential figures of a Silesian circle of poets. One of the most important collections, published in Breslau and printed in Leipzig in 1630, is *Haus- und Hertz-Musica. Das ist: Allerley Geistliche Lieder aus den Heiligen Kirchenlehrern*, written by Heermann while he was pastor at Köben an der Oder. Included here is the chorale *Was willst du dich betrüben*, based on "Gott verlässet keinen" (God forsakes no one), the motto of Herr Georgius von Kottwitz. Kottwitz, earlier the manorial lord of Köben, had recommended Heermann for the leadership post of the Lutheran congregation there.

Heermann places the exhortation to trust in God at the head of his hymn text:

> Was willst du dich betrüben,
> O meine liebe Seel?
> Ergib dich, den zu lieben,
> Der heißt Immanuel.
> Vertraue ihm allein;
> Er wird gut alles machen
> Und fördern deine Sachen,
> Wie dirs wird selig sein.

> Why do you grieve,
> O my dear soul?
> Devote yourself to loving him
> Who is called Immanuel.
> Trust in him alone;
> He will make all things good
> And so support your affairs
> As will be a blessing to you.

Strophe 2 offers the basis for the exhortation with the assurance of God's faithfulness:

> Denn Gott verlässet keinen,
> Der sich auf ihn verläßt,
> Er bleibt getreu den seinen,
> Die ihm vertrauen fest.
> Läßt sichs an wunderlich,
> So laß dir doch nicht grauen;

> Mit Freuden wirst du schauen,
> Wie Gott wird retten dich.
>
> For God forsakes no one
> Who trusts in him.
> He remains true to those of his
> Who trust him firmly.
> If things seem strange,
> Then do not allow yourself to be afraid.
> With joy you will see
> How God will rescue you.

Strophe 3 calls for boldness while referring to the immutability of God's will; strophe 4 points to the powerlessness of Satan himself; in strophe 5 Bach paraphrases the chorale melody on the last line, "Was Gott will, das geschicht" (What God wishes, is done); and from all this strophe 6 sums up:

> Drum ich mich ihm ergebe,
> Ihm sei es heimgestellt,
> Nach nichts ich sonst mehr strebe,
> Denn nur was ihm gefällt.
> Drauf wart ich und bin still,
> Sein Will der ist der beste,
> Das glaub ich steif und feste,
> Gott mach es, wie er will!
>
> Therefore, I surrender myself to him,
> On him reliance may be placed.
> I strive after nothing more
> Than only what pleases him.
> For this I wait and am calm,
> His will it is the best,
> This I believe strongly and truly,
> May God act as he wills!

An expression of thanksgiving for the Trinity follows in the concluding strophe.

Bach places the expected concerted arrangement of the chorale at the top of his composition. The cantus firmus is the melody *Von Gott will ich nicht lassen* (I shall not abandon God), originally from the sixteenth century and secular in origin. It is presented in large note values in the soprano with occasional ornamentation. The larger part of the opening movement—more than two-thirds of its entire scope—is carried by the orchestra: strings, two oboi d'amore, and two transverse flutes, which Bach decided to include only after the compositional work was finished; it was only the first time in Leipzig that he entrusted them with such a challenging task.

The second movement, the only recitative in the cantata, clearly reveals the problematic nature of the source text, as well as Bach's overcoming of it. As a result of the all-too-regular versification, a certain monotony threatens the declamation. Bach countered this by structuring it as *Accompagnato* and juxtaposing the bass voice with a persistently maintained rhythmic figure in the oboi d'amore. Near the end, a passage on the keyword "Freuden" (joys) calls for greater variety, and the last verse, "Wie Gott wird retten dich" (How God will deliver you), draws the voice into the security of a four-part texture. Here, at the latest, it becomes clear that from the beginning the oboi d'amore with their warm coloration have functioned literally "as accompaniment"— as drawn from the first line, "Denn Gott verlässet keinen" (For God forsakes no one).

The first aria, "Auf ihn magst du es wagen" (You may stake everything on him), in A major, is the most distant from the cantata's opening key. The bass voice is joined by a figure in the basso continuo that returns frequently, energetically circling and inviting, as well as the string ensemble with its linking of striking chords and quick passages that dare to penetrate higher registers and thereby underscore the key ideas in the text. The second aria, with its dark minor mode, its restriction of accompaniment to the basso continuo, and its stubbornly persistent return of a figure in the bass rising from the dark depths, seems to be given its character by the line of text "Wenn auch gleich aus der Höllen" (When even right out of hell). When at the end the voice takes up the bass theme in its unchanged form, it becomes clear that the movement is focused on overcoming the tempter and that the verse "Denn dein Werk fördert Gott" (For God supports your work) is to be seen as the key textual component.

The third aria, for soprano and two obbligato oboi d'amore, leads back to the initial key of B minor; it is lent a pastoral coloration by the filigree of the high voices, the moderate leading of the bass, and the self-contained repose of the $\frac{12}{8}$ meter. At the end, the voice leaves this tranquility as, energetically and tolerating no dissent, it recalls the chorale melody on the phrase "Was Gott will, das geschicht." With that, the cue is given for the last of the four arias. Here, the tenor, assisted by an obbligato part comprising muted violins and both transverse flutes, performs its "Drum ich mich ihm ergebe" (Therefore, I surrender myself to him) with decisiveness. The aria is in a major key and therefore relatively distant from the original chorale melody, which returns in the concluding chorale as expected. However, instead of the familiar simple four-part setting, it is embedded in a buoyant pastorale. In contrast to the opening movement, the voices take on more significance, although without endangering the balanced interaction between instruments and voices.

Jesu, der du meine Seele
BWV 78 / BC A 130

Fourteenth Sunday after Trinity, September 10, 1724

Johann Sebastian Bach wrote the cantata *Jesu, der du meine Seele* BWV 78 (Jesus, you who my soul) for the fourteenth Sunday after Trinity in his second year of service as cantor of St. Thomas School in Leipzig. In accordance with his concept of the second annual cycle of cantatas, it is tailored textually and musically to a specific church hymn. Johann Rist wrote the poem "Jesu, der du meine Seele" in 1641; not until 1662 was it paired with a melody associated with Georg Philipp Harsdörffer's hymn *Wachet doch, erwacht, ihr Schläfer*. Johann Rist was born near Hamburg in 1607, became a pastor in Wedel, Schleswig-Holstein, in 1635, and in his day was known as the "Nordischer Apoll, Fürst aller Poeten, großer Cimberschwan" (Northern Apollo, Prince of All Poets, Great Swan of the Elbe). In 1660, seven years before his death, he founded an academy for poetry known as Elbschwan-Orden (Order of the Elbe Swan), whose goal was to overcome the excessive floridness of the poetry of his era and return to simplicity. Of his over 650 sacred poems, hardly any of which have fewer than ten strophes, only a handful have been preserved in collections, among them *O Ewigkeit, du Donnerwort*, *Ermuntre dich, mein schwacher Geist*, and *Werde munter, mein Gemüte*. Johann Rist's hymn *Jesu, der du meine Seele* (also found with the melody *Alle Menschen müssen sterben*) is not among the hymns for the fourteenth Sunday after Trinity. Instead, it is found in hymn collections beneath the rubric "Von der Buße und Beichte" (Of penance and confession) or "Sonderbare Trost-Lieder" (Exceptional songs of consolation) with the subheading "Sincere Penitent and Prayer Song of a Sinner, to His Most Beloved Lord Jesus, for Forgiveness of His Many and Multifarious Sins."[5]

We do not know who reshaped the twelve-strophe hymn to become a seven-movement cantata libretto. The arranger was faced with the task of producing a source text in the mold of Bach's chorale cantatas, in which opening and closing strophes were adopted without change. The other chorale strophes were recast in the form of recitatives and arias, wherein shorter or longer quotations of the original chorale were possible or even desirable. Further, a connection to the Gospel reading of the day needed to be produced. The reading, found in Luke 17, gives the account of the healing of the ten lepers.

Elements of this lesson were included in the cantata text, although its connection to the fourteenth Sunday of Trinity is not clear-cut. Instead, its character is derived from Rist's hymn; hence, it stands much closer to the Passion than to the healing of the ten lepers.

The very first strophe of Rist's chorale—and the first movement of the cantata—evokes the mood of the Passion story:

> Jesu, der du meine Seele
> Hast durch deinen bittern Tod
> Aus des Teufels finstern Höhle
> Und der schweren Seelennot
> Kräftiglich herausgerissen
> Und mich solches lassen wissen
> Durch dein angenehmes Wort,
> Sei doch itzt, o Gott, mein Hort!
>
> Jesus, you who my soul,
> Have through your bitter death,
> Out of the devil's dismal cave
> And heavy affliction of the soul,
> Powerfully torn out
> And let me know this
> Through your propitious word,
> Be even now, O God, my refuge!

The second movement of the cantata, a freely versified aria, contains only a subtle allusion to the chorale text, whose second strophe begins with the words "Treulich hast du ja gesuchet / Die verlorenen Schäfelein" (Truly you have sought / The lost little sheep). The concern of the Sunday Gospel reading is ever present in the aria:

> Wir eilen mit schwachen, doch emsigen Schritten,
> O Jesu, o Meister, zu helfen zu dir.
> Du suchest die Kranken und Irrenden treulich.
> Ach höre, wie wir
> Die Stimmen erheben, um Hilfe zu bitten!
> Es sei uns dein gnädiges Antlitz erfreulich.
>
> We hasten with weak yet diligent steps,
> O Jesus, O Master, for help to you.
> You seek the ill and erring faithfully.
> Ah hear how we
> Lift our voices to pray for help.
> May your gracious countenance be encouraging to us.

In the third movement, a recitative, one finds the procedure often seen in Bach's chorale cantatas in which verses from the chorale are included literally in the recitative and are interleaved with lines of free poetry, all while overarching rhyme schemes and grammatical correspondences are inseparably woven together. The remarkable aspect of this recitative is that, of its seventeen lines of text, six come from Johann Rist's chorale—but they are taken from three different strophes. Two lines each go back to the beginning of the fourth strophe, the middle of the fifth, and the end of the sixth. Corresponding to their chorale strophes, they are placed, respectively, in the beginning, the middle, and the end of the recitative.

The second aria, whose text begins "Das Blut, so meine Schuld durchstreicht / Macht mir das Herze wieder leicht" (The blood that cancels out my sin / Makes my heart light again) and closes with "So stehet Jesus mir zur Seite, / Daß ich beherzt und sieghaft sei" (Then Jesus stands at my side, / So that I am valiant and victorious) turns out to be a very free paraphrase of the sixth and seventh strophes of Rist's chorale, whose beginning and end, respectively, read "Jesu, du hast weggenommen / Meine Schulden durch dein Blut" (Jesus, you have taken away / My debt through your blood) and "Ach, so hilf, Herr Jesu, siegen, / O du meine Zuversicht, / Laß mich ja verzagen nicht" (Ah, then help me, Lord Jesus, to be victorious, / O you who are my assurance, / Do not let me despair). Like the first recitative, the second also combines several strophes of the chorale source text. It begins:

> Die Wunden, Nägel, Kron und Grab,
> Die Schläge, so man dort dem Heiland gab,
> Sind ihm nunmehro Siegeszeichen
>
> The wounds, nails, crown, and grave,
> The blows they gave the savior there
> Are now his signs of victory

This goes back to the beginning of the eighth chorale strophe:

> Deine rotgefärbte Wunden,
> Deine Nägel, Kron und Grab,
> Deine Schenkel fest gebunden,
> Wenden alle Plagen ab.
>
> Your red-stained wounds,
> Your nails, crown, and grave,
> Your tightly bound thighs
> Ward off all troubles.

Afterward, the contents of the ninth strophe—the threatening judgment and the savior's act of redemption—are recounted, and at the end of the recitative the conclusion of the tenth chorale strophe is quoted literally. The next to last cantata movement, again an aria, is a paraphrase of the next to last chorale strophe: "Nun ich weiß, du wirst mir stillen / Mein Gewissen, das mich plagt" (Now I know you will quiet / My conscience, which torments me). The aria text begins: "Nun du wirst mein Gewissen stillen, / So wider mich um Rache schreit" (Now you will quiet my conscience, / Which cries against me for vengeance). Rist's concluding strophe, "Herr, ich glaube, hilf mir Schwachen" (Lord, I believe; help me in my weakness), forms the conclusion of the cantata libretto.

In every conceivable way, Bach's composition does justice to this wide-ranging and meaningful text. This applies in particular to the opening movement, in which Bach enriches his usual approach to the chorale cantatas by adding a new dimension. The chorale cantus firmus in one of the choral voices; motet-like counterpoint in the other voices; a unified orchestral part that enhances overall coherence: all these elements are found here. In addition, the entire movement is arranged as a kind of passacaglia above a continuously recurring pattern in the bass. At the heart of this pattern is a chromatic descent through the interval of the fourth. Rich in tradition, it is known as the *lamento* bass. It is found throughout Bach's oeuvre, from the early Capriccio in B-flat Major BWV 992, up to the composer's very last period in the Crucifixus of the Mass in B Minor BWV 232, in the Three-Part Invention in F Minor BWV 795, and in the famous chaconne from the Partita no. 2 for Solo Violin BWV 1004. To couple this *lamento* bass with a chorale melody while including occasional harmonic modulations, the possibility of contrary motion, and the transposition to an upper voice requires a mastery of artistic means that few of Bach's contemporaries could have shown.

The other movements have a hard time holding their own against this weighty opening movement. With imitation and parallel voice leading in the two high voices, coupled with the busy, continuous figuration of the basso continuo, the playfully cheerful duet, "Wir eilen mit schwachen doch emsigen Schritten," provides a contrast that was probably unavoidable. The dramatic impetus of the first recitative is unusual; its active melody and heavily drawn harmonies would not be out of place in Passion music. In contrast, the aria for tenor and obbligato flute, "Das Blut, so meine Schuld durchstreicht," brings about a brightening of mood; its character is rather more in keeping with the second verse, "Macht mir das Herze wieder leicht." The bass recitative, "Die Wunden, Nägel, Kron und Grab," proves itself a worthy counterpart to the opening movement. Its harmonic wealth and graphic interpretation of the text culminate in the last twelve measures in a way that anticipates the Last Supper scene in the St. Matthew Passion. Like the preceding tenor aria, the superficial concertante bass aria, "Nun du wirst mein Gewissen stillen," is an element of encouragement and consolation. It is followed by a four-part closing chorale, which avoids any depiction of "sin," "death," or "despair."

Liebster Immanuel, Herzog der Frommen
BWV 123 / BC A 28

Epiphany, January 6, 1725

This cantata was first performed on January 6, 1725, in Leipzig. As part of Bach's chorale cantata annual cycle, it makes use of all strophes of a chorale, retaining the first and last as originally written and paraphrasing the others to be set as recitatives and arias. Ahasverus Fritsch was the author of the hymn *Liebster Immanuel, Herzog der Frommen* (Dearest Emmanuel, prince of the devout), first printed in the 1670s. Born in 1629 in Mücheln near Geiseltal, then in Saxony, now Anhalt-Saxony, Fritsch had experienced firsthand the horrors of the Thirty Years' War in his childhood and youth. The description of those sufferings could just as easily fit events of the late twentieth century:

> When he was only two years of age, the horrors of war forced his parents to flee with him . . . just as his home town went up in flames, and four houses burned; they lost everything. Erratically, they fled from one place to another while surrounded by plundering, robbery, burning, and murder. Fritsch had to spend his youth wandering in forests and fields, hiding himself in a ruin at one moment, then in an excavated grave, then in cellars and bushes; as soon as he was discovered or hunger drove him from hiding, he was attacked by soldiers and robbed of his clothing, left with nothing more than his shirt in the winter, or savagely beaten. He fell into enemy hands no fewer than six times. At the age of fourteen, he lost his father, whose heart was broken by the interminable succession of fire, flight, starvation, tribulation, and misery.

In the midst of these deprivations, his mother made it possible for him to attend school in Halle; while suffering continuous need, he studied at the University of Jena. A position as tutor at the court of Rudolstadt was the beginning of a continuous ascent through the positions of court and judicial counselor, court clerk, chancellery director and president of the consistory, and finally the position of chancellor. His contact with the countesses Ludämilia

Elisabeth and Ämilie Juliana influenced his religious poetry; Ludämilia Elisabeth's two hundred Jesus hymns achieved recognition during her own lifetime. Fritsch's wrestling with the expression of personal devoutness—even without unconditionally adopting the trappings of Pietism—can be seen against the background of church life during the Thirty Years' War and its aftermath. It is only in this context that such exuberant formulations such as the title of the hymn collection make sense: "One hundred twenty-one new heavenly sweet Jesus hymns, in which the most exquisitely sweet powerful name of Jesus is found over seven hundred times, in deepest honor of our most worthy savior and redeemer, also the awakening of most holy devotion and joy of the soul, partly written, partly collected by Ahasverus Fritsch."[6] Passages in the associated foreword include examples such as this one: "All is vanity, all is misery and wretchedness. But our Jesus is everything in all. Jesus is the faithful soul's sugar and milk, manna, milk and wine, cinnamon, cloves, and balsam. Blessed is he who feels this heavenly sweetness of Jesus powerfully in his soul."[7]

The six strophes that underlie our cantata are marked by strongly accentuated personal piety. The title line takes up a keyword from the Gospel reading for Epiphany from Matthew 2, in which a quotation from the prophet Micah appears in connection with the description of the visit of the Wise Men from the Orient: "Und du Bethlehem in jüdischen Lande bist mitnichten die kleinste unter den Fürsten Juda's; denn aus dir soll mir kommen der Herzog, der über mein Volk Israel ein Herr sei" (6; And you Bethlehem, in the land of Judah, are not the least among the princes of Juda: for out of you shall come a prince that shall rule my people Israel). There is clearly a world of difference between this text and the ecstatic verses of Ahasverus Fritsch.

> Liebster Immanuel, Herzog der Frommen,
> Du meiner Seele Heil, komm, komm nur bald!
> Du hast mir, höchster Schatz, mein Herz genommen,
> So ganz vor Liebe brennt und nach dir wallt.
> Nichts kann auf Erden
> Mir liebers werden,
> Als wenn ich meinen Jesum stets behalt.
>
> Beloved Emmanuel, prince of the devout,
> You, my soul's salvation, come, come but soon!
> You, highest treasure, have taken my heart from me,
> Which so entirely burns of love and beats for you.
> Nothing on Earth can
> Become dearer to me
> Than if I always keep my Jesus.

With a vocabulary that seems to come from the Song of Songs, the second strophe continues:

> Dein Nam ist zuckersüß, Honig im Munde
> Holdselig, lieblich, frisch wie kühler Tau,
> Der Feld und Blume netzt zur Morgenstunde:
> Mein Jesus ist nur, dem ich vertrau.

> Your name is sweet as sugar, honey in the mouth,
> Charming, lovely, fresh as the cool dew
> That moistens field and flower at the morning hour:
> My Jesus is the only one whom I trust.

The unknown librettist working for Bach did not want to continue in that vein; instead, in the first recitative, he checks the enthusiasm in favor of a widened theological horizon:

> Die Himmelsüßigkeit, der Auserwählten Lust
> Erfüllt auf Erden schon mein Herz und Brust,
> Wenn ich den Jesusnamen nenne
> Und sein verborgnes Manna kenne:
> Gleichwie der Tau ein dürres Land erquickt,
> So ist mein Herz
> Auch bei Gefahr und Schmerz
> In Freudigkeit durch Jesu Kraft entzückt.

> The heavenly sweetness, the delight of the chosen,
> Fills already on Earth my heart and breast
> When I call the name of Jesus
> And know his hidden manna.
> Just as the dew refreshes a dry landscape,
> Thus my heart,
> Even in danger and pain,
> Is delighted in joy through Jesus's power.

The librettist's task was not only to adapt sections of seventeenth-century poetry to the language of the eighteenth and to make it suitable for use in contemporary musical forms but also now and again to create a connection to the Gospel readings of the period after Christmas and for Epiphany. The latter could hardly be expected of Fritsch's hymn, for in hymnals of the period it appears under the neutral rubric of "Jesus Hymns" (*Jesuslieder*) without any particular connection to a specific point in the church year. The third strophe offered an opportunity for clarification:

> Und ob das Kreuze mich gleich zeitlich plaget,
> Wie es bei Christen oft pflegt zu geschehn;
> Wenn meine Seele nur nach Jesu fraget,
> So kann das Herze schon auf Rosen gehn,
> Kein Ungewitter
> Ist mir zu bitter,
> Mit Jesu kann ichs fröhlich überstehn.
>
> And if the cross here in this life torments me,
> As it often happens to Christians,
> If my soul only asks after Jesus,
> Then can my heart go along the path of roses.
> No thunderstorm
> Is for me too bitter.
> With Jesus I can happily endure it.

An aria text was drawn from this with an allusion to the flight of the Holy Family:

> Auch die harte Kreutzesreise
> Und die Tränen bittre Speise
> Schreckt mich nicht.
> Wenn die Ungewitter toben,
> Sendet Jesus mir von oben
> Heil und Licht.
>
> Even the painful journey of the cross
> And the bitter meal of tears
> Do not frighten me.
> If storms thunder,
> Jesus sends me, from above,
> Salvation and light.

Strophe 4 of the hymn and the fourth movement of the cantata, a recitative, deal with the threat of hell, enemies and death, and salvation through Jesus. The scorn and persecution of the world, loneliness, and sadness but also the faithful company of Jesus are objects of the next movement. The last strophe of Ahasverus Fritsch's hymn, adopted without change, deals with renunciation of the vanity of the world and complete submission to Jesus; it closes the sequence of ideas in the cantata libretto.

Bach's composition is dominated, as usual, by its broad, well-developed opening movement, in which the chorale melody is presented by the soprano in large note values, while the other voices provide a motet-like contrapuntal accompaniment, and the whole is lent contour and coherence by a motivically unified instrumental texture. The $\frac{9}{8}$ meter of the pastorale and the simple harmonies, with thirds and sixths predominant, give the movement a touch of tranquil inwardness. The first aria is sharply differentiated, as described by Arnold Schering:

> The various vivid and powerful expressions (hard, cross, tears, bitter, horrify, thunderstorm) awakened in Bach just as much richness of musical expression and imagery. Weary and tortuous, in a bitter F-sharp minor, from the third bar on, the sharp oboes perform the thorny, chromatic theme, disturbing one another. Its complete expressive power is unleashed only with the entrance of the human voice, and the tritone F-sharp / B-sharp is connected with the word "hard" and the arrival at high A with "cross." It is a nice touch when, in the postlude, the often-heard main theme does not appear in the upper voices but is instead given to the bass, and it is entirely in keeping with the Baroque style's predilection for violent expression that the thunderstorm episode that follows suddenly storms four measures ahead into the Allegro.[8]

The second aria does not deliver a similar multitude of correspondences. Even so, the verse "Laß, o Welt, mich aus Verachtung / In betrübter Einsamkeit" (Out of contempt, O world, leave me / In distressed solitude) prompted the composer to give the voice, the bass, only a solo flute in accompaniment, thus illustrating the situation of loneliness. The illustration of sadness through harmonic cloudiness was just as obvious a choice. With an effect common for the period—if rare in Bach's cantatas—the closing chorale is lengthened. Not only the *Stollen* (the chorale's opening section) is repeated here but also, exceptionally, the *Abgesang* (closing section) and, indeed, *piano*. The inward demeanor fits the closing verses well:

> Mein ganzes Leben
> Sei dir ergeben,
> Bis man mich einsten legt ins Grab hinein.

> May my entire life
> Be surrendered to you
> Till one day I am laid in the grave.

Herr Jesu Christ, wahr' Mensch und Gott
BWV 127 / BC A 49

Estomihi, February 11, 1725

The cantata *Herr Jesu Christ, wahr' Mensch und Gott* BWV 127 (Lord Jesus Christ, true human and God) is one of the last works in Johann Sebastian Bach's annual cycle of chorale cantatas. It was performed for the first time on Estomihi Sunday, February 11, 1725. The chorale on which it is based was published by Paul Eber in 1562; although it is a funeral hymn, it appears among Passion hymns in the collections of Bach's time. The reason a Passion hymn is used in a cantata for Estomihi can be seen in the nature of this Sunday, whose Gospel reading from Luke 18, depicting the journey to Jerusalem, clearly foreshadows the Passion story. The blurred line between funeral and Passion hymn stems from the doctrine that Christ truly walked the path to death and that it is possible for the believer to emulate Christ in their own death.

In the manner typical for the cycle, the unknown cantata librettist left the first and last strophes untouched and reshaped the inner strophes to form recitatives and arias. Accordingly, Paul Eber's first strophe in its original wording stands at the beginning:

> Herr Jesu Christ, wahr' Mensch und Gott,
> Der du littst Marter, Angst und Spott,
> Für mich am Kreuz auch endlich starbst
> Und mir deins Vaters Huld erwarbst,
> Ich bitt durchs bittre Leiden dein:
> Du wollst mir Sünder gnädig sein.

> Lord Jesus Christ, true human and God,
> You who suffered torture, fear, and mockery,
> Finally also died on the cross for me
> And earned for me your father's favor.
> I ask, through your bitter suffering,
> That you would be gracious to me, a sinner.

The ensuing recitative combines the content of the second and third strophes, following the depiction of the pains of death in the chorale, a depiction that spans the strophes and pleads for an end to the torture. Eber's fourth strophe prays for the assistance of Christ:

> Bis sich die Seel vom Leib abwendt,
> So nimm sie, Herr, in deine Hand;

Der Leib hab in der Erd sein Ruh
Bis sich der jüngst Tag naht herzu.

Until the soul turns away from the body,
So take it, Lord, in your hand.
The body will have its rest in earth
Until the last day approaches.

The aria text derived from this is vividly formulated:

Die Seele ruht in Jesu Händen,
Wenn Erde diesen Leib bedeckt.
Ach ruft mich bald, ihr Sterbeglocken,
Ich bin zum Sterben unerschrocken,
Weil mich mein Jesu wieder weckt.

The soul rests in Jesus's hands,
When earth covers this body.
O call me soon, you funeral bells,
I am of dying unafraid,
Because my Jesus wakes me again.

The contrast between chorale strophe and cantata text is even stronger in the ensuing recitative. Eber's simple opening verses in the fifth strophe, "Ein fröhlich Auferstehung mir verleih, / Am jüngsten G'richt mein Fürsprecher sei" (Grant me a joyous resurrection. / May you be my advocate at the Last Judgment), are transformed into an impressive scenario of the Last Judgment:

Wenn einstens die Posaunen schallen,
Und wenn der Bau der Welt
Nebst denen Himmelsfesten
Zerschmettert wird zerfallen,
So denke mein, mein Gott, im besten;
Wenn sich dein Knecht einst vors Gericht stellt,
Da die Gedanken sich verklagen,
So wollest du allein,
O Jesu, mein Fürsprecher sein
Und meiner Seele tröstlich sagen:
Fürwahr, fürwahr, euch sage ich:
Wenn Himmel und Erde im Feuer vergehen,
So soll doch ein Gläubiger ewig bestehen.
Er wird nicht kommen ins Gericht
Und den Tod ewig schmecken nicht.

> When once the trumpets sound
> And when the foundations of the world
> Beside that of the firmament,
> Dashed to pieces, will collapse,
> Then think of me, my God, for good;
> When your servant one day stands before judgment,
> Where his thoughts accuse him,
> Then would you alone,
> O Jesus, be my advocate
> And to my soul, in consolation, say:
> Truly, truly, I say to you:
> When heaven and Earth pass away in fire,
> Yet shall the faithful one withstand in eternity.
> He will not come before judgment
> And shall not eternally taste death.

Parts of the promise beginning with "fürwahr" (truly) are taken literally from Eber's sixth strophe; the closing lines depend on his seventh strophe:

> Ich breche mit starker und helfender Hand
> Des Todes gewaltig geschlossenes Band.

> I break, with strong and helping hand,
> Death's powerful, closed snare.

The closing strophe of this funeral and Passion hymn remains unchanged:

> Ach Herr, vergib all unsre Schuld,
> Hilf, daß wir warten mit Geduld
> Bis unser Stündlein kömmt herbei
> Auch unser Glaub stets wacker sei,
> Dein'm Wort zu trauen festiglich,
> Bis wir einschlafen seliglich.

> O Lord, forgive us all our sins.
> Help, that we await with patience
> Until our hour of death arrives
> And always keep our faith brave,
> To trust your word to trust absolutely,
> Until we fall blessedly into death's sleep.

The opening movement of Johann Sebastian Bach's setting of this libretto stands out because of its unusually multileveled structure. It exhibits the expected pattern: here as in most of its sister works, the soprano presents the chorale melody in relatively large note values, while the other voices provide imitative counterpoint to the cantus firmus in the manner of a motet, and a motivically unified instrumental texture serves to unify these divergent components. In fact, the instrumental ensemble—two recorders, two oboes, and strings—fulfills this function from the very beginning, in particular by way of a rhythmically pregnant motive, as well as a figure that clearly refers to the beginning of the chorale melody, with both components remaining present throughout the entire course of the movement.

But the matter does not end there. Beginning with the strings in the first measure and later taken up by the oboes and recorders, the ancient melody of the "German Agnus Dei," *Christe, du Lamm Gottes* (Christ, you lamb of God), is heard as a second cantus firmus. By doing this, Bach makes a connection to a somewhat older Estomihi cantata, *Du wahrer Gott und Davids Sohn* BWV 23 (You true God and David's son), which he composed in 1723 in conjunction with his application for the position of cantor of St. Thomas School. Here also, the ancient *Christe, du Lamm Gottes* is inserted as a purely instrumental quotation, without words, creating the effect of multitextuality in the recitative in which it appears. In the same way, the opening chorus of the cantata *Herr Jesu Christ, wahr' Mensch und Gott* actually integrates two text levels: the chorale poetry of Paul Eber from the second half of the sixteenth century, as well as Luther's translation of the Agnus Dei from about a decade earlier, based on the instrumental quotation. Musically, there are actually three historical levels represented here: the liturgical melody of the Agnus Dei; the cantus firmus to Paul Eber's chorale melody, taken from a French psalter; and the motet-like, concerted composition of Johann Sebastian Bach.

Following a brief tenor recitative, a haunting dialogue unfolds in the aria "Die Seele ruht in Jesu Händen" (The soul rests in Jesus's hands), between the lonely and imploring soprano voice and a faithful and consoling oboe by its side, while the unceasing toll of the funeral bell can be heard in the endless staccato of the recorders, later in the pizzicato of the strings. The penultimate cantata movement, a hybrid of recitative and aria, allows two opposing components to clash with one another: on the one hand, the depiction of the Last Judgment, with wide intervals in the vocal part, impassioned tone and chord repetitions in the strings, and fanfares in the trumpet that signal danger; and on the other, the calming and soothing promise of salvation in the stepwise-moving voice, accompanied only by the basso continuo. The beginning of the last third of the movement anticipates the chorus "Sind Blitzen, sind Donner in Wolken verschwunden" (Have lightning and thunder vanished in clouds) of the St. Matthew Passion BWV 244/27b, several years before it came into being. After the triumphant conclusion of this drama-filled movement, the concluding four-part chorale, "Ach Herr, vergib all unsre Schuld," seems rather humble.

The cantata as a whole occupies a unique position in Bach's oeuvre, which can be seen in the fact that the opening movement—transposed to E-flat major and with minor changes*—was taken into a pasticcio Passion music that is largely the work of Carl Heinrich Graun and is contained in a manuscript from the estate of Bach's son-in-law Johann Christoph Altnickol.** The second part of the Passion, to be performed after the sermon, begins with "Herr Jesu Christ, wahr' Mensch und Gott." It is possible that Altnickol was following a suggestion from Johann Sebastian Bach in making this addition. It is even conceivable that Bach not only offered encouragement but also acted directly as a model, in that he himself added his own chorale movement to a Passion that has not survived, thereby giving it a special place among his cantatas.

---
*Dürr (1988).
**Wollny and Glöckner (1997).

Wie schön leuchtet der Morgenstern
BWV 1 / BC A 173
Annunciation, March 25, 1725

With his composition of the cantata *Wie schön leuchtet der Morgenstern* BWV 1 (How lovely gleams the morning star) in March 1725, Johann Sebastian Bach brought his cycle of chorale cantatas to a premature conclusion. He had begun work on it the summer before, surely with the intention of creating a complete annual cycle. We do not know what caused him to halt work on the cycle just before its final quarter. It is conceivable that the librettist, who refashioned chorale strophes into recitatives and arias for the nearly forty preceding chorale cantatas, was no longer available.[9] But it also seems possible that a certain exhaustion had set in for the composer, who was faced with the task of creating new compositions, often with little lead time, week after week, while dealing with many other pressing issues and not once being able to go back to an existing composition.

If this assumption approaches the truth, it does so only in general—and certainly not with respect to the cantata *Wie schön leuchtet der Morgenstern*. For here we have a masterpiece of incomparable freshness of invention that serves not just as a conclusion but also as a crown and that, long afterward in 1850, received the honor of being the first work published in the complete edition of all of Bach's compositions. The richness and freshness of the ideas could, in this special case, also have to do with the fortunate time of origin. For in Leipzig, the feast day of Annunciation was the only holiday during the several weeks of Lent when concerted music was permitted. Normally, during the music-free weeks of the *tempus clausum*, the busy *Thomaskantor* would concentrate on preparing Passion music and church music for the three Easter holidays afterward. In 1725 Bach was preparing the second version of the St. John Passion, a work that for the most part had been composed and performed the previous year. Its revision was restricted to inserting older choral movements and arias. Hence there was enough time for the composer to painstakingly prepare a particularly sumptuous cantata for the Marian feast, which coincidentally fell on Palm Sunday.

As is the case for most of its companion works in the chorale cantata annual cycle, the source text for Bach's cantata was a main hymn for the feast day, in this case, Philipp Nicolai's *Wie schön leuchtet der Morgenstern*. Nicolai was born in Westphalia in 1556 and died in 1608 as senior pastor in Hamburg. He authored this hymn, together with the equally well-known *Wachet auf, ruft uns die Stimme* (Awaken, calls to us the voice), as pastor in Unna during a plague and published them in his collection *Freuden-Spiegel des ewigen Lebens* (Joyful reflection of the eternal life). This work went through many editions in a very short time, probably because it preserved the spirit of the Reformation to an unusually high degree, even though it was written half a century after Luther's death.

The person who reshaped Nicolai's seven-strophe hymn into a six-movement cantata libretto remains unknown. Outwardly, we have here the least complicated example, whereby the interior strophes are refashioned into recitatives and arias and only the external strophes contain Nicolai's original text, so that Nicolai's opening strophe becomes the first movement:

> Wie schön leuchtet der Morgenstern,
> Voll Gnad und Wahrheit von dem Herrn,
> Die süße Wurzel Jesse!
> Du Sohn David aus Jakobs Stamm,
> Mein König und mein Bräutigam,
> Hast mir mein Herz besessen,
> Lieblich,
> Freundlich,
> Schön und herrlich,
> Groß und ehrlich,
> Reich von Gaben,
> Hoch und sehr prächtig erhaben.

> How lovely gleams the morning star,
> Full of grace and truth from the Lord.
> The sweet root of Jesse!
> You son of David from Jacob's lineage,
> My king and my bridegroom,
> You have taken possession of my heart,
> Lovely,
> Friendly,
> Beautiful and glorious,
> Great and noble,
> Rich with gifts,
> Highly and most splendidly exalted.

In the following text, a recitative, the libretto alternates between a strict and freer reshaping of the source text. The second chorale strophe begins:

> Ei, mein' Perle, du werte Kron,
> Wahr' Gottes und Marien Sohn,
> Ein hochgeborner König.
>
> Ah, my pearl, you precious crown,
> True son of God and Mary,
> A king of noble birth.

In the recitative that beginning becomes:

> Du wahrer Gottes und Marien Sohn,
> Du König derer Auserwählten,
> Wie süß ist uns dies Lebenswort,
> Nach dem die ersten Väter schon
> So Jahr als Tage zählten.
>
> You true son of God and Mary,
> You king of their elect,
> How sweet is to us this living word
> By which the first fathers
> Counted years as well as days.

The Gospel reading of the feast day, the account in Luke 1 of how the angel Gabriel announced the birth of Jesus to Mary, is interwoven with the recitative text.

From the phrase "Flamme deiner Liebe" (Flame of your love), briefly mentioned in the third chorale strophe, the librettist produces an unexpectedly emphatic aria text:

> Erfüllet, ihr himmlischen, göttlichen Flammen,
> Die nach euch verlangende gläubige Brust!
> Die Seelen empfinden die kräftigsten Triebe
> Der brünstigsten Liebe
> Und schmecken auf Erden die himmlische Lust.
>
> Fill, you heavenly, divine flames,
> The faithful breast longing for you!
> Our souls feel the most powerful urges
> Of ardent love
> And taste on Earth heavenly delight.

Any doubts arising as to what "auf Erden" (on Earth) might entail are energetically dispelled by the ensuing recitative:

> Ein ird'scher Glanz, ein leiblich Licht
> Rührt meine Seele nicht;
> Ein Freudenschein ist mir von Gott entstanden,
> Denn ein vollkommnes Gut,
> Des Heilands Leib und Blut,
> Ist zur Erquickung da.
>
> An earthly brilliance, a corporeal light
> Does not stir my soul;
> A joyful light from God has arisen for me,
> For a perfect Good,
> The Savior's body and blood,
> Is here for refreshment.

The source chorale as formulated by Nicolai is less pretentious:

> Von Gott kommt mir ein Freudenschein,
> Wenn du mit deinen Äugelein,
> Mich freundlich tust anblicken.
> O Herr Jesu, mein trautes Gut,
> Dein Wort, dein Geist, dein Leib und Blut
> Mich innerlich erquicken.
>
> From God comes to me a joyful light,
> When you with your little eyes
> Look upon me with friendship.
> O Lord Jesus, my trusted Good,
> Your word, your spirit, your body and blood
> Refresh me within.

Nicolai's next to last strophe is an invitation to sing praises and to "Zwingen," here meaning to sound string instruments:[10]

> Zwingt die Saiten in Cythara
> Und laßt die süße Musica
> Ganz freudenreich erschallen.
> . . . .
> Singet,
> Springet,
> Jubilieret,
> Triumphieret,
> Dankt dem Herren:
> Groß ist der König der Ehren.
>
> Pluck the strings of the zither
> And let sweet music
> Resound rich with joy.
> . . . .
> Sing,
> Leap,
> Rejoice,
> Triumph,
> Thank the Lord:
> Great is the king of the honorable.

The second aria in the cantata text echoes this invitation to make music:

> Unser Mund und Ton der Saiten
> Sollen dir
> Für und für
> Dank und Opfer zubereiten.
> Herz und Sinnen sind erhoben,
> Lebenslang
> Mit Gesang
> Großer König, dich zu loben.
>
> Our voices and sounds of strings
> Shall for you
> Forever and ever
> Prepare thanksgiving and offerings.
> Heart and mind are lifted
> Lifelong
> With singing,
> Great king, in praise of you.

As usual, the final strophe remains unchanged:

> Wie bin ich doch so herzlich froh,
> Daß mein Schatz ist das A und O,
> Der Anfang und das Ende;
> Er wird mich doch zu seinem Preis
> Aufnehmen in das Paradeis,
> Des klopf ich in die Hände.
> Amen,
> Amen!
> Komm du schöne
> Freudenkröne,
> Bleib nicht lange,
> Deiner wart ich mit Verlangen.

> How sincerely glad I am indeed
> That my treasure is the alpha and omega,
> The beginning and the end;
> He will indeed, to his praise,
> Take me up in paradise,
> For which I clap my hands.
> Amen,
> Amen!
> Come, you lovely
> Crown of joy,
> Do not long delay,
> I await you with longing.

Bach's composition is dominated by the expansively designed opening chorus. The chorale melody is extensive but well articulated. Its heritage has roots in Strasbourg that can be followed even farther back to Hans Sachs and the Meistersingers. It is clearly focused on the main key, and, with its folklike major tonality, it allows little opportunity for modulatory excursions. This posed a challenge for the *Thomaskantor*. He met it with an aural panorama of exquisite beauty that makes literal the "morning star," the metaphorically meant image for Christ. Two horns in their higher ranges, as well as two oboi da caccia, woodwind instruments similar to horns in form with a husky timbre in a rather deep range, provide the breadth of the timbral space, and the glistening figuration of two solo violins evokes the serene brilliance of the morning star. In conjunction with the other strings, this setting makes a wide variety of timbral combinations available, which the composer exploits extensively in the course of the opening movement's over one hundred measures in $\frac{12}{8}$ meter.

A concise, vivid tenor recitative is followed by the first aria, in which the "kräftigsten Triebe der brünstigen Liebe" (most powerful urges of ardent love) seem restrained, mostly due to the disciplined effect of the obbligato instrument, the oboe da caccia in its deep register. In contrast to this strict setting, the tenor aria, "Unser Mund und Ton der Saiten" (Our mouth and the sound of strings), has a dancelike character that approaches that of the minuet. It affords the string instruments every conceivable opportunity for development, of which the solo and ripieno violins engage themselves in multifarious contrapuntal and timbral combinations. With its gesture of delight in making music, it proves to be a performance of "Musik in der Musik" (music within the music).

Essentially, the closing chorale presents itself as a simple four-part texture, but it comes across as not quite as contemplative as might be expected. The reason lies with the brass. While the first horn has to follow the chorale melody strictly, Bach allows the second enough room to be a countervoice while being mindful of its restricted sound quality in its lower range. This not only results in a five-part texture but also effects a subtle reminiscence on the distinctive timbres of the first movement.

Ihr werdet weinen und heulen
BWV 103 / BC A 69
Jubilate, April 22, 1725

This cantata was heard for the first time on April 22, 1725, presumably in Leipzig's St. Thomas Church. It thus belongs to a period in which a significant change took place in Johann Sebastian Bach's composition of cantatas. One month before our cantata was performed for the first time, the *Thomaskantor* had broken off work on his annual cycle of chorale cantatas, bringing the most comprehensive compositional project of his career to a premature end. We have no idea what caused him to discontinue the chorale cantata series, begun two weeks after Pentecost 1724, before its expected conclusion in late May 1725. It is conceivable that the unknown librettist or librettists responsible for adapting chorale strophes to the modern forms of recitative and aria were no longer available. But the reason might lie with Bach himself. In a period of less than ten months he had realized the concept of chorale cantata in at least forty instances, and, in particular, he had set the opening movements according to a model: cantus firmus in large note values in one of the voices; motet-like counterpoint in the other voices; and a motivically unified, concerted orchestral part. The possibility should not be ignored that a certain fatigue had set in, coupled with the composer's desire to construct large forms not bound to chorales.

Through coincidence or a systematic search, it must have been during this period that the cantor of St. Thomas came into contact with a female Leipzig poet who up to that point had never been engaged in creating texts for *Kirchenstücken*, or church cantatas: Christiane Mariane von Ziegler. Born in 1695 in Leipzig, she grew up in a middle-class family that was in equal measure wealthy, highly intellectual, and interested in music. Twice married and twice widowed, she had returned to Leipzig in 1722 after years of absence in order to overcome her loneliness in social engagement and take part in poetic and musical activities. Moreover, the arrest of her father by order of the Saxon elector and his lifelong imprisonment in the castle at Königstein without an explanation of the charges and without a trial was a stroke of fate she had yet to overcome.[11]

Although Christiane Mariane von Ziegler's writing career lasted less than two decades, she flourished in the circle of Johann Christoph Gottsched in Leipzig, and in spite of occasional criticism she earned high honors. In November 1733 the Saxon press reported: "Frau Christiana Mariana von Ziegler, a daughter of the erstwhile mayor of Leipzig, Herr Romani, in the month of October has been named Royal Poet Laureate by the Philosophical Faculty of the University of Wittenberg because of her strong and fully developed poetry, an honor that, at least within the entire University, has never been granted to a person of her gender."[12]

Frau Ziegler published nine church cantata texts in her first work, *Versuch in gebundener Schreib-Art*, which appeared in Leipzig in 1728. Within a period of only five weeks in 1725, Johann Sebastian Bach set all nine to music and performed them. The composer must have received the texts from the librettist in advance of their publication in 1728. It is less likely that she coincidentally happened to have them on hand and helped the cantor of St. Thomas in his unforeseen need for cantata texts than that Bach asked for an unbroken sequence of texts from Jubilate Sunday to Trinity in order to be able to fill out the interrupted cantata cycle in advance. In addition, it is noteworthy that Frau Ziegler, in the second and last part of her *Versuch in gebundener Schreib-Art*, published in 1729, expanded the sequence of previously published texts to a complete annual cycle, though without printing the libretti set by Bach a second time. However, Bach evidently made no use of this extensive new offering.

The question whether Frau Ziegler wrote the nine cantata texts on commission for Johann Sebastian Bach or whether he responded to her offer of texts and therefore allowed his chorale cantata cycle to languish is of some significance because the texts printed in 1728 differ in many cases from those composed by Bach in 1725. It is conceivable that the poet revised her texts before publishing them, but it is just as possible that Bach or someone working for him arranged the texts for composition (and must not have been particularly squeamish about doing so).[13] Still, the Ziegler text for Jubilate Sunday is certainly the least affected by this.

The libretto for *Ihr werdet weinen und heulen* BWV 103 (You shall weep and wail) begins with a New Testament dictum taken from the Sunday Gospel reading in John 16, which continues the farewell speeches of Jesus: "Über ein kleines, so werdet ihr mich nicht sehen; und aber über ein kleines, so werdet ihr mich sehen, denn ich gehe zum Vater" (16; For a little while, you will not see me; however, for a little while, you shall see me, for I am going to the Father). The Sunday Gospel reading closes: "Wahrlich, wahrlich ich sage euch: Ihr werdet weinen und heulen, aber die Welt wird sich freuen; ihr aber werdet traurig sein; doch eure Traurigkeit soll in Freude verkehret werden" (20; Truly, truly I say to you: you shall weep and wail, but the world shall rejoice; you, however, shall be sorrowful, yet your sorrow shall be turned into joy). Frau Ziegler's free poetry takes up the lament of the dictum in a brief recitative and, in the ensuing aria, paraphrases the *Suchmotiv* (search motive), "Verbirgst du dich, so muß ich sterben" (If you hide yourself, then I must die).[14] The aria begins:

> Kein Arzt ist außer dir zu finden,
> Ich suche durch ganz Gilead;
> Wer heilt die Wunden meiner Sünden,
> Weil man hier keinen Balsam hat?

> No physician other than you is to be found,
> I search through all Gilead;
> Who will heal the wounds of my sins,
> Since one has no balsam here?

The passage referred to is found in chapter 8, verse 22, of the book of the prophet Jeremiah: "Mich jammert herzlich, daß mein Volk so verderbt ist; Ich gräme mich und gehabe mich übel. Ist denn keine Salbe in Gilead, oder ist kein Arzt da? Warum ist denn die Tochter meines Volks nicht geheilt?" (I am greatly distressed that my people are so corrupted; I grieve and conduct myself badly. Is there then no balm in Gilead, or is no physician there? Why then is the daughter of my people not healed?). "Du wirst mich nach der Angst auch wiederum erquicken" (You will, after my distress, revive me again) reads the recitative that follows in reference to a verse from Psalm 138. The rest of the recitative text is shortened by several lines compared to the printed version, yet without any loss of substance; hewing closely to the dictum at the beginning, it reads:

> Ich traue dem Verheißungswort,
> Daß meine Traurigkeit
> In Freude soll verkehrt werden.
>
> I trust the word of promise,
> That my sorrow
> Shall be transformed to joy.

"Sorrow and joy" is also the theme of the ensuing aria text, which begins "Erholet euch, betrübte Sinnen" (Recover, distressed minds). A strophe from Paul Gerhardt's hymn *Barmherz'ger Vater, höchster Gott* (Merciful father, highest God) draws together the train of ideas in the text once again: "Ich hab dich einen Augenblick, / O liebes Kind, verlassen" (I have, for a moment, / Dear child, left you).

In Bach's wide-ranging composition of the opening movement, the instrumental introduction anticipates the phrase "aber die Welt wird sich freuen" (but the world shall rejoice). Strings, two oboi d'amore, and a solo instrument (in the first version a piccolo recorder, in the later version a solo violin or transverse flute) join together in a lively ensemble of inner cheer that could hardly be allowed to end with the return of the initial phrase, "Ihr werdet weinen und heulen." This appears in a brief fugal exposition full of intense chromaticism that just as quickly resolves into a confident "Aber die Welt wird sich freuen." Upon its reappearance, the joy motive is given along with the sorrowful fugue theme in counterpoint from the start, and here, in a third, identical exposition, now with the text "Doch eure Traurigkeit soll in Freude verkehrt werden," the joy theme—quite in the spirit of the text—proves itself the strongest. On the other hand, the bass arioso at the beginning of the last third of the movement, with its repeated warning, "Ihr aber werdet traurig sein" (You, however, shall be sorrowful), has little effect.

The ensuing recitative, though brief, is quite vivid in its dramatic gesture; in the sorrowful aria that follows, the solo instrument originally planned, the piccolo recorder, illustrates the search "durch ganz Gilead" (through all of Gilead) with its animated passages, while its ingratiating tone is meant to lend emphasis to the plea for compassion. In the tenor aria, self-confident fanfare motives and twisted harmonic progressions conflict with one another until the cantata concludes in a simple chorale movement on the melody *Was mein Gott will, das g'scheh allzeit* (What my God wills, that shall forever be).

Unser Mund sei voll Lachens
BWV 110 / BC A 10

Christmas Day, December 25, 1725

The high feast days, to which Christmas has belonged since time immemorial, regularly presented Bach—as well as his predecessors and successors—with a formidable challenge as far as the organization of church music was concerned. In Leipzig there was a long-standing custom known as *doppelte Kirchenmusik* (doubled church music); that is, on the most important holidays the cantor needed to provide festive music not just for one of the two main churches but also for the other church. In practice this meant that the most important music took place in the morning of the first holiday in the preferred church—in Bach's era this was St. Nicholas, residence of the superintendent—and a composition of lesser significance was heard in the other church, St. Thomas. In the afternoon the circumstances were reversed: in the vespers service, the more challenging, higher-profile work from the morning at St. Nicholas was repeated at St. Thomas, and the less significant work was heard at St. Nicholas. On the second holiday, the sequence in morning and afternoon at the two churches was reversed, and on the third holiday, music was restricted to only one of the two churches. On the first holiday, there was an additional burden for the cantor of St. Thomas: by tradition he was obligated to provide music to St. Paul, the church associated with the university, as well. It may be for this reason that the work performed early in the morning and repeated in the afternoon in the city churches was also offered in the late morning. As the cantata or "main music" (*Hauptmusik*) was not the only demand on the cantor of St. Thomas School, his choir, the soloists, and the instrumental musicians, one can only imagine how much all participants were expected to do during the high feast days of the church year, since doubled church music required the careful allocation of all available musicians.

The cantata *Unser Mund sei voll Lachens* BWV 110 (May our mouth be full of laughter), composed in 1725, also belongs to this context. Bach took the libretto from a collection of texts that he had occasionally drawn upon a decade earlier during his Weimar period. Appearing in 1711 in Darmstadt under the title *Gottgefälliges Kirchen-Opffer* (Church offering pleasing to God), the collection was the work of the librarian and court poet there, Georg Christian Lehms. Lehms, born in Silesia and educated at the University of Leipzig, was already known as an author of opera libretti when he took on the task of creating a double annual cycle of texts for church cantatas. The annual text cycle of 1711 deserves the title "doubled," because for every Sunday and holiday of the church year there is a "devotion" (*Andacht*) in the form of a cantata, as well as a similar "afternoon devotion" (*Nachmittagsandacht*). On only one occasion did Johann Sebastian Bach set such a devotion or, more precisely, "morning devotion": in the case of the cantata *Unser Mund sei voll Lachens*. A distinguishing aspect of the text is that it lacks freely written recitatives altogether; it includes only biblical text, chorale strophes, and freely written arias.

The opening movement is designated by Lehms as Psalm 126, verses 2 and 3. The cantata libretto reads: "Unser Mund sei voll Lachens und unsere Zunge voll Rühmens. Denn der Herr hat Großes an uns getan" (May our mouth be full of laughter and our tongue full of praise. For the Lord has done great things for us). On the other hand, the psalter reads, beginning with the end of verse 1:

> Wenn der Herr die gefangenen Zions erlösen wird, so werden wir sein wie die Träumenden. Dann wird unser Mund voll Lachens und unsre Zunge voll Rühmens sein. Da wird man sagen unter den Heiden: Der Herr hat Großes an ihnen getan! Der Herr hat Großes an uns getan: des sind wir fröhlich.

> When the Lord will release the captives of Zion, we will be like them who dream. Then will our mouth be filled with laughter and our tongue with praise. Then will it be said among the Gentiles: The Lord has done great things for them! The Lord has done great things for us, whereof we are glad.

The poet can certainly be seen to have taken a rather independent approach with the biblical text. This is seen not only in wording but also in traditional interpretation, for to use Psalm 126 for the first day of Christmas and the birth of Christ as described in the feast day Gospels is—to put the matter carefully—unusual. The method of commenting upon the Christmas story from the outside, so to speak, continues in the first aria, which praises the event with these words:

> Ihr Gedanken und ihr Sinnen,
> Schwinget euch anitzt von hinnen!
> Steiget schleunigt himmelan
> Und bedenkt was Gott getan!
> Er wird Mensch, und dies allein,
> Daß wir Himmels Kinder sein.

> You thoughts and you senses,
> Swing up away from here.

> Climb swiftly to heaven
> And consider what God has done!
> He becomes human, and for this alone:
> That we may be heaven's children.

It is not the only aria that describes the birth of Christ as God's deed. The biblical quote that follows was also selected for this purpose. Jeremiah 10:6 reads as follows: "Dir, Herr, ist niemand gleich, du bist groß und dein Name ist groß und kannst's mit der Tat beweisen" (To you, Lord, there is none like. You are great and your name is great and you can prove it with your deeds.) The poet chooses God's greatness and the lowliness and highness of the Son of Man, following Psalm 8, to extend his train of thought. The psalm text reads, "Was ist der Mensch, daß du seiner gedenkst, und des Menschen Kind, daß du dich seiner annimmst?" (4; What is man, that you are mindful of him? and the child of humankind, that you care for him?), but it becomes, in the rhymed form of the aria,

> Ach, Herr, was ist ein Menschenkind,
> Daß du sein Heil so schmerzlich suchest?
> Ein Wurm, den du verfluchest,
> Wenn Höll und Satan um ihn sind,
> Doch auch dein Sohn, den Seel und Geist
> Aus Liebe seinen Erben heißt.

> O Lord, what is a child of humankind
> That you seek his salvation so painfully?
> A worm, that you curse
> While hell and Satan surround him,
> But even your son, whom soul and spirit,
> Out of love, call their inheritance.

This is the moment to weave in a small part of the Gospel reading for the feast day (Luke 2:14): "Ehre sei Gott in der Höhe und Friede auf Erden und den Menschen ein Wohlgefallen" (Glory to God in the highest and peace on Earth and goodwill to men). To attach a distinctly musical text here would seem obvious; Lehms rhymes, roughly and not exactly with inspiration:

> Wacht auf, ihr Adern und ihr Glieder,
> Und singt dergleichen Freudenlieder,
> Die unserm Gott gefällig sein.
> Und ihr, ihr andachtsvollen Saiten,
> Sollt ihm ein solches Lob bereiten,
> Dabei sich Herz und Geist erfreun.

Awaken, you veins and you limbs,
And sing the sort of joyful songs
As are pleasing to our God.
And you, you strings full of devotion,
Shall prepare for him such praise
As heart and spirit delight.

The fifth strophe from Kaspar Füger's hymn *Wir Christenleut* (We Christian people) closes the cantata libretto.

Of the three biblical verses in his text, Bach set only the middle one to newly composed music: the passage from Isaiah "Dir, Herr, ist niemand gleich" appears as a brief recitative for bass with sharply defined motives in the accompanying strings. In the two other cases, Bach drew upon existing compositions. For the text belonging to the Christmas story from the Gospel of Luke, "Ehre sei Gott in der Höhe," Bach drew upon the duet "Virga Jesse Floruit," one of the four inserted movements for Christmas from his Magnificat in E-flat Major BWV 243.1, composed in 1723. Aside from the transposition from A major to F major and the resulting changes in setting (soprano and tenor appear in place of soprano and bass), the piece appears to have undergone only very minor changes. This is fortunate, since the Latin first version of the duet is only partially preserved but clearly can be reliably reconstructed due to its very minor deviations from the cantata version. Bach acquired the festive, broadly conceived opening movement, "Unser Mund sei voll Lachens," from the overture from his Orchestral Suite in D Major BWV 1068. In its fast, fugal, concerto-like middle section, he partly inserted newly composed vocal parts and partly formed them from excerpts of the quick, animated parts for strings and oboes. The addition of flutes, as well as trumpets and drums, obligatory for a feast day, required a bit more compositional investment. From all appearances, neither instrumental group was envisaged in the original version of the orchestral suite. Certainly, neither instrumental group appeared in the original orchestral suite version, the trumpets and tympani at least not in the form they had in the cantata.

In addition to the simple closing chorale, the three arias are newly composed: the introverted "Ihr Gedanken und ihr Sinnen" for tenor and two concertante transverse flutes; the rueful "Ach Herr was ist ein Menschenkind" for alto and obbligato oboe d'amore, which characterizes "Höll und Satan" (Hell and Satan) through increasing chromaticism in its middle section; and the heroic, extroverted "Wach auf, ihr Adern und ihr Glieder" for bass and virtuoso trumpet.

CHAPTER 5

Bach's Fourth Year at Leipzig from the First Sunday after Trinity 1726 to Trinity Sunday 1727

Brich dem Hungrigen dein Brot
BWV 39 / BC A 96
First Sunday after Trinity, June 23, 1726

As was customary for the era, the contents of this cantata are closely connected to the Gospel reading for the Sunday after Trinity, the parable of the rich man and the pauper Lazarus in Luke 16. However, due to a remarkable misunderstanding, for decades the cantata was regarded as "political" music, as a kind of commentary by Bach on events in Leipzig during his time there. It was the Dresden musicologist Rudolf Wustmann who put this idea forward. In a presentation entitled "Bachs Musik im Gottesdienst" (Bach's music in worship) to a church choral association convention in Dessau in 1909, Wustmann carefully ventured the suggestion that Bach might have composed the large, beautiful cantata for a "great celebration of Protestant charity" on June 15, 1732. Rudolf Wustmann may have gotten the idea for this hypothesis from a publication by his father, Gustav Wustmann, Leipzig librarian and director of the city archive. In 1889 the elder Wustmann published an essay in an anthology, *Quellen zur Geschichte Leipzigs* (Sources for the history of Leipzig), in which he reproduced numerous extracts from a handwritten chronicle by a certain Johann Salomon Riemer.[1] A part of this text is concerned with a group known as the Salzburg Emigrants, whose fate was closely bound to a late Counter-Reformation edict by Archbishop Leopold Ernst von Firmian of Salzburg that required Lutheran inhabitants to convert to Catholicism or leave the country. As a result of the edict, almost twenty thousand people emigrated in 1731 and 1732, many of them seeking a new homeland in the thinly settled eastern provinces of Prussia. On their journey to the North, several refugee caravans stopped in Leipzig.

This placed the city in a particularly unenviable position. In 1697 the Saxon elector, Friedrich August I, had converted to Catholicism in service of his effort to gain the Polish crown. Leipzig, at the time a stronghold of Lutheran orthodoxy, felt itself increasingly called upon to take the sensitivities of the sovereign into consideration in order to preserve a certain measure of independence. Although the Salzburg Emigrants were shown great compassion by city, church, and citizenry, the authorities avoided issuing an official greeting because, as an official report reads, "Leipzig is under rulers who profess the Catholic religion, which our Salzburg Emigrants have abandoned."[2]* Nevertheless, it can be neither confirmed nor refuted that the cantata *Brich dem Hungrigen dein Brot* BWV 39 (Break your bread with the hungry) could have been performed on the first Sunday after Trinity in 1732. In any case, Bach cannot have designated the work for this special occasion; instead, the composition and first performance belong in 1726.[3] On the other hand, if one supposed that Bach scheduled a reperformance exactly six years later, with or without foreknowledge of the arrival of the exiles, then one would have to assume that he was confident that his choir at that time could master the tricky and challenging opening movement. In June 1732 this would not have been clear at all. For the faculty and students of Leipzig's St. Thomas School, it was the end of an era marked by unrest and inadequate space situations caused by the extensive renovation of the school building.

If, despite this long-held belief, Bach did not mean his cantata for the Salzburger Emigrants, the text has even less to do with that external circumstance. It appears in a cantata text cycle printed in Meiningen in 1704; one must wonder whether the author is to be sought in that southwestern Thuringian capital.

The layout of the cantata libretti in the anonymous annual cycle is in many cases similar to that of our cantata: at the beginning, a passage from the Hebrew Bible, followed by recitatives and arias; a New Testament passage is followed by recitatives and arias, with a chorale strophe at the end.** In this case, two verses from Isaiah 58 provide the evocative introduction:

> Brich dem Hungrigen dein Brot, und die, so im Elend sind, führe ins Haus. So du einen nackend siehst, so kleide ihn, und entzeuch dich nicht von deinem Fleisch. Alsdann wird dein Licht hervorbrechen wie die Morgenröte, und deine Besserung wird schnell wachsen, und deine Gerechtigkeit wird vor dir hergehen, und die Herrlichkeit des Herrn wird dich zu sich nehmen. (7–8)

Break your bread with the hungry, and those who are in misery, take into your house. Should you see a naked person, clothe him, and do not withdraw yourself from those of your own flesh. And then your light will break forth like the dawn, and your recovery will quickly increase, and your righteousness will go before you, and the glory of the Lord will take you to itself.

Building on these words, the unknown librettist formulates an elaborate admonition to active compassion and empathy in recitatives and arias. In the first recitative, the unknown poet, a lover of the Alexandrine verse form, indulges his predilection for long lines:

> Der reiche Gott wirft seinen Überfluß
> Auf uns, die wir ohn ihn auch nicht den Odem haben.
> Sein ist es, was wir sind; er gibt nur den Genuß,
> Doch nicht, daß uns allein nur seine Schätze laben.
>
> Bounteous God casts his abundance
> Upon us, who without him do not even have breath.
> It is his, what we are; he gives only pleasure,
> Yet not that his treasures should bless us alone.

At the close the text reads:

> Barmherzigkeit, die auf dem Nächsten ruht,
> Kann mehr als alle Gab ihm an das Herze dringen.
>
> Compassion that falls upon one's neighbor
> Can, more than all gifts, penetrate his heart.

The associated aria generalizes these ideas:

> Seinem Schöpfer noch auf Erden
> Nur im Schatten ähnlich werden,
> Ist im Vorschmack selig sein.
> Sein Erbarmen nachzuahmen,
> Streuet hier des Segens Samen,
> Den wir dorten bringen ein.
>
> To become like one's creator still on Earth,
> Though only in shadowy similarity,
> Is a foretaste of blessedness.
> To emulate his mercy
> Sows the seeds of blessing here,
> Which we will harvest there.

The New Testament passage comes from Hebrews 13: "Wohlzutun und mitzuteilen vergesset nicht; denn solche Opfer gefallen Gott wohl" (16; To do good and to share, do not forget, for such offerings please God well). The ensuing aria puts these possibilities into perspective:

> Höchster, was ich habe,
> Ist nur deine Gabe.
> Wenn vor deinem Angesicht
> Ich schon mit dem deinen
> Dankbar wollt erscheinen,
> Willst du doch kein Opfer nicht.

> Highest, whatever I have,
> Is only your gift.
> If, before your visage,
> I should, with all that is yours,
> Wish to appear thankful,
> You still want no offering.

The personal mode of address and the promise to exercise compassion continue in the recitative, once again in Alexandrines:

> Wie soll ich dir o Herr! denn sattsamlich vergelten,
> Was du an Leib und Seel mir hast zugut getan?

> How should I, O Lord! sufficiently repay you
> For what you have done for me in body and soul?

The long text concludes:

> Ich bringe, was ich kann, Herr! laß es dir behagen,
> Daß ich, was du versprichst, auch einst davon mög tragen.

> I bring what I can, Lord! may it please you
> That I may one day gain from it what you promise.

A strophe from David Denicke's 1648 hymn *Kommt, laßt euch den Herren lehren* (Come, let the Lord teach you) summarizes the thread of ideas:

> Selig sind, die aus Erbarmen
> Sich annehmen fremder Not,
> Sind mitleidig mit den Armen,
> Bitten treulich für sie Gott.
> Die behülflich sind mit Rat,
> Auch womöglich mit der Tat,

Werden wieder Hülf empfangen
Und Barmherzigkeit erlangen.

Blessed are they who, out of mercy,
Attend to the affliction of others,
Who are compassionate with the poor,
Pray faithfully for them to God.
Those who are helpful with their counsel
And, where possible in action,
Will in turn receive help
And themselves gain mercy.

The richness of text in the opening passage from Isaiah informs the conception of the opening movement in Bach's composition. The complex movement, 218 measures in length, begins with an instrumental section whose "broken" manner can certainly be understood in relation to the gestures of the breaking and distribution of bread. As the instruments are joined by the choir, the first paragraph of the Isaiah passage is further developed. The gravity and seriousness of "Brich dem Hungrigen dein Brot" call for and receive a fugal treatment in the central part of this first section. The rest of the text, beginning with "So du einen nackend siehest," is instead treated line by line, in the manner of a motet, and is more withdrawn compared to the fugal texture. The same gradation between fugal and chordal textures defines the closing section, beginning at the shift to $\frac{3}{8}$ meter. In contrast to the other text passages, the opening and closing sections are powerfully emphasized by their fugal treatment: "Alsdann wird dein Licht hervorbrechen, wie die Morgenröte," as well as "und die Herrlichkeit des Herrn wird dich zu sich nehmen."

The first recitative for bass, simply declaimed, is followed by the alto aria "Seinem Schöpfer noch auf Erden." It is a truly characteristic movement in Bach's cantatas, in which the buoyant charm of a dance type, here situated between minuet and passepied, is united with strict counterpoint to lend the text a particular emphasis.

With the New Testament passage, Bach begins the second half of the cantata, customarily performed after the sermon in Leipzig—and, with this division, he deviates from the intentions of the librettist. The text "Wohlzutun und mitzuteilen" is given to the bass, the *vox Christi*, which, as so often, is accompanied only by the basso continuo. Through a subtle technique of repetition and variation, voice and accompaniment strive to clarify the gravity of the biblical passage. A lighter contrast is afforded by the setting of the aria "Höchster, was ich habe" (Highest, whatever I have) with soprano and obbligato recorders. The last recitative, with its quite personal expression, is embedded in chords in the strings before the four-part concluding chorale on the melody *Freu dich sehr, o meine Seele* (Rejoice greatly, O my soul) leads to a confident conclusion.

---

*Casper (1982).
**Blankenburg (1977); Schulze (2002a).

Es erhub sich ein Streit
BWV 19 / BC A 180

St. Michael's Day, September 29, 1726

Bach's cantata *Es erhub sich ein Streit* BWV 19 (A battle arose) was composed in 1726 for St. Michael's Day on September 29. Our cantata has well-known predecessors by Heinrich Schütz and by Bach's uncle Johann Christoph Bach, an organist active in Eisenach and a "great and expressive composer," as a family chronicle describes him.[4] All begin with the same passage from the Revelation of St. John. It is uncertain whether Johann Sebastian was aware of the Schutz composition, although he could have encountered it during his school days at Lüneburg, presuming he had access to the music collection of the St. Michael's School. We are better informed as to his knowledge of the Michaelmas work by the Great Eisenacher, Johann Christoph Bach. Sebastian Bach's second-oldest son, Carl Philipp Emanuel, wrote about this to the Göttingen music historian Johann Nikolaus Forkel in the late summer of 1775 while sending several musical items from the Ancient Bach Archive (Alt-Bachisches Archiv): "The twenty-two-part work is a masterpiece. My blessed father performed it on one occasion in church, and everyone was astonished by its effect. I do not have enough singers here; otherwise, I would gladly perform it one day."[5]

That such expressive and elaborately set works for St. Michael's Day existed has to do with the particular nature of the feast day. In the words of Friedrich Smend, one of the most important Bach researchers of the twentieth century, the church announced:

> According to Holy Scripture, hell and the devil were disempowered by Christ's death and resurrection; that in the end times the ultimate destruction of the Antichrist shall first occur; that therefore today on earth the battle rages between Godly and ungodly forces. . . . The church in Bach's time, and in particular Johann Sebastian himself, were aware of this battle

and celebrated the day of the archangel Michael as a feast of triumph, at which at the same time God was called upon for assistance through angelic forces in the struggles of this life. However, the idea of the angels directed one's attention to one's own death; indeed, Jesus himself had said in the parable that the pauper Lazarus was carried to the bosom of Abraham by the angels. Beside this peaceful image of dying there appears the awesome depiction of the prophet Elijah, who travels toward heaven in his chariot pulled by fiery steeds. To be borne by angels to the same place, where the *Ecclesia triumphans* (church triumphant) celebrated, was therefore the prayer of every Christian during this period.

It is unusual that the relevant biblical text is found not in the Gospel reading for the day but in the Epistle. The twelfth chapter of the Revelation of St. John reads:

> Und es erhub sich ein Streit im Himmel: Michael und seine Engel stritten mit dem Drachen; und der Drache stritt und seine Engel, und siegten nicht, auch ward ihre Stätte nicht mehr gefunden im Himmel. Und es ward ausgeworfen der große Drache, die alte Schlange, die da heißt der Teufel und Satanas, der die ganze Welt verführt, und ward geworfen auf die Erde, und seine Engeln wurden auch dahin geworfen. Und ich hörte eine große Stimme, die sprach im Himmel: Nun ist das Heil und die Kraft und das Reich unsers Gottes geworden und die Macht seines Christus, weil der Verkläger unserer Brüder verworfen ist, der sie verklagte Tag und Nacht vor Gott. Und sie haben überwunden durch des Lammes Blut und durch das Wort ihres Zeugnisses und haben ihr Leben nicht geliebt bis an den Tod. Darum freuet euch, ihr Himmel und die darin wohnen! (7–12)

> And a battle arose in Heaven: Michael and his angels battled with the dragon; and the dragon fought and his angels, and did not prevail, also their home was no longer found in heaven. And the great dragon was thrown out, the old snake, who there is called the Devil and Satan, who seduced the entire world, and was thrown upon the earth, and his angels were also thrown there. And I heard a great voice, that spoke in heaven: Now is the salvation and the power and the kingdom of our God, and the authority of his Christ, for the accuser of our brother is cast out, which accuses them before our God day and night. And they have overcome because of the blood of the Lamb and through the word of their testimony, and they did not love their life even unto death. Therefore rejoice, you heavens, and those who live in them!

The cantata text composed by Bach follows the beginning of this epistle, but in rhymed paraphrase, with the exception of the first line:

> Es erhub sich ein Streit.
> Der rasende Schlange, der höllische Drache,
> Stürmt wider den Himmel mit wütender Rache.
> Aber Michael bezwingt,
> Und die Schar, die ihn umringt,
> Stürzt des Satans Grausamkeit.
>
> A battle arose.
> The raging snake, the hellish dragon,
> Storms against the heavens with furious vengeance.
> But Michael conquers,
> And the army that surrounds him
> Topples the savagery of Satan.

The author of this rhymed paraphrase cannot be identified with certainty. The text for Bach's cantata has a somewhat peculiar and convoluted history. Many of its formulations are found in a seven-strophe poem with the title *Erbauliche Gedancken auf das Fest Michaelis* (Edifying thoughts on St. Michael's Day), which the Leipzig occasional poet Christian Friedrich Henrici published in his *Sammlung Erbaulicher Gedancken über und auf die gewöhnlichen Sonn- und Fest-Tage* (Collection of edifying thoughts about and on the usual Sundays and feast days). However, Henrici's poem was not intended for use as a cantata libretto; instead, it was to be sung to the melody *Allein Gott in der Höh sei Ehr* (Honor only to God on high). It is one of countless efforts to enrich and update the contents of contemporary hymn collections.

This source text was reshaped to become a cantata libretto with recitatives and arias, following in principle the procedure so often seen in Bach's chorale cantatas.[6] However, in this case the revision avoids the characteristic retention of the opening and closing strophes of the chorale text. Instead, the cantata text begins with the rhymed paraphrase of the Epistle's beginning just described. It closes with the ninth strophe from the 1620 chorale *Freu dich sehr o meine Seele*, whose text begins:

> Laß dein Engel mit mir fahren
> Auf Elias Wagen rot
> Und mein Seele wohl bewahren,
> Wie Laz'rum nach seinem Tod.
>
> Let your angel journey with me
> On Elijah's red chariot
> And preserve my soul well
> Like Lazarus after his death.

The second movement of the cantata text is also a paraphrase of part of the Epistle:

> Gottlob, der Drachen liegt.
> Der unerschaffne Michael
> Und seiner Engel Heer
> Hat ihn besiegt.
> Dort liegt er in der Finsternis
> Mit Ketten angebunden,
> Und seine Stätte wird nicht mehr
> Im Himmelreich gefunden.
>
> Praise God, the dragon lies.
> The uncreated Michael
> And his host of angels
> Have conquered him.
> There he lies in the darkness
> Bound with chains,
> And his home will no longer
> Be found in the kingdom of heaven.

With the third movement, we are on solid ground with respect to authorship. It matches Christian Friedrich Henrici's St. Michael's Day text of 1725 word for word:

> Gott schickt uns Mahanaim zu;
> Wir stehen oder gehen,
> So können wir in sichrer Ruh
> Vor unsern Feinden stehen.
> Es lagert sich, so nah als fern,
> Um uns der Engel unsers Herrn
> Mit Feuer, Roß und Wagen.
>
> God sends Mahanaim to us;
> Whether we stand or go
> We can in secure repose
> Stand before our enemies.
> Encamped around us, near and far,
> Is the angel of our Lord
> With fire, steed, and chariot.[7]

In part, the image of the barricade of wagons refers to Psalm 34:7, which reads, "Der Engel des Herrn lagert sich um die her, so ihn fürchten, und hilft ihnen aus" (The angel of the Lord encamps around those who fear him and helps them out), and partly to 2 Kings 2:11, depicting the separation of the prophets Elijah and Elisha: "And as they went with one another and talked, see, there came a fiery chariot with fiery horses, they separated the two from each other, and Elijah went up in a whirlwind to heaven." The first line of the aria refers to Jacob's encounter with the angels, as described in Moses 32:1–2, with the mention of Mahanaim: "Jacob, however, went on his way, and the angels of God met him. And as he saw them, he said: This is the army of God, and called the place Mahanaim." This name can mean not only "army camp" but also "two armies." In 1711 Erdmann Neumeister, later the senior pastor in Hamburg, created the following cantata text:

> So laß auf beiden Seiten
> Die Mahanaim mich begleiten.
> Wird mir von Feinden nachgestellt;
> So laß die Feuer-Roß' und Wagen
> Ihr Lager um mich schlagen.
>
> So let on both sides
> The Mahanaim accompany me.
> Should I be chased by enemies;
> Then may the fire steeds and chariots
> Close their camp around me.

He had used similar expressions in a cantata libretto in 1702. There is every reason to suppose that Henrici, nearly thirty years younger, borrowed extensively from the older poet.

The same applies to the fourth movement of the cantata, a recitative whose text begins, "Was ist der schnöde Mensch, das Erdenkind" (What is this vile person, the child of Earth), in which the angels are described as a protecting, vigilant, and defending army. On the other hand, no model for the fifth movement, an aria in which the angels are sought to aid in praising God, can be found in either Neumeister or Henrici:

> Bleibt, ihr Engel, bleibt bei mir.
> Führet mich auf beiden Seiten,
> Daß mein Fuß nicht möge gleiten.
> Aber lernt mich auch allhier
> Euer großes Heilig singen
> Und dem Höchsten Dank zu singen.
>
> Abide, you angels, abide with me.
> Lead me on both sides,
> That my step might never slip.

But train me even here
To sing your great "Holy"
And sing thanksgiving to the most high.

The problematic language and awkward rhyme structure in the last three lines point to a self-taught nonprofessional. We cannot say whether the cantor of St. Thomas took pen in hand himself in this instance or if he asked someone nearby for the still missing aria text. In contrast, the sixth movement, the last recitative before the closing chorale, whose text begins, "Laßt uns das Angesicht / Der frommen Engel lieben" (Let us adore the countenance / Of the devout angel), proves to be a conflation of two text strophes from Henrici's poem of 1725.

Bach's composition begins suddenly, in the apocalyptic tumult of battle, with thick, fugue-like attacks of hammering repeated tones and ravaging passages intertwined with one another and above the whole the gleaming high trumpets, voices of war. Their limited tonal ambitus imposes boundaries on the harmonic unfolding; even more in that regard occurs in the middle section, with vivid language unfurling a series of images of the dangerously chaotic scene. With the return of the opening section and its text, "Es erhub sich ein Streit," the architecture of the overall movement is completed, on the one hand, but it becomes clear that there can be no talk of a plotlike "course of action," on the other hand.

A brief bass recitative is followed by the first aria, "Gott schickt uns Mahanaim zu," for soprano and two oboi d'amore. The soft coloration of the woodwinds suggests warmth and intimacy; the dense, attentive texture with abundant imitation and parallel thirds and sixths suggests security and assurance. The string-accompanied tenor recitative, with its air of self-accusation, brings this idyll to an end. But the aria "Bleibt, ihr Engel, bleibt bei mir" leads into a new world of enchantment. From beginning to end it is dominated by the hovering, $\frac{6}{8}$ Siciliano rhythm familiar from the Christmas Oratorio, associated with the angels, begun by the string instruments and the basso continuo and taken over by the tenor soloist. In addition, a high trumpet sounds the melody "Herzlich lieb hab ich dich, o Herr" (Sincerely I love you, O Lord). The aria's free text is strongly associated with the third chorale strophe:

Ach Herr, laß dein lieb Engelein
Am letzten Tag die Seele mein
In Abrahams Schoß tragen

Ah Lord, may your dear little angel
On my last day carry this soul of mine
To the bosom of Abraham.

The relatively large number of chorale lines, the slow tempo of the aria, and the virtually instrumental demands upon the voice make this movement a true challenge for the singer. This seems to have been a problem in Bach's time as well, since there are certain indications that at the first performance both of the arias for tenor were omitted. Toward the end things become less challenging, with an uncomplicated soprano recitative and the joyful closing chorale, to which the brass once again lends a radiant brilliance.

Wer weiß, wie nahe mir mein Ende
BWV 27 / BC A 138

Sixteenth Sunday after Trinity, October 6, 1726

This cantata was composed in the autumn of 1726 for the sixteenth Sunday after Trinity. The Gospel reading for this Sunday is found in Luke 7:11–17 and gives the account of Jesus raising the boy at Nain from the dead:

> And it happened afterward that he went into a city called Nain; and his disciples went with him and many people. But as he came near the city gate, behold, a corpse was carried out who was the only son of his mother, and she was a widow, and many people of the city went with her. And as she saw the Lord, she cried to him, and he said to her: Do not cry! And he went close and touched the bier, and the bearers stood. And he spoke: Young man, I say to you, stand up! And the dead one arose and began to speak; and he gave him to his mother. And there came upon everyone a great fear, and they praised God and spoke: A great prophet has appeared among us, and God has visited his people! And this talk of him was heard in the entire land of Judea and in all surrounding lands.

The unknown author of our cantata's text takes up this reading and its interpretive tradition and concentrates on fear of death and preparation for it, salvation, longing for heaven, and a blessed departure from the world. The libretto begins with a chorale strophe interleaved with freely versified lines of recitative, thus reviving the tradition of Bach's chorale cantata annual cycle. The chorale is a funeral hymn written by Ämilie Juliane, countess of Schwarzburg-Rudolstadt, in 1686. Its first strophe reads:

> Wer weiß, wie nahe mir mein Ende?
> Hin geht die Zeit, her kommt der Tod,
> Ach wie geschwinde und behende
> Kann kommen meine Todesnot!
> Mein Gott, ich bitt durch Christi Blut,
> Machs nur mit meinem Ende gut!

Who knows, how near to me is my end?
Time goes forth, death approaches.
Ah, how speedily and agilely
My agony of death can come!
My God, I pray through the blood of Christ,
Only make my end good!

The interpolation of recitatives creates a complex structure:

Wer weiß, wie nahe mir mein Ende?
    Das weiß der liebe Gott allein,
    Ob meine Wallfahrt auf der Erden
    Kurz oder länger möge sein.
Hin geht die Zeit, her kommt der Tod,
    Und endlich kommt es doch so weit,
    Daß sie zusammentreffen werden.
Ach wie geschwinde und behende
Kann kommen meine Todesnot!
    Wer weiß, ob heute nicht
    Der Mund die letzten Worte spricht.
    Drum bet ich allezeit:
Mein Gott, ich bitt durch Christi Blut,
Machs nur mit meinem Ende gut!

Who knows how near to me is my end?
    Dear God alone knows that,
    Whether my pilgrimage on Earth
    Might be short or longer.
Time goes forth, death approaches,
    And at last it will come so far
    That they will meet together.
Ah, how speedily and agilely
My agony of death can come!
    Who knows whether or not today
    My mouth will speak its final words.
    Therefore, I pray for all time:
My God, I pray by the blood of Christ,
Only make my end good!

The first recitative concerns a blessed death as the goal of life. At its close it reads:

Drum leb ich allezeit
Zum Grabe fertig und bereit,
Und was das Werk der Hände tut,

> Ist gleichsam, ob ich sicher wüßte,
> Daß ich noch heute sterben müßte;
> Denn Ende gut, macht alles gut!

> Therefore, I live at all times
> Ready and prepared for the grave,
> And what the work of my hands does,
> Is as if I surely knew
> That even today I had to die;
> For a good end makes everything good!

The associated aria harks back to an idea that appeared shortly after 1700 in the cantata libretti of Erdmann Neumeister. Neumeister's aria begins:

> Willkommen! Will ich sagen,
> Sobald der Tod ans Bette tritt.
> Er bringt den Himmelswagen
> Zu meiner frohen Abfahrt mit.

> Welcome! I will say
> As soon as death steps to my bed.
> He brings along the heavenly wagon
> For my happy departure.

In our cantata, this becomes:

> Willkommen! Will ich sagen,
> Wenn der Tod ans Bette tritt.
> Fröhlich will ich folgen, wenn er ruft,
> In die Gruft,
> Alle meine Plagen
> Nehm ich mit.

> Welcome! I will say
> When death steps to my bed.
> Happily I will follow when he calls
> Into the tomb.
> All my troubles
> I will take with me.

Flight from the world, longing for death, and, in particular, separation from the vanities of earthly existence: these characterize the second recitative-aria pair. The recitative reads:

> Ach wer doch schon im Himmel wär!
> Ich habe lust zu scheiden

> Und mit dem Lamm,
> Das aller Frommen Bräutigam,
> Mich in der Seligkeit zu weiden.
> Flügel her!
> Ach wer doch schon im Himmel wär!
>
> Ah, were one already in heaven!
> I have desire to depart
> And with the Lamb,
> The bridegroom of all the devout,
> To pasture myself in salvation.
> Wings, come!
> Ah, were one already in heaven!

The aria begins with the traditional farewell of the soul:

> Gute Nacht, du Weltgetümmel!
> Itzt mach ich mit dir Beschluß;
> Ich steh schon mit einem Fuß
> Bei dem lieben Gott im Himmel.
>
> Good night, you worldly tumult!
> I now make an end with you;
> I already stand with one foot
> Beside dear God in heaven.

The first strophe of Johann Georg Albinus's hymn *Welt, ade! Ich bin dein müde* (World, adieu! I am weary of you) concludes the libretto and summarizes its train of ideas.

In the vocal part of the opening movement, Bach's composition combines the simply harmonized melody *Wer nur den lieben Gott läßt walten* (Whoever only lets dear God rule) with expressive, concentrated recitative episodes and, in the instrumental realm, wide-ranging, bell-like basses, as well as rapid chord progressions in the strings in resolute descending motion with short, pleading motives and sighing passages in the oboes. The greeting of welcome in the first aria appears with an unusually songlike melody in the voice, as well as the darkly tinged obbligato part in the oboe da caccia. When the cantata was reperformed, a second obbligato part for organ was implemented. By all appearances it seems originally to have been meant for cembalo. Even more plausible, not in terms of range but with regard to key and instrumental idiom, would be an obbligato lute or similar plucked instrument due to the timbral symbolism associated with its manner of playing. In that light, the cembalo—and, later, the organ—would perhaps not have provided an entirely satisfactory replacement.

The second aria is characterized by an abrupt change from the "good-night greeting of the soul," with its calm harmonies and slow dance rhythms of the sarabande, to the banal depiction of the "worldly tumult" to be left behind. Remarkably, the aria is given not to the soprano, the soul's usual personification, but to the bass. For the closing chorale, instead of the familiar simple four-part texture we have a somewhat more challenging five-part composition by Johann Rosenmüller, who composed it in 1649 for the burial of a young daughter of the Leipzig archdeacon Abraham Teller and performed it again three years later for a similar memorial. Finding this work, nearly three-quarters of a century old, caused Bach little trouble; the *Neu Leipziger Gesangbuch* by Gottfried Vopelius of 1689 contained a recent reprint.

Ich will den Kreuzstab gerne tragen
BWV 56 / BC A 146

Nineteenth Sunday after Trinity, October 27, 1726

From today's perspective, Bach's *Kreuzstab Cantata* occupies a certain position of privilege in his vocal works not only musically but also with regard to its text. It originated in the autumn of 1726 in close temporal proximity to several other solo cantatas for the late Trinity period. In contrast to these, however, it is the only one that bears the original designation *cantata*. Its assignment to the nineteenth Sunday of Trinity suggests a relation to the Gospel reading of that Sunday, which gives the account in Matthew 9:1–8 of Jesus's healing of the palsy-stricken person.

> And he entered the boat and crossed back over and came into his own city. And behold, they brought him a man sick with palsy, lying on a bed. As now Jesus saw their faith, he spoke to the one sick with palsy: Be of good cheer, my son; your sins are forgiven. And see, several of the lawyers spoke among themselves: This man blasphemes God! However, as Jesus saw their thoughts, he said: Why do you think such evil in your hearts? What is easier to say: Your sins are forgiven, or to say: Stand up and walk? But so that you know that the Son of Man has the power to forgive sins on earth (he said to the one sick with palsy): Stand up, pick up your bed, and go home! And he stood up and went home. As the people saw that, they marveled and praised God, who had given such power to men.

The unknown librettist of our cantata relies only in part upon the Gospel reading.[8] He entirely avoids the account of the healing of the sick and instead places all the more importance upon certainty of faith and the forgiveness of sins. The origin of the title line has caused headaches for Bach researchers. It undoubtedly references the first movement of a solo cantata libretto written by Erdmann Neumeister in 1702 for performance at the court of Weissenfels: "Ich will den Kreuzweg gerne gehen: / Ich weiß, da führt mich Gottes Hand" (I will gladly go the way of the cross: / I know God's hand leads me there). Documentation for the word "Kreuzstab," on the other hand, is not easy to produce, even if recent research has made us aware that the concept has a firm place in Catholic tradition. In the Lutheran hymnal, however, the word "Kreuzstab" appears only rarely. The following strophe is found in Paul Gerhardt's hymn text "Gib dich zufrieden und sei stille" (Be contented and be still) of 1666:

> Es kann und mag nicht anders werden,
> Alle Menschen müßen leiden.
> Was webt und lebet auf der Erden
> Kann das Unglück nicht vermeiden.
> Des Kreuzes Stab schlägt unsre Lenden
> Bis in das Grab, da wird sichs enden.
> Gib dich zufrieden!

> It can and may not be different,
> All people must suffer.
> Whatever moves and lives upon the earth
> Cannot avoid misfortune.
> The cross's beam strikes our loins
> Until the grave, then it will end.
> Be contented!

Beyond Bach's profound knowledge of the Lutheran hymnal in general, his knowledge of this hymn in particular is seen in the fact that he entered it twice in the 1725 notebook he prepared for his wife, Anna Magdalena. Another instance is provided by the hymn *Ach Gott, wird denn mein Leid* (Ah God, will then my suffering), which appears in hymnals beneath the heading "Trost-Lied eines betrübten Creuz-Trägers" (Song of consolation of a sorrowful cross bearer) and which refers to verses in Psalm 77. One strophe reads:

> Du Herr probirest mich
> Mit deinem Kreuzesstabe,
> Ob ich auch werde dich
> Fest lieben bis zum Grabe;
> Ob ich auch, liebster Gott,
> Dir werde treu verbleiben,

> Und nimmer keine Not
> Von dir mich lassen treiben.
>
> You, Lord, you test me
> With your cross's beam,
> Whether I will also love you
> Truly until the grave,
> Whether I also, dear God,
> Will remain ever true to you
> And never let distress
> Drive me away from you.

Here again, a connection to Bach is easily produced: the chorale is found in what is known as the Wagner Hymnal. It appeared in eight volumes in Leipzig in 1697, it is known to have been in Bach's possession, and he is known to have drawn upon it in other contexts.

In the cantata text, the word "Kreuzstab" refers not only to carrying the cross but also to pilgrimage, the way to heaven:[9]

> Ich will den Kreuzstab gerne tragen,
> Er kommt von Gottes lieber Hand,
> Der führet mich nach meinen Plagen
> Zu Gott, in das gelobte Land.
> Da leg ich den Kummer auf einmal ins Grab,
> Da wischt mir die Tränen mein Heiland selbst ab.
>
> I will gladly carry the cross's beam,
> It comes from God's loving hand,
> It leads me, after my torments,
> To God in the promised land.
> There I lay my troubles all at once in the grave,
> There my savior himself wipes my tears away.

In changing the meter in the strophe's last two lines, the librettist once again follows the example of a cantata libretto published in 1702 by Erdmann Neumeister. It remains uncertain whether this closing expression refers to the Revelation of St. John, which in two places (7:17, 21:4) reads, "Gott wird abwischen alle Tränen von ihren Augen" (God will wipe away all tears from their eyes), or to Isaiah 25:8, which reads, "Der Herr wird die Tränen von allen Angesichtern abwischen und wird aufheben die Schmach seines Volks in allen Landen" (The Lord God will wipe the tears from all faces and will take away the rebuke of his people in all lands). In the cantata's second movement, a recitative, the librettist takes up the familiar trope of the seafarer and compares the "Wandel auf der Welt" (journey in the world) to a sea voyage, whereby cross and tribulation appear as dangerous waves and the mercy of God as a life-saving anchor. The promise "Ich will dich nicht verlassen noch versäumen" (I will not forsake or abandon you) is found in this wording in Hebrews 13:5, but it essentially goes back to an account in Joshua.[10] Near the end of the recitative, the line "So tret ich aus dem Schiff in meine Stadt" (I shall step off the ship into my city) recalls the beginning of the Sunday Gospel reading.

The second aria proves to be a paraphrase of a verse from Isaiah 40: "Die auf den Herrn harren, kriegen neue Kraft, daß sie auffahren mit flügeln wie Adler, daß sie laufen und nicht matt werden, daß sie wandeln und nicht müde werden" (31; They who await upon the Lord receive new strength, that they soar up with wings like eagles, that they run and do not faint, that they walk and do not grow weary). In the aria text, this reads:

> Endlich, endlich wird mein Joch
> Wieder von mir weichen müßen.
> Da krieg ich in dem Herren Kraft,
> Da hab ich Adlers Eigenschaft,
> Da fahr ich auf von dieser Erden
> Und laufe sonder matt zu werden.
> O gscheh es heute noch.

> Finally, finally, my yoke must
> Fall away from me again.
> Then I shall in the Lord gain strength,
> Then I shall have the eagle's nature,
> Then I shall soar aloft from this earth
> And run without becoming faint.
> O may it happen even today.

The last recitative begins with "Ich stehe fertig und bereit" (I stand ready and prepared), and it ends with "Wie wohl wird mir geschehn, / Wenn ich den Port der Ruhe werde sehn" (How good it will be for me / When I see the haven of rest) and immediately harks back to the opening aria: "Da leg ich den Kummer auf einmal ins Grab, / Da wischt mir die Tränen mein Heiland selbst ab." In closing, the sixth strophe of Johann Franck's 1653 hymn, "Du o schönes Weltgebäude" (You, O beautiful world building) encapsulates all the ideas of the entire cantata text, including the seafarer allegory:

> Komm, o Tod, du Schlafes Bruder,
> Komm und führe mich nur fort;

Löse meines Schiffleins Ruder,
Bringe mich an sichern Port!
Es mag, wer da will, dich scheuen,
Du kannst mich vielmehr erfreuen;
Denn durch dich komm ich herein
Zu dem schönsten Jesulein.

Come, O death, you brother of sleep,
Come and just lead me away;
Release my little ship's rudder,
Bring me to safe haven!
Let whoever wishes shun you,
You can instead delight me;
For through you I enter in
To the loveliest little Jesus.

This expressive libretto is entirely successful, conceptually as well as linguistically, and Bach's composition exhausts its potentialities in every conceivable way. In the opening movement, the composer juxtaposes descending, heavily burdened figures ridden with sighs against a theme that struggles to remain upright with virtually herculean effort. If the word "Kreuz" (cross) in the text is associated with a note with a sharp in front of it, this might be seen as somewhat naive symbolism. But it is surely more significant that this *Kreuz-Ton* (sharped note) is reached by a leap of an augmented interval, so that—exactly in the sense of the text—the exertion of energy and self-discipline is felt almost physically. In its conflict between exuberant forging ahead and softly submissive lament, the movement reaches its culmination at the text line "Da leg ich den Kummer auf einmal ins Grab" in a serene cheerfulness, like smiling through tears. The first recitative, with the allegory of the seafarer, is accompanied by wave-like tone-painting figures in the strings. At the line "Und wenn das wütenvolle Schäume sein Ende hat" (And when the raging surf comes to an end), the musical wave motion also ends, and serene chords accompany the line "So tret ich aus dem Schiff in meine Stadt."

The second aria is filled with an unbuttoned, joyous, concerted interplay between the obbligato oboe and the voice. The virtuosity demanded of the singer shows that Bach was dealing with a master of his craft. By all appearances, it was none other than Johann Christoph Samuel Lipsius, who began his studies at the University of Leipzig during Bach's first year as cantor, participated in Bach's church music as a bass and received a financial grant in return, and later became a member of the court chapel at Merseburg.* The virtuoso bass aria stands in sharp contrast to what came before, as well as what follows. The final recitative, accompanied by strings, refers back after only a few measures to the opening movement's conclusion, as suggested by the text. And only now does the enraptured "Da leg ich den Kummer auf einmal ins Grab" truly reach its conclusion—and with such intensity that the aria that follows runs the danger of seeming only like an intermezzo.

The concluding chorale movement, removed from everything of this world, needs no commentary. It is among the most perfect that Johann Sebastian Bach ever wrote.

*Schulze (1984a, esp. 49).

Vereinigte Zwietracht der wechselnden Saiten
BWV 207.1 / BC G 37

University of Leipzig, December 11, 1726

It is fairly certain that the homage cantata *Vereinigte Zwietracht der wechselnden Saiten* BWV 207.1 (Concordant discord of changing strings) owes its existence to a commission from a group of students at the University of Leipzig. The occasion was a promotion in the law faculty of the group's Leipzig alma mater. Gottlieb Kortte, born in 1698 in Beeskow Lausitz, earned a master's degree in 1720 after studying theology, philology, and jurisprudence. Four years later he had earned the title of doctor of canon and civil law at Frankfurt an der Oder, and in late 1726 he became a professor at the University of Leipzig. He delivered his inaugural address in Latin on December 11 of that year; it is reported that he must have spoken from memory, because he had been in such a hurry that he left his notes at home. It remains uncertain whether the twenty-eight-year-old actually appeared the absent-minded professor or whether he only faked his forgetfulness in order to display his capabilities in the proper light by delivering his disquisition from memory. Unfortunately, Kortte was granted only a brief period in his new position; death took him in April 1731. It was said that the "beacon of hope" of the faculty was "deeply mourned by the studious young, before whom he had stood to great applause, and all who knew his deep and thorough learning."

Eleven years after Kortte's death, a memoir extended to the citizenry of Dresden demonstrated what this loss meant for the university and its law faculty in particular.* Under the title *Thränen und Seuffzer wegen der Universität Leipzig* (Tears and sighs over the University of Leipzig), a private lecturer named Johann Gottlieb Reichel unsparingly criticized everything and everyone and hauled the legal faculty over the coals. Avarice and accumulation of responsibilities—or empire building—were, in his view, the reasons for the virtually unparalleled indifference of the professors and the decline of the faculty. The full professor Carl Otto Rechenberg in particular was shown no mercy. A quarter century earlier, he had attended Bach's examination of the organ in St. Paul's Church as representative of the university. Reichel wrote of him:

> Lord Privy Councilor Rechenberg is the chair and full professor of the law faculty and the superior expert on law, indeed, as learned and capable a man as can be found anywhere in the world, a man whom everyone talks about, a respected man who can accomplish more in an hour than others can in an entire day, all of which we must say in his honor. But my God! We could also say that he reads as little as Dr. Börner, and we cannot say which of these is the laziest. Before he became a professor he held a collegium now and then, but afterward, once he had achieved his goal of becoming a full professor, he reads nothing at all; if indeed he starts something, it's not as if he wants to read seriously but rather only pro forma in front of others, as if he had read it, though he only wanted to do so but did not actually do it, and how does it help us, in the four weeks that he reads, we will certainly not learn very much, and easily one hundred students leave Leipzig having heard him at most only two or three times, others have never had the good fortune to hear him even once. Shall we ask the reason, where indeed this astonishing laziness comes from? There is none other than this, that one has given himself entirely over to salaciousness, and that one views his profession as only a side job that one does not have to attend, and that brings in only six to eight hundred reichsthalers.

It goes on for pages this way. Gottfried Kortte, highly gifted but cut down in his prime, would certainly have been spared a scolding of this sort. The text of our homage cantata gives one a sense in several places what high hopes his colleagues had for him. The unknown librettist is not at all sparing with encomiums, suggestions, and admonitions from the mouths of the allegorical figures Fortune, Gratitude, Industry, and Honor, but only after the customary invitation to a happy gathering:

> Vereinigte Zwietracht der wechselnden Saiten,
> Der rollenden Pauken durchdringender Knall,
> Locket den lüstern Hörer herbei,
> Saget mit euren frohlockenden Tönen
> Und doppelt vermehrendem Schall
> Denen mir emsig ergebenden Söhnen,
> Was hier der Lohn der Tugend sei.

> Concordant discord of changing strings,
> The rolling drums' penetrating boom,
> Entice the pleasure-seeking listener hereby,
> Tell, with your exultant tones
> And doubly multiplied sound,
> To my sons, diligently devoted to me,
> What the reward for virtue here shall be.

The phrase "vereinigte Zwietracht" turns out to be the German version of the Latin *concordia discors*, found in Ovid's *Metamorphoses* as *discors concordia* and, in the seventeenth and eighteenth centuries, widely used as a motto for single compositions or entire work cycles. From this perspective it is not terribly significant that in March 1738, nearly twelve years after the homage cantata for Gottlieb Kortte was first performed, there was a Leipzig musical celebration for the name day of the Saxon prince elector beginning with the words:

> Ergetzender Wohlklang vereinigter Seyten,
> Der wechselnden Töne durchdringender Schall!
> Locket den lüsternen Hörer herbey.
>
> Delightful euphony of unified strings,
> The changing tones' penetrating sound!
> Entice the pleasure-seeking listener hereby.

Even so, the commonalities with the text set to music by Bach can scarcely be denied. When we recall that the author of the more recent libretto, Heinrich Gottlieb Schelhafer, in later life a professor in Hamburg, was studying law in Leipzig at the time in question (1726) and is known to have met the then new professor Kortte, we are tempted to suspect that he may have taken part in the congratulatory cantata, may have known its text, and might even be its author.[**]

The opening ensemble is followed by an extended recitative and aria voiced by the allegorical figure Diligence, who promises rich rewards for those following the stony path:

> Zieht euren Fuß nicht zurücke,
> Ihr, die ihr meinen Weg erwählt.
> Das Glücke mercket eure Schritte,
> Die Ehre zählt die sauren Tritte,
> Damit, daß nach vollbrachter Straße
> Euch werd in gleichem Übermaße
> Der Lohn von ihnen zugezählt.

> Do not draw back your foot,
> You who choose my path.
> Fortune takes note of your steps,
> Honor counts the painful treads
> So that, after the road has been completed,
> You will be paid in equal superfluity
> The reward for them.

Honor and Fortune join in with a dialogue and then unite their voices in a duet. Thereafter, Gratitude comes into play, first with a verbose recitative and then with an aria:

> Ätzet dieses Angedenken
> In den härtsten Marmor ein!
> Doch die Zeit verdirbt den Stein.
> Laßt vielmehr aus euren Taten
> Eures Lehrers Tun erraten.
> Kann man aus den Früchten lesen,
> Wie die Wurzel sei gewesen,
> Muß sie unvergänglich sein.

> Etch this commemoration
> In the hardest marble!
> Indeed, time erodes the stone.
> Instead, let from your deeds
> Your teacher's action be divined.
> If one can tell from the fruit
> What the root was like,
> It must then be everlasting.

Diligence, Honor, Fortune, and Gratitude each takes the floor in a recitative, after which, all together, a "Kortte lebe, Kortte blühe" (Long live Kortte, may Kortte flourish) introduces the finale. Here again, in the closing ensemble, the four allegorical figures step forward individually, Honor with "den mein Lorbeer unterstützt" (he whom my laurel favors), Fortune with "der mir selbst im Schoße sitzt" (he who sits in my own bosom), Diligence with "der durch mich stets höher steigt" (he who climbs ever higher through me), Gratitude with "der die Herzen zu sich neigt" (he who inclines our hearts to himself). The one so acclaimed must, as the closing text says,

> In ungezählten Jahren
> Stets geehrt in Segen stehn
> Und zwar wohl der Neider Scharen,
> Aber nicht der Feinde sehn.

> Must for countless years
> Stand ever honored in blessing
> And probably see crowds of the envious
> But not of enemies.

Unfortunately, Gottlieb Kortte was not granted "countless years," but the music composed and performed in his honor certainly was. The venture was probably financed by a collection taken among students. The result must have been quite a respectable sum, since otherwise the opulent setting of the opening and closing movements with trumpets, drums, flutes, oboes, and strings could not have been realized. With his strategy in the opening chorus, Bach created a remarkable combination of reduced workload and increased difficulty for himself. Reduced workload, because he brought into the cantata the second fast movement from his F-major concerto, known today as the First Brandenburg Concerto BWV 1046; increased difficulty, because he transposed it to D major, traded the pair of horns for trumpets and drums, and, in particular, with a scarcely imaginable degree of artistic craftsmanship, replaced the solo violino piccolo with a four-part choral texture. (The last word has not yet been spoken with regard to the possibility, occasionally ventured, that the concerto movement was actually the result of the revision of a vocal-instrumental ensemble work and that, in our cantata, Bach simply restored, mutatis mutandis, the original state of affairs.)***

In the middle of the cantata, Bach once again drew upon the concerto previously mentioned. After the duet for Fortune and Honor, represented by soprano and bass, there follows an instrumental postlude entitled "Ritornello." This turns out to be a variant of the second trio for two horns, three oboes in unison, and basso continuo from the F-major concerto; here the horns are replaced by trumpets, and the piece is transposed from F to D major.

The first of the two arias, for tenor and strings, is rather neutral thematically, a consequence of the didactic nature of its text. The second, for alto and two obbligato flutes, is characterized by the remarkable discrepancy between the broad arabesques of melody for voice and flutes, on the one hand, and the strings in unison, on the other. The goal of the rhythmically emphasized repetitions in the strings is clearly meant to recall the "härtesten Marmor" (hardest marble) alluded to in the text—sculpturally, please note, rather than the poetic paraphrase "Ätzen" (etch) in the text. The closing ensemble presents itself as a comparatively undemanding, harmonious conclusion. The echo effects might point to an outdoor performance, perhaps aided by relatively mild December weather.

In any case, a march for many instruments from Bach would have sounded well in the open air. Moreover, the organizers would have requested it in order to parade in front of the honoree's house. And although this sort of thing was not at all uncommon in Leipzig, the procession would have aroused considerable notice, perhaps from "crowds of the envious" as well: at least among those members of the professorship for whom a comfortable life—supported financially by empire building—was more important than the pedagogical instruction expected of them, which should actually have led them to Fortune and Gratitude through Diligence and Honor.

---

*Reichel (1929).
**Schulze (1969, 27ff.).
***Boyd (1993); Talbot (1999, 271–76).

Ich bin in mir vergnügt
BWV 204 / *BC* G 45

For Various Purposes, 1726 or 1727

Among the secular vocal works of Johann Sebastian Bach, the solo cantata for soprano *Ich bin in mir vergnügt* BWV 204 (I am content within) is the great unknown. If nothing else, this is because scarcely anything at all is known for certain about its origin. The reason for the work's creation, probably in 1726 or 1727, has not been determined. It is often suggested that it was for music making in the Bach household, in spite of—or perhaps because of—its sedate, old-fashioned manner and that it was meant for Anna Magdalena Bach, who was a soprano. There is a plausible connection to the Leipzig Collegium Musicum, at which students and other music lovers gathered weekly for their own enjoyment and that of their listeners. Although Bach first took on leadership of this organization officially in 1729, before that point he seems to have provided them with his own compositions now and then as a guest.

Above all, the "Cantata von der Vergnügsamkeit" (cantata of contentment), as Bach himself inscribed it, can be regarded as little known, because today it is seldom performed, in contrast to several of its secular sibling works.

This neglect has nothing to do with its musical qualities but rather with the problematic nature of its text, which turns out to be a rambling "Loblied auf das Mittelmaß" (paean to the average). Substantial portions of this paean are to be found in the printed oeuvre of one of the era's most popular poets, although it can be doubted that he would have approved of the text ultimately set by Bach. In any case, when Bach composed his cantata, Menantes was no longer among the living.

Menantes, whose real name was Christian Friedrich Hunold, was a few years older than Bach and, like him, came from Thuringia. Hunold also had in common with the future *Thomaskantor* that he lost his parents early and was sent away to northern Germany at a young age, returning later to his Thuringian hometown. Nothing is known of any personal relationship, but there is much to support the supposition that Hunold and Bach may have met one another, if not in Hamburg around 1700, then in Arnstadt in 1707. At this time, Bach's professional ascent was proceeding along an assured path, while Hunold had long been searching in vain for a new position. In Hamburg the fun-loving and temperamental law student Hunold had begun a promising career as a writer, making a name for himself in 1703 and 1704 with the opera libretti *Salomon* and *Nebucadnezar*, written for Reinhard Keiser. Satires, all too candid, and habitual indebtedness forced him to flee Hamburg in June 1706 and return to Thuringia. Finally, in late 1708 he was able to gain a foothold in Halle, where he enjoyed a reputation as a popular writer and literary theorist until his early death in August 1721. In the last years of his life Hunold provided numerous cantata texts to the nearby court of Köthen, where Bach was responsible for their composition beginning in late 1717.

In contrast to the Hunold cantatas of 1718–20, in the "Cantata von der Vergnügsamkeit" we have the last of Bach's compositions on Hunold texts and, at the same time, the earliest Hunold text he composed. The source Bach used was a collection published in 1713 in Halle and Leipzig entitled *Menantes Academische Neben-Stunden allerhand neuer Gedichte nebst einer Anleitung zur vernünftigen* (Menantes Academic Interludes of All Sorts of New Poems Together with an Introduction to Rational Poetry). In 1726, five years after the poet's death, the collection was republished. It can be shown, however, that Bach used the older print of 1713. The famous Hamburg opera composer Reinhard Keiser set several cantata texts from this collection shortly after they appeared; in 1714 he published them under the title *Musikalische Landslust . . . in moralischen Cantaten* (Musical country pleasures . . . in moral cantatas). The attractiveness of the texts—and their quick appropriation by Keiser—may have had something to do with the fact that Hunold himself was not only a poet but also a great lover of music; according to contemporary reports, he "played various instruments pleasantly and to perfection, in particular the violin and viola da gamba."

"Moral cantatas"—among them Bach's "Cantata von der Vergnügsamkeit"—followed a trend of the period, particularly in Hamburg and Leipzig.

In 1725 the Hamburg music director Georg Philipp Telemann made a request to the Frankfurt scholar Uffenbach for "a half or whole dozen cantatas of sacred moral content so that they can be performed in church as well as private concerts."[11] And as late as 1740 Telemann asked the poet Albrecht von Haller, then active in Göttingen, for "moralischen Oden" in order to set them in the style of Sperontes's *Singende Muse an der Pleiße* (Singing muse on the Pleisse). In 1735 and 1736 Telemann published two collections of six "moralischen Cantaten" each; he was given the texts for the first group by Daniel Stoppe, the Gottsched follower active in Hirschberg, Silesia.*

It is not difficult to see a parallel to literature and philosophy of the time, in particular, the circulation of "moralische Wochenschriften" after the British "moral weeklies." Tailored to the growing importance of the middle class, these publications were concerned with the improvement of moral standards and a rational existence oriented to striving for earthly happiness. The ideas of Stoic or Epicurean ethics made frugality and accommodation to existing conditions seem to be virtues. On the way to an "enlightened happiness," Johann Christoph Gottsched sought, as its protagonist, "to root out unreason and vice and instead foster reason and virtue among his countrymen."[12] Thus it was just as important to demonstrate the negative effects of envy, slander, arrogance, self-love, and avarice as it was to show the positive effects of modesty, sincerity, love of one's neighbor, and generosity.

Bach's cantata follows this noble objective, but textually it is a bit too much of a good thing. The core of the libretto is a "Cantata der Zufriedenheit" (cantata of contentment), as per Hunold's heading above the text. In plainly classical concentration, it comprises only three arias and two recitatives. A formal and intellectual frame is provided by a short motto placed at the beginning: "Ein edler Mensch ist Perlen-Muscheln gleich: In sich am meisten reich" (A noble person is like pearl oysters: in himself most rich), together with the last aria's final lines:

> In sich selber muß man finden
> Perlen der Zufriedenheit.
>
> In oneself one must find
> Pearls of contentment.

It seems that this text did not match Bach's wishes. In order to expand it to four each of recitatives and arias, at the libretto's beginning he himself or someone commissioned by him placed a poem found elsewhere in Hunold's collection entitled "Der vergnügte Mensch" (The contented person), written in Alexandrines. Moreover, the motto with the comparison of the noble person with pearl oysters was moved to the cantata's conclusion, where, excessively, it was combined with several naively rhymed strophes of unknown origin.

In other similar revisions to his libretti, Bach showed a much more assured hand, particularly in the *Trauerode* BWV 198 (Mourning ode) of 1727 for the Saxon electress, as well as the expansion of the text for the Coffee Cantata BWV 211, composed only a few years later. Where Hunold's original cantata contains fruitful oppositions, if only incipiently, the expanded libretto slides completely into a low-contrast "paean to the average."

Bach's composition must overcome the weaknesses of the overall concept through a carefully planned sequence of keys, richly varied instrumentation, and subtle deployment of dance types. The penultimate recitative can still be helped by the transition to the songlike arioso, but the Alexandrines of the opening movement with their many caesuras remain unintegrated. The lively final ensemble also fails to provide a definitive answer to the questions to what extent Bach intended in this cantata to "amuse" his listeners (i.e., to satisfy them) and to what extent he counted on a certain degree of *Vergnügsamkeit* (amusement): what is meant here is an undemanding contentment that the librettist at least began to preach only after his Hamburg excesses had brought him to the brink of catastrophe.

---

*Schulze (1978).

Ich habe genung
BWV 82 / BC A 169

Purification of Mary, February 2, 1727

The cantata *Ich habe genung* BWV 82 (I have enough) is among the very few true solo cantatas composed by Johann Sebastian Bach. It is for the first Marian feast in the church year, the Purification of Mary. This feast, celebrated since the seventh century, concerns the codes of conduct for those who have recently given birth, as recorded in Leviticus 12. This is also the basis for the Gospel reading of the day, found in Luke 2:22–32, the presentation of the infant Jesus in the temple. Verse 22 reads: "And as the days of her purification according to the law of Moses were accomplished, they brought him to Jerusalem, to present him to the Lord." Following a discussion of the animal sacrifice customary for this occasion, verses 25–32 continue:

> And behold, there was a man in Jerusalem whose name was Simeon; and this man was righteous and devout, and waiting for the consolation of Israel,

and the Holy Spirit was upon him. And it was revealed to him by the Holy Spirit that he should not see death before he had seen the Christ of the Lord. And he came, prompted by the Spirit, into the temple. And when the parents brought the infant Jesus into the temple to do for him as one does according to the law, he took him in his arms and praised God and said: Lord, now let your servant depart in peace, as you have said; for my eyes have seen your savior, which you have prepared before all peoples, a light to enlighten the Gentiles, and for the glory of your people Israel.

At first glance, most music texts for this feast do not seem to have anything to do with a feast in honor of Mary. Almost all of them focus on the words of Simeon: the fulfillment of his dearest wish for an encounter with the savior and his longing for death. The unknown poet responsible for the text of our cantata holds fast to this tradition as well.[13] Even in the first aria, obviously spoken by Simeon, one can see in which direction he plans to channel his thoughts:

> Ich habe genung,
> Ich habe den Heiland, das Hoffen der Frommen,
> Auf meine begierigen Arme genommen;
> Ich habe genung,
> Ich hab ihn erblickt,
> Mein Glaube hat Jesum ans Herze gedrückt;
> Nun wünsch ich, noch heute mit Freuden
> Von hinnen zu scheiden.
> Ich habe genung!

> I have enough,
> I have taken the savior, the hope of the devout,
> Into my eager arms;
> I have enough,
> I have seen him,
> My faith has pressed Jesus to my heart;
> I only wish, even today, with joy
> To depart from this life.
> I have enough!

Beginning with the second movement, a recitative, the longing for a blessed departure from this world is generalized; hence, Simeon is spoken about in the third person:

> Ich habe genung,
> Mein Trost ist nur allein,
> Daß Jesus mein und ich sein eigen möchte sein.

> Im Glauben halt ich ihn,
> Da seh ich auch mit Simeon
> Die Freude jenes Lebens schon.
> Laßt uns mit diesem Manne ziehn!
>
> I have enough,
> My consolation is but alone
> That Jesus might be mine and I his own.
> In faith I hold him,
> For I too see, with Simeon,
> The joy of that life already.
> Let us go with this man!

Increasingly, the movements that follow are filled with hope for "the joy of that life." The second aria longs for the sleep of death as the first step in separation from this world:

> Schlummert ein, ihr matten Augen,
> Fallet sanft und selig zu!
> Welt, ich bleibe nicht mehr hier,
> Hab ich doch kein Teil an dir,
> Das der Seele könnte taugen.
> Hier muß ich das Elend bauen,
> Aber dort, dort werd ich schauen
> Süßen Friede, stille Ruh.
>
> Fall asleep, you weary eyes,
> Fall softly and blessedly closed!
> World, I remain here no longer,
> I have indeed no part of you
> That could be of use to the soul.
> Here I must bear misery,
> But there, there I will see
> Sweet peace, still repose.

The last recitative alludes to Luther's hymn *Mit Fried und Freud ich fahr dahin* (With peace and joy I depart), his translation of the ancient Canticum Simeonis:

> Mein Gott! Wenn kömmt das schöne: Nun!
> Da ich im Friede fahren werde
> Und in dem Sande kühler Erde
> Und dort bei dir im Schoße ruhn?
> Der Abschied ist gemacht,
> Welt, gute Nacht.

> My God! When might come that lovely: Now!
> When I shall depart in peace
> And rest in the sand of the cool earth
> And there within your bosom?
> The departure is made,
> World, good night.

Longing for death, hinted at by the opening aria, becomes the main idea in the closing aria:

> Ich freue mich auf meinen Tod,
> Ach hätt er sich schon eingefunden.
> Da entkomm ich aller Not,
> Die mich noch auf der Welt gebunden.
>
> I look forward to my death,
> Ah, had it already arrived!
> There I will escape all distress,
> Which still binds me in the world.

The remarkable change in perspective between the first movement and the second can perhaps be explained by the fact that the text Bach used, expressly for a solo cantata, is a revision and expansion of an older text, which is preserved in a reprint of 1744.* This version, for several voices, began with the dictum from Luke 2:29, "Herr, nun läßest du deinen Diener im Friede fahren" (Lord, now let your servant depart in peace); closed with a chorale; and contains, in addition to one recitative, only a single aria, "Schlummert ein, ihr matten Augen."

Bach's composition of this libretto, not particularly rich in contrast but well-balanced and thematically self-contained, comes from 1727. It has been reasonably suggested that Bach composed the earliest version of the St. Matthew Passion in the weeks immediately before or afterward. Should this be the case, then our cantata can be associated broadly with that work's conceptual preparation, and this exceptional status can be seen in the effusive or ecstatic opening movement; the "heavenly length" of the "Schlummer" aria; and the closing movement, which gradually turns inward with anticipation.

Bach conceived the first version (BWV 82.1) of the cantata in 1727 for the bass voice, string instruments, and one oboe. Four years later, there followed a transposition from C minor to E minor (BWV 82.2), a soprano replaced the bass, and a transverse flute took the place of the oboe. At about the same time, Anna Magdalena Bach began copying the solo part of movements 2 and 3 along with an accompaniment into her 1725 notebook. Four years later, Bach assigned the solo voice to a mezzo soprano and returned to the original key of C minor (BWV 82.3). About a decade later, we have evidence of two performances, in which the bass recovered its rightful place and the instrumental ensemble was augmented in various ways. The soloist in these performances, probably after 1745, is likely to have been Johann Christoph Altnickol, Bach's student and later his son-in-law. In May 1747 Bach himself confirmed in writing that although Altnickol was a skilled performer of violin and cello, he mostly participated in the chorus (*choro musico*) as a bass singer in order to help with the lack of bass voices at the St. Thomas School. Johann Elias Bach, a cousin of the cantor of St. Thomas, spent several years as his secretary and in-house tutor for the children in the Leipzig household. In 1741 he briefly mentioned a "Basso solo" that Johann Sebastian Bach had lent a Weissenfels singer but had not yet received back, so that further lending was not contemplated at the moment. Although this work cannot at present be identified more precisely, it may have been the cantata *Ich habe genung*.

In any case, this composition was clearly one of Bach's favorite pieces, and he performed it often with pleasure. Whether he undertook the revisions for soprano and mezzo soprano in order to address problems of setting, we do not know. It is just as plausible that highly capable singers asked Bach to arrange the cantata for their specific voice ranges in order to test their ability to master demanding parts in three of the most different aria characters and successfully meet the challenge of this consummate masterpiece. This is still possible today. Although the original—and final—version for bass is the only complete one, the alternative versions for higher voices can be convincingly reconstructed with minimal effort, making them readily available to performers.

*Wollny (2000, 54–57).

O ewiges Feuer, o Ursprung der Liebe
BWV 34.2 / *BC* A 84

Pentecost, June 1, 1727

In its form for the first day of Pentecost, this cantata (BWV 34.2) belongs to Bach's late period and, by all appearances, was first performed in May 1746 or 1747. It is unlikely that the cantata was first performed in either of Leipzig's main churches, St. Thomas and St. Nicholas, but rather—if we are not completely mistaken—the Church of Our Lady (Liebfrauenkirche), in nearby Halle.[14] These inferences are prompted by several remarkable aspects of Bach's holograph manuscript.

The *Thomaskantor* was quite sparing in his use of expensive manuscript paper, and there are over one hundred cases of his using the lower staff systems on a page, left vacant after writing out a complex movement with many voices, to notate a separate piece with fewer parts. Whether these are fair copies or composing scores has no bearing on the situation. In the case of our Pentecost cantata, however, the composer set up a foolproof notational scheme in which he wrote the first recitative on the same page as the middle portion of the first movement, with the instruction "Recitativ so nach dem ersten folget" (Recitative thus follows the first). To drive the point home, there is, at the da capo sign after the end of the middle section just mentioned, the notation "Nach Wiederhohlung des Da Capo folgt sub signo . . . das Tenor Recitativ und die Alt Aria et sic porro" (After repetition of the da capo there follows below the sign . . . the tenor recitative and the alto aria and so forth). It is scarcely imaginable that Johann Sebastian Bach would have used these notes and explanations for a composition of his own with only five movements. More plausibly, the score was to be loaned or given away, and the annotations were meant for the manuscript's receiver, quite likely Wilhelm Friedemann Bach, who added to the score at several places where his father had entered very simple notation.

The evidence for May 1746 as the performance date in Halle is that only a few weeks earlier Wilhelm Friedemann had taken office as organist and music director of the Church of Our Lady, and his father may have wanted to ease his son's first steps in a new field of activity.[15] However, there does exist a cantata by Wilhelm Friedemann for the first day of Pentecost in 1746 whose text begins "Wer mich liebet, der wird mein Wort halten" Fk. 72 (Whoever loves me will hold my word). One would therefore have to assume that Bach's son had performed two cantatas on May 29, 1746. However, no new composition by Wilhelm Friedemann is documented for the following year, and this could speak for a performance on May 21, 1747. The memorable meeting between J. S. Bach and the king of Prussia took place only two weeks before the putative performance date.[16] Father and son undertook the journey to Potsdam together, and one can easily imagine that Friedemann might have taken the occasion to ask his father for the favor of a cantata dedicated to the quickly approaching high holiday.

The annotations to the score mentioned above also support the conclusion that Wilhelm Friedemann received only the score from Leipzig and had to arrange for the preparation of performance parts himself. Fully copied parts would have required no instructions as to the sequence of movements. It is possible that J. S. Bach may have had parts prepared for his own use, but this question must remain open. In this case, simultaneous performances in

Halle and Leipzig would have occurred. A Leipzig performance—if it in fact took place—would have been only in part a first performance. Only the two recitatives were newly composed for Pentecost. All of the other movements go back to a wedding cantata of the same name (BWV 34.1), which Bach seems to have reused several times. The wedding version, only fragmentarily preserved, was evidently first prepared for the nuptials of a clergyman. In any case, its concluding movement is eloquent:

> Gib, höchster Gott, auch hier dem Worte Kraft,
> Das so viel Heil bei deinem Volke schafft:
> Es müße ja auf den zurücke fallen,
> Der solches läßt an heilger Stätte schallen. . . .
> Sein Dienst, so stets am Heiligtume baut,
> Macht, daß der Herr mit Gnaden auf ihn schaut.

> Give, Most High God, here too power to the word
> That creates so much salvation for your people:
> It must indeed redound upon those
> Who let it resound in holy places. . . .
> His service, ever cultivated in the sanctuaries,
> Makes the Lord look upon him with grace.

For a reperformance of the wedding cantata, these specific formulations were replaced by more general expressions, such as:

> Ein Danklied soll zu deinem Throne dringen
> Und ihm davor ein freudig Opfer bringen.

> A song of thanks shall reach your throne
> And bring a joyful offering before him.

Of the seven movements in the first version, three were adopted in the Pentecost cantata: the opening and closing choruses of the first part, to be performed before the ceremony, and the aria at the beginning of the second part, to be performed afterward. Where possible, the unidentified librettist of the Pentecost cantata took characteristic and formative language from the original, thus demonstrating considerable understanding of the connection between text and music. Overall, the new libretto concerns the popular metaphor of the human heart as the dwelling of God. It immediately takes up the beginning of the reading from John 14:23: "Wer mich liebet, der wird mein Wort halten, und mein Vater wird ihn lieben, und wir werden zu ihm kommen und Wohnung bei ihm machen" (Whoever loves me will keep to my word, and my father will love him, and we will come to him and make our dwelling with him). The juxtaposition of "Tempeln" (temples) of the soul and "Hütten" (refuges) of the heart, long familiar in the early Bach cantatas, is seen once again in this relatively late cantata text.[17] The opening movement of the wedding cantata begins:

> O ewiges Feuer, o Ursprung der Liebe,
> Entzünde der Herzen geweihten Altar.
>
> O eternal fire, O source of love,
> Enkindle our hearts' consecrated altar.

It became:

> O ewiges Feuer, o Ursprung der Liebe,
> Entzünde die Herzen und weihe sie ein.
> Laß himmlische Flammen durchdringen und wallen,
> Wir wünschen, o Höchster, dein Tempel zu sein,
> Ach laß dir die Seelen im Glauben gefallen.
>
> O eternal fire, O source of love,
> Enkindle our hearts and consecrate them.
> Let heavenly flames pervade and seethe,
> We wish, O Most High, to be your temple.
> Ah, let our souls please you in faith.

The first recitative then clearly states:

> Drum sei das Herze dein;
> Herr, ziehe gnädig ein.
>
> Therefore, may my heart be yours;
> Lord, enter it with grace.

The following aria, "Wohl euch, ihr auserwählten Seelen, / Die Gott zur Wohnung ausersehn" (Blessed are you, you chosen souls, / Whom God has selected for his dwelling), had in its original version the bucolic image of Jacob and Rachel from the fourth book of Moses as its theme:

> Wohl euch, ihr auserwählten Schafe,
> Die ein getreuer Jakob liebt.
> Sein Lohn wird dort am größten werden,
> Den ihm der Herr bereits auf Erden
> Durch seiner Rahel Anmut gibt.
>
> Blessed are you, chosen flock,
> Whom a faithful Jacob loves.

His reward will be at its greatest,
Which the Lord, already on Earth
Gives to him, through his Rachel, grace.

The last recitative of the Pentecost cantata also stays with the image of the dwelling of God but translates it to the church:

Erwählt Gott die heilgen Hütten,
Die er mit Heil bewohnt,
So muß er auch den Segen auf sie schütten,
So wird der Sitz des Heiligtums belohnt.
Der Herr ruft über sein geweihtes Haus:
Das Wort des Segens aus:
Friede über Israel.

If God chooses the holy tabernacles,
Which he inhabits with salvation,
Then he must also pour blessings upon them,
That the seat of the sanctuary be rewarded.
The Lord calls out over his consecrated house
These words of blessing:
Peace upon Israel.

"Peace upon Israel": this word of blessing from the psalmist is paraphrased differently in the wedding and Pentecost cantatas, but always in accordance with the concern of the work.

Bach's composition presents a large festive ensemble setting in the broadly executed opening chorus, evoking the image of eternally blazing flames, as well as in the terse, powerful closing movement. As Arnold Schering wrote, its "fiery start and agility of the instruments [free themselves] of the 'Hurry to those holy steps' (Eilt zu denen heiligen Stufen) of the original version and meet here, with the feeling of thanksgiving in the highest degree. Earlier, this chorus ended the first part of the wedding cantata, before the sermon. Bach left alone its powerful terseness and homophonic form, which, in the Pentecost cantata, brings the whole to an almost unexpectedly quick conclusion."[18] The alto aria in the middle of the cantata is, in Schering's words, "a world-famous piece, and one of the most beautiful that Bach ever wrote."[19] It unites, in the attachment to the original wedding text, "pastoral idyll and devoted shepherd love": "This lovely mutual swaying of the two-part melody structure above the tranquil bass, the tender, swelling bending of the motive itself, the duetting... finally finding one another in thirds and sixths—hardly ever has a lovers' dalliance been more delightfully represented with sonorous enchantment."[20]

CHAPTER 6

Bach at Leipzig after Trinity 1727

Schwingt freudig euch empor
BWV 36 / BC A 3.4/5
First Sunday of Advent, 1726–1730

In a truly unparalleled fashion, the Advent cantata *Schwingt freudig euch empor* BWV 36.4/5 (Soar joyously aloft) illustrates J. S. Bach's management of his creative work as a composer over his lifetime, as well as the intertwining of the sacred and secular in his vocal works. A secular cantata of the same name (BWV 36.1) is the starting point in a series of at least five related works; it was composed in early 1725 for Leipzig students to honor a university teacher who unfortunately remains unknown. In November of the same or the following year, the cantata was reperformed (BWV 36.2) outside Leipzig to honor Princess Charlotte Frederike Wilhelmine, the second wife of Bach's earlier patron, Leopold of Anhalt-Köthen. The opening and closing ensembles remained essentially unchanged but with new text, as did the three arias. Newly composed, on the other hand, were four recitatives, as well as the recitative interpolations in the final movement.

A bit later, Bach fashioned an Advent cantata (BWV 36.4) from the opening movement and the arias by making some changes to the text. All the recitatives were dropped from the new work, and the composer omitted the closing movement entirely because of its all-too-pronounced dance character. The capstone was now formed instead by a setting of Philipp Nicolai's chorale *Wie schön leuchtet der Morgenstern* (How brightly gleams the morning star) using the seventh stanza of the chorale, "Wie bin ich doch so herzlich froh" (How am I indeed so sincerely happy). In 1731 the cantata was copied out in this form by Christoph Nichelmann, then fourteen years old, preserving it for future generations. Nichelmann, later a musician at the court of Frederick the Great, was a student at St. Thomas School at the time. A few musical and textual errors can probably be ascribed to the inexperience of the young copyist. It is also conceivable, too, that this early Advent version was not prepared by Bach himself but merely assembled at his direction, perhaps by someone else substituting for him.

The original secular version was by no means sidelined by its transformation into a church cantata, a process completed by 1730 at the latest. On the contrary: it was apparently performed a second time early in the 1730s, to honor the St. Thomas School rector, Johann Matthias Gesner, possibly at his fortieth birthday celebration in April 1731. Toward the end of the same year, Bach created an expanded, final version of the Advent cantata (BWV 36.5), now with eight movements as opposed to five in the first version. Nor did this new Advent version result in the original secular version being shelved. The cantor of St. Thomas dedicated it, with text once again reworked and newly composed recitatives (BWV 36.3), to a member of the Rivinus family of scholars in Leipzig in the summer of 1735.[1] The honoree was possibly the law professor and university rector Johann Florens Rivinus, whom we find in September of the same year among the godparents of Bach's youngest son, Johann Christian. In total, the two Advent versions of the cantata stand next to three secular works, as well as a reperformance. Thus it becomes clear that Bach regarded not only his sacred works but also significant portions of his secular oeuvre to be essential components of his repertoire and managed them accordingly.

Bach's handling of these various cantata versions and their continuing presence in his repertoire are reflected in a remarkable way by the interweaving of the gradually accumulated text versions. The unknown author of the libretto for the Advent cantata (BWV 36.4) clearly was able to draw not only on the secular first version of the work (BWV 36.1) but also on the second text by Christian Friedrich Henrici for the birthday of the Köthen princess (BWV 36.2). Only in the opening chorus did he restrict himself to the oldest version of the cantata. The poetically effusive text reads:

> Schwingt freudig euch empor und dringt bis an die Sternen,
> Ihr Wünsche, bis euch Gott vor seinem Throne sieht!
> Doch, haltet ein! ein Herz darf sich nicht weit entfernen,
> Das Dankbarkeit und Pflicht zu seinem Lehrer zieht.
>
> Soar joyfully aloft and press onward to the stars,
> You wishes, till God sees you before his throne!

> But stop! A heart need not travel far
> That to its teacher's drawn by gratitude and duty.

The Advent text is unmistakably drawn from this:

> Schwingt freudig euch empor zu den erhabnen Sternen,
> Ihr Zungen, die Ihr itzt in Zion fröhlich seid!
> Doch, haltet ein! Der Schall darf sich nicht weit entfernen,
> Es naht sich selbst zu euch der Herr der Herrlichkeit!

> Soar joyfully aloft unto the exalted stars,
> You tongues who are now so joyful in Zion!
> But stop! The sound need not travel far;
> He himself draws near to you, the Lord of Glory!

The situation is different in the first aria. The congratulatory cantata praises the love and reverence inspired by the teacher yet also raises a warning index finger:

> Die Liebe führt mit sanften Schritten
> Ein Herz das seinen Lehrer liebt.
> Wo andre auszuschweifen pflegen,
> Wird dies behutsam sich bewegen,
> Weil ihm die Ehrfurcht Grenzen gibt.

> Love leads with gentle steps
> A heart that loves its teacher.
> While others mean to go astray,
> This one will move with caution,
> For reverence sets boundaries for it.

The version meant for Köthen replaces this with a comparison with the solstice:

> Die Sonne zieht mit sanftem Triebe
> Die Sonnenwende zu sich hin.
> So, große Fürstin, deinen Blicken,
> Die unser ganzes Wohl beglücken,
> Folgt unser stets getreuer Sinn.

> The sun draws with gentle desires
> The solstice to its full extent.
> Just as, great Princess, your glances,
> Which favor our whole well-being,
> Are followed by our ever-loyal mind.

Finally, the Advent cantata uses imagery and comparisons from both of the secular forms.

> Die Liebe zieht mit sanften Schritten
> Sein Treugeliebtes allgemach.
> Gleichwie es eine Braut entzücket,
> Wenn sie den Bräutigam erblicket,
> So folgt ein Herz auch Jesu nach.

> Love draws with gentle steps
> Its true beloved gradually,
> Just as it entrances a bride
> When she catches sight of the bridegroom,
> So a heart follows Jesus.

The second aria, whose text begins with "Willkommen, werter Schatz" (Welcome, worthy treasure), also cannot hide its ancestry in two secular cantata texts, if, in this case, it is less the vocabulary than the syntax that provides evidence for the reworking procedure. The approach is even easier to understand in the third aria, with its play with contrasts between the internal and external. Here is the first version:

> Auch mit gedämpften, schwachen Stimmen
> Verkündigt man dem Lehrer preis.
> Es schallet kräftig in der Brust,
> Ob man gleich die empfundne Lust
> Nicht völlig auszudrücken weiß.

> Also with muted, weak voices
> One proclaims the teacher's praise.
> It sounds with power within the breast,
> If one can't immediately express
> The passion felt within.

Henrici/Picander provided the aria with the following verses (which are not readily understandable):

> Auch mit gedämpften, schwachen Stimmen
> Wird, Fürstin, dieses Fest verehrt.
> Denn schallet nur der Geist darbei,
> So heißet solches ein Geschrei,
> Das man im Himmel selber hört.

> Also with muted, weak voices,
> Princess, this fete is honored.

> For if the spirit only resounds with it,
> As such a din may be called,
> That one hears it in heaven itself.

The author of the Advent cantata text appears to have favored this peculiar version of the text over the poetically clear reading of the first version. And so he contented himself with a minor adjustment and with the exchange of the most important vocabulary:

> Auch mit gedämpften, schwachen Stimmen
> Wird Gottes majestät verehrt.
> Denn schallet nur der Geist darbei,
> So ist ihm solches ein Geschrei,
> Das er im Himmel selber hört.
>
> Also with muted, weak voices
> God's majesty is honored.
> For if the spirit only resounds with it
> It becomes such a din to him
> That he hears it in heaven itself.

Whether these verses improve upon the clarity of those by Christian Friedrich Henrici (Picander) remains an open question.

To a certain extent, the problems described in the poetic parts are mitigated by the enrichment of the cantata libretto by chorale strophes. Martin Luther's German version of the ancient church hymn *Veni redemptor gentium*, the Advent chorale *Nun komm der Heiden Heiland* (Now come, the Gentiles' savior) of 1524, is represented with three verses; in addition, there is the sixth strophe of Philipp Nicolai's *Wie schön leuchtet der Morgenstern* of 1599.

The cantata libretto takes on a rather old-fashioned appearance with its restriction to chorale strophes and arias and its total lack of recitatives. The musical image, however, is quite heterogeneous due to the secular origins of the opening chorus and all three arias. The opening movement combines a delicate instrumental texture with the lively interplay of chordal and polyphonic choral sections, in which the oboe d'amore dominates and the strings must remain subdued. The chamber music character of the original secular version matched this completely; a performance in church would have encountered several problems with the balance of sonorities. The *Thomaskantor* took this into account by doubling the oboe d'amore—as opposed to his original intent. In the second movement a change to the serious realm of strict vocal polyphony follows directly, as the Advent hymn *Nun komm der*

Heiden Heiland is heard in various canonic constructions in dense three-part counterpoint. In just as immediate a fashion, the tenor aria takes the listener back to the previous milieu. Voice and oboe compete with one another, carried along by the gentle dance rhythms of the passepied. The first part of the cantata closes with a simple four-part chorale.

The second half of the cantata, to be performed after the sermon, opens with a powerful, buoyant bass aria whose bright and festive character is created by the strings, led by the joyfully animated concerted first violin. Once more, in sharp contrast to the preceding, there follows a choral arrangement of *Nun komm der Heiden Heiland*, this time as a quartet in which the two oboi d'amore and basso continuo perform the imitative contrapuntal accompaniment, while the tenor presents the ancient melody in large note values. In a gently glowing atmosphere, soprano and solo violin then lead a sonorous interplay between lovely melody and instrumental figuration, which, in the aria's central section, dissolves into teasing echo effects. At last, the ancient *Nun komm der Heiden Heiland* is heard for a third time, now in simple four-part texture and devoid of any ambitions to an elaborate arrangement of the chorale.

Laß, Fürstin, laß noch einen Strahl
BWV 198 / BC G 34

Funeral, Electress Christiane Eberhardine, October 17, 1727

The work known as the Trauerode BWV 198 (Mourning ode) to Christiane Eberhardine of Brandenburg-Bayreuth, the electress of Saxony, is traditionally included among the church cantatas of Johann Sebastian Bach. However, it is in fact a secular composition, even though it was meant to be performed in a church. The first indication of this work's existence came in 1802 from the Bach biographer Johann Nikolaus Forkel:

> Among many occasional pieces that he composed in Leipzig, I mention only two funeral cantatas: the one of which was performed at Cöthen, at the funeral ceremony of his beloved Prince Leopold; the other in the Paulinerkirche at Leipzig, at the funeral sermon upon the death of Christiane Eberhardine, Queen of Poland and Electress of Saxony. The first contains double choruses of uncommon magnificence and the most affecting expression; the second has indeed only simple choruses, but they are so appealing that he who has begun to play one of them will never quit it until he has finished it. It was composed in October 1727.[2]

In describing the funeral music for Prince Leopold as having two choirs, Forkel in part fell victim to an error—and in part compounded this error through a misreading. The manuscript in his possession at that time does in fact name Johann Sebastian Bach as composer—wrongly—but it correctly refers to the funeral for the duke of Meiningen, Ernst Ludwig. Hence, it is actually a work by Bach's Meiningen cousin Johann Ludwig Bach from 1724.* On the other hand, Forkel's observations about the funeral music for the Saxon electress are on the mark. For matters concerning the work's genesis and function, Forkel could rely upon the best of all sources: the composer's autograph manuscript, also in Forkel's possession, whose title page exhaustively describes the reasons for the work's composition: "Funeral Music for the Homage and Eulogy upon the Death of Her Royal Majesty and Electoral Serenity of Saxony, Madame Christiane Eberhardine Queen of Poland etc. and Electress of Saxony etc. Duchess of Brandenburg-Bayreuth, by Mr Kirchbach Esq. held in St. Paul's Church in Leipzig, Performed by Johann Sebastian Bach anno 1727 on October 18."[3]

It is evident from the inaccurate date that Bach formulated this title afterward: all contemporary accounts place the funeral ceremony on October 17. Aside from this, there is an unmistakable pride in this title's elaborate verbosity, a pride in taking a crucial role in an artistic and political event of the highest order.

This event's background reaches well into the late seventeenth century. In the course of his efforts to gain the Polish crown, August the Strong, elector of Saxony, converted to Catholicism—but not at all to the delight of his mostly Lutheran subjects in Saxony. When his consort, Christiane Eberhardine, refused to follow him and remained Lutheran, her popular regard rose all the higher. The "mother of her country" died under somewhat mysterious circumstances on September 5, 1727, while at Castle Pretsch, not far from Torgau. Two days later, a country-wide period of mourning was decreed during which even church music fell silent.

For Leipzig, the obvious thing to do would have been to hold a dignified celebration worthy of the departed. The tolerant policies of the elector toward the Lutherans would certainly have permitted something of the sort. But both the city and the university regarded it as prudent to wait and proceed carefully. Previous experience suggested that taking full advantage of the available leeway could lead to the elector asking the city for a financial loan, which, on the one hand, could not and should not be refused but which, on the other, was unlikely to be repaid. A way out of the confused situation presented itself a few days later, when a young nobleman studying at the University of Leipzig, Hans Carl von Kirchbach, took the initiative and requested the university's permission to hold a memorial service for the electress at St. Paul's Church. The late Gothic church was used by the university partly for academic religious services and partly, as in this case, as an auditorium, a venue for events of all kinds. The noble edifice, decorated with many art treasures, withstood the Battle of Nations (Völkerschlacht) in 1813, as well as the bombardment of Leipzig in the Second World War. It was reserved for those in power in the years afterward, despite widespread protests by the population, to dynamite this architectural treasure in order to create space for a hideous new building. With that, an irreplaceable workplace of Johann Sebastian Bach was lost forever.

As for the activities of Kirchbach and his colleagues in early September 1727, the university felt itself unable to take a decision for or against the proposal. And so, on the spur of the moment in early October, Kirchbach turned to Dresden, secured permission immediately, and began preparations for the funeral service. Despite academic tradition, Latin would not be used either for the eulogy or for the funeral music; instead, the German language, in accordance with the aims of the German Society, headquartered in Leipzig, would be used. To create a libretto, Kirchbach engaged Johann Christoph Gottsched, the staunch champion of language reform; for its composition, he chose Bach, the cantor of St. Thomas School.

While these preparations were still under way in the first half of October 1727, the organist at St. Nicholas and the university music director, Johann Gottlieb Görner, got wind of the affair and intervened with the university. Although the event was private, the university authorities took up the matter and attempted to enforce Görner's claim to the production of all academic musical events, including the one in preparation. Kirchbach did not get involved and accepted a settlement, under which he compensated Görner financially. In spite of this quarrel, Bach pressed on with the composition, which he completed on October 15, two days before the planned performance.

The ceremony itself went forward in deepest solemnity. The city council and university faculty marched in procession from St. Nicholas to the university church, which was draped in black. Contemporary accounts praise the quality of the eulogy and the wealth of invention displayed in the funerary art, and they mention the splendor of the mourning gathering: "Aristocratic persons, high ministers, cavaliers, and other foreigners could be found on the fairway, along with a great number of prominent women, as well as the entire laudable university and a high noble and wise councilor."[4] What seemed outwardly to be the result of a private initiative in fact took on the significance of a state function. It is all the more significant that—contrary to contemporary custom—the composer of the funeral music is also mentioned in the accounts. A Leipzig university chronicler expressed himself in considerable detail about the role of the music in the proceedings: "When, then, everyone had taken his place, there had been an improvisation on the organ, and the Ode of Mourning written by Magister Johann Christoph Gottsched, a member of the *Collegium Marianum*, had been distributed among those present by the Beadles, there was shortly heard the Music of Mourning, which this time Capellmeister Johann Sebastian Bach had composed in the Italian style, with *Clave di Cembalo* [harpsichord], which Mr Bach himself played, organ, violas di gamba, lutes, violins, recorders, transverse flutes, &c., half being heard before and half after the oration of praise and mourning."[5]

The account of performance in two parts is accurate, as is the exquisite instrumental ensemble—although the only preserved source, Bach's autograph score, fails to distinguish between organ and cembalo, on the one hand, or flutes and recorders, on the other. The chronicler's remark about the composition being "in the Italian style" is intended as a critical jab: Bach did not set the carefully stylized strophes in Gottsched's ode as written but separated the strophes and took other measures of articulation to create a version of the libretto that he could set in the form of choruses, recitatives, and arias—very much in the style imported from Italy.

In view of this music's context, it is no wonder that it is among the finest and most ambitious to flow from Bach's pen. Bach himself adopted parts of the composition two years later for funeral music for Prince Leopold of Köthen.[6] Two years after that he used the same parts along with still others for his St. Mark Passion BWV 247, later unfortunately lost. In the nineteenth century, the Trauerode was regarded as unperformable for textual reasons. A "rescue" was attempted by paraphrase for All Saints' Day. The work's original form was recovered only in our era; it has enriched the Bachian repertoire with a priceless jewel. That the editors of the Bach-Gesellschaft editions of the nineteenth and twentieth centuries introduced a grotesque transcription error in the text of the eighth movement, a tenor aria, because they assumed that Bach had deviated from Gottsched's text with a downright vulgar expletive** underscores how difficult it has been even for Bach experts to comprehend the event of October 17, 1727. Bach's music was the centerpiece of a first-class funeral ceremony for the "mother of her country," beloved for her unshakable faith, an event that, for reasons outward as well as inward, can be assumed to be a high point that the cantor of St. Thomas School may perhaps never have experienced again.

---

*Hofmann (1983).
**The sixth strophe of Gottsched's ode begins:

> Der Ewigkeit saphirnes Haus
> Zieht deiner heitern Augen Blicke,
> Von der verschmähten Welt zurücke
> Und tilgt der Erden Denckbild aus.
>
> Eternity's saphire house
> Draws your serene glances
> Back from the spurned world
> And erases the mental image of the earth.

Bach's text underlay in his composition score reads:

> Der Ewigkeit saphirnes Haus
> Zieht, Fürstom, deine heitern Blicke
> Von unsrer Niedrigkeit zurücke
> Und tilgt der Erden Denckbild aus.
>
> Eternity's sapphire house
> Draws your serene glances
> Back from our lowliness
> And erases the mental image of the earth.

The editors of the Bach-Gesellschaft volume in the nineteenth and twentieth centuries believed that Bach's rather shakily written "Denckbild" should instead read "Dreckbild" (image of filth) in the unspoken yet mistaken assumption that it was an instance of acceptable Baroque "strong language" (*Kraftwort*) and without being clear as to the context in Leipzig's St. Paul's Church. The assumption that a composer of Bach's rank might permit himself anything of the sort before the "pillars of society" is a characteristic example of the hagiography of the nineteenth century and even into the twentieth.

Sehet, wir gehn hinauf gen Jerusalem
BWV 159 / *BC* A 50

Estomihi, February 27, 1729

This cantata probably originated in February 1729.[7] Johann Sebastian Bach drew its text from a collection that the Leipzig postal secretary and gifted poet Christian Friedrich Henrici (Picander) had begun to publish in the early summer of 1728. He provided a foreword to the collection that overtly stated the goal of the publication: "In honor of God, in response to the desire of good friends, and to promote much devotion, I have decided to prepare the present cantatas. I have undertaken this plan even more happily, since I may flatter myself that perhaps whatever is lacking in poetic charm will be replaced by the loveliness of the incomparable Herr Music Director Bach and that these songs will resound in the most important churches of devout Leipzig."[8] It remains unclear whether Henrici/Picander completed his plan with the agreement of the cantor of St. Thomas, whether Bach promised him compositions for the entire annual cycle, or to what extent Bach was subsequently in a position to fulfill such a promise.[9] The texts appeared in four parts from 1728 to 1729 and again later in a different order. At present, Bach scholars are not agreed as to whether they provided the basis for a fourth annual cycle of cantatas by Bach or whether he was content to set only a selection from Picander's offering.* If Bach did in fact set Picander's cycle in its entirety, then this part of his oeuvre must be considered lost, for the most part. At present, we have evidence of barely ten compositions, roughly a sixth of an entire cycle.

In the case of our cantata, then, we are dealing with one of those works that may be all that remain from a much larger set of compositions. The beginning of the text refers to the Gospel reading of Estomihi Sunday: the account in Luke 18 of the journey to Jerusalem that signals the beginning of Passiontide. The other account in the Gospel reading, the healing of the blind man by the wayside, can be only dimly perceived in Picander's cantata libretto. Otherwise, the text concentrates on the beginning of the suffering of Christ and attempts, wherever possible, to emulate the diction of Passion settings. Since two versions of Bach's St. John Passion had been heard in Leipzig in 1724 (BWV 245.1) and 1725 (BWV 245.2), and the St. Matthew Passion on Picander's text had perhaps received its first performance in 1727 (BWV 244.1), with another performance envisioned for 1729, it is in no way odd that Picander would have referred back to such models for his Estomihi cantata.

Picander places a part of the Lord's word at the beginning, combining it with recitative interpolations of his own invention, as well as a longer closing section. He thereby achieves a dialogue, however unbalanced it might be, that points forward in its last verses to the act of salvation:

> "Sehet!"
> Komm, schaue doch, mein Sinn,
> Wo geht dein Jesus hin?
> "Wir gehn hinauf"
> O harter Gang! Hinauf?
> O ungeheurer Berg, den meine Sünden zeigen!
> Wie sauer wirst du müßen steigen!
> "Gen Jerusalem!"
> Ach, gehe nicht!
> Dein Kreuz ist dir schon zugericht',

Wo du sollst zu Tode bluten;
Hier sucht man Geißeln vor, dort bindt man Ruten;
Die Bande warten dein;
Ach gehe selber nicht hinein!
Doch bliebest du zurücke stehen,
So müßt ich selbst nicht nach Jerusalem,
Ach, leider in die Hölle gehen.

  "See!"
Come, but behold, my soul,
Where is your Jesus going?
  "We are going up"
O difficult journey! Up there?
O monstrous mountain that my sins display!
How painfully you will have to climb!
  "To Jerusalem!"
O do not go!
Your cross is ready for you,
Where you shall bleed to death;
Here they seek whips, there they bind rods,
Bonds await you;
O do not go there yourself!
But were you to stay back,
Then I myself would have to go not to Jerusalem
But unfortunately down to hell.

An even higher degree of verbal artistry is seen in the ensuing aria, in which a strophe from Paul Gerhardt's hymn *O Haupt voll Blut und Wunden* (O head full of blood and wounds), whose text beginning "Ich will hier bei dir stehen" (I will stand here beside you) is expanded with interleaved, freely versified lines, thereby addressing the "follower" theme from two sides:

  Ich folge dir nach
Ich will hier bei dir stehen
Verachte mich doch nicht!
  Durch Speichel und Schmach;
  Am Kreuz will ich dich noch umfangen,
Von dir will ich nicht gehen
Bis dir dein Herze bricht
  Dich laß ich nicht aus meiner Brust,
Wenn dein Haupt wird erblassen
Im letzten Todesstoß
  Und wenn du endlich scheiden mußt,
Alsdenn will ich dich fassen,

>   Sollst du dein Grab in mir erlangen.
> In meinen Arm und Schoß.
>
>   I follow after you.
> I will stand beside you here.
> Do not despise me!
>   Through spitting and insult
>   On the cross I will still embrace you,
> From you I will not go
> Until your heart breaks.
>   I do not let you leave my breast
> When your head will turn pale
> In the last stroke of death.
>   And when you finally must depart,
> Even then I will embrace you.
>   You shall find your grave in me,
> In my arm and bosom.

The two movements that follow, recitative and aria, are dedicated to the renunciation of the world's vanities and the assurance of salvation through the martyr's death of Jesus. The aria in particular anticipates the events of the Passion:

> Es ist vollbracht,
> Das Leid ist alle,
> Wir sind von unserm Sündenfalle
> In Gott gerecht gemacht.
> Nun will ich eilen
> Und meinem Jesu Dank erteilen,
> Welt, gute Nacht!
> Es ist vollbracht.
>
> It is accomplished,
> The suffering is over.
> From our sinful fall we have been
> Justified in God.
> Now I will hurry
> And to Jesus thanks to give.
> World, good night!
> It is accomplished.

In Picander's libretto there is a recitative that follows this aria, with its clear textual link to Bach's St. John Passion, that is missing from Bach's composition—at least in the form passed down to us in copies:

Herr Jesu, dein verdienstlich Leiden
Ist meine Herrlichkeit,
Mein Trost, mein Ruhm, mein Schmuck und Ehrenkleid.
Daran erhalt ich mich, drauf leb ich allezeit,
Drauf will ich auch dereinst verscheiden.

Lord Jesus, your meritorious suffering
Is my glory,
My consolation, my praise, my jewel, my raiment of honor.
By it I am maintained, on it I live forever,
Upon it I will also one day depart.

Picander's libretto closes with the next-to-last strophe from Paul Stockmann's Passion hymn *Jesu Leiden, Pein und Tod* (Jesus's suffering, pain, and death).

In Bach's composition the opening movement is a dialogue between Jesus (represented by the bass, the *vox Christi*) and the soul (assigned here, atypically, to the alto). The soul's reflections are set as powerfully expressive, often dramatically pointed recitatives that, however, enjoy, so to speak, the constant protection of the accompanying chords in the strings. By contrast, the "Sehet, wir gehn hinauf gen Jerusalem" is executed as a lonely, pain-filled arioso whose only austere support is an arduously rising and falling again motive in the basso continuo. The second movement has a dance character somewhere between gigue and pastorale, at least as far as the two freely formed parts, alto and basso continuo, are concerned. As might be expected, these two convert the "follower" theme mentioned in the text into various imitative sequences. In the soprano, supported by an oboe, the ancient melody *Herzlich tut mich verlangen* (Sincerely do I long) unswervingly traces its course. After a brief tenor recitative, the bass and oboe engage in a stirring dialogue in the aria "Es ist vollbracht" (It is accomplished), whose gravitas is relieved only briefly by the middle section, with figuration depicting the keyword "eilen" (hurry). With the same accumulated gravitas, a four-part chorale movement concludes this work on the threshold of Lent, a period without music.

---

*Häfner (1975), as well as Scheide (1980, 1983).

Geschwinde, geschwinde, ihr wirbelnden Winde
(*Der Streit zwischen Phoebus und Pan*)
BWV 201 / BC G 46
For Various Purposes, Autumn 1729

The dramma per musica *Der Streit zwischen Phoebus und Pan* BWV 201 (The contest between Phoebus and Pan) gives the lie to the view that Bach's secular cantatas are written, one and all, for particular occasions and are bound to them for all time.[10] Instead, this work was conceived from the beginning as a repertoire piece, particularly in view of its universally applicable text content, its musical qualities, and its rewarding solos.

The libretto is the work of Bach's "house poet" in Leipzig, Christian Friedrich Henrici; it takes a motif from the *Metamorphoses* of Ovid and develops it into a small dramatic plot about a singing competition between Phoebus Apollo, the god of the arts, and Pan, the god of shepherds and flocks. Without too much consideration for ancient mythology, these two protagonists are joined by the legendary kings Tmolus of Lydia and Midas of Phrygia, who serve as judges (or, actually, advocates or seconds); in addition, there are appearances by Momus, personification of ridicule, and Mercury, messenger of the gods. These six characters are faced with no deeply rooted conflicts to resolve, and there can be no expectation that Pan, the pastoral naif, will emerge victorious from the competition. Greater opposites are scarcely conceivable: the sensitive love song of Phoebus, with its exquisite timbral robes, and Pan's rustic, boisterous dance tune, with its superficial tone painting. Moreover, the mythological ranking of the two deities absolutely forbids any competition between them on an equal footing. In spite of all this, the action is no mock battle. Yet the most important events are moved off to a side stage: the competition between the two singers, whose outcome is never in doubt for the insightful, devolves into a rivalry between the two seconds/critics. Tmolus, associated with Phoebus, turns out to be competent, while his adversary, Midas, is uneducated and unaware. Consequently, he is awarded donkey ears, and Momus writes a mnemonic jingle—in no way time bound—for him in the official record:

> Der Unverstand und Unvernunft
> Will jetzt der Weisheit Nachbar sein,
> Man urteilt in den Tag hinein,
> Und die so tun,
> Gehören all in deine Zunft.

> Folly and unreason
> Would now be the neighbors of wisdom.
> People judge at random,
> And those who do so
> All belong to your guild.

The first performance of this dramma per musica—which, with its six arias, seven recitatives, and two ensemble movements, approaches the dimensions of an opera act—may have taken place in the autumn of 1729. A few months earlier, the cantor of St. Thomas had taken over the directorship of the Collegium Musicum, reestablished by Georg Philipp Telemann in the early eighteenth century. The main motivation for creating *Der Streit zwischen Phoebus und Pan* seems to have been to repudiate the dangerous tendency toward simplification by presenting, after a period of preparation and practice, an extensive new work with this ensemble advocating high musical standards.* The work was performed again several times in the 1730s and in 1749; this fact shows that the defense of "noble music" lost none of its currency in later years.

---

*According to Hans Joachim Kreutzer (2005, 92ff.), *Der Streit zwischen Phoebus und Pan* is Picander's (and hence Bach's) answer to Gottsched's criticism of Picander in the first edition of the *Versuch einer Critischen Dichtkunst*, which is dated 1730 but which appeared at Michaelmas 1729. Johann Christoph Gottsched's *Versuch einer Critischen Dichtkunst für die Deutschen* (Essay on the criticism of poetry for the Germans) is his principal effort to reform German poetry, rejecting the perceived bombast and absurd affectations of the Second Silesian School in favor of highly stylized French classicism.

Weichet nur, betrübte Schatten
BWV 202 / BC G 41

Secular Wedding, before 1730

Among the secular cantatas by Johann Sebastian Bach, the wedding cantata *Weichet nur, betrübte Schatten* BWV 202 (Retreat, you gloomy shadows) enjoys a special popularity. This is due, on the one hand, to its high musical qualities and, on the other, to the truly timeless effect of its text, which is easily grasped by those not familiar with Baroque language. Even so, there is a complication: this particular solo cantata, performed so frequently in our time, yields very few hints as to the secret of its origin. Its rather peculiar transmission also leaves several questions unanswered. This simple fact alone is nearly incomprehensible. This unique work survived only because of a stroke of luck: a thirteen-year-old prepared a copy during the composer's lifetime, and this singular copy fell into the hands of knowledgeable collectors during the nineteenth century, who preserved it for posterity.

The search for the origins of this crucial copy of the cantata leads one to Gräfenroda in Thuringia. About halfway between Ohrdruf and Ilmenau, Gräfenroda was a relatively small settlement during the eighteenth century, with only a few hundred inhabitants. It was the birthplace and center of activity for Johann Peter Kellner, one of the most enthusiastic and industrious collectors and performers of Bach's compositions in his era. Kellner, born in 1705 and thus twenty years younger than Johann Sebastian Bach, began amassing a comprehensive collection of his organ, harpsichord, and violin works as a young man. In his autobiography, published in 1760, Kellner remarked: "I had once seen and heard a great deal about a great master of music and found exceptional pleasure in his work. I refer to the late Capellmeister Bach in Leipzig. I longed for the acquaintance of this excellent man and was so fortunate as to enjoy it. In addition to him, I have had the honor of hearing the famous Herr Handel, capellmeister in London, and getting to know him as well as still other living masters of music."[11]

Kellner's own role in the preservation of our cantata remains open to conjecture. One of his students is more important in this connection: Johannes Ringck, born in 1717 in Frankenhain, a village near Gräfenroda. In 1730, when he was only thirteen, he copied not only our Bach cantata with all the care he could muster but also an extremely long organ work by Dieterich Buxtehude, a *Te Deum Laudamus*, no fewer than 268 measures in length. Several years later, Johannes Ringck went to Gotha in order to continue his training with the famous court music director and composer Gottfried Heinrich Stölzel. Shortly after 1740 we find him in Berlin, first as music teacher and opera composer and then, after 1755, as organist at St. Mary's Church, where he played the Joachim Wagner organ, still extant today. In October 1772 the English music scholar Charles Burney judged Ringck's musical capabilities thusly: "In the church of St. Mary, there is a fine organ, built by Wagner; Mr. Ringck, the organist, is much esteemed as a performer of *ex tempore* fugues, though he is possessed of less brilliancy of finger than the organist of St. Peter."[12] After Ringck died in the summer of 1778, Wilhelm Friedemann Bach—now sixty-eight years old and without a position—sought to succeed him, but without success.* As late as 1829 Ringck's name is found in a letter to Goethe from the Berlin building contractor and director of the Sing-Akademie, Carl Friedrich Zelter. A month after Mendelssohn's sensational revival of the St. Matthew Passion, Zelter looked back with pride upon the continuity of the Bach tradition in Berlin in a letter received by Goethe: "For fifty years I have been accustomed to honoring the genius of Bach; Friedemann died here; Emanuel Bach was royal chamber musician here; Kirnberger, Agricola were students of old Bach; Ringck, Bertuch, Schmalz, and others performed scarcely anything other than pieces by old Bach; I myself have been teaching [Bach's music] for thirty years and have students who play all of Bach's things well."[13] At the time Zelter wrote this, when a good measure of Prussian hegemony was in the air, Ringck had died half a century before, and his copy of the cantata *Weichet nur, betrübte Schatten* was twice as old as that.

No tradition tells us whose wedding Bach composed this work for, who provided the text, or who sang the challenging soprano solo. It has been suggested that Johann Peter Kellner, only twenty-five years old in 1730 and still working as a cantor's assistant in Gräfenroda, may have had another score at his disposal that he presented to his pupil Ringck for copying and that has been since lost; but this does not lead any further either. The only certainty is that the work existed before 1730. Whether it was composed after 1723 in Leipzig or earlier in Köthen, as is often suggested, remains unclear at this time.

As might be expected, the names of the wedding couple remain shrouded in darkness, as well as nearly all accompanying circumstances. The text of the sixth movement does provide a rather vague clue:

> Und dieses ist das Glücke,
> Daß durch ein hohes Gunstgeschicke
> Zwei Seelen einen Schmuck erlanget,
> An dem viel Heil und Segen pranget.
>
> And this is good fortune,
> That through a lofty, benevolent fate
> Two souls attain an ornament
> On which much salvation and blessing are emblazoned.

With a little imagination, one might interpret "hohes Gunstgeschicke" to be an allusion to the permission to marry from the authorities, which might indicate a rural situation. What is missing from the final movement may offer another clue. Ribald wishes for the quick appearance of progeny, so typical of the era, are found here only cryptically:

> Sehet in Zufriedenheit
> Tausend helle Wohlfahrtstage,
> Daß bald bei der Folgezeit
> Eure Liebe Blumen trage.

> May you see in contentment
> A thousand bright days of well-being,
> So that in the near future
> Your love may bear flowers.

This abundance of good taste and consideration is easier to ascribe to an amateur librettist than a professional poet. In any case, a concluding movement of this sort made sense because the entire cantata text takes place in a natural idyll in which Flora, the ancient Italian goddess of blossoms and flourishing, plays the lead role.

The change of seasons and the transitoriness of their splendor is the widely varied theme of the unknown librettist. The beginning of the libretto indicates a wedding in the early months of the year, as in the first aria:

> Weichet nur, betrübte Schatten,
> Frost und Winde, geht zur Ruh.
> Florens Lust
> Will der Brust
> Nichts als frohes Glück verstatten,
> Denn sie träget Blumen zu.
>
> Retreat, you gloomy shadows,
> Frost and wind, retire to bed.
> Flora's delight
> Will grant the breast
> Nothing but happy fortune,
> For she brings flowers.

Then, with a recitative:

> Die Welt wird wieder neu,
> Auf Bergen und in Gründen
> Wird sich die Anmut doppelt schön verbinden,
> Der Tag ist von der Kälte frei.
>
> The world becomes new again,
> In the mountains and in valleys
> Loveliness clings with doubled beauty,
> The day is free of chill.

And once again in an aria that brings the sun god Phoebus into the scenario:

> Phoebus eilt mit schnellen Pferden
> Durch die neugeborne Welt.

Ja, weil sie ihm wohlgefällt,
Will er selbst ein Buhler werden.

Phoebus hastens with quick horses
Through the newborn world.
Yes, because she pleases him
He himself would become a lover.

A spring panorama is assumed in what follows, in which the goddess of flowers, Flora, and the sun god, Phoebus, are joined by the god of love, who is introduced in a recitative and extolled further in an aria:

Wenn die Frühlingslüfte streichen
Und durch bunte Felder wehn,
Pflegt auch Amor auszuschleichen,
Um nach seinem Schmuck zu sehn,
Welcher, glaubt man, dieser ist,
Daß ein Herz das andre küßt.

When the breezes of spring caress
And waft through colorful fields,
Even Cupid is wont to sneak out
To look for his prize,
Which, it is thought, is this,
That one heart another kisses.

Ultimately, the god Cupid commands the field and enjoys the advantage over the other deities—as in the next to last aria:

Sich üben
Im Lieben
In Scherzen sich herzen
Ist besser als Florens vergängliche Lust.

To practice
In love
In playfulness to embrace
Is better than Flora's ephemeral delight.

    The way that Johann Sebastian Bach uncovers ever new facets of this rather restrained libretto truly deserves admiration as he transforms the subtle intimations of the libretto into different characters. The three-part opening movement is the composition's crown jewel. Its gently ascending chords in the strings and the rhapsodically hovering melodies of voice and obbligato oboe evoke the departing "gloomy shadows"; it changes to a cheerful scenario in the quick middle section, and, after this brief foretaste of longed-for blossoming splendor, it returns to the dark mood of the beginning. The second aria, accompanied only by basso continuo, depicts the "swift horses" of the sun god, Phoebus. The dance type that predominates here is that of the gigue, whose main characteristics are, according to Johann Mattheson, a Hamburg contemporary of Bach, "the most extreme speed and volatility, but mostly in a flowing and not impetuous way: like the smoothly shooting arrow of a stream."[14] The third aria, with obbligato violin solo, takes a more careful pace: no wonder, since it depicts the god Cupid, who is "wont to sneak out" (auszuschleichen pflegt) to be on the lookout for victims for his arrows. The fourth aria, "Sich üben im Lieben" (To practice love), is once again in a faster tempo; the soprano and oboe compete with one another in the dance character of a passepied. The concluding gavotte is designed as a stylized dance song: instrumentally compact in the framing sections, and with a more relaxed movement when the soprano enters. Its distinct three-part structure serves as a cheerful reminiscence of the cantata's beginning, and the soprano voice, joined with the broken chords in the high string instruments, evokes once again the wintry gloom of the opening movement, now, however, on the firm ground of the irreversible change of season.

*Henzel (1992).

Jauchzet Gott in allen Landen
BWV 51 / BC A 134

Fifteenth Sunday after Trinity, September 17, 1730

In various regards, the cantata *Jauchzet Gott in allen Landen* BWV 51 (Rejoice to God in every land) occupies a special place in the vocal works of Johann Sebastian Bach. First of all, this applies to the generic term "cantata," which stands as the work's title on the manuscript's first page. Apart from his secular works, Bach was quite sparing in his use of the term. It is found in several compositions that flawlessly embody the type defined around 1700, consisting only of recitatives and arias that use freely versified text. In addition, it is also found in several works that include chorale strophes in their texts, whether these are set in four parts or transferred to the solo voice, as in the case of our cantata.

Also unusual are the demands on the solo soprano in terms of staying power, skill at coloratura, and vocal range. Even so, Johann Adolph Scheibe's

1737 complaint proves unjustified, namely, that Bach's pieces were too difficult to perform because the composer demanded that singers and instrumentalists match with their throats and their instruments what he was able to play on the keyboard, and that was impossible. In our cantata, one never meets the kind of mischievously amassed difficulties of the sort found in the solo cantatas of the Hamburg opera composer and Bach contemporary Reinhard Keiser.* Except for the high C (two octaves above middle C) that appears one time each in the opening and closing movements, the demands do not exceed the level required of choral sopranos in certain parts of the B-Minor Mass.

Moreover, the combination of solo soprano and concertante trumpet** is unique in the works of Bach, particularly in view of the hardly understaffed ensemble of string instruments. The era was indeed quite familiar with the combination of soprano and trumpet, as seen in Alessandro Scarlatti's cantata *Su le sponde del Tebro* or the oft-recounted story of the competition between the castrato Farinelli and a famous trumpeter in Rome in the 1720s. Still, no companion piece to *Jauchzet Gott in allen Landen* can be found in Bach's oeuvre. Instead, when matching the power of one to three trumpets, Bach generally prefers the greater volume of the bass voice.

Also without parallel in Bach's oeuvre is the virtuoso mien of the entire cantata. It pays tribute to the skill of both soloists, and in doing so it runs the risk of slipping too close to a certain undesirable superficiality. Also significant in this regard is the remarkable effort to couple a concerto for two violins with a chorale cantus firmus. This constellation certainly has something to do with the fact that at roughly the same time as the first performance, about 1730, Bach composed his famous Concerto for Two Violins in D Minor BWV 1043 (or reperformed it, in the event it had been written earlier).

In keeping with the composition's tendency toward virtuosity, there is a peculiarity of the text that has long vexed Bach scholarship: while the libretto of the cantata *Jauchzet Gott in allen Landen* is entirely devoted to praise and adoration, it has scarcely anything to do with the Gospel reading of the fifteenth Sunday after Trinity. However, this exact assignment to the church calendar is a late addition; the original assignment read "In ogni Tempo" (for all times) in the church year, a relatively rare carte blanche in Bach's cantatas.

The secondary nature of the assignment just mentioned results in an ambiguity that is difficult to resolve regarding the work's genesis and, in particular, its performers. Based on his profound understanding of Leipzig music history, Arnold Schering suggested that "a particularly skilled young choirboy, . . . or, what is more likely, a student falsettist" might have taken over the challenging solo soprano part.[15] Then the trumpet part would have fallen to the senior member of the *Stadtpfeifer* (city pipers) ensemble, Gottfried Reicha. Decades later, the American musicologist Robert Marshall considered the possibility of a more professional performer, pointing to a soprano known to be active in Dresden around 1730, the castrato Giovanni Bindi—though without credibly explaining his participation in a Protestant Church cantata. Therefore, Klaus Hofmann of Göttingen proposed considering the possibility that the Leipzig *Thomaskantor* may have received a commission from outside the city and suggested a connection to the nearby court of Weissenfels, where there was a long tradition of birthday and other congratulatory musical pieces for soprano and trumpet. Furthermore, in Weissenfels, as well as in Hamburg and Darmstadt but not in Leipzig, female singers could take part in church music.

Nevertheless, it is worth considering whether a particularly gifted St. Thomas soloist could have ventured the challenging soprano solo. To date we have no documentary evidence of this, but that is due to the particular nature of source transmission. In memoranda preserved in the archive of the Leipzig city hall, Bach and several of his predecessors describe the condition of the St. Thomas School and its choir in dismal terms, for well-considered reasons. Thus Johann Kuhnau, cantor of St. Thomas in 1717, complained about the excessive strain on students exposed to wind and weather without consideration for the effect on the most sensitive descant voices. The voices, he explained, were lost even before the singers had gained the ability to capably perform an easy short concert at sight with confidence, a goal that required longer training and often eluded even professional singers. The possibility mentioned almost accidentally by Kuhnau of achieving a certain level of perfection in spite of strenuous work as a musician echoes a remark by Johann Mattheson in Hamburg, who had been able to have women singers appear, at least in the cathedral. Mattheson wrote in 1739: "The boys are of little use, I mean, the chapel boys. Before they have attained a reasonable ability to sing, the descant voice is gone. And if they know a bit more or have a mature voice, more so than others, they work so hard to develop themselves that their voice [*Wesen*] is unpleasant and has no staying power."[16] Mattheson obviously wanted to highlight his innovation. His words need to be put into perspective, just as should the oft-cited negative judgment of falsetto singing by Johann Adam Hiller, a successor to Bach as cantor of St. Thomas at the end of the eighteenth century. According to Hiller, concerts in Leipzig had "never had other singers than when one came forward from the viola or violin and, with a screeching falsetto voice, wanted to sing an aria in the manner of Salinbeni, which, into the bargain, he could not read correctly."[17] Here again we have a transparently self-interested remark, for it was Hiller himself who, shortly after the end of the Seven Years' War, allowed women to appear at Leipzig concerts.

As far as the capabilities of boy sopranos are concerned, we must consider that on average in the eighteenth century the change of voice happened considerably later than it does today. For example, in 1763 the seventeen-year-old son of Cantor Doles at St. Thomas School was still able to sing a soprano solo in a church celebration of the end of the Seven Years' War. Bach himself, arriving in Lüneburg in 1700, was admitted to the matins choir as a soprano at the age of fifteen. Sometime later, it is plausibly reported, his voice broke, and his "uncommonly beautiful soprano voice" was gone. While it is only since the early nineteenth century that we have accounts of remarkable achievements by boy sopranos and altos in the Leipzig St. Thomas Choir, nothing speaks against the assumption that this is a continuation of a tradition that could develop, because, as it was said, "the school was a quasi conservatory and the students stayed in school longer than they do today."

The abilities of a similar boy soloist are described in the autobiography of one Pastor Christian Heinrich Schreyer.*** Born in 1751, he was admitted at the age of twelve years and three months to the choir school at St. Anne's Church in Dresden and in a short time advanced to first soloist: "I was able to climb up to high f with equal strength, without falsetto. My narrow chest became even more so through the strains of breathing, and I was capable of singing runs of three to four measures without pause and of holding single tones even longer that earlier would have exhausted all my breath."[18] This refers to supplemental cadenzas, interpolation of higher pitches, and other means of demonstrating an exceptional artistic skill.

One cannot dismiss the possibility that there were excellent soprano soloists in Leipzig as well during Johann Sebastian Bach's time, around 1730 and later, who were equal to the demands of the cantata *Jauchzet Gott in allen Landen*. Further, while the reason for the work's composition in any case is best sought outside Leipzig, this does not preclude possible reperformances there. It appears that there were at least three of these. One is attested to by several textual changes by Bach that focus on a *Herrschaft* (lordship; not more closely defined); a second, possibly, by the revised assignment to the fifteenth Sunday after Trinity. A third is documented by several changes in instrumentation undertaken by Wilhelm Friedemann Bach in Halle. A 1784 account attests that superb soprano soloists were available there as well from time to time. It mentions "a certain young man [who], roughly in his seventeenth year, has the great fortune of still singing the first soprano parts.... His voice is bright, with a very great range. His trills were—at least as of a year ago—uncommonly clear and large. He has a very high degree of expression in his power."[19]**** Almost all of these are exceptional cases. But this is exactly what an exceptional work such as *Jauchzet Gott in allen Landen* requires.

---

*Scheibe (1737, 36); Kümmerling (1955); Lindner (1855, 186).
**Wolf (1997); Hofmann (1989); Marshall (1976).
***Schulze (1987, 191ff.).
****Serauky (1942, 184).

Wachet auf, ruft uns die Stimme
BWV 140 / BC A 166

Twenty-Seventh Sunday after Trinity, November 25, 1731

Johann Sebastian Bach composed his cantata *Wachet auf, ruft uns die Stimme* BWV 140 (Awaken, calls to us the voice) for the twenty-seventh Sunday after Trinity, an occasion that makes its appearance quite rarely in the church calendar. Heard for the first time on November 25, 1731, it was a belated addition to the cycle of chorale cantatas from 1724 and 1725. It is based on Philipp Nicolai's *Wächterlied* (Watchmen's song), which was published in 1599 as an addendum to his *Freuden Spiegel des ewigen Lebens* (Joyful reflection of the eternal life) but must have been written somewhat earlier. In the original it appears beneath the heading "Ein anders—geistlich Braut-Lied—von der Stimm zu Mitternacht und von den klugen Jungfrauwen die ihrem himmlischen Bräutigam begegnen Matthäus 25" (Another—spiritual bride song—from the voice at midnight and by the clever virgins who meet their heavenly bridegroom Matthew 25). What is meant here is the parable of the wise and foolish virgins, the Gospel reading for the twenty-seventh Sunday after Trinity, Matthew 25:1–13:

> Then the Kingdom of Heaven shall be likened to ten virgins who took their lamps and went out to meet the bridegroom. But five among them were foolish, and five were clever. The foolish ones took their lamps, but they did not take oil with them. The wise ones, however, took oil in their vessels together with their lamps. Because now the bridegroom delayed, they all became drowsy and slept. But at midnight there came a cry: See, the bridegroom comes; go out to meet him! Then all those virgins arose and trimmed their lamps. But the foolish ones said to the wise: Give us some of your oil, for our lamps are going out. Then the wise ones answered and spoke: But

no, lest there not be enough for us and you; but go to the shopkeepers and buy for yourselves. And while they went out to buy, the bridegroom came, and those who were ready went in with him to the marriage feast, and the door was closed. At last the other virgins came and said: Lord, Lord, open to us! He, however, answered and said: Truly, I say to you: I do not know you. Therefore, watch, for you know neither day nor hour in which the Son of Man will come.

The three stanzas of Philipp Nicolai's poetic paraphrase of this Gospel text provide the cornerstones for our cantata. With its reference to slumbering Jerusalem at midnight, the waiting virgins, and the calling watchmen, the opening strophe focuses on the kingdom of blessed sleepers who await the Last Judgment and the return of Jesus Christ:

> Wachet auf, ruft uns die Stimme
> Der Wächter sehr hoch auf der Zinne,
> Wach auf, du Stadt Jerusalem!
> Mitternacht heißt diese Stunde;
> Sie rufen uns mit hellem Munde:
> Wo seid ihr klugen Jungfrauen?
> Wohlauf, der Bräutgam kommt;
> Steht auf, die Lampen nehmt!
> Alleluja!
> Macht euch bereit
> Zu der Hochzeit,
> Ihr müsset ihm entgegen gehn!
>
> Awaken, calls to us the voice
> Of the watchmen very high on the battlement,
> Awaken, you city of Jerusalem!
> The hour is midnight;
> They call to us with a clear voice:
> Where are you wise virgins?
> Get up, the bridegroom comes;
> Stand up, take your lamps!
> Hallelujah!
> Make yourselves ready
> For the wedding.
> You must go to meet him!

The second strophe describes the meeting of the "Auserwählten Seelen" (chosen souls) as royal bride and Jesus Christ as royal bridegroom; accompanied by the host of the faithful, they enter the hall of eternal joys to have the evening meal (Communion, or the Lord's Supper):

> Zion hört die Wächter singen,
> Das Herz tut ihr vor Freuden springen,
> Sie wachet und steht eilend auf.
> Ihr Freund kommt vom Himmel prächtig,
> Von Gnaden stark, von Wahrheit mächtig,
> Ihr Licht wird hell, ihr Stern geht auf.
> Nun komm, du werte Kron,
> Herr Jesu, Gottes Sohn!
> Hosianna!
> Wir folgen all
> Zum Freudenhaus
> Und halten mit das Abendmahl.
>
> Zion hears the watchmen singing,
> Her heart leaps for joy,
> She wakes and stands quickly up.
> Her friend comes from heaven in splendor,
> Strong in grace, mighty in truth,
> Her light brightens, her star ascends.
> Now come, you worthy crown,
> Lord Jesus, Son of God!
> Hosanna!
> We all follow
> To the hall of joy
> And join in the Lord's Supper.

The third strophe of the chorale functions as a conclusory Gloria, sounded before the throne of the Most High, the redeemed of the Lord, and the choir of angels.

This chorale text is expanded with free poetry: two recitative-aria movement pairs. These freely versified movements take up the ideas of the chorale text in continuation of the tradition inherited from the Middle Ages of the *unio mystica* and draw upon the bridal mysticism of the Song of Songs to formulate dialogues between Jesus and the soul. The only exception is the first recitative, which, from a narrator's perspective, depicts the arrival of the bridegroom with flowery language such as the following:

> Der Bräutigam kommt, der einem Rehe
> Und jungen Hirsche gleich
> Auf denen Hügeln springt
> Und euch das Mahl der Hochzeit bringt.
>
> The bridegroom comes, who, like a deer
> And young buck,

Springs upon the hills
And brings to you the wedding feast.

The associated duet indeed allows bride and bridegroom to meet one another—but it remains in a state of suspense and impatient waiting:

Wenn kömmst du, mein Heil?
Ich komme, dein Teil.
Ich warte mit brennenden Öle.
Eröffne den Saal
Zum himmlischen Mahl!
Komm, Jesu—komm, liebliche Seele.

When will you come, my salvation?
I am coming, your portion.
I wait with burning oil.
Open the hall
For the heavenly meal!
Come, Jesus—come, lovely soul.

In the second recitative, Jesus speaks with language from the Song of Songs:

So geh herein zu mir,
Du mir erwählte Braut!
Ich habe mich mit dir
Von Ewigkeit vertraut.
Dich will ich auf mein Herz,
Auf meinem Arm gleich wie ein Siegel setzen
Und dein betrübtes Aug ergötzen.
Vergiß, o Seele, nun
Die Angst, den Schmerz,
Den du erdulden müssen;
Auf meiner Linken sollst du ruhn,
Und meine Rechte soll dich küssen.

So come in here to me,
You, my chosen bride!
I have myself with you
Eternally betrothed.
I will place you just like a seal upon my heart,
Just like a seal upon my arm,
And delight your saddened eye.
Forget now, O soul,
The fear, the pain
That you have had to endure;

> Upon my left hand you shall rest,
> And my right hand shall cushion you.

The duet that follows depicts the lovers united:

> Mein Freund ist mein,
> Und ich bin sein.
> Die Liebe soll nichts scheiden.
> Ich will mit dir in Himmels Rosen weiden,
> Da Freude die Fülle, da Wonne wird sein.
>
> My beloved is mine,
> And I am his.
> Nothing shall separate the love [of God from us].
> I will revel with you in heaven's roses.
> There shall be complete pleasure and delight.

Bach begins his composition with an extended vocal-instrumental chorale arrangement as found so often in his chorale cantatas. In view of the movement's unusual length, Nicolai's chorale melody proves to be a true touchstone for this plan. With its multipartite structure, the tune points back to examples from Strasbourg; in remarkable ways it recalls the "Silberweise" by Hans Sachs.[20] Bach approaches his task by means of exemplary concentration on the instrumental component. A solemn march rhythm and a leaping, urgently syncopated figure, both led by the triadic beginning of the chorale melody, pervade the entire extraordinarily extensive movement of over two hundred measures. The cantata's center is similar, though reduced to three parts. Above a neutral foundation bass, the chorale is engaged in counterpoint by a sweeping melody whose naturally flowing appeal scarcely allows one to sense the intensity and rigor of the setting.

Embedded between these two chorale settings, as well as the closing chorale as a third cornerstone, are the two recitative-aria pairs, which bear no relation to the chorale tune. The two arias, both duets for soprano and bass, are very different in design and stand in a relationship of hope and fulfillment. The first duet, whose vocal component operates as a dialogue, approaches the character of the slow movement of a sonata or concerto, with its theme's wistful upward leap of the sixth and the virtuoso arabesques by the obbligato instrument. The distinctive timbre of the violino piccolo, pitched a minor third above the standard instrument, can be heard to symbolize the increasing impatience, although an inference can also be drawn from its appearance in serenades: that the C-minor duet can be understood as a true *Nachtstück* (evening piece). In contrast, the second duet, with its parallel leading of the voices and the joyous oboe ritornello, is entirely concerned with the joy of the united couple.

Schweigt stille, plaudert nicht
BWV 211 / BC G 48
For Various Purposes, mid-1734

The cantata *Schweigt stille, plaudert nicht* BWV 211 (Be quiet, stop chattering), also known as the *Coffee Cantata*, is without doubt the most famous homage to that brown elixir of the gods—but hardly the earliest.* That right of primogeniture belongs instead to the French composer Nicolas Bernier, who published a collection of *cantates profanes* (secular cantatas) shortly after 1700—and in Paris, of course—that included a cantata entitled *Le caffé* for soprano and violin or flute with basso continuo. By contrast, Johann Sebastian Bach's composition, younger by a generation, remained unpublished, at least so far as the music was concerned.

The text itself fared somewhat better. On May 5, 1732, one day after the beginning of the Jubilate or Easter trade fair, the Leipzig newspapers reported the appearance of the third volume of Picander's *Ernst-Schertzhafften und Satirischen Gedichten* (Earnest-jocular and satyric poems). This is the continuation of the "collected works" by the erstwhile student, now awaiting his advancement in the postal service, the popular and successful occasional poet Christian Friedrich Henrici. Announced in early 1731 but not complete until a year later, this third collection of his poetry presented verses touching on all possible vicissitudes of human existence, as well as a long series of musical texts. Among these is a reprint of a Passion after the evangelist Mark, composed by Bach but lost; a complete annual cycle of church cantatas; and a few secular cantatas at the end. The last of these is a dialogue piece with four each of recitatives and arias beneath the unpretentious heading "Über den Caffe. CANTATA." This text, beginning with "Schweigt stille, plaudert nicht" and ending with Lieschen's aria "Heute noch, lieber Vater, tut es doch" (Even today, dear father, do it please), evidently inspired a whole array of composers in the second third of the eighteenth century. However, the uncertain and in part fragmentary transmission of these cantatas permits scarcely any conclusions as to their authors' names or even why and how they originated.

Strictly speaking, the same is true of Picander's libretto: the only available version of 1732 does not reveal whether it is a first edition or a simplified republication of a single print. In the latter case, one would suspect that the text had been set to music for the first time and performed publicly before 1732. However, this hypothetical composition would have had nothing to do with Bach's Coffee Cantata. Instead, the *Thomaskantor* seems to have decided only in 1734 to give Picander's verses the attention the poet had been hoping for. The reason, first and foremost, was the activity of the Collegium Musicum, whose leadership Bach had assumed in early 1729 and which performed weekly concerts: in the summer in Zimmerman's coffee garden at the Grimma Gate and in the winter at Zimmerman's coffeehouse in the Katherinenstraße.

Bach's second-oldest son, Carl Philipp Emanuel, participated in writing out the performing parts, and on September 9, 1734, he left for the university in Frankfurt an der Oder. This excludes a date much later than that for a performance, and it suggests that it probably took place during the warmer months and probably outside. As he began work on the composition Bach kept to the letter of the printed text and simply named his work *Cantata a Soprano e Baßo con stromenti diversi* (Cantata for soprano and bass with various instruments). Later, his final title became *Schlendrian mit seiner Tochter Ließgen—Dramma per musica* (Schlendrian and his daughter, Lieschen—Dramma per musica). The choice of this designation, "dramma per musica," was justified, since in Bach's version—and only in this one—text and action undergo a significant expansion. Picander's modest morality, according to which Lieschen must sacrifice her coffee obsession for the prospect of a husband, is turned on its head in Bach's version. An interpolated recitative informs us that, with regard to Lieschen's hand in marriage, the only men with any hope of success are those willing to expressly guarantee her right in the marriage contract to drink coffee. To what extent this reversal, as well as the closing aria, focused on laissez-faire—"Die Katze läßt das Mausen nicht" (The cat doesn't give up mousing)—might be ascribed to Bach's account, thus establishing his abilities as a poet, must once again be left to the realm of speculation.

On the other hand, it is quite certain that Bach's Coffee Cantata was performed outside Leipzig. An announcement appeared in the *Wochentlichen Frankfurter Frag- und Anzeigungsnachrichten*: "On Tuesday, April 7, a foreign musician will perform a concert in the shopping quarter among the grocers, in which, among other things, *Schlendrian mit seiner Tochter Ließgen* will be offered in a drama. Whoever chooses to listen can acquire tickets at thirty Kreutzer and the text at twelve Kreutzer in the store at St. Nicholas Church in Schrott-Hauß auf dem Römerberg. Beginning precisely at six o'clock in the evening. No one without tickets will be admitted."[21] The wording of the work's title leaves no doubt that the piece in question is Johann Sebastian

Bach's composition. Whoever may be hiding behind the phrase "foreign musician" can no longer be determined due to the extensive destruction of Frankfurt archives in World War II. Also unanswerable is the question whether the audience in the hall of the Great Shopping Center with the address Neue Kräme 7 beside St. Paul's Church may perhaps have included Goethe's father.

Another riddle is a remark in a letter from the Berlin music theorist Friedrich Wilhelm Marpurg, who wrote to an unidentified person on August 18, 1757, perhaps the Leipzig publisher Breitkopf: "I had promised you a French parody of the Coffee Cantata, but it turned out to be so truly terrible that I gave it back to the Mr. Frenchman. There, no long and short syllable had been attended to properly and so forth. It was awful."[22] Marpurg knew Bach personally and treasured his works. It remains somewhat unclear whether Johann Sebastian Bach's composition is meant by the expression "Coffee Cantata" and why a French text might have been added to it. It is possible that Marpurg was thinking of a work by his Berlin contemporary Johann Friedrich Agricola.

In any case, the designation "Coffee Cantata" is documented at the time. Christian Friedrich Penzel, a passionate admirer of Bach who studied at St. Thomas School from 1751 to 1756, copied out an anonymous composition on Picander's "coffee" text as well as Bach's cantata in early April 1754 to which he gave the title "Coffee Cantata / Herr Schlendrian mit seiner Tochter Ließgen."

The universally comprehensible text, the adept diction, and the skillful musical characterization by the *Thomaskantor* all garnered the Coffee Cantata a certain popularity for some time in the eighteenth century. The Bach Renaissance of the nineteenth century embraced the piece rather quickly: it was published as early as the 1830s, long before such pinnacles as the Christmas Oratorio and the D-major Magnificat. Then as now, its cryptic humor demands subtle highlighting on the part of the performers and undivided attention on the part of the audience. Nothing here will tolerate crude contours: neither Schlendrian's blustery entrance, nor Lieschen's yearning song of praise for sweet coffee, nor Schlendrian's desperate brooding over the thickheadedness of young girls, nor Lieschen's triumphant jubilation at the prospect of a quick wedding. For that reason, a staged performance seems superfluous. Everything that needs to be said is communicated by the text and, above all, by the music.

---

*Extensively discussed in Schulze (1985).

Jauchzet, frohlocket, auf, preiset die Tage
BWV 248 Part I / BC D 7 I

Christmas Day, December 25, 1734

The cantata *Jauchzet, frohlocket, auf, preiset die Tage* BWV 248 Part I (Exult, rejoice, arise, praise the days) is for the first day of Christmas and was first performed on December 25, 1734, in St. Nicholas, the main church of Leipzig. With it, Johann Sebastian Bach began to realize his plan to provide a musical arrangement for the first of the three high feasts of the church year: instead of single cantatas independent of one another, a complete cycle for the longer period from Christmas to Epiphany. The models for such an ambitious sequence of cantatas—aside from Bach's own works, such as the chorale cantata annual cycle, composed in 1724 and 1725—include the multipart Lübeck *Abendmusiken*, as well as other Passion cantata series and multipart Passion oratorios whose performances since the end of the seventeenth century are documented at the Thuringian court of Gotha in particular.

Whether Bach intended at the outset to call his cycle of six cantatas an oratorio is open to question. The original numberings in his autograph scores only begin with the third cantata. The reason for Bach's momentary uncertainty can be seen clearly in the original print of the text of 1734. Its title unmistakably reads: *ORATORIUM, Welches Die heilige Weyhnacht über In beyden Haupt-Kirchen zu Leipzig musicieret wurde* (ORATORIO, which was set to music over holy Christmas Night in both main churches in Leipzig).[23] However, it is clear from the headings in the individual cantatas that one can speak of a cyclical performance only within certain limitations. According to the traditional schedule for concerted music at the main churches, St. Nicholas and St. Thomas, the St. Nicholas congregation heard the first, third, and fifth cantatas in the main worship service in the mornings and the other cantatas at vespers on the second day of Christmas, New Year's Day, and Epiphany. Worshipers at St. Thomas, on the other hand, were able to hear only the first, second, fourth, and sixth cantatas. There was, therefore, a good bit of artistic idealism lurking in Bach's conception of performing the Christmas story from the birth of Christ to the appearance of the wise men from the East.

Even so, long-term planning can be assumed here, although it remains unclear that Bach considered every detail well in advance. In addition to the arrangements for performance just described, with their unavoidable preference for St. Nicholas Church, the treatment of the Gospel narratives raises several questions. Bach allocated the text belonging to the first day of Christmas in equal parts to the first two cantatas and the text for the second day to the third cantata. In similar fashion, the last two cantatas share the Gospel text for Epiphany, while the account of the flight to Egypt, expected on the Sunday after New Year's Day, is missing entirely. It would appear that Bach managed the specific layout of the 1734–35 end-of-year season rather idiosyncratically: there was no Sunday after Christmas but a Sunday between New Year's Day and Epiphany.

What is the earliest evidence of Bach's plan to structure the cantata cycle later called the Christmas Oratorio? The question is of some importance because its answer could help to clarify the classic question of how the parody procedure, which Bach turned to so frequently in the Christmas Oratorio, should be assessed from Bach's perspective as well as that of later generations. Since before 1850 Bach scholarship has been aware that the majority of the arias and choral movements come from secular festive cantatas and are simply supplied with new text. Although scholars had to take this into account relatively early, it has often proven difficult for them to come to terms with this knowledge. In 1880 Philipp Spitta hoped to solve the question by maintaining that Bach was scarcely able to write anything outside of a religious context: "His secular occasional works were, rather, nonsecular, and as such they did not fulfill their purpose. The composer returned them to their true home when he transformed them to church music."[24] Later, Albert Schweitzer complained that through retexting, word and tone had become alienated from one another at many points. In contrast, more recent Bach scholarship has shown with many examples how sensitively and conscientiously Bach and his librettists proceeded in most cases, even if the results might differ in quality. Accordingly, the richness and complexity of Bach's music produce a "musical surplus" that allows the individual movement to be open to very different texts. As Ludwig Finscher wrote in 1969, "The musical greatness of Bach's works is the prerequisite of their suitability for parody."*[25]

It is worth asking whether Bach's Christmas Oratorio owes its origins to the composer's more or less coincidental recourse to several congratulatory cantatas, as well as to a church cantata of unknown purpose from 1733–34, or whether in conceptualizing those works Bach did so with their reuse in mind as part of a larger cantata cycle. Since Bach began relying on parody frequently and deliberately no later than the start of his tenure at Leipzig, he can hardly have begun considering the future uses of works for one-time occasions only after he had finished composing them.

With regard to the Christmas Oratorio, this could mean that the cantatas *Laßt uns sorgen, laßt uns wachen* BWV 213 (Let us care for, let us watch) and *Tönet, ihr Pauken, erschallet, Trompeten* BWV 214 (Sound, you drums, ring out, trumpets) were designed with their reusability in mind. However, one objection would be that even if Bach thought through a secular work's reuse, he prepared it only in a generalized sense. Even when setting the text for a one-time performance for a specific occasion, Bach did so with all his powers and artistic acumen. That the high compositional standard accommodated other and partially divergent text relationships was desirable, but ultimately it was a side benefit.

The first cantata of the oratorio demonstrates in exemplary fashion what obstacles were still to be overcome in spite of all Bach's foresight. Bach composed the movement "Tönet, ihr Pauken" from the 1733 cantata for the queen of Poland (BWV 214) with its use as an opening movement in mind. His librettist, unfortunately unknown, skillfully prepared a new version in which the triad "tönet," "erschallet," "erfüllet" (sound, ring out, fill) is replaced by "jauchzet," "preiset," "rühmet" (exult, praise, extoll). What could not be repaired was the deep beginning of the vocal part with what had been an imitation of drum beats. A second problem arose from the adoption of the alto aria from the cantata *Herkules auf dem Scheideweg* BWV 213 (Hercules at the crossroads), also of 1733. The brusquely defensive "Ich will dich nicht hören, ich will dich nicht wissen, verworfene Wollust, ich kenne dich nicht" (I will not hear you, I will not recognize you, depraved Pleasure, I know you not) was replaced with "Bereite dich Zion, mit zärtlichen Trieben, den Schönsten, den Liebsten bald bei dir zu sehn" (Prepare yourself, Zion, with tender urges, to see the most beautiful, the dearest beside you). This required a change in instrumental accompaniment as well as numerous performance markings in order to alter the character of the aria radically without touching the compositional substance. The adoption of the aria "Fama" from the queen's cantata was less difficult. The original "Cron und Preis gecrönter Damen" (Crown and trophy of royal ladies), gleaming with the sound of trumpets, could be recycled with a clear conscience to "Großer Herr, o starker König" (Great Lord, O powerful king) in praise of the savior. Newly composed, therefore, were the evangelist's role, the accompanied recitatives, and the chorales. In this effort, Bach had to keep in mind the existing material, taken from the secular first version, as he sought to integrate it within the new composition. The success of this comprehensive awareness remains undisputed over generations.

---

*Finscher (1969, 105).

Gott ist unsere Zuversicht
BWV 197.2 / *BC* B 16

Wedding Ceremony, 1736–1737

Bach inscribed his autograph score of the cantata *Gott ist unsere Zuversicht* BWV 197 (God is our assurance) with the words *In diebus nuptiarum* (On wedding days). Hence, it is for wedding celebrations and belongs to the not particularly comprehensive group of *Trauungskantaten* (wedding ceremony cantatas) or, in the terminology of Bach's day, *Brautmessen* (bridal masses). Furnishing wedding ceremonies and celebrations with festive music was an ancient tradition, and the "better society" of Leipzig saw no reason to give it up or restrict its use. On the contrary: the annual average of such commissions was relatively stable, making it possible to calculate Bach's supplemental income as a nearly constant amount. Regarding these fees, a regulation at St. Thomas School observed tersely that "with respect to the bridal masses, the cantor has until now been given one reichsthaler for each, with which he shall also henceforth be satisfied and shall not demand more."[26]

In practice, however, a more lucrative arrangement was in force. Former St. Thomas School students described it when they were asked in 1781, when disagreements about fee amounts arose. Gottlob Friedrich Rothe, sexton at St. Thomas Church and later known as a friend of the writer Johann Gottfried Seume, went on record saying: "In previous times, the cantors Kuhnau, Bach, Harrer, along with the organists, served in person at bridal masses and afterward held a banquet as recreation. For the sake of convenience, the old Martius told the groom to give a thaler instead of this banquet. Since that time the thaler has always been given to those people."[27] The concern here is for catering in addition to cash benefits, for the participation of cantors and organists in celebratory meals, and, later, for the more popular, time-saving option of receiving monetary compensation in lieu of participating in the wedding reception feast. The "alte Martius," responsible for the new regulation of 1730, functioned in Bach's day in Leipzig as director of weddings and funerals. Rothe's colleague Carl Ephraim Haupt, sexton of St. Nicholas Church, unearthed another memory in 1781: "For a full bridal mass the Herr Cantor received two thalers, which he always kept, and one thaler instead of a double flask of wine (which I myself, as a student, many times gave the blessed Herr Cantor Bach in kind; the food has long since ceased)."[28] And so, contrary to the stipulation in the school regulations, the cantor of St. Thomas School received three thalers, one of which was paid in kind for some time and later was paid as a cash benefit. Two thalers went to the St. Thomas School students and five to the city musicians, or eight, in case trumpets and drums were involved. Hence, it was understandable that often the fathers of brides avoided these expenses and, under various pretexts, arranged *stille Trauungen* (silent weddings) without music or had the ceremony performed out of doors in the countryside. Just as understandably, the clergy and musicians tried to collect the fees to which they were entitled and that they had already taken into account in calculating their basic salaries; many legal disputes were fought over this.

These relatively high fees were incurred by the *ganze Brautmessen* (full bridal masses)—or, in today's terminology, *Trauungskantaten* (wedding ceremony cantatas). *Halben Brautmessen* (half bridal masses) were less lavish, financially as well as musically. These involved the performance of several wedding chorales with instrumental accompaniment. These obligations were less profitable and productive in every respect, and the *Thomaskantor* made every effort to pass them off to a substitute. That person, most frequently a prefect in St. Thomas School, would then find out how well he could get along with the mischievous band of singers. In the early summer of 1736, the only way Gottfried Theodor Krauß, then twenty-two years old, knew how to earn respect was through corporal punishment. This touched off a long-lasting dispute between the cantor and rector of St. Thomas School that has come to be known in Bach biography as the *Präfektenstreit*, or "prefects' battle." In one of his missives to the Leipzig town council, the rector remarked, viciously, that the "misfortune" (*Unglück*) of the prefect, who ultimately had to leave the school, was

> to be attributed solely to the negligence of the Cantor. For if he had gone to the wedding service as he should have, since there was nothing wrong with him, instead of thinking it was beneath his dignity to conduct at a wedding service where only chorales were to be sung (for which reason he has absented himself from several such wedding services, including the recent one for the Krögels, in connection with which, as I could not help hearing, the musicians in service to Your Magnificences and You, Noble Sirs, complained to other people)—then the said Krause would have had no opportunity to indulge in those excesses, both in the Church and outside.[29]

The cantata *Gott ist unsre Zuversicht* is a true full bridal mass. It was composed during the tension-filled years 1736 and 1737, when the prefects' battle threatened to shake the foundations of musical tradition at Leipzig's St. Thomas School. Who the bridal couple may have been cannot be established today. The unknown librettist crafted his text in such a general fashion that any search for clues has little hope of success. Perhaps this is in fact an advantage of the libretto, reflecting Bach's intention to use the cantata over and over. The opening movement begins with a phrase in the first verse of Psalm 46:

> Gott ist unsre Zuversicht,
> Wir vertrauen seinen Händen.
> Wie er unsre Wege führt,
> Wie er unser Herz regiert,
> Da ist Segen aller Enden.
>
> God is our assurance,
> We trust his hands.
> As he guides our ways,
> As he governs our heart,
> There is blessing for all purposes.

Next, two recitatives surround an aria before the cantata's first part, performed before the ceremony, closes with the third strophe from Luther's chorale *Nun bitten wir den Heiligen Geist* (Now we implore the holy spirit): "Du süße Lieb, schenk uns deine Gunst" (You sweet love, grant us your favor).

The aria in this first part of the cantata is striking; its text begins with these peculiar lines:

> Schläfert allen Sorgenkummer
> In den Schlummer
> Kindlichen Vertrauens ein.
>
> Put to sleep all care and sorrow
> In the slumber
> Of childlike trust.

This is an indication of parody, the retexting of existing music already on hand. The model is easily identified: it is found in what would later be known as Bach's Easter Oratorio BWV 249 in the tenor aria "Sanfte soll mein Todeskummer" (Gentle shall my deathly trouble), which in turn goes back to a lullaby (*Schlummerarie*) in the secular model for the oratorio, the so-called Shepherd Cantata BWV 249.1. Bach obviously planned to adapt this music, composed in 1725, and instructed his librettist accordingly. His efforts to create an appropriate new text were unrewarded, however, and Bach decided against his original intention in favor of new composition.

Bach proceeded differently in the second part, performed after the ceremony. Here both arias go back textually as well as musically to a Christmas cantata that probably originated in 1728, *Ehre sei Gott in der Höhe* BWV 197.1 (Glory to God in the highest). The greeting to the infant Jesus, "O du angenehmer Schatz" (O you charming treasure), became "O du angenehmes Paar" (O you charming couple). These lines in the original are just as purposeful:

> Ich lasse dich nicht,
> Ich schließe dich ein
> Im Herzen durch Lieben und Glauben.

> I will not let you go,
> I enclose you
> In my heart through love and faith.

They became these more general and less pointed lines:

> Vergnügen und Lust,
> Gedeihen und Heil
> Wird wachsen und stärken und laben.

> Pleasure and delight,
> Prosperity and salvation
> Will grow and strengthen and nourish.

The second part of the cantata closes with a strophe from Georg Neumark's *Wer nur den lieben Gott läßt walten* (Whoever only lets dear God rule). Bach's score is silent as to which text is intended. Another rather uncertain tradition presents Neumark's seventh strophe in a partially paraphrased version:

> So wandelt froh auf Gottes Wegen,
> Und was ihr tut, das tut getreu.
> Verdienet eures Gottes Segen,
> Denn der ist alle Morgen neu:
> Denn welcher seine Zuversicht
> Auf Gott setzt, den verläßt er nicht.

> Then wander happily on God's ways,
> And whatever you do, do it faithfully.
> Earn your God's blessing,
> For it is every morning new:
> For whoever places his trust
> In God, he will not forsake him.

As discussed, there are two layers of different ages in Bach's composition. The younger one includes the opening chorus, first aria, all the recitatives, and, mutatis mutandis, both choral movements. The older one is represented by the two arias in the second part, albeit with some alterations. The first of these arias, "O du angenehmes Paar" (O you charming pair), for bass, obbligato oboe, two muted violins, bassoon, and basso continuo, was scored for alto and two transverse flutes in the Christmas cantata; the original key, G major, was kept. The second aria, whose text begins "Verngügen und Lust" (Pleasure and delight), was originally scored in D major for bass and obbligato oboe d'amore. In the new version, it was transposed to G major and arranged for soprano, solo violin, and two oboi d'amore. The two oboes are only entrusted with filler parts, owing to the higher ranges of singing and instrumental obbligato parts. The wind parts in low register now do not allow the distance to the continuo bass to seem too large.

The most important of the newer group of movements are the opening chorus and first aria. Accompanied by a large festival orchestra with trumpets and drums, as well as woodwinds and strings, the chorus enters after an instrumental introduction of twenty-four measures with the obligatory fugal exposition on the earnest text beginning "Gott ist unsre Zuversicht, / Wir vertrauen seinen Händen." But this episode flows directly into several sustained chords, after which all polyphonic ambitions seem tossed aside. The loose interplay of vocal and instrumental parts gives hardly any hint that this is a church cantata for a particular occasion. Instead, the writing reminds us of Bach's secular cantatas between 1730 and 1740.

Similar features are found in the third movement, the "slumber aria," scored for alto, oboe d'amore, strings, and basso continuo. But here Bach's intentions with respect to an adequate realization of the textual content can be clearly felt and easily comprehensible. If the aria in the Weissenfels *Tafelmusik* (banquet music) of 1725 had a unified scope, a certain degree of contradiction crept into the new version of the text for Easter of the same year, seen in the words "Todeskummer" (death throes) and "Schlummer" (slumber), on the one hand, and "tröstlich" (comforting) and "erfrischend" (refreshing), on the other. The librettist of the wedding cantata followed this tendency blindly; to the beginning section, with its "Schläfert alle Sorgenkummer," he added a contrasting continuation with the words "Gottes Augen, welche wachen" (God's eyes, which watch). Perhaps unwittingly, he failed to accomplish his task, thereby challenging the cantor of St. Thomas to compose a new composition, which had not been his initial intention. In this way, the contradiction intended by the text—but basically unintentional—is elevated to a principle, and the middle part of the aria is distinguished from the external parts by the change of key, meter, tempo, and thematic material.

Kommt, eilet und laufet, ihr flüchtigen Füße
BWV 249.4 / BC D 8

Easter Sunday, April 6, 1738

Compared to its well-known sibling work, the Christmas Oratorio (BWV 248.2), the Easter Oratorio BWV 249.4 is clearly less popular with the public. The reasons for this certainly do not lie with the music and its quality. With its catchy freshness of invention, it lacks nothing in comparison to its younger but much better known sibling. The text, however, poses problems, if only at first glance. It certainly found no favor with the classic Bach biographer of the nineteenth century, Philipp Spitta: "It cannot but surprise us to find that Bach could have been satisfied with such a text," reads the summary from his rather unsympathetic overview:

> The text, of which the author is unknown ... begins with a duet between John and Peter, who are informed of Christ's resurrection by the women, and who run joyfully to the sepulcher to convince themselves (John 20, 3 and 4). There Mary the mother of James, and Salome, reproach them with not having also purposed to anoint the body of the Lord and thus testifying their love for Him. The men excuse themselves, saying that their anointing has been "with briny tears, and deep despair and longing." Then the women explain that these, happily, are no longer needed, since the Lord is risen. They gaze into the empty tomb; John asks where the Saviour can be, to which Mary Magdalene replies what the men have long known: "He now has risen from the dead. / To us an angel did appear, / Who told us, lo He is not here." Peter directs his attention to the "linen cloth," and this leads him to recall the tears he had shed over his denial of Jesus, a very tasteless episode. The women next express their longing to see Jesus once more; John rejoices that the Lord lives again, and the end is a chorus: "Thanks and praise / be to Thee for ever, Lord! / Satan's legions now are bound, / his dominion now hath ceased, / let the highest heaven resound / with your songs, ye souls released. / Fly open, ye gates! / Open radiant and glorious! / The Lion of Judah comes riding victorious."[30]

Spitta and others were prevented from issuing a more just assessment of the Easter Oratorio by what they could not know, namely, its origin as a secular cantata, a *Tafelmusik* (banquet music) of 1725 for Duke Christian of Saxe-Weissenfels. This was discovered in about 1940, when Friedrich Smend came across evidence of a relationship between the Easter music and a lost "shepherds' colloquy" (*Schäfergespräch*) by Christian Friedrich Henrici. Even so, at first the knowledge of the Easter Oratorio's secular parentage was hardly useful. The persistent prejudice against anything resulting from what is called "parody procedure"—supplying existing music with a new text—simply opened the libretto to further criticism. It was seen as reflecting a profoundly meaningful event for the church, but without Gospel narratives or chorale strophes, and thus it was reduced to an intermediate text prepared with nonchalance and without sympathy in order to make good use of an elaborate composition that would otherwise have lain idle.

More recently, studies from the theological side have highlighted how the new text, focused on the feast of the Resurrection, draws upon the centuries-old tradition of Easter plays in many different ways and perhaps in all of its aspects.* In doing so, it consciously avoids any attempt at a dramatic fiction: neither angels nor the Risen One are included in the action. Even so, the play is at once a dramatic realization and a proclamation of praise. Thus the first vocal movement takes up the race between Peter and John to the grave of Jesus from the book of John; but with its text beginning "Kommt eilet und laufet" (Come, make haste and run) it also functions as an appeal to *meditatio*, comparable to the opening of the St. Matthew Passion's opening chorus, "Kommt, ihr Töchter hilft mir klagen" (Come, you daughters, help me lament). The tone of the "mysticism of the bride," going back to the Song of Songs, is hard to ignore in the recitatives (the first, in particular), as well as in Maria Jacobi's aria "Seele, deine Spezereien" (Soul, your spices [shall no longer be myrrh]). The connection to medieval traditions is particularly strong in Peter's aria and its associated recitative, whose meditations include Jesus's cast-off grave clothes and mention his shroud in particular. The linkage of the stories of the disciples at the grave of Jesus and the awakening of Lazarus in John 11 and 20, respectively, follow ancient tradition. The account of Lazarus was understood as an anticipation of the Resurrection of Jesus and the reawakening of the dead and thus symbolizes the hope for a resurrection to eternal life. In this sense, the cast-off grave clothes in Peter's aria become recognized as a sign of the Resurrection of the Lord and convey the certainty that one's own death will be but a sleep.

On the whole, the unidentified librettist deserves every recognition for his work to appropriately transform the arias and ensembles of the secular original into the subject matter of Easter with verbal skill and fealty to content.

In 1725 Bach's efforts were confined to the composition of recitatives and the arrangement of the voices in the arias and ensemble movements. At first probably designated as a cantata for Easter (BWV 249.3), the work was reperformed in 1738 (BWV 249.4) with minor alterations but with the title *Oratorio*. Whether the role designations Maria Jacobi, Maria Magdalena, Petrus, and Johannes were still used at this time cannot be known for certain, but they were certainly omitted in the final performances in 1745 and April 1749 (BWV 249.5).

Significantly, in this late version the original duet for Peter and John was refashioned as a four-part chorus, so that the motif of the disciples' race recedes even further behind the invitation to contemplation.

Otherwise, there was little change to the core musical substance, which goes back to the Weissenfels *Tafelmusik* of 1725. The work begins with two instrumental movements: a cheerful concertante Allegro that exploits timbral contrasts between instrumental groups (trumpets and drums, oboes with bassoon, and string instruments), as well as a mournful Adagio with an expressive solo for oboe (flute in a later version). Both movements may go back to an earlier instrumental concerto. This is perhaps also true of the first vocal movement, which seems to have an unusually robust instrumental accompaniment for a duet. The later transformation to a four-part chorus mitigates this discrepancy somewhat. In the soprano aria, voice and flute compete in a vivid representation of love for Jesus. Peter's slumber aria unfolds in beguiling coloration, with layered timbres of string instruments and recorders in octaves, radiating a heavenly serenity. The alto aria is situated between energetic focus and sensitive encouragement. The work concludes with an ensemble that, by combining a solemn, hovering opening with a brisk fugal ending, follows the model of the Sanctus of 1724 (232.1), later incorporated in the Mass in B Minor (BWV 232.4).

---

*Steiger (1983).

Lobet Gott in seinen Reichen
BWV 11 / *BC* D 9

Ascension Day, May 15, 1738

The Ascension Oratorio BWV 11 of 1735 belongs to a trilogy of impressive compositions for the high feasts of the church calendar.[31] Among its sister works, the Christmas Oratorio BWV 248, which originated a few months earlier, consists of a series of six cantatas for the feast days from Christmas through Epiphany. It coheres through tonal and architectonic relationships and in particular through the biblical accounts from Luke 2 and Matthew 2. On the other hand, the other sibling work, for Easter, ten years older, initially consisted only of a single, one-part, festive cantata (BWV 249.3); it received the designation Easter Oratorio only upon being reperformed in

1738 (BWV 249.4).[32] In contrast to the Christmas Oratorio, the work for Easter contains no original evangelist narrative but only rhymed paraphrases. With the Ascension Oratorio, the situation is different yet again. Here, in the traditional manner, a tenor serves as narrator, who presents the account divided into four parts:

> [Lukas 24:50–51] Der Herr Jesus hub seine Hände auf und segnete seine Jünger, und es geschah, da er sie segnete, schied er von ihnen. [Apostelgeschichte 1:9] Und ward aufgehoben zusehends und fuhr auf gen Himmel, eine Wolke nahm ihn weg vor ihren Augen, [Markus 16:19] und er sitzet zur rechten Hand Gottes. [Apostelgeschichte 1:10] Und da sie ihm nachsahen gen Himmel fahren, siehe, da stunden bei ihnen zwei Männer in weißen Kleidern, [11] welche auch sagten: Ihr Männer von Galiläa, was stehet ihr und sehet gen Himmel? Dieser Jesus, welcher von euch ist aufgenommen gen Himmel, wird kommen, wie ihr ihn gesehen habt gen Himmel fahren. [Lukas 24:52] Sie aber beteten ihn an, [Apostelgeschichte 1:12] wandten um gen Jerusalem von dem Berge, der da heißet der Ölberg, welcher ist nahe bei Jerusalem und liegt einen Sabbater-Weg davon, [Lukas 24:52] und sie kehreten wieder gen Jerusalem mit großer Freude.

> [Luke 24:51] The Lord Jesus lifted his hands and blessed his disciples, and it happened, that as he blessed them, he departed from them. [Acts 1:9] And was lifted as they were looking and traveled up to heaven; a cloud took him away before their eyes, [Mark 16:19] and he sits at the right hand of God. [Acts 1:10] And as they watched him travel to heaven, behold, there stood two men beside them in white clothing, [11] who also said: You men of Galilee, why do you stand and look toward heaven? This Jesus, who was taken from you to heaven, will come, as you have seen him travel to heaven. [Luke 24:52] They however prayed to him, [Acts 1:12] and returned to Jerusalem from the mountain called the Mount of Olives, which is near Jerusalem and lies a sabbath-day journey away, [Luke 24:52] and they returned to Jerusalem with great joy.

Nevertheless, this text has long posed a riddle for Bach scholarship, because although all its components are found in the New Testament, it was not clear who might have assembled and altered the sections from Luke 24, Mark 16, and Acts 1 in different ways. We are indebted to the Leipzig theologian Martin Petzoldt for pointing out the so-called *Evangelien-Harmonie* (Harmony of the Gospels) of Johann Bugenhagen, a contemporary and colleague of Martin Luther. In Bach's day these *Evangelien-Harmonie* were to be found in nearly every hymnal, although reduced in most cases to the Passion story and without the section on the Ascension of Christ. Furthermore, the version set to music by Bach has several minor abbreviations and rearrangements compared to Bugenhagen's version, as well as reformulations, mostly in agreement with the original Gospel text.

There are two chorales in Bach's Ascension Oratorio: in the middle of the work, following the Evangelist's text "eine Wolke nahm ihn weg vor ihren Augen, und er sitzet zur rechten Hand Gottes" (a cloud took him away before their eyes, and he sits at the right hand of God), the fourth strophe from Johann Rist's 1641 hymn *Du Lebens-Fürst, Herr Jesu Christ* (You prince of life, Lord Jesus Christ):

> Nun lieget alles unter dir,
> Dich selbst nur ausgenommen.
>
> Now all lies beneath you,
> You yourself alone excepted.

The entire work concludes with the seventh strophe from Gottfried Wilhelm Sacer's 1697 hymn *Gott fähret auf gen Himmel* (God goes up to heaven), whose text begins:

> Wenn soll es doch geschehen,
> Wenn kömmt die liebe Zeit,
> Daß ich ihn werde sehen
> In seiner Herrlichkeit?
>
> When shall it come about,
> When might the dear time come,
> When I will see him
> In his glory?

With regard to free poetry, the Ascension Oratorio contains two each of recitatives and arias, as well as the opening chorus. The chorus consists of six verses, of which the first three seem superior to the others linguistically and in content:

> Lobet Gott in seinen Reichen,
> Preiset ihn in seinen Ehren,
> Rühmet ihn in seiner Pracht.
>
> Laud God in his kingdoms,
> Praise him in his honors,
> Extol him in his splendor.

Then the continuation:

> Sucht sein Lob recht zu vergleichen,
> Wenn ihr mit gesamten Chören
> Ihm ein Lied zu Ehren macht!

> Seek to justly compare his praise
> When you, with entire choirs,
> Make a hymn to honor him!

Next to the powerful sequence "laud," "praise," "extol," the effects of "comparing" praise and the "making" of a hymn seem unnatural and weakened.

The explanation for this is found in the background of Bach's composition. Shortly after 1900 the French Bach specialist André Pirro pointed to a text that could fit perfectly beneath the music of the opening movement of the Ascension Oratorio. The verses are by Johann Heinrich Winckler, at the time a teacher at the St. Thomas School and later a professor at the University of Leipzig, where he encountered the young student Johann Wolfgang von Goethe. The occasion for Winckler's poetic activity was the consecration of the renovated St. Thomas School in 1732. The festival music for the occasion consisted of a two-part cantata libretto by Winckler; Johann Sebastian Bach was expressly named as the work's composer.[33] The song of praise for the school, the authorities, the aristocracy, and the creator of all things begins with these lines:

> Froher Tag, verlangte Stunden,
> Nun hat unsre Lust gefunden,
> Was sie fest und ruhig macht.
> Hier steht unser Schulgebäude,
> Hier erblicket Aug und Freude
> Kunst und Ordnung, Zier und Pracht.

> Happy day, hoped-for hours,
> Now our delight has discovered
> What will make it secure and serene.
> Here stands our school building,
> Here beholds eye and pleasure,
> Art and order, ornament and splendor.

A year later, Bach incorporated this movement along with all the recitatives and arias into a congratulatory cantata for the name day of the Saxon prince elector.[34] Two years later and with a third text, the opening chorus found its way into the Ascension Oratorio.

Only relatively recently has Bach scholarship addressed the question of whether other movements in this work, in particular the two arias, might have older origins. In 1950 the Berlin theologian and supreme Bach expert Friedrich Smend successfully demonstrated that Johann Christoph Gottsched's text for the "Serenade auf des Herrn geheimen Kriegsraths von Hohenthal Vermählung in Leipzig, 1725" (Serenade for the wedding of Lord Privy Councillor of War von Hohenthal in Leipzig, 1725) must have been composed by Bach and that, ten years later, two of its arias were incorporated in the Ascension Oratorio.[35*]

Lord Privy Councillor of War von Hohenthal was the Leipzig merchant-lord Peter Hohmann the Younger, later ennobled, who in November 1725 married Christiana Sybilla Mencke, daughter of University of Leipzig professor Johann Burkhard Mencke. Gottsched, then twenty-five years old, lived in the Menckes' house; Menke fostered the young scholar in many ways. The text for Gottsched's serenade is a conversation between the personifications of Nature, Virtue, and Modesty. Nature's aria, "Entfernet euch, ihr kalten Herzen, entfernet euch, ich bin euch feind" (Remove yourselves, you frigid hearts, remove yourselves, I am your foe) became, in the Ascension Oratorio, "Ach bleibe doch, mein liebstes Leben, ach fliehe nicht so bald von mir" (Ah, but stay, my dearest life, ah, do not flee so soon from me). The aria for Modesty, "Unschuld, Kleinod reiner Seelen, schmücke mich durch deine Pracht" (Innocence, jewel of pure souls, adorn me with your splendor) was refashioned to become "Jesu, deine Gnadenblicke, kann ich doch beständig sehn" (Jesus, your glances of grace I can indeed see constantly).

Like its sister work for Christmas, the Ascension Oratorio combines original movements along with those that have been adopted or revised. Joy, pride, and confidence characterize the cheerfully concerted opening chorus with its undemanding choral component, catchy fanfare motives and scales, and, in particular, the bouncing Lombard syncopations. Following a brief evangelist narrative, a recitative for bass sensitively laments the departure of Jesus. With the motivic unity of the accompanying flutes and the vocal motifs that anticipate the following aria, it recalls the compositional methods of the St. Matthew Passion. The farewell aria, "Ach bleibe doch, mein liebstes Leben," for alto and the sonorous accompanying unison violins, goes back to a wedding serenade, in which its cutting dissonances must have sounded exceptional. In 1749 Bach incorporated a shorter version, revised in crucial ways, into the closing portion of his Mass in B Minor BWV 232 as the Agnus Dei. A brief evangelist's recitative and a simple four-part chorale close the first part of the oratorio.

The second part begins with the account of the appearance of the "two men in white clothing" and their announcement. The announcement itself is sung in two-part counterpoint, a strict canon at the fifth that symbolizes integrity of the statement, on the one hand, and its unassailability, on the other. The second aria, set for soprano, flutes, one oboe, and strings, omits the normally obligatory bass foundation in what is known as "bassetto effect," a procedure that for Bach is almost always meant symbolically. It can mean very different things: innocence, purity, clarity, incomprehensibility; however, it may simply be a feature of a serenade movement. In the wedding cantata, the luminosity of the upper voices symbolized innocent purity; in the oratorio, the effect has more of the quality of hovering, of being heaven-directed, as it were. For the concluding chorale, Bach unites the chorus and the entire festival orchestra. In doing so, the composer embedded a chorale in B minor into an orchestral movement in D major—a feat he had managed with great success in the last movement of the sixth cantata of his Christmas Oratorio.

*Smend (1950).

Ein feste Burg ist unser Gott
BWV 80 / BC A 183b

Reformation Day, 1739?

The cantata *Ein feste Burg ist unser Gott* BWV 80 (A mighty fortress is our God) is for Reformation Day, celebrating Martin Luther's renowned posting of theses in Wittenberg on October 31, 1517, regarded as the spark that ignited the Reformation, led by Luther. Johann Sebastian Bach first encountered this feast day tradition, essentially restricted to the territory of Electoral Saxony, in 1723 after moving from Köthen to Leipzig. In 1667, 150 years after the posting at Wittenberg, the elector of Saxony, Johann Georg II, decreed October 31 to be a half holiday thenceforth, independent of the day of the week. It remained that way even in 1697, when the Saxon elector Friedrich August I converted to Catholicism for the sake of his efforts to gain the Polish crown. Leipzig, at the time a stronghold of Lutheran orthodoxy, found it necessary to take the sensibilities of the ruler into consideration in order to preserve its independence. For instance, a prime example occurred in 1732 when Salzburg archbishop Leopold von Firmian drove many established Lutheran residents in his lands to emigrate in an anachronistic counter-Reformation show of force. On their way to Prussia, many refugees stopped in Leipzig, and the city, church, and citizenry showed the travelers every conceivable generosity. No official greeting was forthcoming, however, since "Leipzig," so the official statement read, "is under a governance that professes the Catholic religion, which our Salzburg Emigrants have abandoned."[36*]

In those years in which Reformation Day fell on a Sunday, it is likely that the official diplomatic accommodations just described included downplaying the holiday by retaining the designation while, in the sermon, using the Gospel reading for the particular Sunday in the post-Trinity period. This happened four times during Bach's tenure in Leipzig. Significantly, this was reversed for St. John's and St. Michael's Days, when the holiday was given preference. In the four years just mentioned, church music would have been subject to the stipulations for the sermon text, and Bach would have had no opportunity to perform a cantata for Reformation Day; instead, he would have produced a cantata for the given Sunday. Hence, there would have been no occasion for a Reformation Day cantata in 1723, Bach's first year at Leipzig. A year later, however, the first version of a cantata on Luther's hymn *Ein feste Burg ist unser Gott* would seem to fit the context of Bach's chorale cantata cycle without difficulty. But it is equally plausible that this cantata originated only later and that another work, since lost, was performed in connection with the chorale cantatas. This hypothesis stems from the fact that the cantata *Ein feste Burg* is particularly heterogeneous in comparison to the other chorale cantatas. In most cases in the chorale cantata annual cycle, the work is based on a chorale text whose first and last strophes are adopted without change, while the others are reshaped as needed to become recitatives and arias. The reverse is true for *Ein feste Burg*. Luther created his paraphrase of Psalm 46 ("Deus noster refugium et virtus") between 1526 and 1528, a time of severe crises both internal and external. Three of the chorale's four strophes found their way into the cantata only belatedly. At first there were two or even only one.

The cantata's first version is a composition for Oculi Sunday that Bach must have performed in early 1715 and whose text is by the secretary of the Weimar High Consistory, Salomon Franck.[37] The Gospel reading for Oculi, found in Luke 7, gives an account of an exorcism and victory over the devil. Accordingly, Franck's text is largely concerned with themes of "war against Satan and his horde and against the world and sin." The libretto's warlike mien may have prompted Bach to repurpose the Weimar Oculi cantata—unusable during Leipzig's *tempus clausum*—to a composition for Reformation Day in Leipzig. He did not have to rely on a librettist to do this; it only required the three missing Luther strophes to be fitted into the appropriate places in Franck's libretto.

As expected, Luther's first strophe stands at the beginning of the Leipzig version:

> Ein feste Burg ist unser Gott,
> Ein gute Wehr und Waffen.

> A mighty fortress is our God,
> A good defense and weapon.

The text continues with what was originally the opening movement, the first aria authored by Franck:

> Alles, was von Gott geboren,
> Ist zum Siegen auserkoren.
> Wer bei Christi Blutpanier
> In der Taufe treu geschworen,
> Siegt im Geiste für und für.

> All that is born of God
> Is elected for victory.
> Whoever, before Christ's lifeblood banner,
> Has in baptism sworn loyalty
> Conquers in spirit for ever and ever.

It was surely Bach's idea—and not that of the Weimar librettist—to attach an instrumental (untexted) quotation of the chorale melody *Ein feste Burg*, thereby producing a multitextual effect through association. In contrast to this feature in the Weimar cantata, an actual second text was added to the Leipzig version, the second chorale strophe:

> Mit unsrer Macht ist nichts getan,
> Wir sind gar bald verloren.

> With our power nothing is done,
> We are indeed soon lost.

In Franck's text and Bach's Weimar composition, this concluded the Oculi cantata. In the Leipzig version, it was moved near the beginning, where it was combined with the freely versified aria text, whose end rhymes match it, astonishingly: "geboren," "erkoren," "verloren," "geschworen." The ensuing recitative-aria pair contrasts love of God and of Jesus against the demand to drive out the devil and the world. Luther's third strophe, another late addition, follows this:

Und wenn die Welt voll Teufel wär
Und wollten uns verschlingen.

And were the world full of the devil
And wanted to devour us.

A final recitative-aria pair culminates in these lines:

Wie selig sind doch die, die Gott im Munde tragen,
Doch sel'ger ist das Herz, das ihn im Glauben trägt.
Es bleibet unbesiegt und kann die Feinde schlagen
Und wird zuletzt gekrönt, wenn es den Tod erlegt.

How blessed indeed are they who carry God in their mouths,
Yet more blessed is the heart that bears him in faith.
It remains undefeated and can strike the enemies
And will at last be crowned, when it conquers death.

In the 1715 version, this aria began with the words "Wie selig ist der Leib, der, Jesu, dich getragen" (How blessed is the body that, Jesus, carried you), but these phrases had to give way to the cantata's new purpose. Luther's fourth strophe provides a powerful conclusion, "Das Wort sie sollen lassen stahn" (They shall let the word abide), with its closing lines certain of victory:

Laß fahren dahin,
Sie habens kein' Gewinn,
Das Reich muß uns doch bleiben.

Let them all pass away,
They have no gain.
The kingdom must certainly remain ours.

As we have seen, Bach's composition developed in two or even three stages. The oldest level comprises the solo movements that come from the Weimar cantata for Oculi of 1715. Included here is the original opening movement, the bass aria "Alles, was von Gott geboren," with the repeated figures and fanfares by the strings that characterize the "Aria with Heroic Affect." All of its parts are characterized by themes derived from the chorale; we can thus speak of a multilayered chorale fantasia with a heavily ornamented cantus firmus presented line by line, performed in Weimar by the oboe and in Leipzig by the soprano as well. Following the bass recitative, the soprano aria "Komm in mein Herzenshaus" (Come into the house of my heart) attempts to reconcile the most contrasting text elements with lighthearted music and intentional naivete. In contrast, the duet "Wie selig sind doch die" (How blessed indeed are they), in which voices and instruments in pairs go their own ways, shows how Bach, even at the beginning of his intensive production of cantatas, knew how to reconcile the interpretation of diverging cornerstones of text through the demands of a unified thematic flow.

When Bach first reshaped the Weimar solo movements to create a Reformation cantata (BWV 80.2), in 1730 at the latest but perhaps as early as 1724, he placed a simple four-part chorale setting of the strophe "Ein feste Burg" at the beginning. Moreover, he may have added the chorale strophe arrangement "Und wenn die Welt voll Teufel wär" at the same time, so that by including the texted cantus firmus in the bass aria as well as in the closing chorale, Bach represented all four strophes of Luther's chorale in the cantata. The chorale arrangement is predicated entirely on the opposition between the battle tumult in the instrumental parts and the unshakable drive of the chorale melody, whose symbolically meant unison effect radiates out over the instruments.

At a later time, presumably after 1735 but perhaps only in Bach's last year of life, he replaced the simple opening chorale movement with the extensive chorale fantasia on *Ein feste Burg ist unser Gott* (BWV 80.3). Every bit as unusual in its dimensions as in its vocal demands, this exceptional movement shows itself related to such late works as the Canonic Variations on *Vom Himmel hoch, da komm ich her* BWV 769 and *The Art of Fugue* BWV 1080. Moreover, it shows that even the motet-like sequencing principle admits an overall unity if the thematic diversity of the individual lines is compensated for by such an artful homogeneity of structure. Self-evidently, as it were, the fugal treatment of the choral voices and an intensive interpretation of the text that fosters diversity combine with the unifying tone symbolism of the chorale melody, which is presented in strict canon between oboes and instrumental basses. There can be no question that this finely woven structure of relationships in this singular artwork is seriously disrupted if one employs the trumpets and drums added by Wilhelm Friedemann Bach between 1750 and 1764. The fact that this unauthorized and coarse arrangement could persist until the present in musical practice indicates a problematic understanding of Bach and Luther as well.

---

*Caspar (1982).

Mer han en neue Oberkeet
BWV 212 / BC G 32

For Members of the Aristocracy, August 30, 1742

The cantata *Mer han en neue Oberkeet* BWV 212 (We have a new squire), also known as the Peasant Cantata, owes its existence to an occasion of rather local significance. Carl Heinrich von Dieskau was a scion of an ancient aristocratic family whose ancestral seat was in Dieskau near Halle. He became *directeur des plaisirs* at the Dresden court and supervisor of Royal Chapel and Chamber Music. In early 1742 he inherited the manor Kleinzschocher, southwest of Leipzig, from his mother and then made plans for festivities to celebrate the traditional hereditary homage. In deference to decorum, he needed to find an occasion that would permit the suspension of the period of mourning prescribed after his mother's death. The justification was provided by the noble gentleman's birthday on August 30, 1742. Although chronicles of the era are silent about details of the celebration, it may have involved—as customary for such festivities—a procession, double ranks of maidens of honor, and, in the evening, a fine fireworks display. For daylight fireworks, the Leipzig cantor of St. Thomas, Johann Sebastian Bach, and his worthy librettist, Christian Friedrich Henrici, came to mind. Whether one or the other took the initiative or whether the two together were represented by someone else, we do not know. As the county tax collector, the poet Henrici/Picander was immediately subordinate to the district captain Dieskau, so that he is most likely to have initiated the musical tribute. It can be safely assumed that such an investment paid off in due course.

As well designed as it is complex, Picander's libretto combines expressions of devotion with the depiction of life in the countryside in the spirit of the approaching Rococo age, induces knowing smiles from insiders of the tax system, and indulges in assorted tomfoolery in keeping with the principle that "im Gedicht duzt der Bauer den König" (in poetry the peasant addresses the king by first name). The beginning—and, unfortunately, only the beginning—is in dialect, as if intended to provide the *Obersächsisches Wörterbuch der Akademie der Wissenschaften* (Upper Saxon dictionary of the Academy of Sciences) with material:[38]

> Mer hahn en neue Oberkeet
> An unsern Kammerherrn.
> Ha gibt uns Bier, das steigt ins Heet,
> Das ist der klare Kern.
> Der Pfarr mag immer büse tun;

> Ihr Speelleut halt euch flink!
> Der Kittel wackelt Mieken schun,
> Das klene luse Ding.

> We have a new squire
> In our chamberlain.
> He gives us beer, which goes to one's head,
> That's the heart of the matter.
> The pastor may well frown;
> You musicians, look sharp!
> Molly's skirt is already swaying,
> The little saucy thing.

The situation is easily clarified with a few words of explanation: a new "Oberkeet" (*Obrigkeit*, "overseer" or "squire"); "Bier" (*Freibier*, "free beer"), "das steigt ins Heet" ("das in den Kopf steigt," or "which goes to one's head"); the anticipation of enjoying a dance; and a frowning clergyman. But before the host and his guests can make their way to the tavern, the Gray Wolf, the soprano and bass have a bit more to hash out with one another. The oafish bass approaches things head-on: "Nu, Mieke, gib dein Guschel immer her" (Now, Mieke, give us a smooch), but is immediately parried:

> Wenns das alleine wär.
> Ich kenn dich schon, du Bärenhäuter,
> Du willst hernach nur immer weiter.
> Der neue Herr hat ein sehr scharf Gesicht.

> If that were only all.
> I know you well, you old bear skin,
> After that you always want more.
> The new boss has a very sharp face.

The last line means that he has very sharp eyes and sees everything that he shouldn't. The bass beats a retreat:

> Ach unser Herr schilt nicht;
> Er weiß so gut als wir, und auch wohl besser,
> Wie schön ein bißchen Dahlen schmeckt.

> Ah, our master won't scold us;
> He knows as well as we, probably better,
> How lovely a bit of cuddling tastes.

Dahlen, vocabulary still used by Goethe, simply means "cuddling" or "billing and cooing"; it is conceivable that the good woman present (the new chamberlain's wife) did not entirely appreciate this wisecrack. But Mieke, the farm girl, is in no mood to abandon the delicate subject:

> Ach es schmeckt doch gar zu gut,
> Wenn ein Paar recht freundlich tut;
> Ei, da braust es in dem Ranzen,
> Als wenn eitel Flöh und Wanzen
> Und ein tolles Wespenheer
> Miteinander zänkisch wär.
>
> Ah, it does feel awfully good
> When a couple gets really friendly;
> Oh, there's roaring in your belly,
> As if stirred-up fleas and bugs
> And a crazy swarm of wasps
> Were all quarreling with one another.

With luck and skill, the bass hits on a new topic and begins to talk about the tax collector, who in this case also acts as law enforcement—policeman and judge in one, without such new-fangled innovations as keeping such powers separate:

> Der Herr ist gut: Allein der Schösser,
> Das ist ein Schwefelsmann,
> Der wie ein Blitz ein neu Schock strafen kann,
> Wenn man den Finger kaum ins kalte Wasser steckt.
>
> The master is good: but the tax collector,
> There is a real devil
> Who can hit you with a big fine like lightning
> When you've hardly stuck your finger in cold water.

What's meant here is clearly a case of unauthorized fishing in the nearby Elster River, along with a draconian fine in the amount of "a new shock," which could easily be as much as sixty groschen or two and a half thalers. Today, the ensuing sorrow-filled aria could easily be entitled "Hochsteuerland" (High tax country):

> Ach Herr Schösser, geht nicht gar zu schlimm
> Mit uns armen Bauersleuten üm.
> Schont nur unsrer Haut;
> Freßt ihr gleich das Kraut
> Wie die Raupen bis zum kahlen Strunk,
> Habt nur genung!

> Ah, Mr. Tax Collector, don't be so hard
> On us poor farming folk.
> Just spare our hides;
> If you must gnaw through our cabbage
> Like a caterpillar, down to the bare stem,
> Let that be enough!

Mieke immediately attempts to defuse the situation:

> Es bleibt dabei,
> Daß unser Herr der beste sei;
> Er ist nicht besser abzumalen
> Und auch mit keinem Hopfensack voll Batzen zu bezahlen.

> The fact remains
> That our master is the greatest;
> No portrait could improve upon him,
> Nor could you pay for him with a gunnysack full of coins.

The reference here is to ancient small coins called batzen with the likeness of a bear named Meister Petz.[39] A brief paean follows:

> Unser trefflicher
> Lieber Kammerherr
> Ist ein kumpabler Mann,
> Den niemand tadeln kann.

> Our excellent,
> Beloved chamberlain
> Is an affable man
> Whom no one can find fault with.

Here, the rhymes sound a bit like Hans Sachs, and the peculiar word *kumpabel*—a mixture of Latin *capabel* (capable) and *Kumpanei* (comradery)—is occasionally found as late as the nineteenth century.

After the praises of the chamberlain's humanity have been sung, next on the agenda is his influence in public affairs, including the conscription of soldiers—here euphemistically called "Werbung" (recruitment)—and, of course, taxes:

> Er hilft uns allen, alt und jung,
> Und dir ins Ohr gesprochen:
> Ist unser Dorf nicht gut genung
> Letzt bei der Werbung durchgekrochen?

> Ich weiß wohl noch ein besser Spiel,
> Der Herr gilt bei der Steuer viel.
>
> He helps us all, old and young,
> And let me whisper in your ear:
> Didn't our village squeak through OK
> In the last recruitment?
> I know an even better game,
> The master has lots of clout with the taxes.

Then as now, in tax matters speech is silver, but silence is gold:

> Das ist galant,
> Es spricht niemand
> Von den caducken Schocken
> Niemand red't ein stummes Wort,
> Knauthain und Cospuden dort
> Hat selber Werg am Rocken.
>
> It is a pretty thing,
> That no one brags
> About those evaded taxes.
> No one breathes a silent word.
> Knauthain and Cospuden there
> Themselves have holes in their clothes.

The manors of Knauthain and Cospuden belonged, like Kleinzschocher, to the Dieskau family estate, and the "caducken Schocken" refer to the taxation of wastelands, in other words, taxes that do not actually need to be paid.

The bass now turns his attention to the "gnädige Frau" (mistress) and considers her with truly dubious praise:

> Und unsre gnäd'ge Frau
> Ist nicht ein Prinkel stolz.
> Und ist gleich unsereins ein arm und grobes Holz,
> So redt sie doch mit uns daher,
> Als wenn sie unsersgleichen wär
> Sie ist recht fromm, recht wirtlich und genau,
> Und machte unserm gnädgen Herrn
> Aus einer Fledermaus viel Taler gern.
>
> And our gracious mistress
> Is not a bit aloof.
> And like our kind is made of poor, crude wood,
> And therefore speaks with us

As if she were just like ourselves.
She's truly fair, truly good-hearted and direct,
And for our gracious master she'd make
Four thalers from a bat.[40]

The financial wishful thinking of the "gracious ones" becomes clearer when we recall that "Fledermaus" (bat) was the slang term for a worn penny. Even so, the aria that follows has to do with the loss of fifty thalers, which has to be made up through redoubled penny-pinching.

After so much depiction of milieu, some music is called for. In honor of the squire, the soprano lets a little song be heard:

Klein-Zschocher müsse
So zart und süße
Wie lauter Mandelkerne sein.
In unsere Gemeine
Zieh' heute ganz alleine
Der Überfluß des Segens ein.

Let Kleinzschocher be
As tender and sweet
As pure almonds.
In our community
Let nothing come today except
A surplus of blessings.

The bass serves up a contrasting program:

Das ist zu klug vor dich
Und nach der Städter Weise;
Wir Bauern singen nicht so leise.
Das Stückchen, höre nur, das schicket sich vor mich:
Es nehme zehntausend Dukaten
Der Kammerherr alle Tag ein.
Er trink ein gutes Gläschen Wein
Und laß es ihm bekommen sein.

That is too smart for you
And in the manner of the city;
We peasants don't sing so soft.
Now listen to this one that's just right for me!
Ten thousand ducats every day
May the chamberlain take in.
May he drink a glass of good wine,
And may he find it good.

Molly doesn't think it's all that good:

> Das klingt zu liederlich.
> Es sind so hübsche Leute da,
> Die würden ja
> Von Herzen drüber lachen;
> Nicht anders, als wenn ich,
> Die alte Weise wollte machen:
> Gib, Schöne,
> Viel Söhne
> Von artger Gestalt,
> Und zieh sie fein alt,
> Das wünschet sich Zschocher und Knauthain fein bald.
>
> That sounds too dissolute!
> There are such fancy people here
> Who would certainly
> Laugh heartily over it;
> No different than if I
> Wanted to offer this old tune:
> Give us, pretty one,
> Many sons
> Of stalwart form
> And bring them up well,
> That's what Zschocher and Knauthain want, very soon.

Whatever is so "liederlich" about the "Dukaten" aria—that is, licentious and self-indulgent—cannot be inferred from the text, nor can the reason for the laughter of the "hübschen" people—that is, polite and well-educated. The chamberlain and his gracious wife will have heard the wish for "many sons" with rather uncomfortable expressions; so far, they have had five daughters—but not the longed-for son and heir.

Be that as it may, the bass gives in:

> Du hast wohl recht.
> Das Stückchen klingt zu schlecht;
> Ich muß mich also zwingen,
> Was städtisches zu singen.
> Dein Wachstum sei feste
> Und lache vor Lust.
> Deines Herzens Trefflichkeit
> Hat dir selbst das Feld bereit',
> Auf dem du blühen mußt.

> You're quite right.
> The little piece sounds too bad.
> I must then force myself
> To sing something more urbane.
> May your increase be steady,
> And laugh with delight.
> The excellence of your heart
> Has itself prepared the field for you
> On which you must certainly blossom.

After more to-and-fro the party is finally ready to move in the direction of the Gray Wolf:

> Wir gehn nun, wo der Tudelsack
> In unsrer Schenke brummt.
> Und rufen dabei fröhlich aus:
> Es lebe Dieskau und sein Haus,
> Ihm sei beschert,
> Was er begehrt
> Und was er sich selbst wünschen mag.
>
> We're going now where the bagpipes
> In our tavern drone.
> As we call joyfully out:
> Long live Dieskau and his house,
> May he be granted
> All that he desires
> And whatever else he might wish for.

Bach's composition, which he himself entitled "Cantate burlesque," shows evidence at many points of close collaboration between composer and poet in preparing the libretto. This is particularly true of the two "urban" arias. Only the soprano's paean to Kleinzschocher is undisguised; its model was an aria from a congratulatory cantata for August the Strong performed in 1732.[41] There, the personified Landes-Vorsehung (National Destiny) begins:

> Ich will ihn hegen,
> Ich will ihn pflegen
> Und seiner Seele freundlich tun.
>
> I want to cherish him,
> I want to care for him
> And be kind to his soul.

In contrast, the bass aria operates with a double-edged sword: the "Dein Wachstum sei feste" (May your prosperity be secure) goes back to the dramma per musica *Der Streit zwischen Phoebus und Pan* BWV 201, where it is connected to the text "Zu Tanze, zu Sprünge, so wackelt das Herz" (For dancing, for leaping, so wobbles the heart). Steadiness here, violent wobbling there: the music intentionally and successfully undermines what the text says. The same thing happens, whenever possible, in the two shorter aria movements. The song of praise to the excellent, companionable, fault-free chamberlain is set to the ancient melody of the "Folie d'Espagne" (Follies of Spain), which otherwise appears with texts such as "Du strenge Flavia, / Ist kein Erbarmen da" (You strict Flavia, / Have you no mercy) or else, particularly in operas of the period, to accompany the entrance of a fool. The "Ducats" aria cites a contemporary hunting song, accompanied by a hunting horn for the sake of authenticity; in the meantime, the heart of the matter is a popular song text "Was helfen uns tausend Dukaten, / Wenn sie versoffen sind" (What good to us are one thousand ducats / When they are drunk?). It's no wonder that the soprano finds this licentious and self-indulgent and fears that nice people will have an unfavorable impression. The "alte Weise" (old ditty) with "viel Söhne" (many sons) may be based on a lullaby that possibly once enjoyed a crude second text. In the first recitative, a so-called *Großvatertanz* (grandfather dance) or *Kehraus* (last dance of the evening) is heard at appropriate spots, usually sung to the words "Mit mir und dir ins Federbett, / Mit mir und dir ins Stroh" (With me and you in the feather bed, / With me and you in the straw).

From the colorful overture to the tuneful ensemble finale, most movements give the impression of having been conceived and composed with double entendres in mind*—and must have been heard as such as well. Unfortunately, many movements have not yet given up their secrets, and so the pleasure of listening to the only apparently ephemeral Peasant Cantata is mixed with perplexity—just as is Mozart's "Musical Joke."

---

*Schulze (1976). Other clues to "borrowed material" appear in Boyd (1993). Dieskau's advancement at the Dresden court may have prompted the librettist to entitle his 1751 republication of the text "Auf eine Huldigung. Cantata burlesque," thus defusing the obvious textual and musical allusions to those in power.

Notes

Translator's Note

1. "Die vorsätzlich oder fahrlässige Nichtachtung der von Johann Sebastian Bach zur Komposition ausgesuchten Texte und die Unterschätzung ihrer—bekannten oder unbekannten—Verfasser kann allerdings leicht in eine Sackgasse führen: Die Fortschreibung der anderweitig überwunden geglaubten Hagiographie wird unvermeidlich den Konnex zwischen Text und Musik lockern und damit einem leichtfertigen Umgang mit diesen Komponenten Tür und Tor öffnen" (Schulze 2006, 7).

Chapter 1. Bach at Arnstadt and Mühlhausen

1. "Auff begehren Titulo Herrn Dr. Georg Christian Eilmars in die Music gebracht von Johann Sebastian Bach, Organista Molhusino."
2. Schering (1913, 52).
3. Schering (1913, 50–51).
4. Please see the addendum to this essay.
5. Schulze (2010, 2011).
6. January 2, 2005, http://bach-cantatas.com/BWV150-D4.htm, accessed August 6, 2010 (H-JS), February 16, 2023 (JABII).
7. See J. H. Zedler, *Universal Lexicon aller Wissenschafften und Künste*, vol. 5 (Leipzig and Halle, 1733; repr., Graz, 1999), cols. 1776–78, s.v. "Cedurs."
8. Schulze (2010, 71).
9. Schulze (2011).
10. "Er führt größtentheils seine eigenen Kompositionen in den Kirchen auf. Und um mehrere Abwechslung willen setzte er seit 1766 Chorale ganz durch, in der Manier des berühmten Kuhnau, nach Gelegenheit des Inhalts der Strophen in Rezitative, Arien, Duette und Chöre, und führte sie mit unter mit vielem Beifalle auf, statt der gewöhnlichen Kirchencantaten."

11. "Er war wo nicht der Anfänger, doch der glücklicher Fortsetzer der Manier von Kirchenkantaten, zu welchen ein Choral als Text, jede Strophe nach ihrem Inhalte, ganz durchgearbeitet wird. Ich besitze auf diese Weise den Choral 'Wer nur den lieben Gott läßt walten' von ihm."

12. In medieval music, a sequence was a type of addition to the official liturgical chant of the Latin church. It was generally sung after the Alleluia.

13. The *alternatim* is the practice of two or more contrasting forces taking turns in performing music for a liturgical text, each taking only one verse or short section at a time. *NHDM*, s.v. "Alternatim," by Bruce Gustafson.

14. Schweitzer (1966, 2:127).

15. Schweitzer (1966, 2:127).

16. Possibilities include Bach's uncle Tobias Lammerhirt (died August 10, 1707) and Adolf Strecker, mayor of Mühlhausen (died September 16, 1708). See Rathey (2006, 79–84); Maul (2022, 70).

17. Schweitzer (1966, 2:125).

18. Schweitzer (1966, 2:126).

19. Details of layout for this and subsequent quotations of the text are provided in Hans-Joachim Schulze's text.

20. *Abendmusiken* were evening concerts featuring elaborate five-part oratorios on the five Sundays before Christmas in the Marienkirche in Lübeck. These concerts came to prominence under Dieterich Buxtehude and would have been heard by Bach during his stay in Lübeck with Buxtehude from late October / early November 1706 to late January / early February 1707.

Chapter 2. Bach at Weimar and Köthen

1. Spitta (1899, 2:576–77).

2. Christian Morgenstern's poem *Die unmögliche Tatsache* (1909) recounts the plight of Palmström, an elderly gentleman who looks the wrong way at a busy intersection and is run over. Railing at the city administration, at the police, at automobile drivers, he nonsensically concludes that cars are not permitted there and that his mishap never happened at all: "Weil, so schließt er messerscharf, / was nicht sein kann, nicht sein darf" (For, he reasons pointedly, / that which cannot, must not be) (Knight 1964, 34).

3. "Am Hoch-Fürstlichen Geburths-Festin Herrn Herrn Hertzog Christians zu Sachsen-Weissenfels nach gehaltenen Kampff-Jagen im Fürstlichen Jäger-Hofe bey einer Tafel-Music aufgeführet."

4. The cantata for St. Michael's Day is *Man singet mit Freuden vom Sieg* BWV 149. The cantata for the city council election is *Herrscher des Himmels, König der Ehren* BWV 1141.

5. Erdmann Neumeister, preface to *Geistlichen Cantaten statt einer Kirchen-Musik*, 2nd ed. (Weissenfels, 1704).

6. "Eine liebliche Frucht anzusehen, weiß und röthlich, wie kleinen Paradisäpfel.

Inwendig aber sind sie voll weisser Körner, wie die unreiffen Äpfel, ohne safft, herb und ungeschmack. Die auf dem Stamme vertrocknen, werden schwärzlich, und wenn man sie aufbricht, stauben sie wie asche. . . . Es gedencket derselben schon Tacitus, fast auf gleiche Weise, und der Jüdische Geschichtsschrieber Josephus. Einige Gelehrte betrachten sie als ein überbleibsel oder denckmal der sodomitischen Verwüstung."

7. Schulze's reference to the "small octave" comes from the Helmholtz system for describing musical pitches and octaves. The "small octave," denoted by lowercase letters without primes, extends below middle C on the piano. Thus Schulze's f is the pitch f below middle C.

8. The permutation technique is "a type of fugue or fugal passage often found in the choral works of Bach in which every voice enters with the same succession of a number of musical ideas equal to the number of voices . . . so that successive entries . . . are marked by a permutation among the voices of material already heard" (*NHDM*, s.v. "Permutation Fugue").

9. *NBR*, 300 (no. 306).
10. *NBR*, 70 (no. 51).
11. *NBR*, 71 (no. 52).
12. *NBR*, 325 (no. 319).
13. "In seinen jungen Jahren war er oft mit Telemannen zusammen, welcher auch mich aus der Taufe gehoben hat" (*BD* III:289 [no. 803]).
14. *NBR*, 113 (no. 113).
15. Schering (1942, 47).
16. Spitta (1899, 1:542).
17. Schering (1942, 129–30). The questions of what Pietism is and Bach's relation to it are complex and controversial. A recent overview of these can be found in Leaver (2021, 219–47).
18. A symbol of calamity.
19. Franck's text for BWV 161 also appears in the annual text cycle *Gott-geheiligte Sabbaths-Zehnden*, published in Nuremberg in 1728 by Christoph Birkmann, who studied at the University of Leipzig from December 1, 1724, to early September 1727 and during that time frequently heard church music performed by Johann Sebastian Bach. Birkmann's cycle contains thirty-one cantatas by Bach known to have been performed at Leipzig during Birkmann's period of study there. Since Franck's text for BWV 161 is also included in the cycle, it is now believed to have been performed in Leipzig on September 16, 1725. See Blanken (2015b, 70).

Chapter 3. Bach's First Year at Leipzig

1. *NBR*, 106 (no. 102).
2. *NBR*, 106 (no. 103).
3. "trat der neue Cantor, Herr Johann Sebastian Bach, sein Amt bey denen Stadt-Kirchen mit der ersten Music der Kirche zu St. Nicolai an" (*BD* II:105 [no. 141]).
4. "Von der unter BWV2 147a überlieferten einteiligen Weimarer Kantate zum 4.

Advent . . . ist nur Satz 1 überliefert. . . . [O]b weitere Sätze vorlagen, läßt sich nicht sicher bestimmen" (The Weimar early version with BWV2 designation BWV 147a . . . is not included in BWV3 because only the first movement is transmitted in the autograph score. . . . [W]hether other movements existed can no longer be determined) (BWV3, 192 [no. 147]).

5. *Choreinbau* (choral embedding) is a technique in which the instruments play the ritornello while the newly added chorus sings independent material.

6. Bach performed *Gott ist mein König* BWV 71 for a council inauguration on February 4, 1708, in Mühlhausen.

7. *NBR*, 212 (no. 222). Johann Elias Bach's letter informing Bach of his wife's illness, draft or copy, is in *BD* II:391 (no. 489).

8. However, it has recently become clear that Bach was indeed absent from his post at St. Thomas for as much as two years (perhaps 1742–43 or sometime between 1743 and 1746). In a letter of application written in 1751 by a former St. Thomas student, Gottfried Benjamin Fleckeisen, to succeed his father as cantor of the small town of Döbeln, Fleckeisen claimed that "I was an *alumnus* [boarder] at the St. Thomas School in Leipzig for nine years and while I was there served for four years as prefect of the choro musico. For two whole years I had to perform and conduct the music at the churches of St. Thomas and St. Nicholas in place of the capellmeister, and without boasting, may say that I always acquitted myself honorably" (translated in Maul 2018, xv). See also Maul (2017).

9. Klaus Hofmann (2016) has taken issue with Alfred Dürr's 1986 assessment that the original version of the first movement was a French overture akin to those in Bach's orchestral suites and that the middle section was newly composed.

10. Early Weimar versions for the other two works, with the BWV2 designations BWV 147a and 186a, are not included in BWV3 because the editors decided against including "Werke, die Bach geschrieben haben *könnte* da sie ebenfalls in den Weimarer Textdrucken von 1714–1717" (works that Bach *could* have written, because their texts are preserved in Weimar publications of 1714–1717) (BWV3, xi). Moreover, "eine Häufung von drei Adventskantaten im Jahre 1716 entspricht aber nicht den Weimarer Gepflogenheiten monatlich neue Stücke [s. Dok. II Nr. 66]; für den 2. Advent 1716 ist bereits die Kantate BWV 70.1 durch Weimarer Stimmen nachweisbar" (a group of three Advent cantatas for the year 1616 does not accord with the stipulations at Weimar for a new cantata every month [cf. Dok II Nr. 66]. BWV 70.1 is already documented for 2. Advent by Weimar performing parts) (BWV3, 232 [no. 186]).

11. Weimar was among a large number of duchies in central Thuringia ruled by descendants of the Ernestine line of the House of Wettin. A helpful overview can be found in Marshall and Marshall (2016, xvi–xviii).

12. Stile concitato: "A style . . . defined by Monteverdi and employed in his *Combattimento di Tancredi e Clorinda* (1624) and *Madrigali guerrieri ed amorosi* to express anger and warfare" (*NHDM*, s.v. "Concitato").

13. Schering (1942, 17).

14. Jesus schläft, was soll ich hoffen? BWV 81.

15. Texte / Zur Leipziger / Kirchen-Music, / Auf den / Andern, dritten, vierdten Sonntage / nach der Erscheinung Christi, / Das / Fest Mariä Reinigung, / Und die Sonntage / Septuagesimae, Sexagesimae, / Esto mihi, / Ingleichen / Auf das Fest / der Erscheinung Mariä 1724. // Leipzig, / Gedruckt bei Immanuel Tietzen.

16. "Am vierdten Sonntag nach der Erscheinung Christi. In der Kirche zu St. Thomae."

17. The soul's search for Jesus in the Christian reading of the Song of Songs.

18. The St. Petersburg pamphlet indeed reads "Wellen." The alternative was suggested by Wustmann (1982, 48).

Chapter 4. Bach's Second and Third Years at Leipzig

1. "Als er nun in der Hölle und in der Qual war, hob er seine Augen auf und sah Abraham von ferne und Lazarus in seinem Schoß."

2. "At the time, a favorite vehicle for the comparison between outward appearance and inner condition . . . was the *Sodomsapfel* (apple of Sodom), the fruit of a shrub living near the Dead Sea." See the discussion of *Wiederstehe doch der Sünde* BWV 54 / BC A 51 in chapter 2.

3. "Und da sie es ausschütteten für die Männer, zu essen, und sie von dem Gemüse aßen, schrieen sie und sprachen: O Mann Gottes, der Tod im Topf! denn sie konnten's nicht essen" (2 Kings 4:40).

4. "Fahre auf die Höhe und werfet eure Netze aus, daß ihr einen Zug tut"; "Meister, wir haben die ganze Nacht gearbeitet und nichts gefangen; aber auf dein Wort will ich das Netz auswerfen" (Luke 5:4–5).

5. "Herzliches Buß- und Bet-Lied eines Sünders, an seinen allerliebsten Herrn Jesum, um Verzeihung seiner viel- und mannigfaltigen Sünden."

6. "Einhundert Einundzwanzig Neue himmelsüße Jesuslieder, darinnen der hochteure süße Kraft-Nahme Jesus über siebenhundertmal zu finden; zu schuldigster Ehre unsres hochverdienten Heylandes und Erlösers, auch Erweckung heiligster Andacht und Seelen-Freude theils abgefaßt, theils colliget von Ahasvero Fritschio."

7. "Alles ist Eitelkeit, alles ist Elend und Jammer. Aber unser Jesus ist alles in allem, Jesus ist der gläubigen Seelen eitel Zucker und Honig, Manna, Milch und Wein, Zimmer, Nelken und Balsam. Selig, der diese himmlische Jesus-Süße in seinem Geist kräftig empfindet."

8. Schering (1950, 25–26).

9. Schulze (1999, 116) suggested that the anonymous librettist of the chorale cantatas would most likely be someone no longer available to Bach after the late winter of 1725, and that one Andreas Stübel (b. 1653), conrector of the St. Thomas School who died on January 31, 1725, was the most likely candidate. However, Schulze made no mention of Stübel in 2006, perhaps because, as Michael Maul writes, there is no evidence that he ever prepared texts for church music, among other reasons (2018, 188–89).

10. *Zwingen* generally means "to force."

11. Franz Conrad Romanus was installed as mayor by the court of August the Strong over the objections of the Leipzig Town Council. In the winter of 1704–5 "it became known that he had forged town council debentures and . . . embezzled money from the municipal treasury and the treasury of St. Nicholas" (Maul 2018, 176).

12. "Die Frau Christiana Mariana von Ziegler, eine Tochter des ehemaligen Herrn Bürgermeisters zu Leipzig, Herrn Romani, von der Philosophischen Facultät der Universität Wittenberg, im Monat October bei Gelegenheit einer volzogenen starcken Dicht-Kunst, zur Kayserlichen gecrönten Poeten erklärt worden, welche Ehre wenigstens von ganzen Universitäten noch keiner Person von ihrem Geschlechte ertheilet worden."

13. Mark Peters (2005) has cogently summarized this long-running debate and argued for Ziegler's authorship of the changes.

14. The *Suchmotiv* is the soul's search for Jesus in the Christian reading of the Song of Songs.

Chapter 5. Bach's Fourth Year at Leipzig

1. The anthology, edited by G. Wustmann, was published in two volumes in 1889 and 1895. The essay is not titled.

2. "Leipzig unter einer Herrschaft stehet, die sich zur Katholischen Religion bekennet, welche unsere Salzburgische Emigranten verlassen haben."

3. The texts for BWV 39, movements 4 through 7, appear in the Christoph Birkmann annual cycle discovered in Nuremberg by Christine Blanken. Birkmann studied at the University of Leipzig from December 1, 1724, to early September 1727. His text cycle includes many works performed by Bach during Birkmann's period of study in Leipzig. It is believed that BWV 39 was performed on June 23, 1726, in Leipzig (Blanken 2015b, 67).

4. *BD* I:265 (no. 184).

5. "Das 22stimmmige Stück ist ein Meisterstück. Mein seeliger Vater hat es einmahl in Leipzig in der Kirche aufgeführt, alles ist über den Efeckt erstaunt. Hier habe ich nicht Sänger genug, außerdem würde ich es gerne einmahl aufführen" (*BD* III:292 [no. 807]). The Alt-Bachisches Archiv was a collection amassed by J. S. Bach of musical works by older family members to document the clan's musical legacy. The collection was preserved by Carl Philipp Emanuel.

6. Christina Blanken (2015b, 55) has demonstrated that Christoph Birkmann is responsible for the arrangement of Henrici's text.

7. According to Daniel Malamed and Michael Marissen,

> This cryptic reference [to Mahanaim] comes from contemporary Lutheran understanding of the idiosyncratic translation of Genesis 32:1–2 in their Luther Bibles, "Jacob aber zog seinen Weg, und es begneten ihm die Engel Gottes. Und da er sie sahe, sprach er: Es sind Gottes Heere, und hiess dieselbe Stätte Mahanaim" ("But Jacob [the father of the nation of Israel] went on his way, and the angels of God

encountered him. And when he saw them, he said: '[They/Here] are God's armies,' and [he] named the selfsame place Mahanaim"). The Hebrew word "mahanaim" is generally understood today to mean "two [army] camps." The Calov Study Bible (owned by Bach, who curiously quilled a now illegible notation into the commentary on Genesis 32:2) explains that "Mahanaim" means "die Engel Heerscharen" ("the legions of angels") and goes on to say that Jacob was protected by "zwei Englische Heer" ("two angel-armies") encamped around him, on the left and the right. (https://bachcantatatexts.org/BWV19, n10)

8. Based on this text's appearance in a recently discovered annual cantata text cycle published in 1728 in Nuremberg by Christoph Birkmann, a theology student at the University of Leipzig from 1724 to 1727, Christine Blanken (2015b, 46–48) argues that Birkmann is likely the text's author.

9. Christine Blanken (2015b, 27) notes that Christoph Birkmann, before turning to theology, completed a disputation in mathematics on the motion of the sun around its own axis, making use of a navigational instrument called the *Kreuzstab* (cross-staff).

10. Joshua 1:5: "Es soll dir niemand widerstehen dein Leben lang. Wie ich mit Mose gewesen bin, also will ich auch mit dir sein. Ich will dich nicht verlassen noch von dir weichen" (There will not be anyone able to stand before you all the days of your life. As I was with Moses, so I will be with you. I will not fail you nor forsake you).

11. "Ein halb oder ganz Dutzend Kantaten von geistlich-moralischem Inhalte, so, daß sie sowohl in der Kirche, als bei Privat Concerten gemacht werden könnten."

12. "Die Unvernunft und das Laster auszurotten, hingegen Verstand und Tugend unter seinen Landsleuten zu befördern."

13. Based on this text's inclusion in an annual cantata cycle published in Nuremberg in 1728 by Christoph Birkmann, a theology student at the University of Leipzig from 1724 to 1727, it is likely that Birkmann is the text's author. See Blanken (2015b, 49ff.).

14. Our understanding of this cantata's date of origin was radically altered by the discovery of a printed text booklet in the Russian National Library in St. Petersburg for use by an audience member at St. Nicholas or St. Thomas Church in Leipzig. The date on the booklet's cover, 1727, shows that the work was composed roughly twenty years earlier than previously thought and only shortly after the secular cantata BWV 34.1, on which it is based. See Schabalina (2008, 65–68).

15. May 1746 is now understood to be the date of reperformance.

16. Schulze here refers to J. S. Bach's visit to King Frederick II of Prussia at Potsdam on May 7, 1747, when the king presented Bach with a theme upon which Bach extemporaneously improvised a fugue. Bach later composed a collection of fugues (or ricercars), canons, and a trio sonata on the "royal theme," which he published in September of that year under the title *Das musikalische Opfer* BWV 1079.

17. See endnote 13.

18. Schering (1950, 92).

19. Schering (1950, 91).

20. Schering (1950, 91).

Chapter 6. Bach at Leipzig after Trinity 1727

1. The copyist of the second violin and viola parts was recently identified as Johann Wilhelm Machts, who entered St. Thomas School on May 31, 1735, at age eleven; his role as copyist is unlikely to have begun before 1737–38. See Wollny (2016, 83–91).

2. *NBR* 451.

3. "Trauer Music, so Bey der Lob- und Trauer Rede, welche auff das Absterben Ihro Königlichen Majestät und churfürstlichen Durchlaucht zu Sachsen, Frauen Christianen Eberhardinen Königen in Pohlen etc. und Churfürstin zu Sachsen etc. gefürsteten Marckgräfin zu Brandenburg-Bayreuth von dem Hochwohlgebornen Herrn von Kirchbach in der Pauliner-Kirche zu Leipzig gehalten wurde, aufgeführt von Johann Sebastian Bach anno 1727 den 18. Octobris."

4. "Was für Fürstlichen Personen, hohen Ministres, Cavalliers und andern Fremden sich dieses mahl auf der Messe befunden, hat sich, nebst einer grossen Anzahl vornehmer Dames, wie auch die gantze löbliche Universität und ein Edler Hochweiser Rath in Corpore dabey eingefunden" (*BD* II:174 [no. 231]).

5. *NBR*, 136–37 (no. 136).

6. Klagt, Kinder, klagt es aller Welt BWV 1143.

7. Or more likely 1727, owing to the presence of Henrici's libretto in a text cycle published by Christoph Birkmann in 1728 that reflects cantatas performed in Leipzig from late 1724 until September 1727. See Blanken (2015b, 42–43n125).

8. "Gott zu Ehren, dem Verlangen guter Freunde zur Folge und vieler Andacht zur Beförderung habe ich entschlossen, gegenwärtige Cantaten zu verfertigen. Ich habe solches Vorhaben desto lieber unternommen, weil ich mir schmeicheln darf, daß vielleicht der Mangel der poetischen Anmuth durch die Lieblichkeit des unvergleichlichen Herrn Capell-Meisters Bachs, dürfte ersetzet, und diese Lieder in den Haupt-Kirchen des andächtigen Leipzigs angestimmet werden."

9. When this essay was written, the only known exemplar of Henrici's 1728 annual cycle had vanished in 1945. In 2009 a partially complete first edition print was discovered in St. Petersburg's Russian National Library; this recently appeared source and other recently discovered prints in St. Petersburg have helped to clarify several questions regarding the so-called Picander Jahrgang (Picander cycle). See Schabalina (2009, 20–30).

10. Der Streit zwischen Phoebus und Pan is the title of the printed text.

11. "Ich hatte sehr viel von einem grossen Meister der Music ehemals theils gesehen, theils gehöret, und fande einen ausnehmenden Gefallen an dessen Arbeit. Ich meyne den nunmehr seligen Capellmeister Bachen in Leipzig. Mich verlangte nach der bekanntschaft dieses vortrefflichen Mannes, und wurde auch so glücklich, dieselbe zu geniessen. Ausser diesen habe auch den so berühmten Herrn Händel, Capellmeister in London, zu hören und ihm, nebst noch andern lebenden Meistern in der Music, bekannt zu werden die Ehre gehabt" (*BD* III:77 [no. 663]).

12. Burney (1775, 2:207).

13. "Ich bin seit 50 Jahren gewohnt, den Bachschen Genius zu verehren; Frie-

demann ist hier gestorben, Emanuel Bach war hier Königlicher Kammermusiker, Kirnberger, Agrikola Schüler vom alten Bach, Ring, Bertuch, Schmalz und Andere ließen fast nicht anderes hören als des alten Bachs Stücke; ich selbst unterrichte seit 30 Jahren darinne und habe Schüler, die alle Bachschen Sachen gut spielen." Zelter sent the letter of April 6, 1829, to Friedrich Konrad Griepenkerl and afterward sent a copy on to Goethe. See Schulze (1984b, 130).

14. "äußerste Schnelligkeit und Flüchtigkeit, doch mehrentheils auf eine fließende und keine ungestüme Art: etwa wie der glattfortschießende Strom-Pfeil eines Bachs."

15. "ein erlesener junger Thomaner, . . . oder, was wahrscheinlicher ist, ein studentischer Falsettist" (Schering 1950, 121).

16. "Die Knaben sind wenig nutz. Ich meine, die Capell-Knaben. Ehe sie eine leidliche Fähigkeit zum Singen bekommen, ist die Discant-Stimme fort. Und wenn sie ein wenig mehr wissen, oder einen fertigen Hals haben, als andre, pflegen sie sich so viel einzubilden, daß ihr Wesen unleidlich ist, und hat doch keinen Bestand."

17. "nie andere Sänger gehabt, als wenn einer von der Bratsche oder Violin vortrat, und mit einer kreischenden Falsettstimme, dem Salimbeni eine Arie nachsingen wollte, die er oben drein nicht recht lesen konnte."

18. "Mit gleicher Stärke war ich ohne Fistel imstande, bis ins dreigestrichene F hinaufzusteigen. Selbst meine bisherige Engbrüstigkeit verminderte sich durch die Anstrengung des Atmens, und ich vermochte Läufer zu drei bis vier Takten lang ohne abzusetzen zu singen und einzelne Töne noch länger auszuhalten, sowie ich vorher vollen Odem geschöpft hatte."

19. "ein gewissen jungen Menschen [der] jetzt ungefähr in seinem 17. Jahre noch immer mit vielem Glück die ersten Diskantrollen [singt]. . . . Seine Stimme ist hell, und von einem sehr großen Umfang. Der Triller war, wenigstens noch vor einem Jahre, ungemein deutlich und groß. Den Ausdruck hat er in einem sehr hohen Grad in seiner Gewalt."

20. "Silberweise" (1512) is the best-known composition by Hans Sachs (1494–1576), member and later head of the master singers guild in Nuremberg and the main character in Richard Wagner's *Die Meistersinger von Nürnberg*.

21. "Dienstags den 7. April wird ein fremder Musicus im Kauffhauß unter den neuen Krähmen ein Concert aufführen, in welchem unter andern der Schlendrian mit seiner Tochter Ließgen in einen Dramate wird gemacht werden, wer Belieben hat solches mit anzuhören, der kann die Billets vor 30 Kreuzer und den Text vor 12 Kreuzer in dem Laden an der Nicolai Kirche im Schrot-Hauß auff dem Römerberg bekommen, und ohne Billet wird niemand eingelassen, der Anfang ist praecise um 6. Uhr Abends."

22. "Ich hatte Ihnen eine Französiche Parodie der Caffee Cantate versprochen; aber sie ist so herzlich schecht geraten, daß ich sie dem Herrn Franzosen zurückgegeben habe. Da war keine lange und kurze Sylbe in Acht genommen etcetera. Es war schlecht."

23. "Weyhnacht" is singular.

24. Spitta (1899, 2:576–77).

25. "Die musikalische Größe der Bachschen Werke ist die Voraussetzung ihrer Parodierbarkeit."

26. "Anlangende die Brautmessen, ist bisher dem Cantori von ieder ein Reichs-Thaler gegeben worden, mit welchem er auch hinführo sich begnügen lassen, und mehreres nicht fordern soll."

27. "In vorigen Zeiten haben die Cantores Kuhnau, Bach, Harrer, die gantzen Brautmessen in der Kirche und im Hauße, so wie die Organisten, in Persohn abgewartet, und nachher zur Recreation, eine Mahlzeit erhalten. Zu mehrerer Bequemlichkeit für solche, hat dann circa 1730, der alte Martius, den Bräutigam disponirt, ihnen statt dieser Mahlzeit einen Thaler zu geben. Seit der Zeit ist dieser Thaler allemal denen Leuten mit liquidiert worden" (*BD* III:342 [no. 852]).

28. "Von einer ganzen Brautmeße bekommt der Herr Cantor 2 Thaler, die er allemal erhalten, und 1 Thaler statt einer Doppel-Flasche Wein (welche ich als Schüler dem seeligen Cantori Bach vielmahl selbst in natura gehohlt habe, die Speisung ist schon längstens abgekommen)" (*BD* III:342 [no. 851]).

29. *NBR*, 181ff. (no. 184).

30. Spitta (1899, 2:591).

31. Peter Wollny has identified the copyist previously known as Anonymous Vj, scribe of the continuo part in BWV 11, as Johann Wilhelm Machts, who arrived as a student at St. Thomas School only two weeks before Ascension 1735. This identification, together with a detailed analysis of the score, led Wollny to conclude that the first performance more likely took place on May 15, Ascension 1738. See Wollny (2016, 83–89).

32. J. W. Machts, the scribe mentioned in notes 17 and 29, also participated in preparing the sources for the Easter Oratorio BWV 249.4; Wollny (2016, 91) proposes April 6, 1738, as the date of its first performance.

33. Froher Tag, verlangte Stunden BWV 1162.

34. Frohes Volk, vergnügte Sachsen BWV 1158.

35. Auf, süß-entzückende Gewalt BWV 1163.

36. "Leipzig unter einer Herrschaft stehet, die sich zur Catholischen religion bekennet, welche unsre Salzburgischen Emigranten verlassen haben."

37. Alles, was von Gott geboren BWV 80.1.

38. The same company published the *Wörterbuch der obersächsischen Mundarten* (Dictionary of Upper Saxon dialects).

39. Meister Petz is the name of a bear in a fable in which various animals have human names: Isegrim the wolf, Lamprecht the hare, Adebar the stork.

40. In other words, the coins would be well-worn.

41. Es lebe der König, der Vater im Lande BWV 1157.

References

Ambrose, Z. Phillip. 1980. "'Weinen, Klagen, Sorgen, Zagen' und die antike Redekunst." *BJ* 66:35–45.
Blanken, Christine. 2015a. "A Cantata Text Cycle of 1728 from Nuremberg: A Preliminary Report on a Discovery Relating to J. S. Bach's So-Called Third Annual Cycle." *Understanding Bach* 10:9–30
Blanken, Christine. 2015b. "Christoph Birkmanns Kantatenzyklus 'GOtt-geheiligte Sabbaths-Zehnden' von 1728 und die Leipziger Kirchenmusik unter J. S. Bach in den Jahren 1724–1727." *BJ* 101:13–74.
Blankenburg, Walter. 1977. "Eine neue Textquelle zu sieben Kantaten Johann Sebastian Bachs und achtzehn Kantaten Johann Ludwig Bachs." *BJ* 63:7–25.
Boyd, Malcolm. 1993. *Bach: The Brandenburg Concertos*. Cambridge: Cambridge University Press.
Boyd, Malcolm, ed. 1999. *Oxford Composer Companions: J. S. Bach*. Oxford: Oxford University Press.
Burney, Charles. 1773. *The present state of music in Germany, the Netherlands, and United provinces. Or, The journal of a tour through those countries, undertaken to collect materials for a general history of music*. 2 vols. London: Printed for T. Becket.
Casper, S. Jost. 1982. "Johann Sebastian Bach und die Salzburger Emigranten—eine unheilige Legende. Zur 250. Wiederkehr des Durchzugs der Salzburger Protestanten durch Leipzig im Juni und September 1732." *Mitteilungen der Gesellschaft für Salzburger Landeskunde* 122:341–70.
Dirksen, Pieter. 2003. "Ein verschollenes Weimarer Kammermusikwerk Johann Sebastian Bachs? Zur Vorgeschichte der Sonate e-Moll für Orgel (BWV 528)." *BJ* 89:7–36.
Dürr, Alfred. 1986. "Zum Eingangssatz der Kantate BWV 119." *BJ* 72:117–20.
Dürr, Alfred. 1988. "Zum Choralsatz 'Herr Jesu Christ, wahr' Mensch und Gott' BWV 127 (Satz 1) und seiner Umarbeitung." *BJ* 74:205–9.

Dürr, Alfred. 2005. *The Cantatas of J. S. Bach*. Translated by Richard D. P. Jones. Oxford: Oxford University Press.

Ernst, H. Peter. 1987. "Joh. Seb. Bachs Wirken am ehemaligen Mühlhäuser Augustinerinnenkloster und das Schicksal seiner Wender-Orgel." *BJ* 73:75–83.

Finscher, Ludwig. 1969. "Zum Parodieproblem bei Bach." In *Bach-Interpretationen (Walter Blankenburg zum 65. Geburtstag)*, edited by Martin Geck, 94–105. Göttingen: Vandenhoeck & Ruprecht.

Glöckner, Andreas. 1985. "Zur Chronologie der Weimarer Kantaten Johann Sebastian Bachs." *BJ* 71:159–64.

Glöckner, Andreas. 1988. "Zur Echtheit und Datierung der Kantate BWV 150 'Nach dir, Herr, verlanget mich.'" *BJ* 74:195–203.

Glöckner, Andreas. 2000. "Eine Michaeliskantate als Parodievorlage für den sechsten Teils des Bachschen Weihnachts-Oratoriums?" *BJ* 86:317–26.

Häfner, Klaus. 1975. "Der Picander Jahrgang." *BJ* 61:70–113.

Henzel, Christoph. 1992. "Zu Wilhelm Friedemann Bachs Berliner Jahren." *BJ* 78:107–12.

Hobohm, Wolf. 1973. "Neue 'Texte zur Leipziger Kirchen-Musik.'" *BJ* 59:5–32.

Hobohm, Wolf. 2000. "Ein unbekannter, früher Textdruck der Geistlichen Cantaten von Erdmann Neumeister." In *Ständige Konferenz Mitteldeutsche Barockmusik, Jahrbuch 2000*, edited by Wilhelm Seidel, 182–86. Eisenach: Verlag Karl Dieter Wagner.

Hofmann, Klaus. 1983. "Forkel und die Köthener Trauermusik Johan Sebastian Bachs." *BJ* 69:115–17.

Hofmann, Klaus. 1989. "Bachs Kantate 'Jauchzet Gott in allen Landen' BWV 51. Überlegungen zu Entstehung und ursprünglicher Bestimmung." *BJ* 75:43–54.

Hofmann, Klaus. 2001. "Über die Schlußchoräle zweier Bachscher Ratswahlkantaten." *BJ* 87:151–62.

Hofmann, Klaus. 2016. "Anmerkungen zu Bachs Kantate 'Preise, Jerusalem, den Herren' BWV 119." *BJ* 102:125–35.

Karstädt, Georg. 1962. *Die "Extraordinairen" Abendmusiken Dietrich Buxtehudes: Untersuchungen zur Aufführungspraxis in der Marienkirche zu Lübeck*. Lübeck: Verlag M. Schmidt-Römhild.

Knight, Max. 1964. *The Gallows Songs: Christian Morgenstern's Galgenlieder, a Selection*. Berkeley: University of California Press.

Koch, Ernst. 1989. "Tröstendes Echo: Zur theologischen Deutung der Echo-Arie im IV. Teil des Weihnachts-Oratoriums von Johann Sebastian Bach." *BJ* 75:203–12.

Koch, Ernst. 1995. "Die Stimme des Heiligen Geistes: Theologische Hintergründe der solistischen Altpartien in der Kirchenmusik Johann Sebastian Bachs." *BJ* 81:61–81.

Krausse, Helmut K. 1986. "Erdmann Neumeister und die Kantatentexte Johann Sebastian Bachs." *BJ* 72:7–31.

Kreutzer, Hans Joachim. 2005. "Weltdichtung und Vollendung der Natur: Aspekte der Literaturtheorie der Bach-Zeit." In *Musik, Kunst und Wissenschaft im Zeitalter Johann Sebastian Bachs*, edited by Ulrich Leisinger and Christoph Wolff, 67–98.

Vol. 7 in the series Leipziger Beiträge zur Bach-Forschung. Hildesheim: Georg Olms Verlagsbuchhandlung.

Krummacher, Friedhelm. 1991. "Bachs frühe Kantaten im Kontext der Tradition." *Die Musikforschung* 44(1): 9–32.

Krummacher, Friedhelm. 1995. *Bachs Zyklus der Choralkantaten: Aufgaben und Lösungen*. Göttingen: Vandenhoeck & Ruprecht.

Kümmerling, Harald. 1955. "Fünf unbekannte Kantaten in Reinhard Keisers Autograph." In *Festschrift Max Schneider zum achtzigsten Geburtstag*, edited by Walther Vetter, 177–81. Leipzig: Deutscher Verlag für Musik.

Leaver, Robin. 2021. *Bach Studies: Liturgy, Hymnology and Theology*. Oxfordshire: Routledge.

Lindner, Ernst Otto. 1855. *Die erste stehende deutsche Oper*. Berlin: Schlesinger'sche Buch- und Musikhandlung.

Marissen, Michael, and Daniel Melamed. n.d. "Texts and Historically-Informed Translations for the Music of Johann Sebastian Bach." Accessed June 16, 2023. www.bachcantatatexts.org.

Marshall, Robert L. 1976. "Bach the Progressive: Observations on His Later Works." *Musical Quarterly* 62(3): 313–57.

Marshall, Robert L., and Traute M. Marshall. 2016. *Exploring the World of J. S. Bach: A Traveler's Guide*. Urbana: University of Illinois Press.

Maul, Michael. 2017. "'Having to Perform and Direct the Music in the Capellmeister's Stead for Two Whole Years': Observations on How Bach Understood His Post during the 1740s." Translated by Barbara Reul. *Understanding Bach* 12:35–58.

Maul, Michael. 2018. *Bach's Famous Choir*. Translated by Richard Howe. Woodbridge: Boydell Press.

Maul, Michael. 2022. *Bach: A Pictorial Biography*. Leipzig: Lehmstedt.

Maul, Michael, and Peter Wollny. 2003. "Quellenkundliches zu Bach-Aufführungen in Köthen, Ronneburg und Leipzig zwischen 1720 und 1760." *BJ* 89:97–141.

Peters, Mark. 2005. "A Reconsideration of Bach's Role as Text Redactor in the Ziegler Cantatas." *JRBI* 36(1): 25–66.

Petzoldt, Martin. 1992. *Bachstätten aufsuchen*. Leipzig: Verlag Kunst und Touristik.

Petzoldt, Martin. 1993. "'Die kräfftige Erquickung unter der schweren Angst-Last': Möglicherweise Neues zur Entstehung der Kantate BWV 21." *BJ* 79:31–46.

Petzoldt, Martin. 2004. *Bach-Kommentar: Theologisch-musikwissenschaftliche Kommentierung der geistlichen Vokalwerke Johann Sebastian Bachs*. Vol. 1, *Die geistlichen Kantaten des 1. bis 27. Trinitatis Sonntags*. Vol. 14.1 in the series Schriftenreihe der Internationalen Bachakademie Stuttgart. Kassel: Bärenreiter.

Rathey, Markus. 2006. "Zur Datierung einiger Vokalwerke Bachs in den Jahren 1707 und 1708." *BJ* 92:65–92.

Reichel, J. G. 1929. *Thränen und Seuffzer wegen der Universität Leipzig. . . .* Leipzig: Ph. Reclam Jr.

Rucker, Henrike, ed. 2000. *Erdmann Neumeister (1671–1756): Wegbereiter der evan-

gelischen Kirchenkantate. Vol. 2 in the series Weißenfelser Kulturtraditionen. Rudolstadt: Hain.
Schabalina, Tatiana. 2008. "'Texte zur Music' in St Petersburg." *BJ* 94:33–98.
Schabalina, Tatiana. 2009. "'Texte zur Musik' in Sankt Petersburg—weitere Funde." *BJ* 95:11–48.
Scheibe, Johann Adolph. 1737. *Der critische Musikus: Sechstes Stück*. Hamburg.
Scheide, William. 1980. "Bach und die Picander-Jahrgang: Eine Erwiderung." *BJ* 66:47–51.
Scheide, William. 1983. "Eindeutigkeit und Mehrdeutigkeit in Picanders Kantatenjahrgangs-Vorbemerkung und im Werkverzeichnis des Nekrologs auf Johann Sebastian Bach." *BJ* 69:109–13.
Schering, Arnold. 1913. "Die Kantate Nr. 150 'Nach dir, Herr, verlanget mich.'" *BJ* 10:39–52.
Schering, Arnold. 1942. *Über Kantaten Johann Sebastian Bachs*. Leipzig: Koehler & Amelang.
Schering, Arnold. 1950. *Über Kantaten Johann Sebastian Bachs*. Leipzig: Koehler & Amelang.
Schulze, Hans-Joachim. 1969. "Neuerkenntnisse zu einigen Kantatentexten Bachs auf Grund neuer biographischer Daten." In *Bach-Interpretationen (Walter Blankenburg zum 65. Geburtstag)*, edited by Martin Geck, 22–28. Göttingen: Vandenhoeck & Ruprecht.
Schulze, Hans-Joachim. 1976. "Melodiezitate und Mehrtextigkeit in der Bauernkantate und in den Goldbergvariationen." *BJ* 62:58–72.
Schulze, Hans-Joachim. 1978. Foreword to *Georg Philipp Telemann, Moralische Kantaten*, edited by Kurt Janetzky. Continuo-Einrichtung von Dietrich Knothe. Leipzig: Deutscher Verlag für Musik.
Schulze, Hans-Joachim. 1984a. "Studenten als Bachs Helfer bei der Leipziger Kirchenmusik." *BJ* 70:45–52.
Schulze, Hans-Joachim. 1984b. *Studien zur Bach-Überlieferung im 18. Jahrhundert*. Leipzig: Edition Peters.
Schulze, Hans-Joachim. 1985. *Ey! Wie schmeckt der Coffee süße: Johann Sebastian Bachs Kaffee-Kantate*. Leipzig: Evangelische Verlagsanstalt. Translated by Alfred Mann in 2001 as "Ey! How Sweet the Coffee Tastes! Johann Sebastian Bach's Coffee Cantata in Its Time." *BACH: The Journal of the Riemenschneider Bach Institute* 32(2): 1–34.
Schulze, Hans-Joachim. 1987. "Das didaktische Modell der Thomaner im Spiegel der deutschen Musikpädagogik." In *Alte Musik und Musikpädagogik*, edited by Hartmut Krones, 185–98. Vol. 1 in the series Wiener Schriften zur Stilkunde und Aufführungspraxis. Vienna: Böhlau.
Schulze, Hans-Joachim. 1995. "Die Handhabung der Chromatik in Bachs frühen Tastenwerken." In *Das Frühwerk Johann Sebastian Bachs: Kolloquium, veranstaltet von Institut für Musikwissenschaft der Universität Rostock 11–13 September 1990*, edited by Karl Heller and Hans-Joachim Schulze, 70–86. Cologne: Studio.

Schulze, Hans-Joachim. 1999. "Texte und Textdichter." In *Die Welt der Bach-Kantaten*. Vol. 3, *Johann Sebastian Bachs Leipziger Kirchenkantaten*, edited by Christoph Wolff and Ton Koopman, 109–25. Stuttgart: Metzler.

Schulze, Hans-Joachim. 2000. "Wann entstand Johann Sebastian Bachs 'Jagdkantate'?" *BJ* 86:301–5.

Schulze, Hans-Joachim. 2002a. "Johann Sebastian Bachs dritter Leipziger Kantatenjahrgang und die Meininger 'Sontags- und Fest-Andachten' von 1719." *BJ* 88:193–99.

Schulze, Hans-Joachim. 2002b. "Johann Sebastian Bach und die norddeutsche Fugenkunst." In *Bach, Lübeck und die norddeutsche Musiktradition: Bericht über das Internationale Symposion der Musikhochschule Lübeck April 2000*, edited by Wolfgang Sandberger, 272–79. Kassel: Bärenreiter.

Schulze, Hans-Joachim. 2006. *Die Bach-Kantaten: Einführungen zu sämtlichen Kantaten Johann Sebastian Bachs*. Leipzig: Evangelische Verlagsanstalt.

Schulze, Hans-Joachim. 2010. "Rätselhafte Auftragswerke J. S. Bachs." *BJ* 96:69–93. Reprinted in Hans-Joachim Schulze. 2017. *Bach-Facetten: Essays- Studien- Miszellen*. Leipzig: Evangelischen Verlagsanstalt.

Schulze, Hans-Joachim. 2011. "Die Bach-Kantate 'Nach dir, Herr, verlanget mich' und ihre Meckbach-Akrostikon." *BJ* 97:255–57. Reprinted in Hans-Joachim Schulze. 2017. *Bach-Facetten: Essays- Studien- Miszellen*. Leipzig: Evangelischen Verlagsanstalt.

Schweitzer, Albert. 1966. *J. S. Bach*. Translated by Ernest Newman. 2 vols. New York: Dover.

Serauky, Walter. 1942. *Musikgeschichte der Stadt Halle*. Vol. II/2. Halle.

Smend, Friedrich. 1950. "Bachs Himmelfahrts-Oratorium." In *Bach-Gedenkschrift*, edited by Karl Matthaei, 42–65. Zurich: Atlantis.

Spitta, Philipp. 1899. *Johann Sebastian Bach: His Work and Influence on the Music of Germany, 1685–1750*. Translated by Clara Bell and J. A. Fuller-Maitland. 3 vols. London: Novello and Co.; New York: H. W. Gray.

Steiger, Lothar, and Renate Steiger. 1983. " . . . angelicos testes, sudarium et vestes: Bemerkungen zu Johann Sebastian Bachs Osteroratorium." *Musik und Kirche* 53:193–202.

Steiger, Renate. 1989. "Actus tragicus und ars moriendi: Bachs Textvorlage für die Kantate 'Gottes Zeit ist die allerbeste Zeit' (BWV 106)." *Musik und Kirche* 59:11–23.

Talbot, Michael. 1999. "Purpose and Peculiarities of the Brandenburg Concertos." In *Bach und die Stile: Bericht über das 2. Dortmunder Bach-Symposion 1998*, edited by Martin Geck and Klaus Hofmann, 255–89. Vol. 2 in the series Dortmunder Bach-Forschungen. Dortmund: Klangfarben Musikverlag.

Wetzel, Christoph. 1985. *Die Psalmen in Bachs Kantaten im Detempore der Leipziger Schaffensperiode*. In *Bach als Ausleger der Bibel: Theologische und musikwissenschaftliche Studien zum Werk Johann Sebastian Bachs*, edited by Martin Petzoldt, 131–50. Berlin: Evangelisches Verlagsanstalt.

Wolf, Uwe. 1997. "Johann Sebastian Bach und der Weißenfelser Hof- Überlegungen anhand eines Quellenfundes." *BJ* 83:145–50.

Wolff, Christoph. 1996. "'Die betrübte und wieder getröstete Seele': Zum Dialog-Charakter der Kantate 'Ich hatte viel bekümmernis' BWV 21." *BJ* 82:139–45.

Wollny, Peter. 2000. "Dokumente und Erläuterungen zum Wirken Johann Elias Bachs in Schweinfurt (1743–1755)." In *Die Briefentwurfe des Johann Elias Bach (1705–1755)*, edited by Evelin Odrich and Peter Wollny, 45–73. Vol. 3 in the series Leipziger Beiträge zur Bach-Forschung. Hildesheim: Olms.

Wollny, Peter. 2001. "Johann Christoph Friedrich Bach und die Teilung des väterlichen Erbes." *BJ* 87:55–70.

Wollny, Peter. 2016. "Neue Erkenntnisse zu einigen Kopisten der 1730er Jahre." *BJ* 102:63–113.

Wollny, Peter, and Andreas Glöckner, eds. 1997. *Passionskantate Wer ist der, so von Edom kömmt (Pasticcio)*. Vol. II/1 in the series Denkmäler Mitteldeutscher Barockmusik. Leipzig: Friedrich Hofmeister Musikverlag.

Wustmann, Rudolf. 1982. *Joh. Seb. Bachs Kantatentexte*. 3rd ed. Wiesbaden: Breitkopf & Härtel. Originally published in Leipzig, 1913.

Index

Abendmusiken, of Lübeck, 21, 218, 248n20
Ach Gott, vom Himmel sieh darein (ancient melody), 112; in *Ich will den Kreuzstab gerne tragen,* 165
Ach Gott, vom Himmel sieh darein (BWV 2), 108–13; archaic aspects of, 112; "Die Armen sind verstört," 110; composition of, 108; copies of, 113; "Das wollst du, Gott, bewahren rein," 110–11; "Durchs Feuer wird das Silber rein," 110, 112; inward/outward opposition in, 108–9; Luther's hymn in, 108–10, 112; opening movement, 112; for second Sunday after Trinity, 108; "Sie lehren eitel falsche List," 108–9; "Tilg, o Gott, die Lehren," 110, 112
acrostics, of *Nach dir, Herr, verlanget mich,* xiii
Acts of the Apostles: in *Gottes Zeit ist die allerbeste Zeit,* 15; in *Lobet Gott in seinen Reichen,* 229; in *Weinen, Klagen, Sorgen, Zagen,* 38
Actus tragicus. See *Gottes Zeit ist die allerbeste Zeit* (BWV 106)
Advent, Bach's cantatas for, 46–51, 186–91
Agricola, Johann Friedrich, 217
Albinus, Johann Georg: *Welt, ade! Ich bin dein müde,* 163
Allein Gott in der Höh sei Ehr (hymn melody), in *Es erhub sich ein Streit,* 156
Also hat Gott die Welt geliebt (BWV 68), 26
Altnickol, Johann Christoph, 135, 181

Ämilie Juliana of Schwarzburg-Rudolstadt, Countess, 127; funeral hymn by, 160
Ancient Bach Archive (Alt-Bachisches Archiv), 154, 252n5
Andachten (devotions), in cantata form, 146
Annunciation: in Leipzig, 136; *Wie schön leuchtet der Morgenstern* for, 135, 137
Arnstadt, Bach at, 6, 175
The Art of Fugue (BWV 1080), 237
Ascencion Oratorio. See *Lobet Gott in seinen Reichen* (BWV 11)
August the Strong (elector of Saxony): congratulatory cantata for, 245–46; conversion to Catholicism, 192
Aus der Tiefen rufe ich, Herr, zu dir (BWV 131), 1–4, 10; autograph score of, 1; biblical passages, 2–3; compositional style of, 3; dedication of, 1; double motive of, 4; "Erbarm dich mein in solcher Last," 3; fugal movement, 4; inscription to Eilmar, 1; libretto of, 2–3; "Meine Seele wartet auf den Herrn," 3; occasion for, 2–3; performance date of, 3; "So du willst, Herr, Sünde zurechnen," 3; "Und er wird Israel erlösen," 4; "Und will ich denn in meinem Sinn," 3; writing for organ in, 3–4

Bach, Anna Magdalena, 80, 113, 250n7; and *Ich bin in mir vergnügt,* 174; notebook of, 165, 180; performances by, 118

Bach, Carl Philipp Emanuel, 37, 46, 80; archives of, 252n5; contribution to *Schweigt stille, plaudert nicht,* 216; on *Es erhub sich ein Streit,* 154, 203
Bach, Catharina Dorothea, 2
Bach, Johann Christian (son of Johann Sebastian), 187
Bach, Johann Christoph (uncle of Johann Sebastian): *Es erhub sich ein Streit,* 154
Bach, Johann Christoph Friedrich (son of Johann Sebastian), 96
Bach, Johann Elias (cousin of Johann Sebastian), 79–80, 181, 250n7
Bach, Johann Ludwig (cousin of Johann Sebastian): funeral music for Prince Leopold, 192
Bach, Johann Sebastian: application at Hamburg, 41, 42; Arnstadt residence, 6, 175; artistic goals, 65; attendance at wedding services, 221, 222; as boy soprano, 209; Calov Study Bible annotations, 253n7; as cantor of St. Thomas School, 41, 51, 61, 65, 102; chronological catalogs of, xi; complete edition of, 135–36; composition obligations, 33; Concertmaster position (Weimar), 32–33, 37; creative milieu of, xii; directorship of Collegium Musicum, 201; estate of, 37, 113; Köthen residence, 41, 64, 118, 175; legacy of, 14; lost works, 23, 193, 194, 196, 215, 234; management of his creative works, 186; manuscripts of, 11, 81–82, 106, 187, 192, 202, 221; meeting with king of Prussia, 182, 253n16; Mühlhausen residence, 1–22, 41, 45; nineteenth-century Renaissance of, 217; notational schemes of, 182; parody technique, xii, 23, 73, 219, 223, 227; patrons of, xii, 42, 186; permutation technique of, 31, 36, 78, 249n8; Pietism and, 249n17; radio broadcasts of, xi; secular works, 23–27, 169–77, 186–95, 201–6, 215–17, 221–25, 238–46; St. Thomas School consecration music, 231–32; supplemental income of, 221; Weimar residence, 23, 27–41, 46–55; "Weimar style" of, 91, 92; Weissenfels *Tafelmusik* of, 225, 226, 227, 228
—friends and associates: Buxtehude, 21, 248n20; Eilmar, 2, 10; Frohne, 2; Johann Ernst of Saxe-Weimar, 42; Kellner, 202
—Leipzig residence: after Trinity 1727, 186–246; first year, 61–101; fourth year, 149–85; second and third year, 102–48
Bach, Maria Barbara, 2
Bach, Wilhelm Friedemann, 202; changes to *Jauchzet Gott in allen Landen,* 209; at the Church of Our Lady, 182; contributions to *Ein feste Burg ist unser Gott,* 237; scores owned by, 113, 182; use of Bach's cantatas, 51; "Wer mich liebet, der wird mein Wort halten," 182
Bach-Archiv (Leipzig), xi
Bach Compendium (Schulze and Wolff), xi
Bach family: 2, 46, 80; cost of support for, 33; Goethe on, 203; household music of, 174; move to Leipzig, 61; use of Bach material, 51
Bach-Jahrbuch (Schulze and Wolff), xi
Baroque era: Song of Songs poetry of, 44; violent expressions of, 130; vocabulary of sin, 28
Becker (paper manufacturer), 1
Bernier, Nicolas: *Le caffé,* 215
Bindi, Giovanni, 208
Birkmann, Christoph, xiii, 253n6; cantata text cycles of, 252n2, 253nn8–9, 13, 254n7; disputation in mathematics, 253n9; *Gott-geheiligte Sabbaths-Zehnden,* 249n19
Blanken, Christine, xiii, 252n3, 252n6, 253nn8–9
boy soloists, 208, 209. *See also* falsettists, male
Brandenburg Concerto, First (BWV 1046), 173
Brautmessen (bridal masses), 221; full and half, 222. *See also* weddings
Breitkopf (firm), publication of Bach, 1
Brich dem Hungrigen dein Brot (BWV 39), 149–54; Alexandrine verse form of, 151, 152; for first Sunday after Trinity, 149; *Freu dich sehr, o meine Seele* melody in, 154; "Höchster, was ich habe," 152, 153–54; *Kommt, laßt euch den Herren lehren* in, 152–53; librettist of, 151, 252n3; parable of Lazarus in, 149; as political music, 149; publication of, 150; "Der reiche Gott wirft seinen Überfluß," 151; "Seinem Schöpfer noch auf Erden," 151, 153; *vox Christi* in, 153
Bruhns, Nicolaus, 11
Bugenhagen, Johann: *Evangelien-Harmonie,* 229–30
Burney, Charles, 202

264 Index

Buxtehude, Dietrich, 21, 248n20; *Te Deum Laudamus,* 202

cantatas: *Acti,* 14; Bach's use of term, 206; chorale, 11; free poetry, 5; mixed texts, 2, 5, 47; moral, 175; northern German masters of, 11

cantatas, Bach's: for Advent, 46–51, 186–91; annual cycles of, 11–12, 13, 46, 113, 118, 135–36, 141, 142, 150, 160, 196, 215, 218, 234; anonymous librettists of, 103, 127, 128, 141, 150, 151, 164, 170, 204, 251n9; biblical passages in, xiv; biographical features of, xii; chorale, 11–13, 102, 103, 109, 112–14, 122, 124, 141, 156, 214, 234; Christmas to Epiphany cycle, 218–19, 228; congratulatory, 171, 188, 208, 219, 231, 245–46; council pieces, xii, 16, 17–18, 79, 80; creative milieu of, xii; difficulties of performance, 206–7; early, 1, 6–7, 12, 13, 24, 28, 32, 45, 51, 184; English translations of, xiii–xiv; free poetry, 5, 9, 62, 88, 95–95, 114, 124, 212, 230; lost, 234; mixed text form of, 2, 5, 47; moral, 175; opening movement models, 141; parody procedures of, xii, 23, 73, 219, 223, 227; Passion, 32, 123, 131, 196, 218; poetic traditions of, xii; range of forms, 13; recent discoveries, xiii; reusability of, 26, 219–20, 223–25, 231–32; secular, 23–27, 169–77, 186–95, 201–6, 215–17, 221–25, 238–46; wedding, xiii, 183, 185, 201, 221; for Weimar, 33–41, 46–51. *See also names of individual cantatas*

Capriccio in B-flat Major (BWV 992), 125

Charles XII (king of Sweden), campaigns against Germany, 20

Charlotte Frederike Wilhelmine of Anhalt-Köthen, Princess: cantata for, 186

Choreinbau (choral embedding), 74, 250n5

Christe, du Lamm Gottes (melody), 134

Christiane Eberhardine of Brandenburg-Bayreuth (electress of Saxony): funeral cantata for, 191–95; Lutheran faith of, 192

Christian of Saxe-Weissenfels, Duke, 24–25; *Tafelmusik* for, 225, 226, 227, 228

Christ ist erstanden (hymn), 12

Christ lag in Todes Banden (BWV 4), 10–13, 51; chorale partita of, 13; chorale text of, 10; composition date, 12; for Easter, 10, 11; last movement, 12; performances of, 11–12; style of, 12

Christmas, Bach's writings for, 145–46, 218–20

Christmas Oratorio, 217; adaptations from cantatas, 219–20; first cantata, xii, 220; "Großer Herr, o starker König," 220; Siciliano rhythm of, 159; sixth cantata, 93, 233. See also *Jauchzet, frohlocket, auf, preiset die Tage* (BWV 248 Part I)

Christus, der ist mein Leben (BWV 95), 84–88; "Ach schlage doch bald, selge Stunde," 86; canticle of Simeon in, 85; chorales of, 84, 87, 88; "Denn ich weiß dies," 86; free verse in, 86; "letzter Glockenschlag" of, 87; librettist of, 84; "Mit Fried und Freud fahr ich dahin," 85; raising of dead in, 84; for sixteeth Sunday after Trinity, 84; "Valet will ich dir geben," 85–86, 87; *Wenn mein Stündlein vorhanden ist* in, 86–87

city councils: Bach's cantatas for, xii, 16, 17–18, 79, 80; inaugurations of, xii, 17, 20n6, 79

Coffee Cantata. See *Schweigt stille, plaudert nicht* (BWV 211)

Collegium Musicum (Leipzig): Bach's directorship of, 201; coffeehouse concerts by, 216; *Ich bin in mir vergnügt* and, 174

Concerto for Two Violins in D Minor (BWV 1043), 207

concordia discors (motto for compositions), 171

Counter-Reformation, Lutheran emigrants from, 149–50, 233–34

Denicke, David: *Kommt, laßt euch den Herren lehren,* 152–53

Deuteronomy, Book of: in *Gott ist mein König,* 20

devotions: in cantata form, 146; *Nachmittagsandacht,* 146

DeWael, Johan, 9

Dieskau, Carl Henrich von, 246; celebratory cantata for, 238

Doles, Johann Friedrich, 209; *Wer nur den lieben Gott läßt walten* performances, 11, 113

Drese, Johann Samuel, 33

Dürr, Alfred, 250n9; *The Cantatas of J. S. Bach,* xiv

Du wahrer Gott und Davids Sohn (BWV 23), 134

Index 265

Easter Oratorio. See *Kommt, eilet und laufet, ihr flüchtigen Füße* (BWV 249.4)
Easter plays, tradition of, 12, 227
Easter Sunday, Bach's compositions for, 10, 11, 51, 223, 226–28
Eber, Paul: text for *Herr Jesu Christ, wahr' Mensch und Gott*, 131–33
Ehre sei Gott in der Höhe (BWV 197.1), 223–24
Eilmar, Georg Christian, 1–2; funeral odes of, 10
Elbschwan-Orden (poetry academy), 122
Die Elenden sollen essen (BWV 75), 61–65; chorale, 64; free poetry in, 62; French overture in, 64; "Gott stürzet und erhöhet in Zeit und Ewigkeit," 63; libretto, 62–63; "Mein Herze glaubt und liebt," 64–65; "Mein Jesus soll mein alles sein," 64; parable of Lazarus in, 62–63, 64; for Sunday after Trinitiy, 61; *Was Gott tut, das ist wohlgetan* strophes in, 64, 65
Enchiridion Oder eyn Handbüchlein (Erfurt, 1524), 12
Epiphany, Bach's music for, 92, 218–19
"Ergetzender Wohlklang vereinigter Seyten" (Leipzig musical celebration), 171
Ernst August of Saxe-Weimar, Duke, 26
Ernst Ludwig of Meiningen, Duke: funeral of, 192
Es erhub sich ein Streit (BWV 19), 154–60; "Ach Herr, laß dein lieb Engelein," 159–60; "Bleibt, ihr Engel, bleibt bei mir," 158–59; *Erbauliche Gedanken auf das Fest Michaelis* strophes in, 156, 157, 158; *Freu dich sehr o meine Seele* strophe in, 156; "Gottlob, der Drachen liegt," 157; "Gott schickt uns Mahanaim zu," 157, 159; "Herzlich lieb hab ich dich, o Herr," 159; "Laß dein Engel mit mir fahren," 156; "Laßt uns das Angesicht," 159; Mahanaim in, 157, 159, 252n7; source text of, 156; for St. Michael's Day, 154–56; "Was ist der schnöde Mensch, das Erdenkind," 158
Es ist gewißlich an der Zeit (melody), 92

falsettists, male, 31, 208–10. See also boy soloists
Fama, allegory of, 74
Farinelli (castrato), competition with trumpet, 207
Ein feste Burg ist unser Gott (BWV 80), 233–37; "Alles, was von Gott geboren," 235, 236; chorale fantasia, 236, 237; composition stages, 236; Franck's contributions to, 234–35; "Komm in mein Herzenshaus," 236; "Mit unsrer Macht ist nichts getan," 235; for Reformation Day, 233–34, 237; "Und wenn die Welt voll Teufel wär," 237; versions of, 234; Weimar Oculi Sunday version, 234–37; "Wie selig sind doch die," 236–37; Wilhelm Friedemann Bach's contributions to, 237
Finscher, Ludwig, 219
Firmian, Leopold Ernst von, Archbishop, 149, 233
Fleckeisen, Gottfried Benjamin, 250n8
"Folie d'Espagne" (ancient melody), 246
Forkel, Johann Nikolaus, 154; on *Laß, Fürstin, laß noch einen Strahl*, 191
Franck, Johann: "Du o schönes Weltgebäude," 167–68; *Jesu, meine Freude*, 99–100, 101
Franck, Salomon, 25; "Adam muß in uns verwesen," 53; Bach libretti of, 37; contributions to *Ein feste Burg ist unser Gott*, 234–35; *Evangelisches Andachts-Opffer*, 52, 55; *Evangelische Sonn- und Fest-Tages-Andachten*, 70, 88, 91; *Geistliche und Weltlichen Poesien*, 24; *Herz und Mund und Tat und Leben* text, 70–72; *Der Himmel lacht, die Erde jubilieret* text, 52; *Himmelskönig, sei willkommen* text, 34; *Komm, du süße Todesstunde* text, 55–58, 249n19; *Wachet! betet! betet! wachet* text, 88–91
Frankfurt, wartime destruction of archives, 217
Frederick II (king of Prussia), meeting with Bach, 182, 253n16
French overture: in *Die Elenden sollen essen*, 64; in *Nun komm der Heiden Heiland*, 50; in *O Ewigkeit, du Donnerwort*, 106
Freu dich sehr, o meine Seele (hymn), 91, 154, 156
Friedrich August I (elector of Saxony), conversion to Catholicism, 142, 150, 192, 233
Friedrich August II (elector of Saxony), 231
Fritsch, Ahasverus: *Liebster Immanuel, Herzog der Frommen*, 126, 127–29; life of, 126–27

266 Index

Frohne, Johann Adolf, 2
Füger, Kaspar: *Wir Christenleut,* 148

Genesis, Book of: in *Gott ist mein König,* 20
Gerber, Ernst Ludwig: on Doles, 10–11
Gerber, Heinrich Nicolaus, 11
Gerhardt, Paul: *Barmherz'ger Vater, höchster Gott,* 144; "Gib dich zufrieden und sei stille," 165; *Ich hab in Gottes Herz und Sinn,* 96; *O Haupt voll Blut und Wunden,* 197–98
Gerstenbüttel, Joachim, 11
Geschwinde, geschwinde, ihr wirbelnden Winde (BWV 201): Henrici's libretto for, 200; mythological characters of, 200; performances of, 201; *Streit zwischen Phoebus and Pan* in, 201; "Der Unverstand und Unvernunft," 200–201; for various purposes, 200
Gesner, Johann Matthias (rector, St. Thomas School), 187
Geystlichen gesangk Buchleyn (Wittenberg, 1524), 12
Goethe, Johann Wolfgang von, 24, 231, 239, 255n13; on Bach family, 203
Görner, Johann Gottlieb, 193
Gotha (Thuringia), Passion music of, 218
Gottes Zeit ist die allerbeste Zeit (BWV 106), 13–16; biblical passages of, 15–16; choral fugue of, 16; compositional style, 13–14; date of composition, 14; "Es ist der alte Bund: Mensch du mußt sterben," 16; "Glorie, Lob, Ehr und Herrlichkeit," 16; instrumental chorale, 16; interiority of, 14; for memorial service, 13, 14–15; publication of, 14; seventeenth-century forms of, 14; soprano solo, 16; use in memorial service, 13
Gottgefälliges Kirchen-Opffer (cantata text cycle), 27
Gott ist mein König (BWV 71), 17–22; biblical passages in, 18–20, 21; "Durch mächtige Kraft" aria, 22; Emperor Joseph I in, 21; fugues, 22; instruments for, 21; libretto of, 18–20; performances of, 18, 21, 250n6; printing of, 18; seventeenth-century elements of, 21–22; strophic passages of, 20; "Tag und Nacht sind dein" arioso, 22; for town council inauguration, xii, 17–18; voices for, 21
Gott ist unsere Zuversicht (BWV 197.2), 221–25; autograph score of, 221; librettist, 222–23, 225; *Nun bitten wir den Heiligen Geist* strophe in, 223; "O du angenehmes Paar," 224, 225; opening chorus, 225; parody procedure in, 223; reused compositions of, 223–25; "Schläfert allen Sorgenkummer," 223, 225; for secular wedding, xiii, 221; "So wandelt froh auf Gottes Wegen," 224; "Verngügen und Lust," 224, 225; *Wer nur den lieben Gott läßt walten* strophe in, 224
Gottsched, Johann Christoph, 142; criticism of Picander, 201; "enlightened happiness" of, 176; libretto for electress Christiane, 193–94; Ode of Mourning, 194; "Serenade auf des Herrn geheimen Kriegsraths von Hohenthal Vermählung in Leipzig, 1725," 232; *Versuch einer Critischen Dichtkunst für die Deutschen,* 201
Gräfenroda (Thuringia), 202
Graun, Carl Heinrich, 135
Graupner, Christoph, 27
Gryphius, Andreas, 119

Halle: Church of Our Lady, 33, 181; soprano soloists of, 209–10
Haller, Albrecht von, 176
Hamburg, Bach's application at, 41, 42
Handel, George Frideric, 42, 202
Harsdörffer, Georg Philipp: *Wachet doch, erwacht, ihr Schläfer,* 122
Haupt, Carl Ephraim, 221
Hauptmann, Moritz, 14
Hebrews, Book of: in *Brich dem Hungrigen dein Brot,* 152; in *Ich will den Kreuzstab gerne tragen,* 167
Heerman, Johannes, 118; *Haus- und Hertz-Musica,* 119; *O Gott du frommer Gott,* 19; *Was willst du dich betrüben,* 119
Henrici, Christian Friedrich (Picander): discoveries in St. Petersburg, 254n9; *Erbauliche Gedanken auf das Fest Michaelis,* 156, 157; *Ernst-Schertzhaften Und Satirischen Gedichten,* 215; Gottsched's criticism of, 201; *Schäfergespräch* of, 226; *Der Streit zwischen Phoebus and Pan,* 201; text *for Geschwinde, geschwinde, ihr wirbelnden Winde,* 200–201; text for *Mer han en neue Oberkeet,* 238–46; text for *Schwingt freudig euch empor,* 186, 189; text for *Sehet, wir gehn hinauf gen Jerusalem,* 195–99; "Über den Caffe," 215–16

Herberger, Valentin, 85–86
Herkules auf dem Scheideweg (BWV 213), adaptation for Christmas Oratorio, 220
Herman, Nikolaus: *Wenn mein Stündlein vorhanden ist*, 54, 55, 86–87
Herr, gehe nicht ins Gericht mit deinem Knecht (BWV 105), 75–80; "Ach Herr, vergib all unsre Schuld," 135; chromaticism of, 79; *Jesu, der du meine Seele*, 77–78; "Kann ich nur Jesum mir zum Freunde machen," 78; librettist of, 75–76; "Mein Gott, verwirf mich nicht," 76; for ninth Sunday after Trinity, 75; "Nun ich weiß, du wirst mir stillen," 78–79; parable of unjust householder in, 75; performances of, 75; *sacrum commercium* in, 75; sin as debt theme, 75; "Wie zittern und wanken der Sünder Gedanken," 76–77, 78; "Wohl aber dem, der seinen Bürgen weiß," 77, 78
Herr Jesu Christ, wahr' Mensch und Gott (BWV 127), 131–35; "Ach Herr, vergib all unsre Schuld," 133; "Bis sich die Seel vom Leib abwendt," 131–32; *Christe, du Lamm Gottes* in, 134; *Du wahrer Gott und Davids Sohn* and, 134; Eber's text for, 131–33; for Estomihi Sunday, 131; Last Judgment in, 132, 134; Luther's Agnus Dei in, 134; opening movement of, 133–34, 135; Passion in, 131, 133, 135; performance of, 131; "Die Seele ruht in Jesu Händen" in, 132, 134; "Wenn einstens die Posaunen schallen," 132–33
Herrscher des Himmels, König der Ehren (BWV 1141), 248n4
Herzlich tut mich verlangen (melody), in *Sehet, wir gehn hinauf gen Jerusalem*, 199
Herz und Mund und Tat und Leben (BWV 147), 70–75; "Bereite dir, Jesu, noch itzo die Bahn," 74; *Choreinbau* technique in, 74; composition of, 70; Franck's text for, 70–72; "Gebendeiter Mund!," 71; "Hilf, Jesu, hilf daß ich auch dich bekenne," 71, 74; "Ich will von Jesu Wundern singen," 73; *Jesu, meiner Seelen Wonne* strophe in, 73; Magnificat in, 71, 72, 73; "music within music" of, 74; parody procedure of, 73–74; reception history of, 75; revisions from *Nun komm der Heiden Heiland*, 70, 71, 72–73, 74; "Schäme dich, o Seele, nicht," 71–72, 74; "Verstockung kann Gewaltige verblenden," 71; for Visitation of Mary, 70, 71
Hiller, Johann Adam: on falsetto singers, 208–9
Die Himmel erzählen die Ehre Gottes (BWV 76), 65–70; chorale, 69; composition of, 65; *Es woll uns Gott genädig sein* strophe in, 68–69; "Hasse nur, hasse mich recht," 68, 69–70; honor of God in, 66; "Hört, ihr Völker, Gottes Stimme," 69; librettist of, 65; "Liebt, ihr Christen in der Tat," 70; performances of, 70; for second Sunday after Trinity, 65; sinfonia, 69
Himmel hoch, da komm ich her (BWV 769), Canonic Variations on, 237
Der Himmel lacht, die Erde jubilieret (BWV 31), 51–55; "Adam muß in uns verwesen," 54; canonic constructions of, 54; for Easter Sunday, 51; "Ein Christe flieht / Ganz eilend von dem Grabe!," 53; Franck's text in, 55; fugue expositions, 54; "Fürst des Lebens, starker Streiter," 54; "Letzte Stunde, brich herein, / Mir die Augen zuzudrücken," 54; performances of, 51; place in Bach's repertoire, 52; soprano aria, 55; tenor aria, 54
Himmelskönig, sei willkommen (BWV 182), 32–37; arias, 35; crucifixion in, 35; instrumentation, 36; "Jesu, laß durch Wohl und Weh," 36; *Jesu Kreuz, Leiden und Pein* in, 36–37; "Leget euch dem Heiland unter," 36; librettist of, 34–36; opening chorus, 36, 37; for Palm Sunday, 32, 34, 37; performances of, 33, 37; permutation fugue of, 36; "So lasset uns gehen in Salem der Freuden," 37; *vox Christi* of, 36
Hofmann, Klaus, 250n9; on *Jauchzet Gott in allen Landen*, 208
Hohmann, Peter, the younger: marriage to Christiana Mencke, 232
Hunold, Christian Friedrich (Menantes): *Academische Neben-Stunden allerhand neuer Gedichte nebst einer Anleitung zur vernünftigen*, 175; Alexandrine verses of, 176; cantatas for Köthen, 175; opera libretti of, 175; text for *Ich bin in mir vergnügt*, 175–77; "Der vergnügte Mensch," 176–77
Hunt Cantata. See *Was mir behagt, ist nur die muntre Jagd* (BWV 208)

hymns, Lutheran, 12–13. *See also* Luther, Martin

Ich bin in mir vergnügt (BWV 204), 174–77; as "Cantata der Zufriedenheit," 176; as "Cantata von der Vergnügsamkeit," 174, 175, 177; Leipzig Collegium Musicum and, 174; "Loblied auf das Mittelmaß" text of, 174–75; Menantes's text for, 175–77; performances of, 174; purposes of, 174; *Vergnügsamkeit* in, 177; versions of, 180–81

Ich habe genung (BWV 82), 177–81; Bach's regard for, 181; canticle of Simeon in, 178–79; "Herr, nun läßest du deinen Diener im Friede fahren," 180; "Ich freue mich auf meinen Tod," 180; librettist of, 178–79; "Mein Gott! Wenn kömmt das schöne: Nun!," 179–80; performances of, 181; for Purification of Mary, 177–78; "Schlummert ein, ihr matten Augen," 179, 180; use of *Mit Fried und Freud ich fahr dahin*, 179–80

Ich hatte viel Bekümmernis (BWV 21), 41–45; "Ach Jesu, meine Ruh," 43–44; affliction in, 43; "Alle eure Sorge werfet auf ihn," 43; Bach's pride in, 42; choral movement, 45; consolation in, 43, 44; Neumark hymn in, 44; performances of, 41, 42; as representational work, 45; search theme of, 43; "Sei nun wieder zufrieden," 45; "Seufzer, Tränen, Kummer, Not," 43; Song of Songs theme, 43–44; soprano aria, 45; tenor aria, 45; textual heterogeneity of, 44; for third Sunday after Trinity, 41, 43; versions of, 42–43; "Was betrübst du dich meine Seele," 43; Weimar performance of, 42–43; *Wer nur den lieben Gott läßt walten* in, 45

Ich will den Kreuzstab gerne tragen (BWV 56), 164–69; concluding chorale, 169; "Da leg ich den Kummer auf einmal ins Grab," 169; "Du Herr probierst mich," 165–66; "Du o schönes Weltgebäude" in, 168; "Endlich, endlich wird mein Joch," 167; "Es kann und mag nicht anders werden," 165; forgiveness of sins in, 164–65; "Ich stehe fertig und bereit," 167; Jesus's healing in, 164; "Komm, o Tod, du Schlafes Bruder," 167–68; *Kreuz-Ton* of, 168; librettist of, 164–67; Neumeister's text in, 165; for nineteenth Sunday after Trinity, 164; sea voyage trope, 167; "Waldel auf der Welt" in, 167

Ihr werdet weinen und heulen (BWV 103), 141–44; *Barmherz'ger Vater, höchster Gott* strophe in, 144; "Ich traue dem Verheißungswort," 144; "Ihr aber werdet traurig sein," 144; joy motive, 144; for Jubilate, 141; "Kein Arzt ist außer dir zu finden," 143; opening movement, 144; performance of, 141; *Suchmotiv* of, 143, 252n13; *Was mein Gott will, das g'scheh allzeit* in, 144; Ziegler's text for, 143–44

Imperial Library (St. Petersburg), *Jesus schläft, was soll ich hoffen* in, 97. *See also* St. Petersburg, Bach discoveries at

Isaiah, Book of: in *Brich dem Hungrigen dein Brot,* 150–51, 153; in *Gottes Zeit ist die allerbeste Zeit,* 15; in *Ich will den Kreuzstab gerne tragen,* 166, 167; in *Sie werden aus Saba alle kommen,* 95; in *Unser Mund sei voll Lachens,* 148

Jahn, Otto, 14

Janus, Martin: *Jesu, meiner Seelen Wonne,* 73

Jauchzet, frohlocket, auf, preiset die Tage (BWV 248 Part I), 218–20; performance of, 218. *See also* Christmas Oratorio

Jauchzet Gott in allen Landen (BWV 51), 206–10; concertante trumpet in, 207; demands on solo soprano, 206–7, 208, 209–10; for fifteenth Sunday after Trinity, 206, 207, 209; revisions to, 209; virtuosity of, 207

Jeremiah, Book of: in *Ihr werdet weinen und heulen,* 143

Jesu, der du meine Seele (BWV 78), 122–26; "Das Blut, so meine Schuld durchstreicht," 124, 125; composition of, 122; "Deine rotgefärbte Wunden," 124; for fourteenth Sunday after Trinity, 122; free poetry in, 124; "Herr, ich glaube, hilf mir Schwachen," 124; *lamento* bass of, 125; "Nun du wirst mein Gewissen stillen," 124; "Nun ich weiß, du wirst mir stillen," 125; opening movement, 125; Passion in, 123, 125; Rist's text for, 122–25; "Wir eilen mit schwachen, doch emsigen Schritten," 123, 125; "Die Wunden, Nägel, Kron und Grab," 124, 125–26

Jesu, meine Freude (BWV 227), 39

Jesus schläft, was soll ich hoffen (BWV 81), 96–101; autograph score, 99; "Belials Bächen" imagery of, 98, 100; calm/agitation tension in, 100; evocation of slumber, 100; first cantata, 97; for fourth Sunday after Epiphany, 96; "Herr, warum trittst du so ferne?," 98; *Jesu, meine Freude* strophes in, 99–100, 101; performance date of, 97; "Die schäumende Wellen von Belials Bächen," 98, 100; "Schweig, aufgetürmtes Meer!," 99, 101; search motif of, 97; Star of Bethlehem in, 98; *vox Christi* of, 100
Johann Ernst of Saxe-Weimar, Prince: death of, 59; patronage of Bach, 42
Johann Georg II (elector of Saxony), 233
Johann Georg of Saxe-Weissenfels, Duke, 24
John, Gospel of: in *Herz und Mund und Tat und Leben*, 71; in *O ewiges Feuer, o Ursprung der Liebe*, 183; in *Weinen, Klagen, Sorgen, Zagen*, 37; in *Widerstehe doch der Sünde*, 29–30
Joseph I, Holy Roman Emperor, 21
Josephus, Flavius, 31
Judges, Book of: in *Komm, du süße Todesstunde*, 56

Keiser, Reinhard: difficult works of, 207; *Musikalische Landslust . . . in moralischen Cantaten*, 175
Kellner, Johann Peter: collection of Bach's works, 202
Keymann, Christian: *Meinen Jesum laß ich nicht*, 91
Ein Kind geborn zu Bethlehem (hymn), 94
Kings, Second Book of: in *Es erhub sich ein Streit*, 158; in *Wer nur den lieben Gott läßt walten*, 117
Kirchbach, Hans Carl von, 192–93
Kirnberger, Johann Philipp, 203
Knoll, Christoph, 58
Knüpfer, Sebastian, 5, 11
Kolrose, Johann: *Ich dank dir, lieber Herre*, 70
Komm, du süße Todesstunde (BWV 161), 55–60; Franck's text for, 55–58, 249n19; "Ich habe lust, von dieser Welt zu scheiden," 59; "Mein Verlangen ist, den Heiland zu umfangen," 59; organ counterpoint of, 59; performances of, 59–60; resurrection in, 55; Samson and the lion in, 56; "Der Schluß ist schon gemacht,"

59; Simeon in, 60; for sixteenth Sunday after Trinity, 55, 60; versions of, 59–60; "Wenn es meines Gottes Wille," 58, 59
Kommt, eilet und laufet, ihr flüchtigen Füße (BWV 249.4), 223, 225, 226–28; alto aria, 228; connection to medieval traditions, 227; for Easter Sunday, 226; instrumental movements, 228; librettist of, 226, 227; origins of, 226; parody procedure of, 227; performances of, 256n32; Peter's aria, 227, 228; reperformance of, 228–29; *Schäfergespräch* and, 226; secular parentage of, 226–27; "Seele, deine Spezereien," 227
Kortte, Gottlieb: death of, 169, 170; homage cantata for, 169, 170–74
Köthen: Bach at, 41, 64, 118, 175; Menantes' cantatas for, 175
Kottwitz, Georgius von, 119
Krauß, Gottfried Theodor, 222
Krebs, Johann Ludwig, 27, 28
Krebs, Johann Tobias the elder, 27–28
Kreutzer, Hans Joachim: on *Der Streit zwischen Phoebus und Pan*, 201
Krieger, Johann Philipp, 11
Kuhnau, Johann, 5, 11, 208, 221

lamento bass, Bach's use of, 40, 125
Lammerhirt, Tobias, 248n16
Laß, Fürstin, laß noch einen Strahl (BWV 198), 177, 191–95; autograph manuscript of, 192; background for, 192; "Der Ewigkeit saphirnes Haus," 195; for funeral of Christiane Eberhardine, 191–95; Leipzig account of, 194; modern recovery of, 194; quarrel over performance, 193; secular character of, 191; title of, 192; transcription errors in, 194
Laßt uns sorgen, laßt uns wachen (BWV 213), adaptation for Christmas Oratorio, 219–20
Lehms, Georg Christian, 27, 28–30; *Gottgefälliges Kirchen-Opffer*, 145–48; *Mein Herze schwimmit im Blut* text, 33–34; *Widerstehe doch der Sünde* text, 34
Leipzig: Annunciation in, 136; Bach's absences from, 80, 250n8; Bach's first year at, 61–101; Bach's fourth year at, 149–85; Bach's second and third year at, 102–48; during Battle of Nations, 193; bombardment in Second World War, 193; bridal masses of, 221; Christmas music of, 218;

church cantatas of, xii, xiii, 11, 41–45, 51; city council inauguration (1723), xii, 79; *doppelte Kirchenmusik* custom, 145–46; election cantatas for, 80; funeral of electress Christiane at, 193–94; *Ich hatte viel Bekümmernis* at, 41; monument to Bach, 84; municipal rituals of, xii, 79–80; Salzburg Emigrants in, 149–50, 233–34; *Stadtpfeifer* of, 208; St. Nicholas Church, 61, 83, 145, 218; St. Paul Church, 145, 193; St. Thomas Church, 84, 145, 218; *tempus clausum* at, 27, 70, 91, 136, 234; *Thürknecht* (door servant) of, 79; town clerk of, 79; women singers of, 209. *See also* St. Thomas School (Leipzig)

Leopold of Anhalt-Köthen, Prince, 186; funeral music of, 194

Leopold of Brandenburg-Bayreuth (elector of Saxony), funeral of, 191, 192

libretti, church: theological ideas in, xii

Liebster Immanuel, Herzog der Frommen (BWV 123), 126–30; "Auch die harte Kreutzesreise," 129; closing chorale, 130; "Dein Nam ist zuckersüß, Honig im Munde," 128; flight of Holy Family in, 129; "Die Himmelsüßigkeit, der Auserwählten Lust," 128; "Laß, o Welt, mich aus Verachtung," 130; opening movement, 129–30; sadness of, 130; Wise Men in, 127

Lipsius, Johann Christoph Samuel, 168

Lobet Gott in seinen Reichen (BWV 11), 228–33; "Ach bleibe doch, mein liebstes Leben, ach fliehe nicht so bald von mir," 232; for Ascension Day, 228; "bassetto effect" in, 233; concluding chorale, 233; copyist of, 256n31; *Du Lebens-Fürst, Herr Jesu Christ* strophe in, 230; free poetry of, 230; *Gott fähret auf gen Himmel* strophe in, 230; Gottsched's "Serenade" text in, 232; "Jesu, deine Gnadenblicke, kann ich doch beständig sehn," 232; "Nun liegel alles unter dir," 230; opening chorus, 230; reused material in, 231–32; "Sucht sein Lob recht zu vergleichen," 231; tenor narrator of, 229; "Wenn soll es doch geschehen," 230

Löwenstern, Matthäus Apelles von, 119

Lübeck, *Abendmusiken* of, 21, 218, 248n20

Ludämilia Elisabeth of Schwarzburg-Rudolstadt, Countess, 126; hymns of, 127

Luke, Gospel of: in Christmas Oratorio, 228; in *Christus, der ist mein Leben,* 84; in *Die Elenden sollen essen,* 62; in *Gottes Zeit ist die allerbeste Zeit,* 15–16; in *Herr, gehe nicht ins Gericht mit deinem Knecht,* 75; in *Herz und Mund und Tat und Leben,* 71, 72, 73; in *Die Himmel erzählen die Ehre Gottes,* 65–66; in *Ich habe genung,* 180; in *Lobet Gott in seinen Reichen,* 229; Simeon in, 60; in *Unser Mund sei voll Lachens,* 147–48; in *Wachet! betet! betet! wachet,* 88–89; in *Widerstehe doch der Sünde,* 28

Luther, Martin: Agnus Dei translation, 134; *Es woll uns Gott genädig sein,* 68–69; *Ein feste Burg ist unser Gott,* 233–37; *Mit Fried und Freud fahr ich dahin,* 16, 179–80; Ninety-five Theses, 233; *Nun bitten wir den Heiligen Geist,* 223; *Nun komm der Heiden Heiland,* 46; *Salvum me fac, Domine* translation, 108–10, 112; Te Deum of, 82–83; *Veni redemptor gentium* version, 47, 190

Machts, Johann Wilhelm, 254n1, 256nn31–32

Magnificat in E-flat Major (BWV 234), 148

Malamed, Daniel, 252n7

Man singet mit Freuden vom Sieg (BWV 149), 248n4

Marissen, Michael, xiv, 252n7

Mark, Gospel of: in *Der Himmel lacht, die Erde jubilieret,* 53; in *Lobet Gott in seinen Reichen,* 229

Marpurg, Friedrich Wilhelm, 217

Marshall, Robert L., 208

Mary, Virgin: Feast of Purification, 60, 177–78

Mass in B Minor (BWV 232): Agnus Dei, 232; Crucifixus, 40; "et Ressurexit," 54; Sanctus, 223

Mattheson, Johann, 206; on boy singers, 208; on *Ich hatte viel Bekümmernis,* 42

Matthew, Gospel of: in Christmas Oratorio, 228; in *Himmelskönig, sei willkommen,* 34, 35; in *Ich bin in mir vergnügt,* 164–65; in *Jesus schläft, was soll ich hoffen,* 99; in *Nun komm der Heiden Heiland,* 46–47; in *Sie werden aus Saba alle kommen,* 92–93; in *Wachet auf, ruft uns die Stimme,* 210; in *Widerstehe doch der Sünde,* 30

Maul, Michael, 251n9
Meckbach, Conrad, 10
Meistersingers, 140
Melamed, Daniel, xiv
Menantes. *See* Hunold, Christian Friedrich
Mencke, Christiana Sybilla: marriage of, 232
Mencke, Johann Burkhard, 232
Mendelssohn, Felix, 11, 202; on *Gottes Zeit ist die allerbeste Zeit,* 14; performance of *Preise, Jerusalem, den Herrn,* 84
Mer han en neue Oberkeet (BWV 212), 238–46; "Ach es schmeckt doch gar zu gut," 240; "Ach Herr Schösser, geht nicht gar zu schlimm," 240; "Ach unser Herr schilt nicht," 239; chamberlain in, 239, 241, 243, 244, 246; conscription in, 241–42; "Das ist galant," 242; "Das ist zu klug vor dich," 243, 244, 246; "Das klingt zu liederlich," 244; "Dein Wachstum sei feste," 246; double entendres of, 246; "Du hast wohl recht," 244–45; "Er hilft uns allen, alt und jung," 241; "Es bleibt dabei," 241; *Großvatertanz* in, 246; Henrici's text for, 238; "Der Herr ist gut: Allein der Schösser," 240; *Kehraus* in, 246; "Klein-Zschocher müsse," 243; for members of the aristocracy, 238; National Destiny in, 245–46; paean to Kleinzschocher, 245–46; Saxon dialect in, 238, 241; taxes in, 240–42; "Und unsre gnäd'ge Frau," 242–43; "Unser trefflicher Lieber Kammerherr," 241; "urban" arias, 245–46; "Wenns das alleine wär," 239; "Wir gehn nun, wo der Tudelsack," 245
middle class, moral standards of, 176
Morgenstern, Christian, 23; *Die unmögliche Tatsache,* 248n2
Mozart, Wolfgang Amadeus, 45; "Musical Joke," 246
Mühlhausen (Thuringia): Bach at, 1–22, 41; City Council Inauguration (1708), 17–18; councilmen of, 18, 79; *Eingepfarrten* of, 12; government of, 17–18; municipal rituals of, xii, 17–18; musical traditions of, 2–3, 12, 21; St. Blasius Church, 10, 12, 18, 21; St. Mary's Church, 18, 21
music, medieval: sequences in, 248n12
Das musikalische Opfer (BWV 1079), 253n16

Nach dir, Herr, verlanget mich (BWV 150), 4–10; acrostic strophes of, xiii, 5–6, 8–10; authenticity of, 4–5; biblical passages, 5, 6; chaconne of, 7, 9; choral movements, 7; compositional style of, 7; date of composition, 5, 6, 10; "Doch bin und bleibe ich vergnügt," 7; free poetry in, 5; fugal passages, 7; lamentation in, 7; libretto of, 5–9; "Meine Tage in dem Leide," 7; occasion for, 10; presentation print of, 10; purpose of, 8; self-confidence of, 7; sister works of, 10; "Zedern müßen von den Winden," 7
Nachmittagsandacht (afternoon devotion), 146
Nain, raising of dead at, 84, 160
Neue Bach-Ausgabe (Schulze and Neumann), xi
Neumark, Georg: *Wer nur den lieben Gott läßt walten,* 44, 113–17, 224
Neumeister, Erdmann, 5, 28; cantata texts of, 34, 46–47, 56–57; *Geistliche Poesien,* 46; "Ich will den Kreuzweg gerne gehen," 165; *Nun komm der Heiden Heiland* libretto, 46; "So laß auf beiden Seiten," 158; "Willkommen! Will ich sagen," 162
Neurmann, Werner, xi
Nichelmann, Christoph, 187
Nicolai, Philipp: *Freuden Spiegel des ewigen Lebens,* 210; *Wächterlied,* 210–11, 214; *Wie schön leuchtet der Morgenstern,* 47, 136–41, 186, 190
Noack, Elisabeth, 27
Nun danket alle Gott (chorale melody), 83
Nun komm der Heiden Heiland (Advent chorale), 190–91
Nun komm der Heiden Heiland (BWV 61), 46–51; church service for, 49–50; entrance of Jesus into Jerusalem, 50; for first Sunday of Advent, 46; French overture form in, 50; human heart metaphor of, 49; libretto, 47–50; "Öffne dich, mein ganzes Herze," 50; performances of, 49–50; revision for Leipzig, 70, 71, 72–73, 74; "Siehe, ich stehe vor der Tür und klopfe an," 50; tenor aria, 50

Obersächsisches Wörterbuch der Akademie der Wissenschaften, 238
octaves, small, 31, 249n7

Oculi Sunday: Bach's compositions for, 234; *Widerstehe doch der Sünde* for, 27, 28, 30

O ewiges Feuer, o Ursprung der Liebe (BWV 34), 181–85; composition of, 182; "Drum sei das Herze dein," 184; "Erwählt Gott die heilgen Hütten," 185; "Gib, höchster Gott, auch hier dem Worte Kraft," 183; holograph manuscript of, 181–82; human heart trope of, 183; Jacob and Rachel in, 184–85; opening chorus, 185; for Pentecost, 181; performances of, 181, 182–83, 253n15; redating of, xiii, 253n14; wedding cantata version, 183, 185; "Wohl euch, ihr auserwählten Seelen," 184–85

O Ewigkeit, du Donnerwort (BWV 20), 102–8; "bound" style in, 107; chorales of, 103, 106; chromaticism of, 107; "Ewigkeit, du machst mir bange," 107; French overture structure, 106; "Gott ist gerecht in senin Werken," 104, 107; holograph score of, 106; Last Judgment in, 105; Lazarus and the rich man in, 103; "O Mensch, errette deine Seele," 107; "O Menschenkind, hör auf geschwind," 105–6, 107; opening movement, 106; Rist's text for, 103–6; "Solang ein Gott im Himmel lebt," 103–4; "Wacht auf, wacht auf, verlorenen Schafe," 105, 108

Olearius, Johann: *Christliche Bet-Schule*, 15, 16

opera, French seventeenth-century, 50

Opitz, Martin, 119

Orchestral Suite in D Major (BWV 1068), 148

Ovid: *discors concordia* of, 171; *Metamorphoses*, 200

Pachelbel, Johann, 4

Palm Sunday, *Himmelskönig, sei willkommen* for, 32, 34, 37

Passion: in Bach's cantatas, 218; in *Herr Jesu Christ, wahr' Mensch und Gott*, 131, 133, 135; in *Jesu, der du meine Seele*, 123, 125; in music of Gotha, 218; in *Sehet, wir gehn hinauf gen Jerusalem*, 196; in *Widerstehe doch der Sünde*, 32

Paul, Epistles of: in *Herr, gehe nicht ins Gericht mit deinem Knecht*, 77

Peasant Cantata. See *Mer han en neue Oberkeet*

Penzel, Christian Friedrich, 4; copying of Bach manuscripts, 5, 9, 217

Peter, First Epistle: in *Ich hatte viel Bekümmernis*, 43

Peters, Mark, 252n13

Petzoldt, Martin, 229

Philippians, Book of: in *Komm, du süße Todesstunde*, 56–57

Picander. See Henrici, Christian Friedrich

Pietism, 55, 127; Bach and, 249n17

Pirro, André, 231

poetry, German: Silesian, 119, 201

Preise, Jerusalem, den Herrn (BWV 119), 79–84; for city council inauguration, xii, 79; closing chorale, 83; "Hilf deinem Volk, Herr Jesu Christ," 82–83; libretto of, 80; Luther's Te Deum in, 82–83; Mendelssohn's performance of, 84; "Die Obrigkeit ist Gottes Gabe," 82, 83; original version, 250n9; press notice of, 84; trumpet fanfares, 83; "Wie kann Gott besser lohnen," 80–81; "Wohl dir, du Volk der Linden," 81

Psalm 8, in *Unser Mund sei voll Lachens*, 147

Psalm 10, in *Jesus schläft, was soll ich hoffen*, 97–98

Psalm 12, in *Ach Gott, vom Himmel sieh darein*, 108–11

Psalm 16, in *Der Himmel lacht, die Erde jubilieret*, 52

Psalm 19, in *Die Himmel erzählen die Ehre Gottes*, 66

Psalm 22, in *Die Elenden sollen essen*, 62

Psalm 25, in *Nach dir, Herr, verlanget mich*, 6

Psalm 31, in *Gottes Zeit ist die allerbeste Zeit*, 15

Psalm 33, in *Preise, Jerusalem, den Herrn*, 81–82

Psalm 34, in *Es erhub sich ein Streit*, 157–58

Psalm 40, in *Himmelskönig, sei willkommen*, 34–35, 36

Psalm 42, in *Ich hatte viel Bekümmernis*, 43, 45

Psalm 46, in *Gott ist unsere Zuversicht*, 223; Luther's paraphrase of, 234

Psalm 51, in *Herr, gehe nicht ins Gericht mit deinem Knecht*, 76, 78

Psalm 74, in *Gott ist mein König*, 19, 20, 21

Psalm 85, in *Preise, Jerusalem, den Herrn*, 80

Psalm 94, in *Ich hatte viel Bekümmernis,* 43
Psalm 116, in *Ich hatte viel Bekümmernis,* 44
Psalm 126, in *Preise, Jerusalem, den Herrn,* 82; in *Unser Mund sei voll Lachens,* 146
Psalm 130, in *Aus der Tiefen rufe ich, Herr, zu dir,* 2–3
Psalm 143, in *Herr, gehe nicht ins Gericht mit deinem Knecht,* 76
Psalm 147, in *Preise, Jerusalem, den Herrn,* 80, 83
psalms, seven penitential, 3
Puer natus in Bethlehem (hymn), 94
Purification of Mary, feast of, 60, 177–78

Rechenberg, Carl Otto, 170
Reformation, Lutheran, 12; under Friedrich August I, 150, 233–34
Reformation Day, cantata for, 233–37
Reicha, Gottfried, 208
Reichel, Johann Gottlieb: *Thränen und Seuffzer wegen der Universität Leipzig,* 169–70
Reusner, Adam: *In dich hab ich gehoffet, Herr,* 16
Revelation of Saint John: in *Es erhub sich ein Stret,* 154–55, 156; in *Gottes Zeit ist die allerbeste Zeit,* 15; in *Der Himmel lacht, die Erde jubilieret,* 52–53; in *Ich hatte viel Bekümmernis,* 44; in *Ich will den Kreuzstab gerne tragen,* 166; in *Nun komm der Heiden Heiland,* 48–49
Riemer, Johann Salomon, 149
Ringck, Johannes, 202, 203
Ringwaldt, Bartholomäus: *Herr Jesu Christ, du höchstes Gut,* 3
Rist, Johann: *Du Lebens-Fürst, Herr Jesu Christ,* 230; *Jesu, der du meine Seele,* 77–78, 122–25; life of, 122; "O Ewigkeit, du Donnorwort," 103–7
Rivinus, Johann Florens, 187
Rodigast, Samuel, 39; *Was Gott tut, das is wohlgetan,* 39–40, 63, 64, 65
Romans, Epistle to: in *Preise, Jerusalem, den Herrn,* 82
Romanus, Franz Conrad, 251n11
Rosenmüller, Johann, 164
Rothe, Gottlob Friedrich, 221

Sabean people, in Isaiah, 93
Sacer, Gottfried Wilhelm: *Gott fähret auf gen Himmel,* 230

Sachs, Hans, 140, 241; "Silberweise," 214, 255n20
Salvum me fac, Domine (hymn), 108
Salzburg Emigrants, 149–50, 233–34
Samuel, Book of: in *Gott ist mein König,* 19
Scarlatti, Alessandro: *Su le sponde del Tebro,* 207
Scheibe, Johann Adolph, 206–7
Schelhafer, Heinrich Gottlieb, 171
Schelle, Johann, 5, 11; *Actus musicus auf Weihnachten,* 14
Schering, Arnold, 4–5; on *Der Himmel lacht, die Erde jubilieret,* 52; on *Jauchzet Gott in allen Landen,* 207; on *Liebster Immanuel, Herzog der Frommen,* 130; on *O ewiges Feuer, o Ursprung der Liebe,* 185; on Pietism, 55; on Three Kings, 93
Schop, Johann: "O Ewigkeit, du Donnerwort," 103
Schreyer, Christian Heinrich, 209
Schübler, Johann Georg: Schübler Chorales, 118
Schulze, Hans-Joachim: on anonymous librettists, 251n9; *Die Bach-Kantaten,* xi–xii; on Frederick of Prussia, 253n16; influence of, xi; radio broadcasts by, xi; on small octave, 249n7
Schütz, Heinrich: *Es erhub sich ein Streit,* 154
Schweigt stille, plaudert nicht (BWV 211), 177, 215–17; Bach's contribution to, 216; date of composition, 216; performances of, 216–17, 254n7; Picander's libretto for, 215–16, 217; popularity of, 217; titles of, 216; for various purposes, 214
Schweitzer, Albert, 219; on Bach's *Actus Tragicus,* 13, 17
Schwingt freudig euch empor (BWV 36), 186–91; "Auch mit gedämpften, schwachen Stimmen," 189–90; bass aria, 191; chamber music character of, 190; copyist for, 254n1; dedication of, 187; for first Sunday of Advent, 186; "Die Liebe führt mit sanften Schritten," 188; "Die Liebe zieht mit sanften Schritten," 189; manuscript copy of, 187; opening movement, 190; performances of, 186; secular/Advent versions, 186–90; "Die Sonne zieht mit sanftem Triebe," 188; tenor aria, 191; *Wie schön leuchtet der Morgenstern* strophe in, 186, 190; "Willkommen, werter Schatz," 189

274 Index

Sehet, wir gehn hinauf gen Jerusalem (BWV 159), 195–99; composition of, 195; "Es ist vollbracht," 198; for Estomihi, 195, 196; Henrici's text for, 195–99; "Herr Jesu, dein verdienstlich Leiden," 199; *Herzlich tut mich verlangen* in, 199; "Ich folge dir nach," 197–98; *Jesu Leiden, Pein und Tod* strophe in, 199; Jesus's dialogue with soul, 199; *O Haupt voll Blut und Wunden* strophe in, 197–98; Passion in, 196; possible losses from, 196; salvation in, 198; second movement of, 199; *vox Christi* in, 199
Sermon on the Mount, in *Die Elenden sollen essen*, 63
Seume, Johann Gottfried, 221
Shepherd Cantata (BWV 249.1), 223
Sie werden aus Saba alle kommen (BWV 65), 92–96; "Des Glaubens Gold, der Weihrauch des Gebets, die Myrrhen der Geduld sind meine Gaben," 96; for Epiphany, 92, 95; free poetry of, 94–95; fugue theme, 94; "Gold aus Ophir ist zu schlecht," 95; *Ich hab in Gottes Herz und Sinn* strophe in, 96; *Ein Kind geborn zu Bethlehem* in, 94; "Die Kön'ge aus Saba kamen dar," 94; "Nimm mich dir zu eigen hin," 96; opening movement, 93–94; Sabean people in, 93; sketches for, 94; Three Kings in, 96; *Was mein Gott will, das g'scheh allzeit* in, 96
Silesia, poets of, 119, 201
Smend, Friedrich, 226; on Ascension Oratorio, 232; on St. Michael's Day, 154–55
Sodomsäpfeln, 30, 110, 251n2
Song of Songs: in *Ich hatte viel Bekümmernis*, 43–44; mysticism of the bride, 212, 227; soul's search for Jesus in, 251n17
Sperontes, *Singende Muse an der Pleiße*, 176
Spitta, Philipp, 23, 219; on *Kommt, eilet und laufet, ihr flüchtigen Füße*, 226; on Salomon Franck, 54–55
Steinbach, Georg Adam, 18
stile concitato, 250n12; of *Wachet! betet! betet! wachet*, 91
St. John Passion (BWV 245), versions of, 136, 196
St. Mark Passion (BWV 247), 194
St. Matthew Passion (BWV 244): earliest version of, 180; "Kommt, ihr Töchter hilft mir klagen," 227; Last Supper, 126; Mendelssohn's revival of, 202; performances of, 196; "Sind Blitzen, sind Donner in Wolken verschwunden," 134
St. Michael's Day, *Es erhub sich ein Streit* for, 154–56
Stockmann, Paul: *Jesu Leiden, Pein und Tod*, 36, 199
Stölzel, Gottfried Heinrich, 202
Stoppe, Daniel, 176
St. Petersburg, Bach discoveries at, xiii, 97, 251n18, 253n14, 254n9
Strattner, Christoph, 33
Strecker, Adolf, 18, 248n16
Der Streit zwischen Phoebus und Pan (BWV 201), 201, 246, 254n10
St. Thomas School (Leipzig): Bach as cantor, 41, 51, 61, 65, 102; Bach's scores at, 113; boy soloists of, 209; corporal punishment at, 222; *Präfektenstreit* at, 222; renovation of, 231; unrest at, 150, 222
Stübel, Andreas, 251n9
Sweelinck, Jan Pieterszoon, 4

Tacitus, 31
Telemann, Georg Philipp, 46, 201; "moralischen Cantaten" of, 176
Teller, Abraham, 164
Thirty Years' War, 118, 126–27
Tönet, ihr Pauken, erschallet, Trompeten (BWV 214): "Fama" aria, 220; reuse in Christmas oratorio, 219–20
Trauerode (BWV 198). See *Laß, Fürstin, laß noch einen Strahl* (BWV 198)
Trauungskantaten (wedding ceremony cantatas), 221. See also *Brautmessen* (bridal masses); weddings
Trio Sonata in E Minor for Organ (BWV 528), 69

Uffenbach, Johann Friedrich Armand von, 176
University of Leipzig: commission for Bach, 169; legal faculty, 169–70
Unser Mund sei voll Lachens (BWV 110), 145–48; "Ach, Herr, was ist ein Menschenkind," 147, 148; for Christmas Day, 145; "Ihr Gedanken und ihr Sinnen," 146–47, 148; Lehms's text for, 145–48; opening movement, 146, 148; "Wach auf, ihr Adern und ihr Glieder," 148; *Wir Christenleut* strophe in, 148

Veni redemptor gentium (hymn), Luther's version of, 47, 190
Vereinigte Zwietracht der wechselnden Saiten (BWV 207.1), 169–74; allegorical figures of, 171–72, 173, 174; "Ätzet dieses Angedenken," 172; closing ensemble, 173; commission for, 169; didactic nature of, 173; F-major concerto passage in, 173; homage to Kortte, 169, 170–74; "In ungezählten Jahren," 172–73; "Kortte lebe, Kortte blühe," 172; opening chorus, 172; performance of, 169, 174; "Zieht euren Fuß nicht zurücke," 171–72
Victimae paschali laudes (hymn), 12
Virgins, wise and foolish: parable of, 210–11
Von Gott will ich nicht lassen (melody), 120
Vopelius, Gottfried: *Neu Leipziger Gesangbuch,* 164
Vulpius, Melchior: *Christus, der ist mein Leben,* 87

Wachet auf, ruft uns die Stimme (BWV 140), 210–15; "Der Bräutigam kommt, der einem Rehe," 212–13; bride of Christ in, 211–13; composition of, 210; counterpoint in, 47, 136–41, 186, 190; free poetry of, 212; "Mein Freund ist mein," 214; *Nachtstück* duet of, 214; Nicolai's *Wächterlied* in, 210–11, 214; performances of, 210; "So geh herein zu mir," 213–14; Song of Songs in, 212, 213; for twenty-seventh Sunday after Trinity, 210; *unio mystica* in, 212; "Wenn kömmst du, mein Heil?," 213; "Zion hört die Wächter singen," 212
Wachet! betet! betet! wachet (BWV 70), 88–92; chorale strophes of, 88, 91, 92; composition of, 88; *Es ist gewißlich an der Zeit* in, 92; free poetry of, 88; *Freu dich sehr, o meine Seele* strophe in, 91; "Freu dich sehr o meine Seele und vergiß all Not und Qual," 92; "Hebt euer Haupt empor," 92; "Laßt der Spötter Zungen schmähen," 90, 92; Last Judgment in, 91; Leipzig recitatives of, 91; *Meinen Jesum laß ich nicht* in, 91; opening chorus, 89, 91–92; performances of, 88; "Seligster Erquickungstag," 90; *stile concitato* of, 91; stylistic differences in, 91; for twenty-sixth Sunday after Trinity, 88; Weimar style in, 91, 92; "Wenn kömmt der Tag, an dem wir ziehen," 89–90, 92; *Wie nach einer Wasserquelle* in, 92
Wagner, Richard, 13–14; *Die Meistersinger von Nürnberg,* 255n20
Wagner Hymnal, Bach's use of, 166
Walter, Johann: *Es woll uns Gott genädig sein,* 69
Walther, Johann Gottfried, 27; *Musikalisches Lexikon,* 28
Was mein Gott will, das g'scheh allzeit (melody), 96, 144
Was mir behagt, ist nur die muntre Jagd (BWV 208), 23–27; autograph score, 24; composition date, 24; dedication of, 24–25; ensemble movements, 26; "Felder und Auen," 26; finale, 26; "Jubilant dispute of the gods," 25, 26; "Lebe, Sonne dieser Erden," 25–26; modifications to, 26; mythological characters, 24, 25–26; occasion for, 24; performances of, 24, 26–27; text of, 24; use in church cantatas, 26
Wass Gott tut, das ist wohlgetan (chorale), "Wir müßen durch viel Trübsal in das Reich Gottes eingehen," 41
Was willst du dich betrüben (BWV 107), 118–22; "Auf ihn magst du es wagen," 118–21; "Denn Gott verlässet keinen," 119–20, 121; "Drum ich mich ihm ergebe," 120, 121; God's will in, 120; Heermann's text for, 118–21; opening movement, 120–21; performance of, 118; for seventh Sunday after Trinity, 118; source text for, 118; *Von Gott will ich nicht lassen* melody in, 120
weddings: cantatas for, xiii, 183, 185, 201, 221; fees for music, 221–22; without music, 222. See also *Brautmessen* (bridal masses)
Weichet nur, betrübte Schatten (BWV 202), 201–6; composition of, 203; dance in, 206; Kellner's preservation of, 202; librettist of, 201, 203–4; manuscript copy of, 202; mythological characters in, 204–6; opening movement, 205–6; origins of, 201–2; "Phoebus eilt mit schnellen Pferden," 204–5; popularity of, 201; seasons in, 204–6; for secular wedding, xiii, 201; "Sehet in Zufriedenheit," 203–4; "Sich üben im Lieben," 205, 206; transmission of, 201–2; "Und

dieses ist das Glücke," 203; "Die Welt wird wieder neu," 204; "Wenn die Frühlingslüfte streichen," 205

Weimar: Advent cantata, 46–51; archives, 32; Bach at, 23, 27–41, 46–55; castle church, 31, 49, 51, 88; castle fire (1774), 32; Ernestine rulers of, 250n11; Kirchen-Cappelle of, 33; musical establishment of, 31; Oculi Sunday in, 27, 234

Weinen, Klagen, Sorgen, Zagen (BWV 12), 37–41; composition of, 37; emulation of Christ in, 38–39; final chorale, 41; "Ich folge Christo nach," 41; for Jubilate Sunday, 37; Kingdom of God in, 38; "Kreuz und Kronen sind verbunden," 38, 40; *lamento* bass variations, 40; libretto of, 37–40; parataxis in, 37–38; "Sei getreu, alle Pein," 39, 41; sinfornia of, 40; "Was Gott tut, das ist wohlgetan," 39–40; "Wir müßen durch viel Trübsal in das Reich Gottes eingehen," 40

Weissenfels: Bach's *Tafelmusik* for, 225, 226, 227, 228; congratulatory music of, 208; Hof-Capelle, 25

Wer nur den lieben Gott läßt walten (BWV 93), 113–18; Bach's regard for, 118; "Denk nicht in deiner Drangsalshitze," 115; "Er kennt die rechten Freudenstunden," 115, 117–18; for fifth Sunday after Trinity, 113; "Man halte nur ein wenig stille," 117; Neumark's chorale in, 113–17; opening movement, 117; performances of, 113; publication of, 118; recitative-aria movements, 117; "Sing, bet und geh auf Gottes Wegen," 115; "Was helfen uns die schweren Sorgen?," 114–15

Wer nur den lieben Gott läßt walten (hymn), in *Ich hatte viel Bekümmernis,* 45

Wer weiß, wie nahe mir mein Ende (BWV 27), 160–64; "Ach wer doch schon im Himmel wär!," 162–63; "Gute Nacht, du Weltgetümmel!," 163, 164; libretto of, 160–63; longing for death in, 162; raising of dead in, 160; for sixteenth Sunday after Trinity, 160; soul's farewell in, 163; timbral symbolism of, 163; *Welt, ade! Ich bin dein müde* in, 163

Widerstehe doch der Sünde (BWV 54), 27–32; alto solo, 31; arias, 28, 29–30; "Die Art verruchter Sünden," 30; defiance in, 29; as fragment, 28; "Laß dich nicht den Satan blenden," 29; manuscript source for, 27; for Oculi Sunday, 27, 28, 30; outward appearance/inner condition in, 30; performances of, 28; permutation technique of, 31; printed text of, 31; resistance in, 31; "Sünde" in, 31; "Teufel" in, 31; text sources for, 28; use in Passion, 32; violas divisi of, 31; vocal-instrumental fugue, 31; "Wer Sünde tut, der ist vom Teufel," 29

Wie nach einer Wasserquelle, 92

Wie schön leuchtet der Morgenstern (BWV 1), 135–41; for Annunciation, 135, 137; Christ imagery in, 140; closing chorale, 141; composition of, 11, 135; "Ei, mein' Perle, du werte Kron," 137; "Ein ird'scher Glanz, ein leiblich Licht," 138; "Erfüllet, ihr himmlischen, göttlichen Flammen," 138; first movement, 136–37, 141; music within music in, 141; Nicolai's text in, 136–40; opening chorus, 140; publication of, 135–36; "Unser Mind und Ton der Saiten," 139, 141; "Von Gott kommt mir ein Freudenschein," 138; "Wie bin ich doch so herzlich froh," 140; "Zwingt die Saiten in Cythara," 139

Wilhelm Ernst of Saxe-Weimar, Duke, 33

Winckler, Johann Heinrich: libretto for *Lobet Gott in seinen Reichen* (BWV 11), 231

Wochenschriften, moralische, 176

Wolff, Christoph, xi

Wollny, Peter, 255n31

Wörterbuch der obersächsischen Mundarten, 256n38

Wustmann, Gustav, 252n1; *Quellen zur Geschichte Leipzigs,* 149

Wustmann, Rudolf, 251n18; "Bachs Musik im Gottesdienst," 149

Zachow, Friedrich Wilhelm, 42

Zelter, Carl Friedrich, 202–3, 255n13

Ziegler, Christiane Mariane von, 252n13; Bach's settings of, 142–43; text for *Ihr werdet weinen und heulen,* 143–44; *Versuch in gebundener Schreib-Art,* 142; writing career of, 141

BWV Index

BWV 1, *Wie schön leuchtet der Morgenstern*, 11, 135
BWV 2, *Ach Gott, vom Himmel sieh darein*, 108
BWV 4, *Christ lag in Todes Banden*, 10, 51
BWV 11, *Lobet Gott in seinen Reichen*, 228, 256n31
BWV 12, *Weinen, Klagen, Sorgen, Zagen*, 37
BWV 19, *Es erhub sich ein Streit*, 154
BWV 20, *O Ewigkeit, du Donnerwort*, 102
BWV 21, *Ich hatte viel Bekümmernis*, 41, 259, 262
BWV 27, *Wer weiß, wie nahe mir mein Ende*, 160
BWV 31, *Der Himmel lacht, die Erde jubilieret*, 51
BWV 34, *O ewiges Feuer, o Ursprung der Liebe*, xii, 181
BWV 36, *Schwingt freudig euch empor*, 186
BWV 39, *Brich dem Hungrigen dein Brot*, 149, 150, 252n3
BWV 51, *Jauchzet Gott in allen Landen*, 206
BWV 54, *Widerstehe doch der Sünde*, 27, 34
BWV 56, *Ich will den Kreuzstab gerne tragen*, 164
BWV 61, *Nun komm der Heiden Heiland*, 46
BWV 65, *Sie werden aus Saba alle kommen*, 92
BWV 70, *Wachet! betet! betet! wachet*, 88
BWV 71, *Gott ist mein König*, xii, 10, 17, 250n6
BWV 75, *Die Elenden sollen essen*, 61, 65
BWV 76, *Die Himmel erzählen die Ehre Gottes*, 65, 237
BWV 78, *Jesu, der du meine Seele*, 122
BWV 80, *Ein feste Burg ist unser Gott*, 233
BWV 81, *Jesus schläft, was soll ich hoffen?*, 96, 250n14
BWV 82, *Ich habe genung*, 177
BWV 93, *Wer nur den lieben Gott läßt walten*, 113
BWV 95, *Christus, der ist mein Leben*, 84
BWV 103, *Ihr werdet weinen und heulen*, 141, 143
BWV 105, *Herr, gehe nicht ins Gericht mit deinem Knecht*, 75
BWV 106, *Gottes Zeit ist die allerbeste Zeit*, 13, 261
BWV 107, *Was willst du dich betrüben*, 118
BWV 110, *Unser Mund sei voll Lachens*, 145
BWV 119, *Preise, Jerusalem, den Herrn*, xii, 79, 257, 258
BWV 123, *Liebster Immanuel, Herzog der Frommen*, 126
BWV 127, *Herr Jesu Christ, wahr' Mensch und Gott*, 131, 257
BWV 131, *Aus der Tiefen rufe ich, Herr, zu dir*, 1, 10

BWV 140, *Wachet auf, ruft uns die Stimme*, 210
BWV 147, *Herz und Mund und Tat und Leben*, 70
BWV 150, *Nach dir, Herr, verlanget mich*, xiii, 4, 258
BWV 159, *Sehet, wir gehn hinauf gen Jerusalem*, 195
BWV 161, *Komm, du süße Todesstunde*, 55, 249n19
BWV 182, *Himmelskönig, sei willkommen*, 32
BWV 197.2, *Gott ist unsere Zuversicht*, xii, 221
BWV 198, *Laß, Fürstin, laß noch einen Strahl*, 177, 191
BWV 201, *Geschwinde, geschwinde, ihr wirbelnden Winde*, 200, 246
BWV 202, *Weichet nur, betrübte Schatten*, xiii, 201
BWV 204, *Ich bin in mir vergnügt*, 174
BWV 207.1, *Vereinigte Zwietracht der wechselnden Saiten*, xiii, 169
BWV 208, *Was mir behagt, ist nur die muntre Jagd*, 23, 24
BWV 211, *Schweigt stille, plaudert nicht*, 177, 215
BWV 212, *Mer han en neue Oberkeet*, 238
BWV 248 Part I, *Jauchzet, frohlocket, auf, preiset die Tage*, 218, 228
BWV 249.4, *Kommt, eilet und laufet, ihr flüchtigen Füße*, 223, 226

HANS-JOACHIM SCHULZE is the leading authority on the music of Bach and its source traditions, on which he has authored over 500 books and articles.

JAMES A. BROKAW II is an independent scholar and translator.

The University of Illinois Press
is a founding member of the
Association of University Presses.
_____

University of Illinois Press
1325 South Oak Street
Champaign, IL 61820-6903
www.press.uillinois.edu